Medley

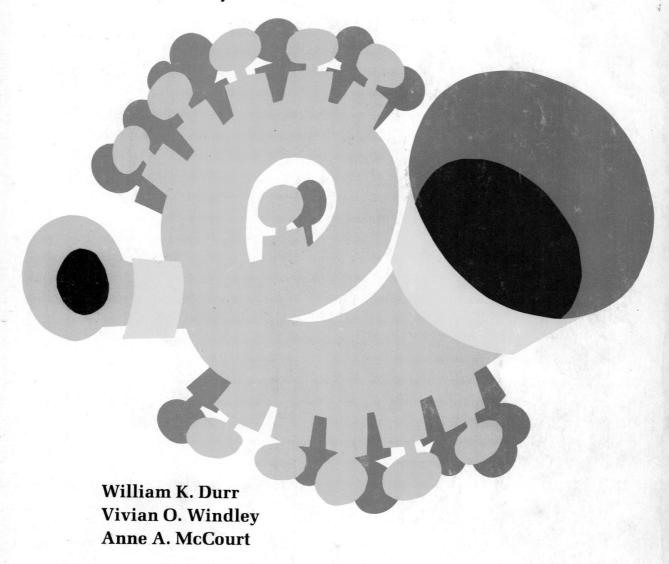

William K. Durr
Vivian O. Windley
Anne A. McCourt

CONSULTANT Paul McKee

HOUGHTON MIFFLIN COMPANY • Boston

Atlanta • Dallas • Geneva, Illinois • Hopewell, New Jersey • Palo Alto • Toronto

Acknowledgments

For each of the selections listed below, grateful acknowledgment is made for permission to adapt and/or reprint original or copyrighted material, as follows:

"Along Sandy Trails," slightly adapted from *Along Sandy Trails* by Ann Nolan Clark with photographs by Alfred A. Cohn. Text copyright © 1969 by Ann Nolan Clark. Photographs copyright © 1969 by Alfred A. Cohn. Used by permission of The Viking Press, Inc.

"Androclus and the Lion," adapted from *Favorite Tales of Long Ago*, retold by James Baldwin. Copyright 1955, by E. P. Dutton and Co., Inc. By permission of the publishers.

"Angry" and "Running Song," by Marci Ridlon from *That Was Summer*, published by Follett Publishing Co. Copyright 1969. By permission of Marci Ridlon.

"Arap Sang and the Cranes," from *Tales Told Near a Crocodile*, by Humphrey Harman. Copyright © 1962 by Humphrey Harman. All rights reserved. Reprinted by permission of The Viking Press, Inc. and Hutchinson Publishing Group, Ltd.

"Askia the Great," from *Black Is the Color* by Ruth Duckett Gibbs and illustrated by Tom Feelings. By permission of the publisher, Center for Media Development, Inc.

"Betsy Has a Birthday," from *Understood Betsy* by Dorothy Canfield Fisher. Copyright 1917, 1945 by Dorothy Canfield Fisher. Abridged and reprinted by permission of Holt, Rinehart and Winston, Publishers.

"The Bronze Hippo," from *The Bronze Zoo* by Shay Rieger, with special thanks to Edgar Tafel. Copyright © 1970 by Shay Rieger. Used by permission of Shay Rieger.

"Chester Makes Some New Friends," from *The Cricket in Times Square*, by George Selden, illustrated by Garth Williams. Copyright © 1960 by George Selden Thompson and Garth Williams. By permission of Farrar, Straus and Giroux, Inc. and J. M. Dent & Sons, Ltd.

"Chinese New Year," abridged with permission of Macmillan Publishing Co., Inc. from *The Chinese in America* by Betty Lee Sung. Copyright © 1972 by Betty Lee Sung.

"Cinder Ellie," from *Track Comes to Lonesome Point* by James Ayars. Copyright © 1972 by James Ayars. Reprinted by permission of the publishers, E. P. Dutton & Co., Inc.

"Cocoon," from *Far and Few* by David McCord. Copyright © 1925, 1929, 1931, 1941, 1949, 1952 by David McCord. This poem first appeared in *The New Yorker*, copyright 1949. Reprinted by permission of Little, Brown, and Co. and Curtis Brown, Ltd.

"The crow flew so fast . . . ," by Richard Wright. Copyright © by Richard Wright. Reprinted by permission of Paul R. Reynolds, Inc.

"Ernestine Rose," from *Women Themselves* by Johanna Johnston. Copyright © 1973 by Johanna Johnston. Reprinted by permission of Dodd, Mead & Company, Inc.

"Esmé on Her Brother's Bicycle," from *The Pedaling Man and Other Poems* by Russell Hoban. Text copyright © 1968 by Russell Hoban. Published by Grosset & Dunlap, Inc., New York. By permission of Grosset & Dunlap, Inc., and World's Work, Ltd.

"First Woman in Space," by Mitchell R. Sharpe. Copyright © 1973 Highlights for Children, Inc., Columbus, Ohio.

"Garbage Boom," adapted from *Read About the Sanitation Man* by Francine Klagsbrun. Copyright 1972 by Franklin Watts, Inc. Used by permission of the publisher.

"Gazinta," from *It Doesn't Always Have to Rhyme*, by Eve Merriam. Copyright © 1964 by Eve Merriam. Used by permission of Atheneum Publishers.

"He Reached for the Stars," from *Pioneers and Patriots* by Lavinia Dobler and Edgar A. Toppin, copyright © 1965 by Doubleday & Co., Inc. Reprinted by permission of Doubleday & Co., Inc.

"How Do We Know About Dinosaurs?" from *Discovering Dinosaurs* by Glenn O. Blough. Copyright © 1960 by Glenn O. Blough. Used with permission of McGraw-Hill Book Company.

"Hughbert and the Glue," from *The Rose on My Cake* by Karla Kuskin. Copyright © 1964 by Karla Kuskin. Reprinted by permission of Harper & Row, Publishers, Inc.

"In This Quiet Hour," by Luis Palés Matos from *The Puerto Rican Poets*, edited by Alfredo Matilla and Iván Silén, published by Bantam Books, Inc. Permission to use a translation of the poem granted by the University of Puerto Rico Press.

"Jack and the Three Sillies," from *Jack and the Three Sillies* by Richard Chase. Copyright 1950 by Richard Chase and Joshua Tolford. Permission by Houghton Mifflin Company.

Jokes: "Mary: You have your shoes . . ." and "Kerry: What do . . . ?" from *The Joke Book*, compiled by Oscar Weigle. Copyright © 1963 by Grosset & Dunlap, Inc. Published by Grosset & Dunlap, Inc., New York.

Joke: "Tourist: Look at that bunch of cows," from *The Real Book of Jokes* by Margaret Gossett. Copyright 1954 by Franklin Watts, Inc. Used by permission of Franklin and Mary Elting Folsom.

"Little Vic's Greatest Race," adapted from *Little Vic* by Doris Gates. Copyright 1951 by Doris Gates. Reprinted by permission of The Viking Press, Inc.

"Loneliness" and "Charlotte," from *Charlotte's Web*, by E. B. White. Copyright 1952 by E. B. White. Used by permission of Harper & Row, Publishers, Inc., and Hamish Hamilton, Ltd.

"Make a Fossil," from *Fossils Tell of Long Ago* by Aliki Brandenberg. Copyright © 1972 by Aliki Brandenberg, with permission of Thomas Y. Crowell Company, Inc., publisher, and John Farquharson, Ltd.

"Mary and the Monster," by Margaret J. Anderson. Reprinted from *Ranger Rick's Nature Magazine* by permission of the publisher, the National Wildlife Federation.

"Meet Delilah," adapted from *Delilah* by Carole Hart. Text copyright © 1973 by Carole Hart. Reprinted by permission of Harper & Row, Publishers, Inc. and McIntosh and Otis, Inc.

"Mrs. Dunn's Lovely, Lovely Farm," from *The Witch of Fourth Street* by Myron Levoy. Text copyright © 1972 by Myron Levoy. Used by permission of Harper & Row, Publishers, Inc.

"The Mystery of the Moon Guitar," adapted from *The Moon Guitar*, copyright © 1969 by Marie Niemeyer. Used by permission of the publisher, Franklin Watts, Inc.

"New Hope for the Whooping Crane," adapted from *The Whooping Crane* by J. M. Roever. Copyright © 1971 by Steck-Vaughn Company.

". . . and now Miguel," from *. . . and now Miguel*, by Joseph Krumgold. Copyright © 1953 by Joseph Krumgold, with permission of Thomas Y. Crowell Company, Inc., publishers, and the Julian Bach Literary Agency.

"Old Bessie, a brown speckled cow . . . ," from *Animal Limericks*, by Edward S. Mullins. Copyright © 1966 by Edward S. Mullins. By permission of Follett Publishing Company.

"Our Court," from *Project Boy* by Lois Lenski. Copyright, 1954 by Lois Lenski. Published by J. B. Lippincott. Used by permission of Henry Z. Walck, Inc., publishers.

"Paul Revere's Big Ride," by Jean Fritz. Abridged and adapted by permission of Jean Fritz and Coward, McCann & Geoghegan, Inc. from *And Then What Happened, Paul Revere?* Text copyright © 1973 by Jean Fritz; illustrations copyright © 1973 by Margot Tomes. Permission also by Russell & Volkening, Inc.

"The People Downstairs," from *The People Downstairs and Other City Stories* by Rhoda Bacmeister. Copyright © 1964 by Rhoda Bacmeister. Adapted by permission of Coward, McCann and Geohegan, Inc.

"Pepe Goes North," from *The Green Song* by Doris Troutman Plenn. Copyright 1954 by Doris Plenn. Published by the David McKay Company, Inc. Reprinted by permission of the publishers and the Evelyn Singer Agency, Inc.

"Races on Wheels," excerpts by permission of Charles Scribner's Sons from *A Great Bicycle Book* by Jane Sarnoff and Reynold Ruffins. Text copyright © 1973 Jane Sarnoff. Illustrations copyright © 1973 Reynold Ruffins.

"Riders on the Goodnight-Loving Trail," from *The Adventures of the Negro Cowboys* by Philip Durham and Everett L. Jones. Copyright © 1965, 1966 by Philip C. Durham and Everett L. Jones. Reprinted by permission of Dodd, Mead & Company, Inc. and Collins-Knowlton-Wing, Inc.

"The Sea Turtle," by Keith Hay. Reprinted from *Ranger Rick's Nature Magazine* published by the National Wildlife Federation.

"Smorgasbord" and "Word Stories," adapted by permission of Pantheon Books, a Division of Random House, Inc. from *Dandelions Don't Bite* by Leone Adelson. Copyright © 1972 by Leone Adelson.

"The Spider, the Cave, and the Pottery Bowl," from *The Spider, the Cave, and the Pottery Bowl* by Eleanor Clymer. Text copyright © 1971 by Eleanor Clymer. Used by permission of Atheneum Publishers.

"Subway Ride," from *This Street's for Me* by Lee Bennett Hopkins. Copyright © 1970 by Lee Bennett Hopkins. Used by permission of Crown Publishers, Inc.

"Taking Away and Putting Into," from *Roosevelt Grady*, by Louisa R. Shotwell. Copyright © 1963 by Louisa R. Shotwell. Reprinted by permission of William Collins & World Publishing Co., Inc., and The Bodley Head.

"A Tame Bear?" adapted from the book *Gentle Ben*, by Walt Morey. Copyright © 1965 by Walt Morey. Adapted and reprinted by permission of E. P. Dutton and Co., Inc. and J. M. Dent & Sons, Ltd.

"Three Strong Women," from *Three Strong Women* by Claus Stamm. Copyright © 1962 by Claus Stamm and Kazue Mizumura. Adapted by permission of The Viking Press, Inc.

"Toad's Tongue Twister," from *Tongue Tanglers* by Charles Francis Potter, copyright © 1962. Reprinted by permission of William Collins & World Publishing Co., Inc.

"The Train That Never Came Back," from *The Train That Never Came Back*, by Freeman H. Hubbard and Kurt Wiese. Copyright 1952 by Freeman H. Hubbard and Kurt Wiese. Used by permission of McGraw-Hill Book Company.

"Treasure Island, USA," by Rafe Gibbs. Used by permission of the author.

"Trip: San Francisco," by Langston Hughes. Copyright 1958 by Langston Hughes. Reprinted by permission of Harold Ober Associates, Inc.

"Undersea Parks—A New Wave in Hawaii," by Lorraine M. Ruff, from *Jack and Jill Magazine*, copyright 1974 by The Saturday Evening Post Company.

"Web Weavers," by Ruth Fagen. Reprinted from *Ranger Rick's Nature Magazine*, published by the National Wildlife Federation.

"Well, hello down there," from *Cricket Songs: Japanese Haiku*, translated and · © 1964 by Harry Behn. By permission of Harcourt Brace Jovanovich, Inc. and Curtis Brown, Ltd.

"What Is the Last Number?" reprinted from *Answers and More Answers*, by Mary Elting. Copyright © 1961 by Mary Elting. Published by Grosset and Dunlap, Inc.

"Wheels," adapted from *Wheels*, by Lisa Miller. Text © 1965 by Lisa Miller. By permission of Coward, McCann and Geoghegan, Inc.

"When Clay Sings," from *When Clay Sings* by Byrd Baylor. Reprinted by permission of Charles Scribner's Sons. Copyright © 1972 Byrd Baylor.

"The Wolf Pack," from *Little House on the Prairie*, by Laura Ingalls Wilder. Text copyright 1935 by Laura Ingalls Wilder. Copyright renewed 1963 by Roger L. MacBride. Used by permission of Harper and Row, Publishers, and Methuen Children's Books, Ltd.

"Words in a Circle," reprinted by permission from *Arrow Book of Word Games* by Murray Rockowitz, © 1964 by Scholastic Magazines, Inc.

Illustrators: PP. 12-25, SUSAN SWAN; PP. 28-34, LYLE MILLER; PP. 35-41, DONN ALBRIGHT; P. 42 *(also* PP. 95, 148, 192, 252, 294, 356, 396, 462, 497) LOU CUNETTE; P. 45, WALLY NEIBART; PP. 48-67, ROBERT ANDREW PARKER; PP. 68-79, DOROTHEA SIERRA; PP. 81-89, SHAN ELLENTUCK; P. 90, IKKI MATSUMOTO; PP. 96-98, WALLY NEIBART; PP. 100-113, GARTH WILLIAMS; PP. 118-120, CHRISTINE CZERNOTA; PP. 121-131, JOHN FREAS; P. 132, LAURENCE SCOTT; PP. 133-141, MICHAEL HAMPSHIRE; PP. 142-146, BILL MORRISON; PP. 149, 150, 152, WALLY NEIBART; PP. 153-168, MARC BROWN; PP. 170-180, WILLIAM NEGRON; PP. 182-189, DIANE SHAPIRO; PP. 190-191, MARC BROWN; P. 195, WALLY NEIBART; PP. 196-213, JOHN FREAS; PP. 218-228, MARGOT TOMES; P. 232, BONNIE UNSWORTH, *designer;* PP. 233-241, WILLI BAUM; PP. 242-247, JEANETTE KEHL; P. 255, WALLY NEIBART; PP. 257-274, RICHARD EGIELSKI; PP. 276-284, GEORGE EISENBERG; P. 285, MARC BROWN; PP. 286-288, REYNOLD RUFFINS; PP. 297, 298, WALLY NEIBART; PP. 300-315, ARVIS STEWART; PP. 340-351, LYDIA DABCOVICH; P. 355, JUDY PELIKAN; PP. 356 (bottom), 357, WALLY NEIBART; PP. 362-370, DAVID JONAS; P. 371, STEVE SNIDER; PP. 372-379, ELEONORE SCHMID; P. 380, YOKO MITSUHASHI; PP. 381-392, PETE HARRITOS; P. 393, LADY McCRADY; PP. 394-395, TECO SLAGBOOM; P. 399, 401, WALLY NEIBART; PP. 402-417, GARTH WILLIAMS; PP. 422-433, BOB BARNER; P. 434, DAVID KELLEY, *designer;* PP. 436-439, KYUZO TZUGAMI; PP. 440-454, ERIC VON SCHMIDT; P. 463, JOHN FREAS; P. 464 (top) RICHARD EGIELSKI, (bottom) BILL MORRISON; PP. 465, 466, ERIC VON SCHMIDT; PP. 468-472, JOEL SNYDER; PP. 480-481, IKKI MATSUMOTO; PP. 482-491, FRANZ ALTSCHULER; P. 492, SUE THOMPSON; PP. 493-496, TAD KRUMEICH; P. 498, SHAN ELLENTUCK; P. 499 (top) GARTH WILLIAMS; P. 499 (bottom) ROBERT ANDREW PARKER; PP. 502-521, JIM CROWELL. p. 76 (top left and bottom) adapted from illustrations by Tom Bahti from *When Clay Sings* by Byrd Baylor by permission of Charles Scribner's Sons. Illustrations copyright © 1972 Tom Bahti.

Photographs: P. 27, TERRY WALKER; P. 80 (top) The Bettmann Archive, (center) GRANT HEILMAN PHOTOGRAPHY; PP. 91, 92-93, Tass from Sovfoto; p. 118, MARTUCCI STUDIOS; P. 169, GEORGE S. SHENG; P. 181, JOHN T. URBAN/Stock, Boston; P. 229, JOHN RUNNING/Stock, Boston; P. 232, BONNIE UNSWORTH; P. 248 (top left) Bituminous Coal Institute, (top right) GEORGE S. SHENG; P. 249 (background) GEORGE S. SHENG, (foreground) CHRISTIAN DELBERT; p. 250, Museum of Science, Boston; p. 275, ERNST HAAS/Magnum; PP. 289, 290, Florida Department of Commerce; p. 291, JESSE O'CONNELL GIBBS; p. 292 (top, center foreground, and bottom) JESSE O'CONNELL GIBBS, (center background) Florida Department of Commerce; p. 293 (top) House of Refuge, Stuart, Florida, (middle and bottom) PETER C. H. PRITCHARD; PP. 320-339, ALFRED A. COHN; P. 352, WERNER STOY/Camera Hawaii; p. 353 (top right) Tom Stack Associates, (center) DAVE LATOUCHE/Tom Stack Associates, (bottom left) Camera Hawaii, (bottom right) Shostal Associates; P. 354, Tom Stack Associates; p. 359, Field Museum of Natural History; p. 434, DAVID KELLEY; P. 455, MARTY STOUFFER; P. 456 (top) MARTY STOUFFER from NATIONAL AUDUBON SOCIETY, (center) MARTY STOUFFER, (bottom) FRED LAHRMAN from NATIONAL AUDUBON SOCIETY; P. 459, *Animals Animals* © 1974 by JERRY COOKE; P. 461, J. BERNDT/Stock, Boston; PP. 473-479, EEVA/Courtesy of the Bronx Zoo; P. 500, ALFRED A. COHN.

Book cover, title page, and magazine covers by GARY FUJIWARA.

Contents

COUNTERPOINT

REFLECTIONS

SYMMETRY

8

Counterpoint

STORIES

ARTICLES

POEMS

JUST FOR FUN

SKILL LESSONS

During the late 1800's and early 1900's, thousands of people from Russia, Italy, Ireland, and other countries came to America to build better lives. Many of these families made their homes in New York City.

In the book THE WITCH OF FOURTH STREET AND OTHER STORIES, *Myron Levoy tells eight slightly true but mostly fanciful tales about these wonderful people. The story you are about to read is one of these tales.*

Mrs. Dunn's Lovely, Lovely Farm

by Myron Levoy

Mrs. Dunn had always wanted a farm. Back in the old country, she had lived in the great city of Dublin with its crowded streets and noisy carts over the cobblestones. She had made her husband promise that when they came to America, they would save every penny they possibly could, so that in time they could buy a farm — a lovely farm with chickens and cows and potatoes, with the smell of sweet clover and the giggle of a brook always beyond the door, where their children, Cathy and Neil, could have good fresh food, could grow and run and tumble — a lovely, lovely farm.

When they arrived in New York, with other thousands from Ireland and Italy and Hungary and Russia, they moved into a little apartment on the third floor of a building near Second Avenue. One of their neighbors was named DeMarco and another was named Kandel. In Dublin everyone had Irish names; this was something new and different, and a little frightening. But the neighbors said hello and smiled and warned them about Mr. Warfield, the terrible, horrible landlord. And Mr. and Mrs. Dunn felt much better, because in Dublin the landlords had been terrible and horrible, too. Things were becoming familiar very quickly.

The next task was for Mr. Dunn to find work. After much searching, he found a job hauling coal. He helped send the coal roaring like a river down a metal chute into the basements of buildings. Sometimes he would stand on the mound of coal in the back of the truck and coax it down through a square hole into the chute. And sometimes he would stand on the coal pile down in the cellar, clearing the coal away from the bottom of the chute so that more coal and still more coal could come roaring down into the coal bin.

Mr. Dunn would come home every night looking just like a great lump of coal, himself. But after a good washing and a hot dinner, Mr. Dunn looked almost like Mr. Dunn again.

And though they could pay the rent and buy coats for the winter, and could afford a little more lamb and butter than they could in Dublin, they couldn't seem to save much money. After a year, Mrs. Dunn counted four dollars and ninety-two cents in her secret empty cereal box, and Mr. Dunn had eight dollars and twelve cents in his shaving mug.

At that rate, they would never have enough for a farm. There were new shoes needed, and a new blanket, and a bigger stew pot, and this, and that, and the other. So Mrs. Dunn made a firm decision. They must buy their farm now, as much of it as they could, or the money would vanish like a mist over the chimneys of Dublin. And Mr. Dunn had to admit she was right.

That very next day, Mrs. Dunn bought a hen. They had told her at the market that it was a good, dependable laying hen, a Rhode Island Red, the best.

Mrs. Dunn wrapped the hen in a scarf, tucked it under her arm, and carried it five blocks back to her kitchen. Then she put the hen on the floor and watched it strut on the yellow linoleum.

The children named it Amelia for no special reason and fed it cereal and corn and crusts of bread. Mr. Dunn brought home scraps of wood from the coalyard and built a coop. Then with more wood and some chicken wire, he built a little barnyard filled with dirt and pebbles in which Amelia could scratch. And he took some old felt hats and shaped them into nice, soft nests.

Soon, Amelia was joined by Agatha, and then Adeline. Now there were two eggs, sometimes three, every morning in the hat-nests, fresh and delicious. Cathy and Neil loved Agatha and Amelia and Adeline as if they were their own sisters. Each hen was different: Amelia was very, very proud and strutted as if she were a rooster; Agatha was a busybody, forever poking into everything; Adeline was shy and loved to sit in the coop and preen.

Soon, the other children in the building started bringing the three hens little presents: Aaron Kandel brought pieces of a huge, flat, dry cracker called *matzo* (maht′suh), which Adeline particularly loved; Fred Reinhardt brought scraps of thick pumpernickel bread; and Vincent De-Marco brought dried seeds called chick peas. And sometimes, Mrs. Dunn would give one of the

children a freshly laid egg to take home.

Now it was time for the vegetables, for who ever heard of a farm without vegetables? Mr. Dunn built large, deep boxes, filled them with earth, and planted seeds. Then he put them on the fire escape outside the bedroom window. When the fire-escape landing was covered with boxes, he put new boxes on the iron stairs leading up to the next landing. Soon, the fire escape was blooming with the green shoots of tomato plants, string beans, potatoes, onions, and parsley. And on every windowsill were pots of herbs: rosemary, thyme, mint, chives.

On weekdays, Mrs. Dunn carefully weeded and watered the fire-escape garden and fed the chickens. On Sundays, after he had tried to wash the last of the coal from his face and hands for the third time, Mr. Dunn would repair the chicken wire, and prop up the growing vegetables with tall sticks and string, and build new boxes. Then he and Mrs. Dunn would walk from room to room, admiring the pots of herbs, the vegetables, the chickens, and the mushrooms growing in flat boxes on the kitchen shelves.

But one day, Mr. Warfield, the terrible, horrible landlord, came to collect the rents. As he was about to enter the building, a sun shower drenched his hat. He took off the hat and looked at it with disbelief, for there wasn't a cloud in the sky. Perhaps a tenant had spilled some dishwater on him from above. He looked up and shook his fist toward the top of the building at the hidden enemy.

His mouth dropped in astonishment, and he forgot to bring down his fist, for up above, three stories up, was a hanging garden twining about the metal bars of the fire escape. A lady was watering the green mirage with a watering can, and some of it had dripped down the fire escape from landing to landing until it finally splashed on Mr. Warfield's head.

"This is an outrage!" Mr. Warfield muttered to himself. "It's completely unreasonable."

Then he plunged into the building and rushed toward the stairs.

"Ah, Mr. Warfield," said Mrs. Callahan at the first landing, "and when, tell me, are you going to fix m'stove? The divil of a thing's got only one burner working. Do you expect me to pay m'rent when I can't cook soup and stew at the same time?"

"Oh blast!" said Mr. Warfield. "I'll see you later. I've got a madhouse here. A madhouse! Let me go by, Mrs. Callahan."

"And what might be the trouble, if I may ask?" said Mrs. Callahan.

"Somebody's growing a tree on the fire escape!"

"Ah, to be sure, to be sure." And with that, Mrs. Callahan nudged her little girl, Noreen, standing next to her. Without a word, Noreen turned and raced up the two flights of stairs to warn her friend Cathy Dunn that Warfield, the monster landlord, was on his way up. "And tell me now, Mr. Warfield, but how would a tree gain the necessary nourishment on a fire escape, do you know?"

"I intend to find out, Mrs. Callahan, if you'll let me get by!"

"But m'stove, Mr. Warfield. I'm paying rent for three rooms and four burners."

"Yes, yes, yes, yes! Very reasonable request. We'll have it fixed in seventy-two hours. Now please let me get—"

"Seventy-two hours, is it now? Make it twenty-four," said Mrs. Callahan.

"But that's only one *day*. That's unreasonable. Make it . . . forty-eight hours."

"Thirty-six, Mr. Warfield, or I'll have the Board of Health, I will."

"Forty!"

"Thirty-eight!"

"All right! We'll have it fixed within thirty-eight hours! Now let me *through*!"

And Mr. Warfield raced up the flight of stairs to the second landing.

"Hello, Mr. Warfield!" Mrs. Grotowski called. "I dreamt about you last night! And what did I dream?"

"I don't care!" said Mr. Warfield. "Let me go by!"

"I'll *tell* you what. I dreamt that I took the money for your rent and tore it up into little shreds. Then I put a little pepper on it, a little salt, stirred in some nice chicken fat, and made you eat every dollar of it until you choked. And *why*?"

"Please, Mrs. Grotowski! This isn't the time for your dreams!"

"I'll tell you why. Because you promised to have my apartment painted two months ago. Two months! Where are the painters? Did they join the Foreign Legion? Or is it possible that they've gone over Niagara Falls in a barrel?"

"We'll have the painters soon."

"When?"

"Soon. Very soon."

"How soon?"

"Very, very soon. Let me go by, Mrs. Grotowski, before I lose my temper."

"This week! I want them *this week*."

"Next week."

"By Friday!"

"By next Wednesday, for sure, Mrs. Grotowski."

"By next Monday, Mr. Warfield, next *Monday*."

"Tuesday."

"All right. But it better be Tuesday," said Mrs. Grotowski.

"Tuesday. Absolutely, positively Tuesday."

Meanwhile, up in the Dunns' apartment, people were flying back and forth. Cathy and Neil had each grabbed a chicken and raced out the door. One chicken went into the DeMarco apartment, the other clucked away in Mrs. Kandel's kitchen. But the chicken left behind, Amelia—or was it Adeline?—had gotten so excited from all the rushing about that she'd flown up to the ceiling and was now roosting comfortably on top of the chandelier in the living room. Mr. Dunn wasn't at home, but Mrs. Dunn took vegetable boxes off the fire-escape landing and slid them under the bed. And from the apartment above, Mrs. Cherney climbed out of her bedroom window onto the fire

escape, took more boxes off the iron stairs, and hid them in her own apartment. But try though they did, there just wasn't enough time to hide everything.

Now Mr. Warfield had finally reached the third floor and was pounding at the Dunns' door. Three Rhode Island Reds answered with a cascade of *berawk-bawk-bawk*s: one in Mrs. Kandel's kitchen, one in Mrs. DeMarco's bathroom, and one on Mrs. Dunn's chandelier. But fortunately, Mr. Warfield knew they weren't chickens, because that would not be possible. It was the children making noises at him. Why did they all hate him? He was a good man. Fair. Reasonable. Wasn't he always reasonable? . . . But what was *this*? There were feathers in the hallway. Children having a pillow fight? Very likely. Ah well, children must play. No harm. Not like trees on the fire escape!

Then Mr. Warfield pounded on the door again; not the dainty tap-tap of a salesman, nor the thump-thump of a bill collector, but the shaboom-shaboom of a landlord. And again, from three apartments, three children in a superb imitation of three chickens, *berawk-bawk*ed away at Mr. Warfield.

"Why?" thought Mr. Warfield. "Why?" He had three children of his own and they *loved* him. Didn't they? Of course they did.

At last the door opened a crack, and Mrs. Dunn's hand appeared with an envelope holding the rent money. She waved the envelope up and down at Mr. Warfield. Mr. Warfield took the envelope but also pushed firmly on the door.

"Mrs. Dunn, I'd like a word or two with you," he said.

"I'm feeling a bit ill today, Mr. Warfield, sir. Would you be so kindly as to stop back next week."

"Mrs. Dunn! There is a tree growing on your fire escape! I saw it with my own two eyes!"

"Mr. Warfield," said Mrs. Dunn rapidly, "you're blessed. There's many a blind man would trade this very building for your keen eyesight. But still, a tree cannot truly grow on a fire escape. Good day to you now."

"Good day, my foot! I demand to see the condition of that fire escape. As landlord, I have the right to enter and inspect the premises at reasonable hours. I'm a reasonable man, and I would never come at an unreasonable hour."

"Why, it's nearly four o' the clock. I've got to do m' husband's supper. 'Tis not a reasonable hour at all," said Mrs. Dunn.

"Either you let me in, Madam, or I'll call the police—*and* the fire department. A tree on the fire escape is a fire hazard. Let me in!"

"Tomorrow."

"NOW!" shouted Mr. Warfield. And with that, the chicken on the chandelier clucked again. "Did you hear that, Mrs. Dunn?"

"Sounded like a cuckoo clock. Cuckoo, cuckoo. 'Tis four o' the clock, you see."

"Nonsense. You have a *chicken* in there! My building has *chickens!*" At that, all three hens in all three apartments *berawk-bawk*ed again. "This isn't an apartment house! It's a zoo!" Then Mr. Warfield pushed his way past Mrs. Dunn and stormed into her living room.

"My chandelier!" shouted Mr. Warfield.

"'Tisn't *your* chandelier. I've

paid the rent. 'Tis *my* chandelier," said Mrs. Dunn.

Mr. Warfield rushed through to the bedroom and stared at the remains of the farm on the fire escape. "My fire escape!" His face was flushed; his eyes were bulging. "Unbelievable! Mrs. Dunn, what are these weeds supposed to *be*?"

"That? Why that's onions, Mr. Warfield."

"*This* is an *onion*?"

"Oh, you can't see it. The onion's beneath the dirt. Least I hope 'tis."

"And *this*?" he said, pointing.

"That's supposed to be potatoes. But I fear for them. The soil's not deep enough."

"Incredible!" he said. "Don't you like geraniums, Mrs. Dunn? I thought people liked to grow geraniums. Look out the window, across the street. See the window-sills? There and there. And over there. Everyone *else* is growing geraniums."

"That's a good *idea*, Mr. Warfield," said Mrs. Dunn. "'Twould brighten up the house. I'll fetch some seed tomorrow."

"No, no. I didn't mean . . . Mrs.

Dunn, look here. This is a fire-trap! And that chicken—"

"I have two more, visiting with the neighbors."

"Well, that, Mrs. Dunn, is a relief. I thought *all* the tenants had gone insane."

"No, 'tis only m'self. But I do think I'm as sane as you, if not a bit saner. Because you see, I shall have the freshest vegetables in the city of New York. I already have the freshest eggs."

"Those chickens, in an apartment, are a health hazard. You'll have to remove them! Sell them to a farmer or a butcher."

"I shan't. They stay right here."

"That's unreasonable. I'm a reasonable man, Mrs. Dunn. Say something reasonable, *ask* something reasonable, and I'll say: *That's* reasonable."

"Very well. Why don't you pretend that you hadn't come at all today. Then you wouldn't have seen anything, would you, and your mind would rest easy," said Mrs. Dunn.

"Completely unreasonable! And *that's* why you tenants don't like me. Because *I'm* reasonable, and you're all *un*reasonable. Simple as that."

"Oh, I like you, Mr. Warfield."

"Nonsense."

"Any landlord who would offer me the use of his roof for a fine little garden must be a very likable *and* reasonable man."

"I didn't offer you any roof, Mrs. Dunn."

"You were going to. I saw it on the tip of your lips."

"My *lips?*"

"And you were going to say how much better 'twould be if the chickens had a much bigger coop up there on the roof."

"*I* was never going to say—"

"Tut tut, Mr. Warfield," said Mrs. Dunn. "You've as good as said it. And I was going to answer that for such generosity you should surely receive some fresh string beans and onions and potatoes in season. And you were going to say, 'Ah, and how lovely the roof would look with greenery all about.' And I was about to answer, 'Yes, Mr. Warfield, and the tenants would surely look at you most affectionately.' Would they not, now?"

"*Hmm*," said Mr. Warfield, thinking.

"Reasonable or unreasonable?" asked Mrs. Dunn.

"*Hmm* . . . well . . . I'd have to give this some thought."

"But you're a man of *action*, Mr. Warfield. You pound on the door like a very tiger."

"Yes. Well . . . it's not *un*reasonable," said Mr. Warfield. "If you didn't already *have* any chickens or trees or onions, I would say no. But since you *do* have all this *jungle* of creatures and vines . . . I would, after careful consideration, being after all a human being, I would . . . *ahem, ahem* . . . say . . . *ahem* . . . yes."

"Oh, you are a darling man, Mr. Warfield. A darling, *darling* man."

"Here, Mrs. Dunn! Watch your language! I mean to say! *Darling man?*"

"Oh, back in the old country, it only means you're nice, that's all."

"Oh. Now do remember, Mrs. Dunn, a bargain's a bargain. I expect one tenth of everything you grow as my roof rent. Is that a deal?"

"'Tis a deal."

"Except the onions. You can keep them all. I hate onions. My whole family hates onions."

And with that, Mr. Warfield slammed his hat on his head, only to find it was still wet from Mrs. Dunn's watering can. Without a word, he turned and stalked out to the living room. At that moment, Amelia—or was it Adeline up on the chandelier?—decided it was time to come down. For there, on top of Mr. Warfield's head, was her nest-shaped-like-a-hat, moving by. And down she came, wings beating, feathers flying, on top of Mr. Warfield's head. "Oh blast!" shouted Mr. Warfield as he raced to the hallway with the chicken flapping on top of him.

"She likes you!" called Mrs. Dunn. "She knows you have a

good heart! Chickens can tell right off!"

But Mr. Warfield didn't hear this very clearly, for as he raced out to the hallway and down the stairs, all three chickens started their *berawk-bawk*ing again, and the loudest of all was the one on top of Mr. Warfield. He finally escaped by leaving his nest-shaped-like-a-hat behind.

And so Mrs. Dunn moved everything to the roof, and Mr. Dunn added still more boxes for vegetables. Cathy and Neil and their friends went up to the roof every afternoon to feed the chickens and water the plants. And Mrs. Dunn had her lovely, lovely farm — or at least she thought she did, which comes to the same thing in the end.

AUTHOR

Myron Levoy was born in New York City. He went to college at Purdue University in Indiana. In college he studied to be a chemical engineer. While working as an engineer, he helped develop an atomic engine for rockets and spaceships.

In addition to working as an engineer, Mr. Levoy has done a lot of writing. He is the author of books, stories, plays, and poetry for adults. *The Witch of Fourth Street*, from which the story you have just read was taken, was his first book for young readers. He has since written another one, *Penny Tunes and Princesses*.

Mr. Levoy, his wife, and children live in New Jersey.

KERRY: What do they do with doughnut holes?
TERRY: They use them to stuff macaroni.

Tourist: Look at that bunch of cows.
Cowboy: Not "bunch"—herd.
Tourist: Heard what?
Cowboy: Herd of cows.
Tourist: Sure I've heard of cows.
Cowboy: No—a cow herd.
Tourist: Why should I care what a cow heard? I've got no secrets from a cow.

MARY: Barry, you have your shoes on the wrong feet.
BARRY: But they're the only feet I have!

Subway Ride

On the subway I can read the ads, count the stops,
   study faces—
      white faces, pink faces,
      brown faces, black faces,
      old faces, new faces,
      and my own face's face in the train window.

I can be a conductor (if I'm in the first car
   or the last) and look out the window at
   the darkness whizzing by.

I can think thoughts—my very own secret
   subway-ride thoughts.
And I ride and ride
Until it's my turn to get off.
Then I leave it all to someone else.

Lee Bennett Hopkins

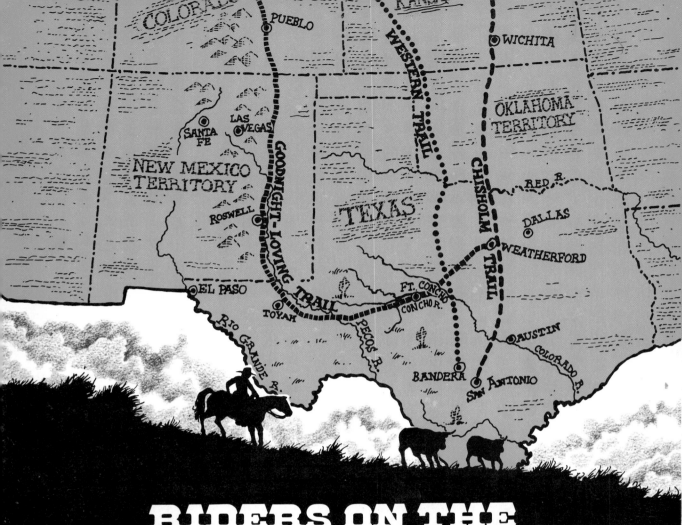

RIDERS ON THE GOODNIGHT-LOVING TRAIL

by Philip Durham and Everett L. Jones

*More than five thousand black cowboys rode the long cattle
trails north from Texas just after the Civil War. The following
article, from* THE ADVENTURES OF THE NEGRO COWBOYS, *tells*

At about the time of the Civil War, the American people began to eat more beef than pork, and there was a great demand for beef. But there were still no railroads going from Texas to the East. Cattlemen could not ship their animals as they can today. Instead, they had to round them up and drive them to railroads and markets in Kansas, Nebraska, or Colorado.

There were three main trails over which cattlemen drove their cattle up from Texas. These were the Chisholm Trail, the Western Trail, and the Goodnight-Loving Trail. They became important as cowboys drove cattle to them from all over the Texas plains.

One cattle trail out of Texas was very different from the trails that went north through Kansas. It went southwest through central Texas to the Pecos River, and then it turned north to go through New Mexico, Colorado, and Wyoming. Instead of running through rolling plains dotted by jack oaks and crossed by many rivers, it led through waterless deserts and over rough mountains.

It was pioneered by Colonel Charles Goodnight and Oliver Loving, two Texas cattlemen. Just after the end of the Civil War, these two men decided to drive their cattle to the army posts of New Mexico and the mining camps of Colorado. They threw their two herds together and began a drive from Weatherford, Texas.

There were several kinds of dangers on all the trails in those days. On the Goodnight-Loving Trail, however, there was a particular danger. Just before the trail reached the Pecos River, it had to go through about eighty miles of waterless desert.

On the trail, a longhorn herd normally needed water every day. In an emergency it could go two days without water, but thirst was hard on a steer. It did not like going without water, so it became hard to handle. Goodnight and Loving knew that to get across the eighty miles of desert, the herd would have to go about five days without water. The cowboys had a problem.

On the first drive, Goodnight and Loving started with a mixed herd that contained cows as well as steers. They knew that they had to move fast and that they could not be slowed down by calves born along the way. So each morning a cowboy had to shoot the calves born during the night.

When the herd came near the long stretch of desert, Goodnight and Loving stopped at the headwaters of the Middle Concho. There they allowed the herd to drink its fill of fresh water and prepare for the long, dry stretch ahead.

As they entered the desert, the trail bosses tried to pace the restless herd. They drove late in the afternoon and in the early morning, hoping to save the strength of the cattle. But the thirsty, restless animals would not bed down at night. They only milled around. So the cowboys found it easier to drive straight through.

Goodnight led the way. Loving stayed with the drag, saving every animal he could. They lost some cattle on the drive across the desert stretch. They lost more at the river, where about five hundred head stampeded after smelling the water of the Pecos. And they lost a few more to the poisoned water of potholes that lined the trail.

That first drive over the Goodnight-Loving Trail made history in the cattle country. One of the cowboys who helped

to make that history was Bose Ikard, a black. When the old cowboy died in Texas in 1929, the saddened Goodnight put up a marker that told about their four years together on the Goodnight-Loving Trail.

Bose was born a slave in Mississippi before the Civil War. He was brought to Texas by his master's family, the Ikards, when he was five years old. Growing up on the frontier near Weatherford, Texas, he learned to ride, rope, and fight. These skills made him a valuable hand later.

Bose Ikard first rode for Oliver Loving. But when Loving died, Bose began to ride for Goodnight.

Goodnight said that there was a dignity and a reliability about Bose that was wonderful. Goodnight went on to say, "I have trusted him farther than any living man. He was my detective, banker, and everything else in Colorado, New Mexico, and the other wild country I was in. The nearest and only bank was at Denver, and when we carried money, I gave it to Bose.

"We went through some terrible trials during those four years on the trail. . . . After being in the saddle for several days and nights at a time . . . and finding that I could stand it no longer, I would ask Bose if he would take my place.

He never failed to answer me in the most cheerful and willing manner and was the most skilled and trustworthy man I had.''

It would take many pages to tell about all the trails that Bose Ikard and Charles Goodnight rode together. One time on the trail, just before dawn, there was a stampede. Because the cattle had been quiet, Goodnight had left Bose alone with the herd and had ridden in to the wagon to wake the cook and get the crew moving. Suddenly something frightened the cattle, which came stampeding down toward the camp.

Goodnight grabbed a blanket and ran out waving it and making as much noise as he could. In this way he was able

to split the herd, which poured around the wagon and the men sleeping on the ground. Then he found his horse, which was still tied to the wagon wheel. He mounted and raced up the side of the stampeding herd.

By now, dawn was near and Goodnight could see. Near the front of the herd he saw Bose, and in a few minutes Bose looked back, saw him, and moved in to turn the leaders. Working together, the two men soon had the herd circled, and the stampede stopped.

Bose Ikard was no coward in other ways, too. When Goodnight was hurt in New Mexico and lay helpless in the shade of the wagon, Bose rode out to stop an outlaw leader from cutting the herd. At the end of one drive, when Goodnight drove from Colorado to Texas carrying all the profits of the year's drives with him, Bose was in the driver's seat, armed and alert.

There were many cowboys who rode along the Goodnight-Loving Trail in New Mexico. One of these, a black cowboy named Add, was range boss of the LFD outfit. Add usually led a crew of southern Texas black cowboys. Howard Thorp, himself a cowboy, said that Add was one of the best cowhands on the Pecos River: "Cowmen from Toyah, Texas, to Las Vegas, New Mexico, knew Add, and many of them at different times had worked on roundups with him." Working as a range boss made Add an expert. He became famous among the cattlemen of the Southwest and once became the subject of a cowboy song.

Add was known and respected all over the Pecos area of New Mexico. It was not surprising that the news of his plans spread rapidly when he told a few friends one fall that he intended to be married on Christmas Day. Widely separated ranchers, all of whom knew and liked him, decided to send presents. Most of them, prompted by their practical wives, decided on the same present. When Add and his bride rode on their wedding day to the Roswell freight station, they found *nineteen* cookstoves waiting for them!

Cowboys like Bose and Add rode on all the trails. Their job was to take beef to a nation of hungry people. Through cloudbursts and burning sun, through mud and dust, these men rode on. They went where the trails went, and they did their jobs.

AUTHORS

Philip Durham and Everett L. Jones teach at the University of California at Los Angeles. They have each written many books for adults. The interest they share in the history of the American West made them decide to work together on a book. *The Negro Cowboys* was first written for adults. Mr. Durham and Mr. Jones knew young readers, too, would be interested in the book, so they wrote another version, which they called *The Adventures of the Negro Cowboys*.

MEET DELILAH

by Carole Hart

Delilah Bush is almost ten years old. She's the tallest girl in her class. She plays basketball and drums. She has two left feet. (They're made of green felt, and they're sewn to the seat of her favorite pair of blue jeans.)

She also has short, very curly, brownish-red-in-winter, reddish-brown-in-summer hair that frames her face. One of Delilah's eyes is gray. The other is gray-green. She is named Delilah because her mother and father were young and silly at the time she was born.

Bounce. Delilah was dribbling her basketball to the playground down the street. *Bounce.* She felt light, as if she were riding on a soft, sighing wind. *Bounce.* She didn't have a care in the world. *Oof.* She rode right into a garbage collector.

"Shee . . ." he said.

"Sorry," she said.

"No mind," he said. Then he grabbed her basketball. And he started dribbling it down the street. Fast.

"Hey!" she said. And she ran after him, feeling slow, and wondering, *Where did the wind go?*

He stopped in the playground. She caught up to him. He smiled. She breathed hard and tried not to show it.

"You wanna play ball?" he asked.

"Sure," she answered. "Let's have a free-throw contest." That's what she did best. She got seven out of ten baskets and won the first round. He got six. The next time they tied. Eight baskets apiece.

"Let's try lay-ups," he said.

"No," she said.

"Why not?" he asked.

"I'm not very good at lay-ups," she said softly.

"What?" he said.

"I'm not very good at lay-ups," she said a little louder.

"I can't hear you," he said.

"I'm not very good at lay-ups," she shouted.

"Well," he said, "if you keep telling yourself you're not any good at lay-ups, you'll never get any better." He laughed and threw her the basketball. "Try one. Let's see."

She charged down the court, and missed—by a mile.

"No wonder you're not good. You move like a hurricane. Take it easy. Pretend you're riding on a soft, sighing wind." And he showed her. Nice and slow and graceful like a dance step.

She tried it his way. It worked. She tried it again. And again. It felt good. She might have played forever. But a loud and awful horn started honking.

"That's for me," he said. So they walked back up the street together to his garbage truck. Behind it there was an old man in a car, leaning on his horn.

"What do you think you're doing, leaving a garbage truck in the middle of the street?" the old man shouted.

The garbage collector climbed into his truck. "Sorry. I wasn't thinking," he told the old man. "So long," he told Delilah. "Thanks for the game."

"See ya," she said, and waved, and went on her way.

Bounce. Delilah was dribbling her basketball to her house up the street. *Bounce.* She felt light, as if she were riding on a soft, sighing wind. *Bounce.* She knew how to do lay-ups.

On the first day of spring, it was beautiful. It made Delilah happy. It made her so happy that she wanted to sing. "Oh, what a beautiful morning," she sang as she put on her favorite pair of jeans.

Her mother came rushing in. "Delilah, what's wrong?" she asked.

"Nothing," Delilah answered. "It's a beautiful day, and I was just singing about it."

"So that's what it was. I thought you were in pain." Delilah blushed. "Delilah, I know it's not right for a mother to be discouraging, but you are the *worst* singer I've ever heard. If you must sing, please sing somewhere else. OK?"

"Somewhere else." Delilah sang the words sweetly.

"That's a very old joke," her mother said, but she laughed anyway. And Delilah went out for a walk.

It *was* a beautiful day. It made Delilah happy. It made her so happy that, despite herself, she burst into song. A police officer passing in his car screeched to a stop. "Whatsa matter, kid?" he asked.

"Nothing," Delilah answered. "It's a beautiful day, and I was just singing about it."

"So that's what it was. It sounded like appendicitis!" Delilah

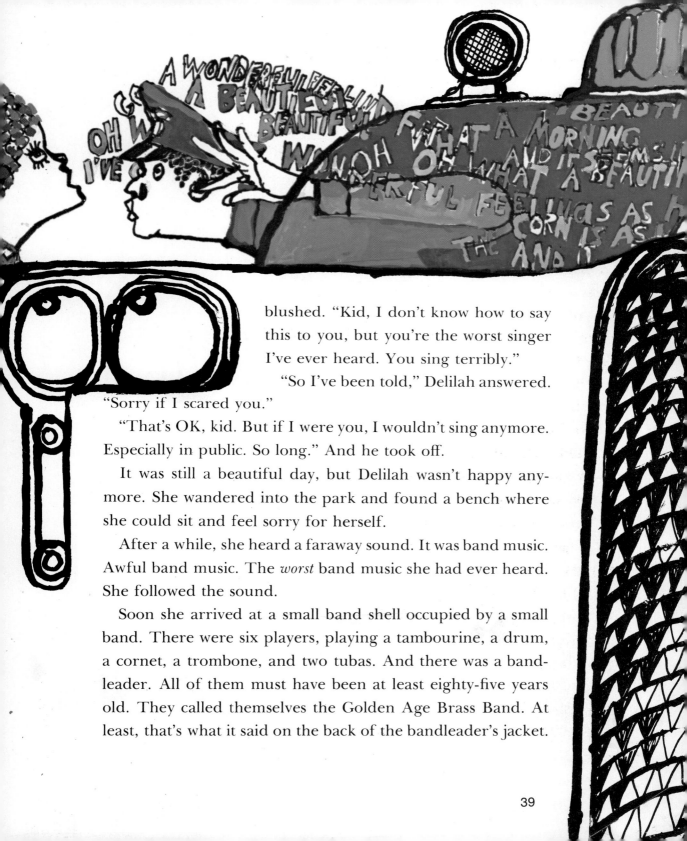

blushed. "Kid, I don't know how to say this to you, but you're the worst singer I've ever heard. You sing terribly."

"So I've been told," Delilah answered. "Sorry if I scared you."

"That's OK, kid. But if I were you, I wouldn't sing anymore. Especially in public. So long." And he took off.

It was still a beautiful day, but Delilah wasn't happy anymore. She wandered into the park and found a bench where she could sit and feel sorry for herself.

After a while, she heard a faraway sound. It was band music. Awful band music. The *worst* band music she had ever heard. She followed the sound.

Soon she arrived at a small band shell occupied by a small band. There were six players, playing a tambourine, a drum, a cornet, a trombone, and two tubas. And there was a bandleader. All of them must have been at least eighty-five years old. They called themselves the Golden Age Brass Band. At least, that's what it said on the back of the bandleader's jacket.

"Hi!" Delilah said when they'd finished their number.

"What'd ya say?" the bandleader asked her.

Delilah moved a little closer. "I said, 'Hi.'"

"I didn't quite get it. Would you mind speaking up? A little hard of hearing, you know."

Delilah grinned. "Can you play 'When the Saints Go Marchin' In'?" she shouted.

"Sure," the bandleader shouted back.

"Would you?" she asked.

"Of course," the bandleader said happily. It was the first time he'd ever been asked to play anything except somewhere else. Delilah climbed onto the band shell. "A-one, a-two, a-three, a-four," the bandleader counted. And the band played. And Delilah sang.

When they finished, they all clapped for each other. "Do you know 'Hail, Hail, the Gang's All Here'?" Delilah shouted.

"Sure do," said the bandleader. And on the first day of spring, Delilah sang for joy.

The story you have just read tells only two of the many adventures Delilah Bush has with her family and friends. You can get to know her better by reading the book DELILAH, *by Carole Hart.*

AUTHOR

Carole Hart has worked on many projects besides books. She was one of the original writers for the well-known television show called *Sesame Street.* She also wrote the children's television special "The Wonderful World of Jonathan Winters" and produced the record "Free To Be . . . You and Me," by Marlo Thomas and Friends.

Like Delilah, Carole Hart lives in Manhattan, in New York City.

LOCATING WORDS AND WORD MEANINGS IN A DICTIONARY

You know that sometimes you can figure out the meaning of a strange word by using the context in which you meet the word. But when the context does not give the help you need, you should try to get the meaning all by yourself in some other way. That is one reason why you should learn how to use a dictionary.

A good dictionary lists many words and tells you what their meanings are. Look at the dictionary page on the opposite page. There you can see that words included in the dictionary list are printed in heavy black print and are placed farthest to the left in each column. You also can see that each word in the list is followed by one or more meanings.

All the words in a dictionary list are placed in the order of the letters of the alphabet. First come all the words that begin with *a*. Then come all those that begin with *b*. The words that begin with *c* come next, and so on through the *z* words, which are the last words in the list.

You can see that in a dictionary list the words *bottle* and *broom* would be among the words which begin with *b*. Which word would come first? The second letter in each word tells

pack (păk) *n.* **1.** A bundle to be carried on the back of a person or animal. **2.** A group of dogs or wolves that hunt together. **3.** A group or set of like things: *a pack of cards.* —*v.* **1.** To place in a box or a trunk. **2.** To crowd together.

pack•age (păk′ĭj) *n.* **1.** A bundle of things wrapped up or tied together. **2.** A box, case, or crate in which things are packed. —*v.* To make up or arrange into a package: *They package a pen with each notebook.*

pack•er (păk′ər) *n.* A person who packs goods, especially meat products, for transportation and sale.

pack•et (păk′ĭt) *n.* **1.** A small package or bundle, as of mail. **2.** A boat that is used to carry mail and cargo as well as people.

pack rat. A North American rat that carries off objects and collects them in its nesting place.

pack•sack (păk′săk′) *n.* A canvas or leather pack carried strapped to the shoulders.

pact (păkt) *n.* A formal agreement, as between nations; a treaty.

pad•dle•fish (păd′l fĭsh′) *n.* A large fish of the Mississippi River and its branches, having a long snout in the shape of an oar.

pad•dock (păd′ək) *n.* **1.** A small enclosed field or pasture. **2.** An enclosed place planted with grass at a racetrack, in which horses are exercised.

pad•dy (păd′ē) *n.* **1.** Rice, whether still growing or harvested. **2.** The land on which rice is grown.

pad•lock (păd′lŏk′) *n.* A removable lock with a curved bar that is hinged at one end. The bar is put through a ring or link and then snapped into a hole in the body of the lock. —*v.* To fasten with a padlock.

pae•an (pē′ən) *n.* A song of joy or praise.

pag•eant (păj′ənt) *n.* **1.** A public entertainment or play, often performed outdoors, consisting of scenes based on historical events. **2.** An elaborate show or spectacle, such as a parade.

pa•go•da (pə gō′də) *n.* A sacred Hindu or Buddhist temple or tower.

pail (pāl) *n.* **1.** A container, usually round, with a flat bottom and curved handle; a bucket. **2.** The amount held by a pail: *I spilled almost a pail of water.*

pain (pān) *n.* An ache; suffering in either the body or the mind. —*v.* To hurt: *The sharp scolding pained him.*

pain•ful (pān′fəl) *adj.* **1.** Full of pain; causing pain. **2.** Needing effort or care: *a painful task.*

pain•less (pān′lĭs) *adj.* Free from pain; causing no pain.

pains•tak•ing (pānz′tā′kĭng) *adj.* Involving or showing great care; careful: *a painstaking study.*

paint (pānt) *n.* **1.** A color or pigment, usually mixed with oil or water, that forms a dry coat when spread over a surface. **2.** A spotted horse; a pinto. —*v.* **1.** To cover or decorate with paint. **2.** To make (a picture) with paints: *She painted four pictures.* **3.** To represent in a painting: *She painted some horses by a river.*

ă pat/ ā pay/ â care/ ä father/ ĕ pet/ ē be/ ĭ pit/ ī pie/ î fierce/ ŏ pot/ ō go/ ô paw, for/
oi oil/ o͝o took/ o͞o boot/ ou out/ ŭ cut/ û fur/ *th* the/ th thin/ hw which/ zh vision/ ə ago,
item, pencil, atom, circus

you. Since *o* comes before *r* in the alphabet, *bottle* comes before *broom* in a dictionary list. Which word comes first in a dictionary list, *glass* or *game?* Why?

Which word would come first in a dictionary list, *paint* or *panda?* When the first two letters in each word are the same, the third letter in each word tells you. Since *i* comes before *n* in the alphabet, *paint* comes before *panda* in a dictionary list. Which word comes first in a dictionary list, *token* or *toast?* Why?

Think of a dictionary as having a front part, a middle part, and a back part. To which part would you open the book to find the word *musket?* To which part would you open to find each of the words *valve, bluejay,* and *orbit?* Why?

Look again at the dictionary page on page 43. Do you see the words *pack* and *paint* at the top of the page? They are called **guide words.** Notice too that the first guide word, *pack,* is the first word in the dictionary list on the page and that the second guide word, *paint,* is the last word in the list. All the other words listed on the page come in alphabetical order after *pack* and before *paint.*

You can use the guide words on a dictionary page to decide quickly whether a word you are looking for is listed on that page. If your word comes between the two guide words in alphabetical order, it will be on that page unless the dictionary you are using does not list it at all. If your word comes before the first guide word in alphabetical order and the dictionary lists it, it will be on some page which comes before the one you are looking at. If your word comes after the second guide word and the dictionary lists it, it will be on some page which comes after the one you are looking at.

Suppose that you opened a dictionary to a page on which the guide words are *game* and *get.* Why would you expect or why would you not expect to find on that page each of the following words: *gate, gem, gander, geyser?*

Sometimes a dictionary gives only one meaning for a word. Often, however, more than one meaning is given. Notice the different meanings that the dictionary page on page 43 gives for the word *pack.*

Look at the *n.* that follows the special spelling of *pack.* The *n.* is an abbreviation that stands for the word *noun.* After the *n.* are three different meanings that the word *pack* can have when it is used as a noun in a sentence.

Find the —*v.* after the third meaning for *pack.* The abbreviation —*v.* stands for the word *verb.* After the —*v.* are two meanings that the word *pack* can have when it is used as a verb in a sentence.

If you know that *pack* is used as a noun in the sentence you are reading, you need only to read the noun meanings and then choose the meaning that makes sense in that sentence. If you know that *pack* is a verb, you need only to read the verb meanings before you choose the one that makes sense in the context of your reading.

Sometimes a word listed in a dictionary is neither a noun nor a verb, but another part of speech. The word may be an adjective. Look at the words *painful* and *painless* on page 43. The abbreviation *adj.* that follows the special spelling of each of those words tells you that it is an adjective.

When you meet a printed word for which you cannot think a meaning that makes sense, try first to use the context to teach yourself what the meaning is. If the context does not give the help you need, use a good dictionary.

Discussion

Help your class answer these questions:

1. When you are reading and meet a word for which you cannot think a meaning that makes sense, what should you try to do first to get the meaning you need? If you cannot get the meaning in that way, what should you do next?

2. In what order are the words in a dictionary list placed? Would *lizard* come after *plot?* Why or why not? Would *bank* come before *beak?* Why or why not? Would *ripe* come before *rinse?* Why or why not?

3. Would you open a dictionary to the front part, middle part, or back part to find *valve? bluejay? orbit?*

4. How can the guide words on a dictionary page help you?

5. In a certain dictionary, the guide words on one page are *game* and *get*. Which of the following words would you expect to find on that page: *gander, gate, geyser, gem, gable, gelatin?* To find each word which you think would not be on the page, would you turn pages toward the front of the dictionary? Toward the back?

6. How can the abbreviations for the parts of speech be helpful when you are looking for word meanings in a dictionary?

On your own

The word *paint* or *pack* is used in each of the numbered sentences that follow. Use the dictionary page on page 43 to help you decide which meaning that word has in each sentence.

Number a sheet of paper from 1 through 5 to stand for the five sentences. After each number, write the part of speech (*noun* or *verb*) and the number of the meaning you chose from the dictionary page for *paint* or *pack* in that sentence.

1. Molly rode the paint down the trail to the stream.
2. The snarling pack began to close in on the wounded buffalo.
3. When I finish building the bookcase, I am going to paint it red.
4. Thousands of people will pack the ball park for the game.
5. The last thing we had to do before the movers came was to pack all the dishes.

Checking your work

If you are asked to do so, read aloud the parts of speech and numbers of the meanings you chose. If you made a mistake in choosing a meaning, find out why it is a mistake.

The Spider, the Cave, and the Pottery Bowl

by Eleanor Clymer

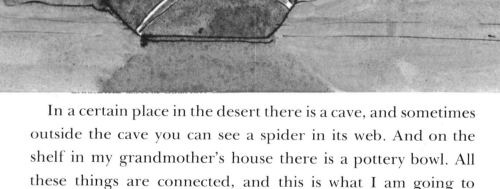

In a certain place in the desert there is a cave, and sometimes outside the cave you can see a spider in its web. And on the shelf in my grandmother's house there is a pottery bowl. All these things are connected, and this is what I am going to tell about. But first I must tell about myself.

I am Indian. My name is an Indian word meaning "One Who Dips Water." But in school they call me Kate. In winter I live with my father and mother and brother Johnny in a town near the edge of the desert. My father works in a store. There is a garage next to the store and he helps there too. We have a garden and peach trees. We have a wooden house. We have running water and electricity. We aren't rich, but we have those things.

But in summer Johnny and I go back to the mesa where my grandmother lives. We used to live there too, but we moved away. Grandmother's house is part of a village built of stone, with many small rooms, all connected, like a wall of houses around an open place. It's a small village. Some of the houses have other houses that were built on top of them when more rooms were needed. The village is very old, many hundreds of years old. When you drive across the desert, you can see the mesa, like a high wall of rock ahead of you. And on top is the village.

I love it on the mesa. It is windy, hot in the sun but cool in the shade of the houses, and you can see far out over the desert—the Painted Desert they call it, because it looks as if it were painted. It is beautiful on the mesa, but it is hard to live there. There is no water. The people must carry water up from springs down below. They must carry up everything they need, and they must go down to tend their gardens, and walk a long way through the desert to find grass or plants for their sheep to eat. It is hard work.

That is why some people moved away. My father doesn't mind hard work, but he needed to earn money for us. So we had to go away to the town.

But every summer we came back, my mother and my brother and I. We stayed in my grandmother's house. My mother helped Grandmother with the summer work. And I helped too. We went down below and worked in the garden, and we dried the corn and squash for the winter. We gathered peaches from the orchard at the foot of the mesa, and we dried them. My brother played with his friends and rode the burros that live in the corral.

We gathered firewood for the stove and for the fireplace and piled it up for the winter. We plastered the walls to make the house look clean. And we went a few miles away and brought home clay for the pottery.

The pottery is what I love most of all. I love to work the cool, wet clay between my hands. When I was little, my grandmother gave me pieces of clay to play with, and I made things out of them. I made little animals: sheep and donkeys and birds.

Then when I got bigger, I watched my grandmother make bowls and jars. She made a flat piece for the bottom. Then she rolled pieces of clay into long rolls between her hands and coiled them on top of the flat piece till she had built up a jar. She smoothed it with a stone or a piece of shell and shaped it in beautiful curves. When it was dry, she painted it with lovely designs. I watched her hand holding the brush of yucca leaves, slowly painting birds and leaves around the curving sides of the bowl. When she had enough bowls and jars, she built a fire and baked them hard.

People came to buy them, and my father took some to sell in the store where he works. But one bowl was never for sale. It stood on the shelf in the corner. It had been there for as long as I could remember.

But this summer was different. My mother could not go to Grandmother's. She had to stay behind and work in a hotel to earn extra money.

She said to me, "Kate, you are big. You will help Grandmother. And Johnny is big enough to bring wood and water."

I promised to help. Johnny was hoping he could go with the big boys to herd sheep. He thought he was big enough this year.

My father drove us to the mesa in the truck. It is about forty miles. We rode across the desert, between red and black and yellow rocks, and sand dunes covered with sage and yellow-flowered rabbit brush.

At last we saw the houses and the store and the school at the foot of the mesa. We took the narrow, rocky road up the side of the mesa, and at last we came out in the open space on top.

It was good to be there. We jumped out of the truck and ran to see our friends. My best friend, Louisa, was there with her mother. She lives on the mesa all the time. I was so glad to see Louisa that we hugged each other. Summer is the only time we can really be together.

My grandmother was waiting for us in the doorway of her house. When I saw her, I was surprised. She looked much older than the last time I had seen her. I had always thought of Grandmother as a strong, plump woman with black hair. This year she looked smaller, thinner, and her hair was gray.

Father noticed, too. He said to her, "Are you all right?"

Grandmother said, "Yes, I am well."

Father carried in the basket of food we had brought, and the boxes with our clothes.

Father asked about Grandmother's garden. But she said she had not planted a garden this year. Then he asked if she had any pottery for him to take back, and she said, "No, I have not made any."

Father said good-by then. As he was leaving, he said to me, "Remember, if you need Mother or me, go down to the store and telephone, and we will come."

The first days passed. I did everything I could think of. I tried to grind corn on the *metate* (the grinding stone), thinking it would please Grandmother. But I did not really know how to do it, and it was easier to cook the ready-made corn meal. I washed the cups and bowls and shook out the bedding. I swept the house. Grandmother did not do much. She rested most of the time.

Nearly every day some tourists came. When the tourists asked for pottery, I had to say that we had none. I wondered when we were going to make some, but I did not like to ask.

Then one day I did. There had been lots of tourists, all looking for pottery. When they went away, I said, "Grandmother, when will we make some?"

She said, "There is no more clay."

I knew there was none in the storeroom. Always before, there had been chunks of the grayish clay there, waiting to be ground up and soaked in water and shaped into bowls.

Grandmother used to carry it herself from a place she

knew, a mile or so from the mesa. Later on, Father had brought it in the truck. But this year she had not asked him to get any.

"The bed of clay is used up," she said.

I said, "But there are other beds. Louisa's mother and the other women know where to get clay. I can go with them and get some."

She said, "The clay that I used was very fine. It needed nothing mixed with it to keep it from cracking."

I knew what she meant. Some kinds of clay will crack in the firing unless they are mixed with sand or ground-up bits of old pottery. But the kind she liked was good enough to be used alone. And there was no more of it.

I said, "Well, I will get some other kind, and you can show me what to do."

She nodded and said, "Perhaps. Perhaps later."

So there was nothing to be done, except to do my work and remind Johnny to do his. But most of the time he was nowhere in sight.

Johnny was disappointed too. There were no big boys for him to go herding with, and none of the men wanted to take him to the cornfields. So all he did was play with the burros.

One day Louisa and I went to get some firewood on the mesa top, beyond the village. We took cloths along and piled juniper twigs in them. It was hot; there was no shade to protect us from the sun. The wind blew, but that only made it hotter.

As we walked back with our firewood, I felt hot and dusty, and I would have liked to have a bath. But on the mesa there was no water for bathing.

As we came toward the village, there was a loud noise: boys' voices shouting and burros' hoofs clattering on the stone. Johnny and three other boys had come running into the plaza. They had let the burros out of the corral and were trying to lasso them. It made a terrible dust, and people began running out of the houses, shouting at them.

In the middle of all this, there were some tourists in a big white car. The people inside the car looked scared.

Louisa's mother came out with a broom and chased the burros away. She told Johnny to go home, and she shouted at the other boys to drive the burros back to the corral.

After I said good-by to Louisa, I went home with my firewood and put it down beside the stove. Johnny was sitting at the table.

Then there was a knock at the door. It was one of the old men of the village.

"Please come in," Grandmother said.

He entered and looked at Johnny. He said, "You and your friends must be more polite. Those strangers are our guests. If you are not careful, the *kachinas* will whip you."

Kachinas are the spirits that take care of people. They bring rain for the cornfields, and they bring gifts for good children and punishment for bad ones.

Johnny looked frightened.

After the old man went away, I wanted to talk about something else to make Johnny feel better, so I went over to the shelf in the corner and lifted the pottery bowl down and held it in my hands.

"Be careful!" said Grandmother.

Johnny asked, "Where did that come from?"

Grandmother said, "It belonged to the Old Ones, our ancestors. Long ago your grandfather was working with some white men in the ruins on the other side of the mesa. He brought it home to me. It was in a cave. There were other bowls, but only this one was perfect. I learned from studying it how to make my own pottery."

Johnny got up and looked into the bowl. There were some smooth stones in it. We both knew what they were. They were Grandmother's polishing stones, the ones she used for rubbing her pottery to make it smooth and shiny. Johnny reached in and took them out and felt them with his fingers.

Grandmother said, "Your grandfather found them in the bowl. A woman used them long ago, and I have used them all these years."

With his finger Johnny traced the design on the bowl. It was a bird with a pointed beak and outspread wings.

"It's pretty," he said.

Then he went to put the stones back into the bowl. In doing so, he pushed my arm. The bowl fell to the floor and smashed.

We both stood there staring at the pieces on the floor. Then we looked at Grandmother. What would she say? I was sure she would be very angry. Maybe the *kachinas* would whip both of us. After all, I had taken the bowl down, so it was my fault just as much as Johnny's.

But Grandmother did not scold us. She only looked very sad for a moment. Then she said, "Pick up the pieces and put them into a basket. Perhaps we can mend it."

I didn't think we could, but I picked them up and put them with the polishing stones into a basket.

When I looked up, Johnny was gone. I thought, "I guess he feels pretty bad. I'll leave him alone for a while."

And I began to get supper ready. When it was done, I went out to call Johnny, but he didn't answer. I asked some of the boys if they had seen him, and they said, "Yes, up by the corral." So I went up there, and he was standing patting his favorite burro. She had her nose on his shoulder as if she were sympathizing with him.

I told him to come home and eat, and he said he wasn't hungry; but I said it was time to come anyhow, so he came with me. I had cooked bacon and corn bread, and we had peaches and cake that I had bought at the store. I noticed Johnny ate quite a lot, though he had said he wasn't hungry.

After supper Grandmother lay down on her bed, but instead of going to sleep, she began to tell stories.

She told some we had heard before, ones we liked to hear again. She told the story about where our people came from. She told about the Spider Woman, the grandmother of us all, who took care of the people and showed them where to live. That was why we must never kill a spider, because it could be Grandmother Spider herself.

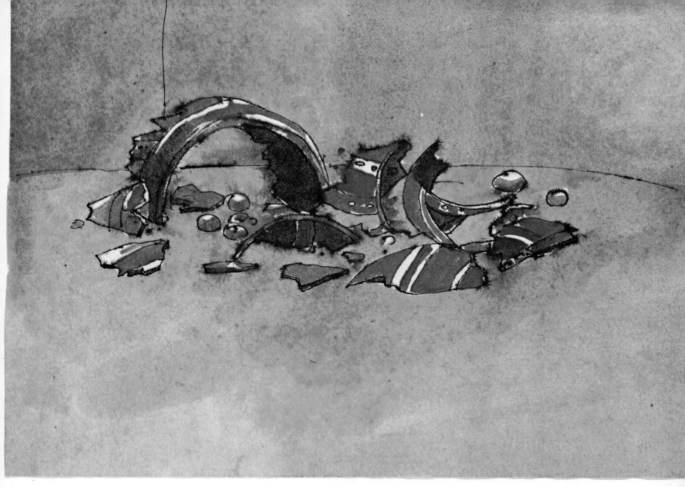

Then she told us a story I had never heard before. She said,
"On the far side of the mesa, there is a path that leads to the
fields below. And beside the path there is a spring. It is not
the spring we all use. It is a very small, secret spring. There is a
hollow place nearby, under the rocks. That is where Grandmother Spider lives. It is her secret house. If you see her there,
spinning her web, you must not stop. You must lay a stick of
firewood beside the path for the Spider Woman and hurry
on. If you stop to talk to her, she may invite you into her
house. Once you go in, you may have to stay there. So be
careful, and do not go that way."

Then she closed her eyes, and I could tell from her breathing that she was asleep. Johnny was almost asleep. I pulled him up and led him over to his bed, and he fell onto it and was sound asleep in a minute.

Then I went to bed myself. I thought about the stories. Why did Grandmother tell us those stories? Especially the one about the spring. Which spring was it? Could it be the one where Louisa and I sometimes went for water? No, it couldn't be. It must be one somewhere else.

I had a strange dream. I dreamed that out of the fireplace came something small and gray. It was a spider. It looked all around and waved its little feet in the air as if it was looking for something. It ran up the wall to the shelf. I looked, and there was the pottery bowl where it had always been. I thought, "Oh, I'm so glad it wasn't broken after all." The spider ran inside the bowl and disappeared, and then I woke up and it was daylight.

Sometimes dreams fade away as soon as you wake up, but this dream was as clear as if it had been real life. The first thing I did was to jump out of bed to look at the shelf, to see if the bowl was there, but of course it wasn't.

Then I saw something else. Johnny wasn't there. I thought it was strange that he should be out so early. Most days it was hard to get him out of bed. I looked outside the door, but he was not in sight. I wondered if he had gone for water, but the pails were empty. So I put my clothes on and went myself.

At the top of the path, I met a couple of men who were going to work in their fields. I could tell because they had their hoes.

One of them was angry. He was saying, "I don't see how she could have gotten out."

I said, "Good morning, did you lose something?"

He said, "Yes, my burro. She got out of the corral somehow. I don't know how, because the others aren't out. Did you see her?"

I said, "No, but I'll look for her." I hurried home. Grandmother was awake. I said, "Did you see Johnny?"

She hadn't seen him. I was sure he had something to do with the burro. It was the one he liked so much.

I said to Grandmother, "One of the neighbors' burros is missing. Maybe Johnny has taken it, not knowing the man wanted it for work this morning. I will go and see if I can find him."

Grandmother nodded and said, "He is troubled about the bowl. Tell him it does not matter. I am not angry. Last night I was sad, but now I think that perhaps it had to be. The Old Ones may have wanted it back."

I was just going when she said, "Wait. Eat first and take some food and water with you. Never go out in the desert without food and water." So I put some corn bread and a bottle of water into a basket.

Then I went to the corral. It was true that the little female burro was gone. But which way did she go? I looked around on the ground and found some little hoofmarks. Then I looked to see which way they went.

Back of the village, the mesa top stretches out for miles. Desert plants grow on it—juniper and sagebrush and some cactus. I started to walk away from the village, and I could see where twigs and leaves had been broken, and I thought that must be the way Johnny went.

I found a path where there were some little hoofprints. I followed them as fast as I could.

The mesa has valleys in it, like big cracks in a table top. We call them washes, because when there is a thunderstorm, the water washes down them like a flood.

I looked up at the sky and thought, "I'm glad it's not going to rain today," though we had all been hoping for rain for many days because it was so dry. But there were only white clouds in the blue sky, the fluffy kind that never do anything.

I was coming to one of those washes. The path led down the slope into the valley. It wasn't steep like the edge of the mesa where the village is; still, it was pretty far down. I squinted my eyes, and yes, down in the valley I saw a boy on a burro. They looked very tiny. I yelled, "Johnny!" But of course he couldn't hear. So I started down. The ground had a lot of loose sand and stones, and I slid partway down, holding on to bushes as I went. At last I got to the bottom.

I was getting tired, and I thought, "Why am I hurrying? Johnny knows the way back, and besides, he has the burro."

But then I looked up at the sky, and I saw that there was good reason to hurry. Instead of the fluffy white clouds, all of a sudden there were thunderclouds, tall gray clouds standing like mountains in the west. The sun was still bright, and as long as the clouds did not cover the sun, I did not feel frightened. But they were moving. In the desert a storm can come up in a few minutes. I began to run and to shout, "Johnny!"

He heard me and stopped, and then turned the burro and came toward me. I ran as hard as I could and pointed to the sky, and he understood. At last I caught up to him. I was out of breath and couldn't talk, but I climbed on the burro and beat her with my heels to make her run. Johnny ran on ahead. We were in the middle of the valley, and it was maybe half a mile to the opposite side, to a higher spot where we would be safe. Just in time we got there.

In a few minutes we heard thunder. Then the cloudburst came. The rain poured down, and in no time the wash was running like a river. Mud and rocks and tree branches came tumbling down in the roaring water.

Then I heard Johnny yell, "Come up here!"

He had found a cave, really an overhanging arch in the rock, and was standing there out of the rain. I pulled the burro and went up there too, and we sat down and watched the rain fall. We sat for a long time. We ate the bread and drank the water I had brought.

I asked, "Where were you going?"

But he wouldn't tell. I said, "Maybe you were going to look for Grandmother Spider."

Then he laughed and said, "No."

I said, "Well, then what?"

He said, "If I tell you, you'll laugh at me."

I promised not to laugh. Then he said, "Grandfather found that bowl in the ruins where the Old Ones used to live. I broke it, so I was going to find another."

I said, "But Johnny, there aren't any left. The white people took them all away long ago."

He said, "White people couldn't find them all. I would find one that they didn't see."

We stood up and looked around at the rock shelter we were in. It might have been a good place for the Old Ones to live, though if their houses had ever been there, they had crumbled away. But at the back, under one end of the arch, there was a crack, really a hole in the rock, partly filled with stones and sand, and we noticed that a trickle of water ran out of it and down the slope.

"There must be a spring in there," I said.

"Let's go in," Johnny said. "It looks like a deep hole. Maybe there are some ruins inside."

Just then I noticed something. Near the entrance, a spider web was stretched across the branches of a little bush. I would not have seen it if the sun hadn't come out and drops of water on the threads sparkled in the light. In the middle of the web was the spider with her legs spread out. Some little flies were buzzing about. One of them hit the web and was trapped. At once the spider pulled in all her legs and jumped on the fly. I thought how clever she was to make her web by the spring where the flies would come.

Then I thought, "Maybe it's the Spider Woman!" And I shouted to Johnny, "Don't go in!" But it was too late. He was inside the hole. "Now," I thought, "the Spider Woman will get him, and he will have to stay in her house forever."

I felt frightened. But I could not let him go in there alone. I tied the burro to a bush and crawled in after Johnny.

It was pretty dark inside. At first I couldn't see anything. Then my eyes got used to the darkness, and I saw Johnny at the back of the cave. The cave was larger inside than I had thought it would be. Its floor was damp with the water that trickled down from the wall. I guess the water flowing for many years had hollowed out the cave.

"Did you find anything?" I asked.

"Yes," said Johnny. "An old basket and a stick."

I went over to look. Somebody had been digging there and had gone away and left the things behind. I tried to lift the basket, but it was heavy. I dragged it to the entrance and looked inside.

Johnny said, "It's just a lot of dirt. I wanted to find pottery."

I said, "Johnny, you did!"

He thought I was joking. He said, "It's only sand."

I said, "It's not sand. It's clay. There's clay in this cave. We can make pottery with it."

The clay was between two layers of rock in the wall at the back of the cave. We took the old digging stick and dug it out. We put it in Johnny's shirt to carry it. We wanted to take the clay we had found in the old basket, but it was heavy. Besides, the basket was rotted with dampness, and I was afraid it would break, so we left it there.

We took as much clay as we could carry and went outside. The sky was blue. The water was still running down the wash, but we could cross it. We loaded our clay on the burro and started home.

Johnny led the burro down the slope, but I stayed behind.

I went back to the place where the spider web hung. The spider had sucked the juice out of the fly and was waiting for another.

I bent down and said, "Thank you, Grandmother Spider. I saw you last night in my dream. I thought you were telling me something. Now I think I understand." Then I looked around for a piece of firewood to lay beside the spring. I couldn't find one, so I laid down the digging stick that I had in my hand.

I ran to catch up with Johnny, and we led the burro down the slope. We climbed the other side of the wash and walked across the mesa to the village. It was getting toward evening. We had been gone a long time.

Grandmother was sitting inside the door waiting for us. She looked sad and small and very old.

I said, "Here we are."

She said, "So you found him. Where did you go?"

I wanted to say, "To Grandmother Spider's house." But I was afraid she would think I was joking. You must not joke

about such things. So I just said, "Across the wash, and we have brought you a present from there."

I laid Johnny's shirt on the floor and untied it. She bent down and took a handful and felt it with her fingers.

"Clay!" she said. "The best kind of clay!" She smiled at me. "Where did you get it?"

I told her, "Across the wash there is a kind of cave, really just a hole in the rocks, with water trickling from it. We found a basket of clay and a digging stick."

Grandmother said, "I know that place. A woman was digging there. She had her child with her, and the child was playing outside. There was a storm, and she ran out to save the child and never went back."

I asked, "Did she save the child?"

She said, "Yes, the child is grown up now. But we never went back. We thought it was bad luck. But you see, after many years it is time for good things to happen. It doesn't hurt to wait." Then she looked at Johnny and asked, "Why did you run away? And why did you take the burro?"

He looked a little scared because he knew he shouldn't have taken the burro without permission. But he was brave.

He said, "I was sorry I broke the bowl. I wanted to find another bowl in the place where the Old Ones lived. But I didn't know how far it would be, so I took the burro. But I didn't find a bowl. Kate says there are no more left. She says the white people took them all away."

Grandmother said, "They could not take them all. There are still many left, but they are buried in the earth. You would have to dig deep to find them. But what you did find is better. We will make our own bowls now."

AUTHOR

Eleanor Clymer was born in New York City and has lived in cities most of her life. She now lives in the country and likes it, but she is still fond of city life. She feels that city children and country children are alike in many ways and that they share the same needs and feelings.

Mrs. Clymer has enjoyed writing from the time she worked on her high-school newspaper. She has written more than thirty-five books for children. Some of them are *Luke Was There; We Lived in the Almont; Me and the Eggman; The House on the Mountain;* and *The Spider, the Cave, and the Pottery Bowl,* from which the story you have just read was taken.

When Clay Sings

by Byrd Baylor

There are
desert hillsides
where
ancient
Indian pottery
still lies
half buried
in the sand
and
lizards
blink at
other dusty lizards
that were painted
on those pots
a thousand years ago.

Now
Indian children
make a game
of searching for
bits of
clay
that were once
somebody's
bowl
or mug
or cooking pot
or dipper.

Their parents
look at what
they find
and tell them:
"Remember, treat
it with respect.
It is so old. . . ."

They say
that every piece
of clay
is a piece of
someone's
life.

They even say
it has
its own
small voice
and sings in
its own way.

So
the children
touch
the pieces
carefully
as they
kneel there
in the hot
dry sand
listening
for whatever
voice
a broken pot
might use—
A windy voice?
A sandy voice?
A voice like
a far bird's
cry?

Sometimes
if they look long enough
and
if they are lucky enough
they can fit
four
or
five
pieces
together
the way you'd do
a jigsaw puzzle.

Then
suddenly
they see
a perky
wide-eyed
bird
look up
at them . . .
surprised.

Maybe
the bowl
with the bird
was dropped
by some other
Indian child
who chased
a rabbit
near these same rocks
then.

When they find
a bowl
that isn't broken
the children can
pretend
that they've just
eaten from it
and that
they're sitting
by some campfire
on a deerskin blanket
and it's
then
not
now

and
they speak
an older
language.

But
they don't need words
to know
that there were
speckled bugs
and spotted bugs
and bugs with
shiny wings
and pinchy bugs

and jumpy bugs
and bugs that had
a thousand legs
that liked to walk
through grass. . . .

They know
the molding of
a lump of clay
has always been
a slow
and gentle
work.
No hurrying.
No rushing.

Hands that
shape
the earth
this way
have time
to know
the cool
touch
of the sand.

Women then
must have
spoken
to the earth
as they took
its clay.
They must have
sung special
songs

for shaping the bowl,
for polishing it,
for baking it
so it would be
strong enough
to last
long after
that tribe
was gone. . . .

Once
somebody
sitting on the ground
outside a high
cold
cliff house
thought:
"I'll make
this bowl
as pretty
as I can."

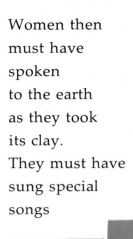

And she painted
what she
liked
the most . . .
stars
and moon
and sun
and whirlwinds.

Was the sun shining
as she worked?
Were her own
brown
naked children
playing near?
Was there a
skinny dog?
Was the smell
of cooking
in the air?
Did a man
come back from
hunting
and shake his head?
And on another day
did she
paint
that hunter
too?

Sometimes
children
may have
said
(but in that
other language):
"Mama, make
a bowl
with pictures
of big animals
for me . . .
big
fierce
creatures
that I'll
hunt someday."

So
she drew
mountain lions
and wildcats
and
even a man
wrestling
a bear.

Or
is it
a bear
wrestling
a man?

The colors
are
still bright—
Reds as deep as
sandstone cliffs,
browns and tans
the shade of
desert earth,
black and white
shiny as
stones
polished
by water
in high
mountain streams.

There were a
thousand
shapes to draw—
Horned toads
and lizards.
Butterflies.
Turtles.
And beautiful
leaping fish.

And deer
and mountain goats
and antelope
that flashed
across
these canyons
always
faster than
the boys
who knew their
trails
and followed them
among the rocks.

They even drew
the
scariest
things
they could
think of.

Call them
monsters.
Call them
night spirits.
Call them
anything.

Children
make them up
today
and they
still have
the same
scary look
in their eyes.

Many a child
must have eaten
rabbit stew
for supper
out of bowls
with rabbits
painted on them.

Here's a hunter
who used
a fine long net
for catching
rabbits . . .
but

what rabbit
couldn't
jump
through
that hole
in the dish?

This child
was sick
and they called
a medicine man
to cure him.

What magic
is he using?

What special
chants
and dances
and whispered words
and feathered wands
may have helped
a boy
get well again?

And
did medicine
made from
dry roots
and flowers
and wild
yellow grasses
taste
like
pink medicine
tastes now?

Indians who find
this pottery today
say
that everything
has its own
spirit—
even a broken pot.
They say
the clay
remembers
the hands
that made it.

Does it
remember
the cornfields too?
And the
summer rains?
And the
ceremonies
that held
life together?

Here are
the masks
and the
costumes
and the
great
dancing
figures.

Here is the
flute player
bent low
over his
song.

Songs
had to be
powerful
enough
to make
rain fall
and winds
blow
and seeds
sprout
in the dark
earth. . . .

Songs
had to be
powerful
enough
to keep
warriors safe

and lead the
hunter
to the deer
and make
summer always
follow
winter
and hold
the sun in its
proper path
across the sky
and keep life
moving on
from tribe
to
tribe.

They say
that even now
the wind sometimes
finds
one of those songs
still in the clay
and lifts it out
and carries it
down the canyon
and across
the hills.

It is a small sound
and always far away
but
they say
sometimes
they hear it.

AUTHOR

Byrd Baylor was born in San Antonio, Texas, and spent most of her childhood in the southwestern United States. She went to college at the University of Arizona and still lives in Arizona.

Her books show her love for the land and people of the Southwest. She is particularly interested in the Papago Indians. Their reservation is northwest of Tucson. Byrd Baylor is the executive secretary of the Association of Papago Affairs. That is a group that works with Indians who have left their reservation and have moved to the city of Tucson.

She has written many books for young readers about the land and the Indians of the Southwest. They include *The Man Who Talked to a Tree, Before You Came This Way,* and *Coyote Cry*.

Byrd Baylor is married and has used her married name, Byrd Baylor Schweitzer, on some of her books.

WORD STORIES by Leone Adelson

Some words tell their own stories. One look at *spring* and *fall*, a second to think, and we know the reason why these names were given to two of our seasons. New plants spring up in the spring; leaves fall in the fall of the year. But other words are harder to understand, and they have to be coaxed to tell us about themselves and where they come from.

The past meaning of the word *bulldozer* is quite different from its present meaning. Today bulldozers are the powerful earth-moving machines that we use in building or road making. But at one time a bulldozer was a man with a very special job. With a noisy crack of his bull whip, he helped to move great herds of cattle across the plains. This was called "giving them a dose of the bull" by the "bull-doser," or bulldozer. A good bulldozer could move cattle safely, without losing

or stampeding them. Because he was such a powerful mover, the same name was given to the great machines that can move mountains of earth and rock.

Caterpillars have been on this earth for as long as there have been insects. In every land they had a name in the language of that land. The English word for these fuzzy creatures comes right from the Old French name *catepelose*. It really means "cat hairy" from *cate* [Old French for "cat"] and *pelose* ["hairy"]. If it sounds better to us as *hairy cat*, it should rightly be *pillarcater*. *Caterpillar* or *pillarcater*, neither one has anything to do with cats. Some words have led puzzling lives.

Imagine now that you are sitting on the floor of a little one-room cabin in the mountain country of the South. In a rocking chair sits an old, old grandmother about to tell you a story. This tale could very well be the one you would hear.

Jack and the Three Sillies

by Richard Chase

Jack? Why, he was a boy lived back in old times. I reckon he lived somewhere here in the mountains. There's a lot of tales on Jack: tales about him outdoin' his two brothers, Will and Tom, and about Jack and some giants, and about him a-courtin' first one girl and then another. I never heard 'em tell but one tale, though, about Jack really gettin' married.

Know it? Oh, you want to hear it. Well, let me see can I recollect how it starts.

Said one time Jack fin'lly got him a woman, and a few days after they'd got married, Jack's wife sent him to sell the cow.

"She's worth fifty dollars, Jack.

Don't ye come back with any less. Ye hear?"

Jack was lazy. He didn't want to walk all the way to the settlement with that cow. But he started off anyhow.

Got along all right till directly his cow started actin' unruly. She went to balkin' and runnin' in and out of the bushes, and Jack couldn't hold her.

Met a man drivin' a pig on a rope.

"Hello, Jack. You havin' a little trouble?"

"I never *saw* such a cow!"

The man helped Jack hold the cow.

"She's sort of puny, Jack. Looks old, too. Now this sow is fat, and hit's a young one. How'd ye like to swap?"

Jack swapped for the pig, and went on.

But it wasn't long till that pig got unruly. Tangled Jack up in the rope. Old woman came along carryin' a goose.

"Havin' trouble, Jack?"

"Sort of," says Jack.

That pig had Jack so tangled and tied up he couldn't move.

"How'd you like to swap your pig for this goose, Jack? It'll not cause ye a bit of trouble. You can tote it under your arm — easy."

Jack swapped. Went on.

But directly the goose started actin' *awful* unruly. It went to floggin' Jack with its wings. Jack held on to it the best he could.

Met a girl carryin' a big cat.

"Havin' some trouble, are ye, Jack?"

Jack had hold of his goose by one leg and was a-dodgin' and a-duckin', and it just a-whoppin' him and a-peckin' him.

"This goose — ouch! — don't

want — ow! — to go — dad burn this thing! — no further. Ouch!"

The girl she helped Jack get the goose's wings folded down again till Jack could get a good grip on it.

"Why don't ye swap me for this cat, Jack? It won't be a bit of trouble to ye. Hit's a good 'un about catchin' rats and mice."

Jack swapped. Took the cat in his arms and went on.

But next thing he knowed, that cat saw a bird on a branch and tried to jump out of Jack's arms. Jack he held it tight, and it started scratchin'. So Jack squeezed it a little tighter, and that old cat went to meowlin' so loud and scratchin' Jack up so bad he was about to turn it loose.

Just about then a young feller came up. Had a big round rock in his hands.

He set the rock down, took hold on Jack's cat, and got it tamed down again.

"A little more and you'd been a goner, Jack. Why don't ye swap me your cat for this round rock? It's an awful handy thing to prop the door back."

Jack figgered a rock wouldn't act unruly or peck him or scratch, so he swapped.

Took that rock and went on back home.

"Where's my fifty dollars, Jack?"

"Fifty dollars? Huh! I never even got to town."

"Where's my cow, then?"

So Jack had to tell his wife how unruly her cow had acted, and how he had to keep on swappin' till he got that rock.

"And hit's just fine to prop the door back. Here." And he handed her that big rock.

She took it and threw it out in the yard.

"I'll say! Prop the door back! I never saw such a silly in all my life. I'll bet there's no man in this whole world has got less sense than you."

"I'll bet there is," says Jack.

"Bet—nothin'! I'm goin' to leave you this minute! That's what! And I'm not goin' to come back to ye neither, unless I find three men as silly as you are— and get my money back, too."

So Jack's wife she left him and started travelin'.

And one day she hadn't found a place to stay the night, but the moon was full so she kept on travelin' right on up in the night. She was walkin' past a millpond, and there was a man over by the edge of the pond a-jumpin' up and down and hollerin' and a-throwin' his hands up and pointin' down in the water. So Jack's wife went and asked him what was the matter.

"It's the moon!" he hollered, and went to jumpin' around some more. "Look! It's done dropped down in the millpond! Right there! You can see it plain!

"Law me! Run get some more folks to help get it out! Get some ropes! Fetch a ladder! We'll have to get it out of there! O Law!

"How'll we know when to plant 'taters and corn unless we get the moon put back?

"Get some ropes! Get a grabble hook! Get a ladder so we can put the moon back up in the sky where it belongs!"

"That's not the moon. That's just where it's shinin' in the water. Look up yonder. There's the moon. Hit's in the sky."

"Look up—nothin'! Why should I look up yonder for it when I can see it right down there in the water? Hunh! You must think I got no sense! O Law! Somebody run here and help me get the moon out!"

Jack's wife could hardly keep from laughin'.

"Don't just stand there!" that man told her. "I'll hire ye to help! Here's ten dollars. Take it! Take it now, and run for help!"

And he went to hollerin' and jumpin' around some more.

Jack's wife she put the ten dollars in her apron pocket and went on. She told everybody she met, and they all went up there to watch that man try to get the moon out of the millpond.

And after she got down the road a piece, she stopped. "Well," she says, "that's one."

So she kept on travelin', and one day she saw an old man and an old woman in a field. The old man was hitched up to a plow and the old woman had hold of the plowlines. She'd flap the lines and whack 'em on the old man's back.

"Get up there!" she'd holler, and the old man would heave on the plow.

Jack's wife looked and saw an old mule grazin' around in the field, so she stopped and watched. The old man would drag the plow a little ways and stop. Then the old woman 'uld holler and rattle the lines on him again, and he 'uld pull and heave the plow on a little further.

"Hey, you-all! Why don't ye hitch up that mule and plow with it?"

"Plow with a mule?" the old woman hollered back. "We *ride* the mule. We don't *never* plow with it. Giddap there!" And she whopped the old man again.

"Most folks do their plowin' with a mule."

"Ye say they do? Well, anyhow, we don't know how to hitch up a mule to make it plow. Get along there, old man!" Kawhop!

"I can show ye how to hitch a mule to a plow."

The old man stopped, hollered out, "You show us that and I'll pay ye fifteen dollars, bedad!"

So Jack's wife she showed 'em how to hitch up that mule, and the old man paid her. Then he took hold on the plow and started to work, and the old woman she went to the house and sat on the porch in her rockin' chair and started rockin'.

Jack's wife went on.

"Humh!" she says. "That's two."

And she counted her money.

So she kept on travelin', kept on travelin', and one day she walked by a house that was close to the road, and all at once she heard somebody holler "Ow!" She looked and there sat a man on the porch. Had a shirt on— sleeves and buttons and all—but his head was down under the cloth. His wife was standin' there behind him with a stick of stove-wood raised up. She bammed him on the head with it, and he hollered again.

"Hold still now, honey. It won't take but a few more licks."

BAM! "OW-W-W-W!"

Jack's wife stopped at the gate. "What's the matter?" she asked 'em.

"Law me!" the woman told

her. "I know everything about makin' a shirt except how to fix the neckhole. I have to beat this old man's head through every time I make him a shirt. I don't make him one but once a year, and hit nearly kills him then. Hold right still, honey. I'm goin' to have to hit it hard this time."

"Wait! I can show ye how to cut the neckhole in a shirt."

That man he hollered out, "Show my wife that, and I'll pay ye twenty-five dollars, I will!"

So Jack's wife showed the woman how to cut and sew the neckhole to a shirt, and her old man paid out the money.

Jack's wife went on.

"Well, now," she says, "I reckon that makes three."

Then she stopped and counted her money "A ten and three fives. That makes twenty-five. And two tens and a five. That's twenty-five more. And that makes fifty."

So she turned around and went on back to Jack.

And the last time I was down there, they were both of 'em gettin' on well.

AUTHOR

While Richard Chase was in college studying to be a scientist, his plans were unexpectedly changed by a chance visit to a Kentucky school. There he discovered the lively tales, songs, and dances that for hundreds of years have been passed from one generation to the next by people of the isolated mountain regions of the South. This folklore was probably brought from England by the first settlers. In time, it became distinctly American as mountain storytellers and performers added to it their own humor and details. From earliest days, the folk ways had never been written down. Children learned them simply by watching and listening to their parents and grandparents.

Mr. Chase has had an interesting life finding out all he can about this folklore; and since 1940, to delighted audiences throughout America, he has retold the tales, sung the songs, and presented the dances that mountain people taught him. So that the folklore will never be lost, he has put much of it into writing, too. "Jack and the Three Sillies," which you just read, and the many stories in his books *The Jack Tales* and *Grandfather Tales* are Mr. Chase's retellings of mountain tales that have been told to him. He is also the author of *Hullabaloo,* a collection of old singing games and dances.

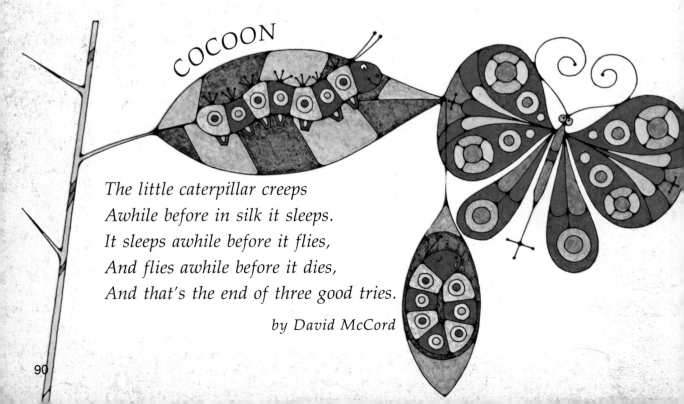

COCOON

The little caterpillar creeps
Awhile before in silk it sleeps.
It sleeps awhile before it flies,
And flies awhile before it dies,
And that's the end of three good tries.

by David McCord

First Woman in Space

by Mitchell R. Sharpe

Liftoff! With a deep rumble the huge white rocket rose slowly off the launch pad. Dust swirled in orange and red clouds across the desert at Tyuratam, the spaceport of the Soviet Union. It was June 16, 1963. Valentina Tereshkova, a twenty-six-year-old Russian woman, was on her way to becoming the first woman in space.

Valya, as her friends called her, began preparing for her journey into space in the tiny village of Maslennikovo. March 6, 1937, was bitterly cold, and snow was still on the ground. The crude log hut had neither electricity nor running water. However, its iron stove kept the hut warm enough on that day when Valentina Vladimirovna Tereshkova was born.

Her father was a tractor driver, and her mother a dairy maid. They both worked on a large farm outside Maslennikovo. However, Valya was to grow up without her father. He was killed during World War II when she was only four years old.

Valya and her girl friend Tonya often played together in the village. Once, on a dare, Valya almost drowned while trying to swim the largest pond near the village. Valya even invented a dangerous game she called parachuting. She and Tonya would climb to the top of the tallest birch trees and swing out from them. Slowly the trees would bend down until the girls let loose and fell the last few feet to the ground. Sometimes Valya's older sister Lyuda would join them.

When World War II ended, the Tereshkova family moved to Yaroslavl. There Mother took a job in a textile factory to provide for her children. While Valya was growing up, she remained very active. When the neighborhood boys dared her to jump from a bridge into the river, she did. Then she climbed back up on it and jumped again—before the first boy ever jumped once!

When she was sixteen years old, Valya tried to find a job. It took a year. She finally went to work in a plant making tires for automobiles and tractors. The work was hard, and the factory was hot and noisy. The odor of hot rubber was everywhere. After a year there, she managed to get a job in the textile plant where her mother and sister worked. Valya was put in the ribbon-winding department.

In 1958 Valya joined the Yaroslavl Air Sports Club and learned to be a *real* parachutist. She learned to jump at night, over land, and into the river. The most dangerous of her sixty-three jumps was from a plane at a very high altitude. She had to fall freely, not pulling the ripcord until the last minute.

On April 12, 1961, following the flight of Yuri Gagarin, the first man in space, Valya wrote a letter to her government. As a parachutist first class, she volunteered to become a cosmonaut. (In the Soviet Union, astronauts are called cosmonauts.) To her surprise, she was accepted for testing as a cosmonaut. For a month, Valya took special physical and mental tests at an air force hospital in Moscow. Other girls were there, too, but Valya was the first to complete the tests and become a cosmonaut.

She was sent to Star Town, a suburb of Moscow. All the cosmonauts live and train there. When she arrived, Valya was met at the door of the dormitory by a handsome but shy young man.

"Hello, Valya," he said. "My name is Andrian Nikolayev. Let's take your suitcases up to the second floor. That's where you women cosmonauts are going to live."

Cosmonaut training began the next day. Valya had to study harder than the other girls because she had not been to college as they had. There were courses in astronomy, physics, biology, and mathematics. In addition, there was a strict course in physical training. Valya had to compete in both indoor and outdoor sports. She became skilled in skiing, basketball, volleyball, hockey, and swimming.

As if all this were not enough, she learned to fly as well. Despite being a parachutist first class, she had to start parachute training all over, from the beginning. When she was not flying, jumping, or studying, she was riding the centrifuge. Whirling around on it, Valya learned what the great force on her body would feel like when her rocket lifted off.

On May 26, 1963, Yuri Gagarin, commander of the cosmonauts, called Valya into his office.

"Valya, tomorrow you and your back-up cosmonaut are to

leave for Tyuratam. Valery Bykovsky and his back-up will be going with you," he said. "As you know, the launch dates for *Vostok 5* and *6* are not far off."

Valya knew then that she was going to be the cosmonaut for *Vostok 6*.

June 14 was bright and sunny, and Valery's *Vostok 5* lifted off without a flaw.

At 12:30 a.m. on June 16, Valya lifted off to join him in space. For three days she circled Earth. In addition to piloting the *Vostok 6*, she took pictures for astronomers. Also, she did special exercises and tests so that doctors could tell whether she could live and work in space. *Vostok 6* returned to Earth on June 19.

When Valya got back to Star Town, she had some news that surprised everyone. She and Andrian Nikolayev were going to be married. After the marriage, she and Andrian went on a honeymoon to India, Nepal, Ceylon, Thailand, and Indonesia.

Then Valya returned to Star Town and her cosmonaut training. She also entered the Zhukovsky Engineering Academy to work on her degree in astronautical engineering. However, on June 8, 1964, her classes were interrupted when her daughter, Yelena Andrianovna Nikolayeva, was born. Yelena is the only person in the world whose mother *and* father have traveled in space.

Today, Valentina Nikolayeva-Tereshkova is still busy. As official hostess of Star Town, she has greeted such distinguished visitors as American astronauts Frank Borman and Neil Armstrong. She graduated from the Zhukovsky Engineering Academy and is now one of the teachers at the Yuri A. Gagarin Cosmonaut Training Center at Star Town.

SKILL LESSON

USING A PRONUNCIATION KEY
IN A DICTIONARY

One day when Mark was reading a short story, he came to a paragraph in which he met the word *pantomime*. Mark did not know what the word meant, and when he tried to use the context to teach himself what the meaning is, he could not find there the help he needed. Also, he did not know whether the pronunciation he had thought for *pantomime* was correct. These are the reasons why Mark looked up the word in the dictionary.

When Mark found the word in the dictionary, this is what he saw:

> **pan•to•mime** (păn′tə mīm′) *n.* **1.** A play in which the actors do not speak. **2.** Movements of the body or face that show meaning without words.

Quickly Mark decided that the second meaning was the one that made the most sense in the paragraph in which he met the word. Then he figured out what the correct pronunciation of *pantomime* is. He did this by using what are called the **special spelling** and the **pronunciation key.**

In a dictionary or a glossary, the correct pronunciation of a word is shown in a special spelling right after the word. You can see in the dictionary entry for *pantomime* on page 95 that the special spelling for that word looks like this:

pan•to•mime (păn′tə mīm′)

Do you know how to use the special spelling to check the pronunciation of a word? In any good dictionary or glossary, usually at the bottom of each page or every other page, is a pronunciation key. The pronunciation key contains rows of words called **key words.** The key words show what sounds to give to vowels and certain other letters in the special spelling. They are common words that you already know how to pronounce. Here is the pronunciation key from the dictionary Mark used, and it is like the ones used in many dictionaries and glossaries:

ă pat/ ā pay/ â care/ ä father/ ĕ pet/ ē be/ ĭ pit/ ī pie/ î fierce/ ŏ pot/ ō go/ ô paw, for/ oi oil/ ŏŏ took/ ōō boot/ ou out/ ŭ cut/ û fur/ *th* the/ th thin/ hw which/ zh vision/ ə ago, item, pencil, atom, circus

In the special spelling of *pantomime*, the first syllable looks like this: **păn′**. Notice the little mark above the *a* in that syllable. Now find the letter *a* with that mark above it in the pronunciation key. What key word comes right after it? Yes, *pat*. Notice that the *a* in *pat* is printed in heavy black print. This means that **ă** in the first syllable of **păn′tə mīm′** is pronounced like the *a* in *pat*, which you already know how to pronounce.

Do you see the mark ə in the second syllable of **păn′tə mīm′**? Find that mark and the key words that follow right after it in the pronunciation key. The key words tell you that ə stands for a sound you often use for different vowels in words. That sound is the sound you hear for the *o* in *atom*, and it is the sound *o* has in *pantomime*.

Look at the last syllable of **păn′tə mīm′**. Notice the little mark above the *i* in that syllable. In the pronunciation key, find the letter *i* with that mark above it. You can see the key word *pie* coming right after it with *ie* in heavy black letters. It tells you that ī in the special spelling stands for the vowel sound you hear at the end of *pie*.

There is one more thing that the special spelling shows you about the pronunciation of a word. Notice the mark that comes after the first syllable in **păn′tə mīm′**. That mark (′) is called the **primary stress mark.** It tells you that the syllable just before it, which is printed in heavy, black letters, should be said with more force, or stress, than the other syllables.

In some longer words, more than one syllable needs to be stressed. Usually in such words, one syllable has a stronger stress than the other stressed syllable. The syllable with the weaker stress is marked with a stress mark that looks like this: (′). It is called a **secondary stress mark.** A secondary stress mark appears after the last syllable in **păn′tə mīm′.** It tells you that the last syllable in that word should be stressed more than the second syllable, which has no stress mark, but not as strongly as the first syllable. Can you pronounce *pantomime* correctly now?

Most dictionaries have the stress mark coming right after the syllable that should be stressed. Some dictionaries, however, place the stress mark *before* the syllable that should be stressed. Just inside the front cover or within the first few pages of every dictionary is a full explanation of all the marks used by that dictionary to show correct pronunciations. Before you look up the pronunciation of any word in a dictionary, check that explanation to find out how that dictionary shows which syllable should be stressed.

Discussion

Help your class answer these questions:

1. Where is the special spelling shown for a word listed in a dictionary or glossary?
2. Where is the pronunciation key shown in most dictionaries and glossaries?
3. How do you use the special spelling and the pronunciation key to learn how to pronounce a word?
4. What does a primary stress mark (′) tell you? A secondary stress mark (′)?

On your own

If you do not know both the meaning and the correct pronunciation of any of the underlined words in the following sentences, use the dictionary page shown on page 43 to get that meaning and that pronunciation.

1. In our history book there is a beautiful picture of a Japanese pagoda.
2. The music teacher taught our class a paean.
3. Our school is going to take part in this year's winter pageant.
4. The horses were led to the paddock.

Checking your work

If you are asked to do so, read one or more of the sentences aloud. If you make a mistake in pronouncing any of the words, find out what that mistake is and correct it.

from

THE CRICKET IN TIMES SQUARE

by GEORGE SELDEN

Mario Bellini was a hardworking boy. He helped his father and mother run a newsstand in the busy Times Square subway station, right in the middle of New York City. One Saturday night, while Mario was taking care of the newsstand alone, he found a cricket. Chester Cricket and Mario quickly became friends.

When Mario's parents came back to close up the stand for the night, he and his father talked Mama Bellini into letting Chester stay. Mario made Chester a fine bed from a matchbox. Then he said good-night and went home with Mama and Papa Bellini, leaving the cricket alone in the locked-up stand.

Chester Makes Some New Friends

Tucker Mouse had been watching the Bellinis and listening to what they said. Next to scrounging, eavesdropping on human beings was what he enjoyed most. That was one of the reasons he lived in the Times Square subway station. As soon as the family disappeared, he darted out across the floor and scooted up to the newsstand. At one side the boards had separated and there was a wide space he could jump through. He'd been in a few times before—just exploring. For a moment he stood under the three-legged stool, letting his eyes get used to the darkness. Then he jumped up on it.

"Psst!" he whispered. "Hey, you up there—are you awake?"

There was no answer.

"Psst! Psst! Hey!" Tucker whispered again, louder this time.

From the shelf above came a scuffling, like little feet feeling their way to the edge. "Who is that going 'psst'?" said a voice.

"It's me," said Tucker. "Down here on the stool."

A black head, with two shiny black eyes, peered down at him. "Who are you?"

"A mouse," said Tucker. "Who are *you?*"

"I'm Chester Cricket," said the cricket. He had a high, musical voice. Everything he said seemed to be spoken to an unheard melody.

"My name's Tucker," said Tucker Mouse. "Can I come up?"

"I guess so," said Chester Cricket. "This isn't my house anyway."

Tucker jumped up beside the cricket and looked him all over. "A cricket," he said admiringly. "So you're a cricket. I never saw one before."

"I've seen mice before," the cricket said. "I knew quite a few back in Connecticut."

"Is that where you're from?" asked Tucker.

"Yes," said Chester. "I guess I'll

never see it again," he added wistfully.

"How did you get to New York?" asked Tucker Mouse.

"It's a long story," sighed the cricket.

"Tell me," said Tucker, settling back on his haunches. He loved to hear stories. It was almost as much fun as eavesdropping—if the story was true.

"Well, it must have been two—no, three days ago," Chester Cricket began. "I was sitting on top of my stump, just enjoying the weather and thinking how nice it was that summer had started. I live inside an old tree stump, next to a willow tree, and I often go up to the roof to look around. And I'd been practicing jumping that day, too. On the other side of the stump from the willow tree, there's a brook that runs past, and I'd been jumping back and forth across it to get my legs in condition for the summer. I do a lot of jumping, you know."

"Me, too," said Tucker Mouse. "Especially around the rush hour."

"And I had just finished jumping when I smelled something," Chester went on. "Liverwurst, which I love."

"You like liverwurst?" Tucker broke in. "Wait! Wait! Just wait!"

In one leap, he sprang down all the way from the shelf to the floor and dashed over to his drainpipe. Chester shook his head as he watched him go. He thought Tucker was a very excitable person—even for a mouse.

Inside the drainpipe, Tucker's nest was a jumble of papers, scraps of cloth, buttons, lost jewelry, small change, and everything else that can be picked up in a subway station. Tucker tossed things left and right in a wild search. Neatness was not one of the things he aimed at in life. At last he discovered what he was looking for: a big piece of liverwurst he had found earlier that evening. It was meant to be for breakfast tomorrow, but he decided that meeting his first cricket was a special occasion. Holding it between his teeth, he whisked back to the newsstand.

"Look!" he said proudly, dropping the meat in front of Chester Cricket. "Liverwurst! You continue the story—we'll enjoy a snack, too."

"That's very nice of you," said Chester. He was touched that a mouse he had known only a few minutes would share his food with him. "I had a little chocolate before, but besides that, nothing for three days."

"Eat! Eat!" said Tucker. He bit the liverwurst into two pieces and gave Chester the bigger one. "So you smelled the liverwurst—then what happened?"

"I hopped down from the stump and went off toward the smell," said Chester.

"Very logical," said Tucker Mouse, munching with his cheeks full. "Exactly what I would have done."

"It was coming from a picnic basket," said Chester. "A couple of tuffets away from my stump, the meadow begins, and there was a whole bunch of people having a picnic. They had hard-boiled eggs, and cold roast chicken, and roast beef, and a whole lot of other things besides the liverwurst sandwiches which I smelled."

Tucker Mouse moaned with pleasure at the thought of all that food.

"They were having such a good time laughing and singing songs that they didn't notice me when I jumped into the picnic basket," continued Chester. "I was sure they wouldn't mind if I had just a taste."

"Naturally not," said Tucker Mouse sympathetically. "Why mind? Plenty for all. Who could blame you?"

"Now, I have to admit," Chester went on, "I had more than a taste. As a matter of fact, I ate so much that I couldn't keep my eyes open—what with being tired from the jumping and everything. And I fell asleep right there in the picnic basket. The first thing I

knew, somebody had put a bag on top of me that had the last of the roast beef sandwiches in it. I couldn't move!"

"Imagine!" Tucker exclaimed. "Trapped under roast beef sandwiches! Well, there are worse fates."

"At first I wasn't too frightened," said Chester. "After all, I thought, they probably come from New Canaan or some other nearby town. They'll have to unpack the basket sooner or later. Little did I know!" He shook his head and sighed. "I could feel the basket being carried into a car and riding somewhere and then being lifted down. That must have been the railroad station. Then I went up again and there was a rattling and roaring sound, the way a train makes. By this time I was pretty scared. I knew every minute was taking me further away from my stump, but there wasn't anything I could do. I was getting awfully cramped, too, under those roast beef sandwiches."

"Didn't you try to eat your way out?" asked Tucker.

"I didn't have any room," said Chester. "But every now and then, the train would give a lurch and I managed to free myself a little. We traveled on and on, and then the train stopped. I didn't have any idea where we were, but as soon as the basket was carried off, I could tell from the noise it must be New York."

"You never were here before?" Tucker asked.

"Goodness no!" said Chester. "But I've heard about it. There was a swallow I used to know who told about flying over New York every spring and fall on her way to the North and back. But what would I be doing here?" He shifted uneasily from one set of legs to another. "I'm a country cricket."

"Don't worry," said Tucker Mouse. "I'll feed you liverwurst. You'll be all right. Go on with the story."

"It's almost over," said Chester. "The people got off one train and walked a ways and got on another even noisier than the first."

"Must have been the subway," said Tucker.

"I guess so," Chester Cricket said. "You can imagine how scared I was. I didn't know *where* I was going! For all I knew, they could have been heading for Texas, although I don't guess many people from Texas come all the way to Connecticut for a picnic."

"It could happen," said Tucker, nodding his head.

"Anyway, I worked furiously to get loose. And finally I made it. When they got off the second train, I took a flying leap and landed in a pile of dirt over in the corner of this place where we are."

"Such an introduction to New York," said Tucker, "to land in a pile of dirt in the Times Square subway station. Tsk, tsk, tsk."

"And here I am," Chester concluded forlornly. "I've been lying over there for three days not knowing what to do. At last I got so nervous I began to chirp."

"That was the sound!" interrupted Tucker Mouse. "I heard it, but I didn't know what it was."

"Yes, that was me," said Chester. "Usually I don't chirp until later on in the summer—but my goodness, I had to do *something!*"

The cricket had been sitting next to the edge of the shelf. For some reason—perhaps it was a faint noise, like padded feet tiptoeing across the floor—he happened to look down. A shadowy form that had been crouching silently below in the darkness made a spring and landed right next to Tucker and Chester.

"Watch out!" Chester shouted. "A cat!" He dove headfirst into the matchbox.

Chester buried his head in the tissue. He didn't want to see his new friend, Tucker Mouse, get killed. Back in Connecticut he had sometimes watched the one-sided fights of cats and mice in the meadow, and unless the mice were near their holes, the fights always ended in the same way.

But this cat had been upon them too quickly. Tucker couldn't have escaped.

There wasn't a sound. Chester lifted his head and very cautiously looked behind him. The cat—a huge tiger cat with gray-green and black stripes along his body— was sitting on his hind legs, switching his tail around his forepaws. And directly between those forepaws, in the very jaws of his enemy, sat Tucker Mouse. He was watching Chester curiously. The cricket began to make frantic signs that the mouse should look up and see what was looming over him.

Very casually Tucker raised his head. The cat looked straight down on him. "Oh, him," said Tucker, chucking the cat under the chin with his right front paw. "He's my best friend. Come out from the matchbox."

Chester crept out, looking first at one, then the other.

"Chester, meet Harry Cat," said Tucker. "Harry, this is Chester. He's a cricket."

"I'm very pleased to make your acquaintance," said Harry Cat in a silky voice.

"Hello," said Chester. He was sort of ashamed because of all the fuss he'd made. "I wasn't scared for myself. But I thought cats and mice were enemies."

"In the country, maybe," said Tucker. "But in New York, we gave up those old habits long ago. Harry is my oldest friend. He lives with me over in the drain-pipe. So how was scrounging tonight, Harry?"

"Not so good," said Harry Cat. "I was over in the ash cans on the East Side, but those rich people don't throw out as much garbage as they should."

"Chester, make that noise again for Harry," said Tucker Mouse.

Chester lifted the black wings that were carefully folded across his back and with a quick, expert stroke drew the top one over the bottom. A "thrumm" echoed through the station.

"Lovely—very lovely," said the cat. "This cricket has talent."

"I thought it was singing," said Tucker. "But you do it like playing a violin, with one wing on the other?"

"Yes," said Chester. "These wings aren't much good for flying, but I prefer music anyhow." He made three rapid chirps.

Tucker Mouse and Harry Cat smiled at each other. "It makes me want to purr to hear it," said Harry.

"Some people say a cricket goes 'chee chee chee,'" explained Chester. "And others say, 'treet treet treet,' but we crickets don't think it sounds like either one of those."

"It sounds to me as if you were going 'crik crik crik,'" said Harry.

"Maybe that's why they call him a 'cricket,'" said Tucker.

They all laughed. Tucker had a squeaky laugh that sounded as if he were hiccuping. Chester was feeling much happier now. The future did not seem nearly as gloomy as it had over in the pile of dirt in the corner.

"Are you going to stay awhile in New York?" asked Tucker.

"I guess I'll have to," said Chester. "I don't know how to get home."

"Well, we could always take you to Grand Central Station and put you on a train going back to

Connecticut," said Tucker. "But why don't you give the city a try? Meet new people—see new things. Mario likes you very much."

"Yes, but his mother doesn't," said Chester. "She thinks I carry germs."

"Germs!" said Tucker scornfully. "She wouldn't know a germ if one gave her a black eye. Pay no attention."

"Too bad you couldn't have found more successful friends,"

said Harry Cat. "I fear for the future of this newsstand."

"It's true," echoed Tucker sadly. "They're going broke fast." He jumped up on a pile of magazines and read off the names in the half-light that slanted through the cracks in the wooden cover. "*Art News, Musical America.* Who would read them but a few long-hairs?"

"I don't understand the way you talk," said Chester. Back in the meadow, he had listened to bullfrogs, and woodchucks, and rabbits, even a few snakes, but he had never heard anyone speak like Tucker Mouse. "What is a longhair?"

Tucker scratched his head and thought a moment. "A longhair is an extra-refined person," he said. "You take an Afghan hound. That's a longhair."

"Do Afghan hounds read *Musical America?*" asked Chester.

"They would if they could," said Tucker.

Chester shook his head. "I'm afraid I won't get along in New York," he said.

"Oh, sure you will!" squeaked Tucker Mouse. "Harry, suppose we take Chester up and show him Times Square. Would you like that, Chester?"

"I guess so," said Chester, although he was really a little leery of venturing out into New York City.

The three of them jumped down to the floor. The crack in the side of the newsstand was just wide enough for Harry to get through. As they crossed the station floor, Tucker pointed out the local sights of interest, such as the Nedick's lunch counter — Tucker spent a lot of time around there — and the Loft's candy store. Then they came to the drainpipe. Chester had to make short little hops to keep from hitting his head as they went up. There seemed to be hundreds of twistings and turnings, and many other pipes that opened off the main route, but Tucker Mouse knew his way perfectly — even in the dark.

At last Chester saw light above them. One more hop brought him out onto the sidewalk. And there he gasped, holding his breath and crouching against the cement.

They were standing at one corner of the Times Building, which is at the south end of Times Square. Above the cricket, towers that seemed like mountains of light rose up into the night sky. Even this late, the neon signs were still blazing. Reds, blues, greens, and yellows flashed down on him. And the air was full of the roar of traffic and the hum of human beings. It was as if Times Square were a kind of shell, with colors and noises breaking in great waves inside it. Chester's heart hurt him and he closed his eyes. The sight was too terrible and beautiful for a cricket who up to now had measured high things by the height of his willow tree and sounds by the burble of a running brook.

"How do you like it?" asked Tucker Mouse.

"Well — it's — it's quite something," Chester stuttered.

"You should see it New Year's Eve," said Harry Cat.

Gradually Chester's eyes got used to the lights. He looked up. And way far above them, above New York, and above the whole world, he made out a star that he knew was a star he used to look at back in Connecticut.

When they had gone down to the station and Chester was in the matchbox again, he thought about that star. It made him feel better to think that there was one familiar thing, twinkling above him, amidst so much that was new and strange.

Chester and his new friends, Tucker and Harry, cause many problems for the Bellinis. But they also bring good fortune in a most unusual way—a way that surprises the whole city of New York. You can read all about it in George Selden's book, THE CRICKET IN TIMES SQUARE.

ABOUT THE AUTHOR

According to its author, the idea for *The Cricket in Times Square* came to him when he heard a cricket chirp in the Times Square subway station late one night. George Selden's full name is George Selden Thompson, but he uses only his first two names when he writes. Mr. Thompson grew up in Connecticut but now lives in New York City. In the story of Chester Cricket, he expressed many of his own feelings about his adopted city.

Mr. Thompson is a graduate of Yale University. After college he studied at the University of Rome, in Italy, for a year. He then moved to New York, where he has devoted all of his time to writing. In addition to some plays for adults, he has written a number of children's books. One, *Oscar Lobster's Fair Exchange*, is a humorous story about a group of seashore animal friends.

After waiting for nine years to be sure that his story idea would be completely fresh, Mr. Thompson wrote another book about the characters in *The Cricket in Times Square*. In *Tucker's Countryside* Tucker Mouse and Harry Cat visit Chester Cricket at his home in Connecticut.

Since *Tucker's Countryside*, the author has written *Harry Cat's Pet Puppy* and *The Genie of Sutton Place*.

BOOKS TO ENJOY

AT THE CENTER OF THE WORLD, *by Betty Baker*

This is an action-filled tale about the early days of the Papago and Pima Indians.

MOON-WATCH SUMMER, *by Lenore Blegvad*

What if you were a real space enthusiast, but you could not watch the first moon walk on TV? Adam has this great problem when he stays with his grandmother at her farm.

SANTIAGO'S SILVER MINE, *by Eleanor Clymer*

In the mountains of Mexico, two boys find a great treasure from the past, which helps their fathers earn a living.

RITA, THE WEEKEND RAT, *by Sonia Levitin*

Cynthia, who is president of the Boys' Club, is determined to show that she can be quite responsible for caring for the classroom pet on weekends.

SCOOP, LAST OF THE BROWN PELICANS,
by Robert McClung

In this nature story about brown pelicans, you will discover the dangers they face and what can be done to protect them.

SQUEALS AND SQUIGGLES AND GHOSTLY GIGGLES,
by Ann McGovern

Here are some spooky limericks, tricks, and games.

THE SEVEN STONE, *by Mary Francis Shura*

Maggie feels left out until she makes friends with the new girl in school, who has a magic stone.

Reflections

Reflections

STORIES

PLAY

ARTICLE

POEMS

JUST FOR FUN

SKILL LESSONS

Is There Life On Other Planets?

Characters   by Marion Lane

HEAD SCIENTIST
FIVE SCIENTISTS

SETTING: *A conference room. The* HEAD SCIENTIST *and the* FIVE
SCIENTISTS *are seated at a long table with their backs to the audience.*

HEAD SCIENTIST *(Rising, with back to audience):* Ladies and
gentlemen, please come to order. I have called you here
today to give you important news. I am sorry to tell you
that after much study, it has been decided that there cannot
possibly be any life on the planet nearest us.

1ST SCIENTIST: What about the changes in color from white
to green that have been seen on the planet's surface?
Don't these show weather changes and some kind of air?

HEAD SCIENTIST: All tests show that there is some air there, but
it is not enough to sustain life as we know it.

2ND SCIENTIST: Then how do you account for the ditches or
canals that have been seen with our telescopes?

HEAD SCIENTIST: Latest viewings show that these are only natural
formations. No one can prove that they are made by any
living beings.

Reprinted from *Skits, Comedies and Farces for Teen-Agers.* A. S. Burack, Editor, Plays, Inc., Publishers, Boston, Mass. 02116. Copyright © 1965 by Plays, Inc.

3RD SCIENTIST: Then the flying saucer stories are all false?

HEAD SCIENTIST: No, of course not. Most of these sightings can be explained logically, and the rest are just imagination.

4TH SCIENTIST: Then all the strange sounds picked up on radios come from our own sending stations or are caused by the weather?

HEAD SCIENTIST: I'm afraid so.

5TH SCIENTIST: I, for one, am very much surprised. I've always been sure we had neighbors on other planets or at least on the one nearest to us. Perhaps not life as we know it, but some kind of life not known to us.

HEAD SCIENTIST: Ladies and gentlemen, I am going to call an end to this meeting. I can see no point in talking about this matter further. The tests have proved that we must accept the fact that there is no life on —

ALL *(Turning to audience to show weird masks or makeup):* **Earth!**

Little Vic's Greatest Race

by Doris Gates

Pony Rivers was the orphan son of a racetrack rider. Little Vic was the son of a great racehorse. Pony and Little Vic met when Little Vic was a newborn colt and Pony was a fifteen-year-old looking for a job on a horse farm in Kentucky's Bluegrass Country. It was love at first sight.

Pony followed Little Vic from one master to another, dreaming of the day when he and Little Vic would stand in the winner's circle after a big race. But Little Vic seemed to miss all his chances to win races, and Pony was told he would have to become a jockey before he could ride Little Vic. Pony worked hard at learning to be a good jockey, but one day while racing he was badly hurt, and he became fearful of riding.

After recovering, Pony once again found a job taking care of Little Vic. This time it was on a ranch in Arizona that was managed by an unpleasant man named Joe Hills, who was not very friendly to Pony.

Pony's life at the ranch was little different from what it had been on the farm in the Bluegrass Country where Little Vic was born. His duties were about the same. And yet, though his life seemed little different, he felt entirely different inside himself. A shadow had been cast over his happiness by Joe Hills. Pony knew that he could never be really happy here as long as Joe Hills felt about him the way he did. However, there was Little Vic, and Pony was quite sure that he would rather take the Joe Hills kind of unhappiness than the sorrow he would feel if he had to be separated from the horse again. So he tried to do his work as well as he could, and he kept out of sight of Joe Hills just as much as possible.

At first he had tried to be content just taking care of the horse. But the longer he was around Little Vic, the more Pony began to wonder if he would ever have the courage to ride him if the chance were given him. The more he

thought about it, the more he wondered. And the more he wondered, the more it seemed to him that he would never be at peace until he had put himself to the test.

One evening Pony disappeared into the night as soon as the dishes were done. The moon was coming up above the rim of mountains to the east. Off to the west there were banks of clouds in the sky. There had been heavy rains in those mountains a short time ago.

This was the night he had decided to find out if he had the courage to ride Little Vic. He would have to be very careful because Joe Hills had told him never to ride the horse. Until now it had been easy to obey that rule. Now, however, Pony knew that he must try to ride Little Vic. If he didn't have the courage to run him, then he could settle down forever, glad just to be the horse's stable hand. But the idea would not die in Pony that perhaps he and the horse were meant to race together. If they were, then he would have to have the courage to race him. Tonight was going to prove to him once and for all which it should be—jockey or stable hand.

The desert floor was white under the moonlight when Pony approached the stables. As he went past the house where the ranch hands slept, Pony looked in the windows and saw Joe Hills sitting at a table with four other men. They were playing cards, and they looked as if they would be sitting there for many hours to come.

Pony went first to the tack room, where he had put his riding things. Then he went to Little Vic's stall and saddled up. He led the horse out and closed the stall door very carefully behind him. Then, still leading the horse, Pony started across the open fields toward the highway. As always, Little Vic went quietly along. Pony knew now that he would have no fear of riding him at a walk. He had the courage to get on. But first he had to find something to stand on in order to get into the saddle. The irons were high up on the horse's side, the

123

way jockeys always have them, and Pony's legs were too short to make the long reach from the ground to where the irons hung.

After walking about half a mile without finding either a tree stump or a rock large enough to be of any use, Pony decided to try to get the horse close enough to the wire fence to let him stand on one of the posts and make a jump for the saddle. It took some time to get Little Vic close to the fence, and an even longer time to get him to stand still long enough for Pony to get into the saddle. Little Vic was not used to this kind of thing. And all the while, Pony's footing on the post was anything but sure. At last, however, he was sitting on the horse's back, very happy to be there after the struggle. Pony did not realize that in his efforts to get on his horse, he had quite forgotten to be afraid.

He guided the horse at a walk a little distance off the highway in the direction of the western mountains. He found it good to be riding again, even at a walk. A smile appeared on Pony's face and stayed there. Suppose he and Little Vic just disappeared into the wide land out beyond. Suppose he just kept on riding west. It was a lovely idea, and for a moment Pony played with it. He was sure the horse would be happier with him than with Joe Hills.

Little Vic's long legs carried him over the ground at a good clip, even at a walk. His steps were wide apart, and he held his head high and looked about him as he went. Pony dared at last to lift himself in the saddle, and Little Vic began to trot. After a bit, Pony pulled him up. It had been all right! He had not been afraid. If only he had the strength of mind to let Little Vic run. But no matter how Pony talked to himself, he couldn't bring himself to the point of letting Vic really go.

Now they were riding along the edge of the draw, a dry riverbed that ran for some miles along the highway. The ground was hard and even. The draw itself was a deep shadow in the moonlight, splitting the desert floor in two.

Suddenly Pony was surprised to see a light up ahead of him. It was an unsteady light and seemed to come from the very bottom of the draw. He moved Little Vic into a trot, and before long came up to where some people had settled themselves around a campfire in the bottom of the draw.

Pony drew up Little Vic and called down to them, "You folks had better not try to camp there."

Now they saw him sitting on his horse just above their heads.

"Why not?" one of the men called out, and a woman laughed.

"It's not safe," Pony told him. "There have been heavy rains in the mountains today, and a flash flood might come down this draw and drown you in your sleep."

The man laughed. "Do you expect us to believe that?"

"It's the truth," said Pony.

"Don't worry," called up another woman. "If the wind should come up, we will be out of it down here. It's a lovely place to camp."

Pony saw that he could not change their plan, so he said no more but trotted Little Vic on past them and their car, which was parked off the highway a little distance from them.

Pony thought he had ridden something over a mile when suddenly Little Vic began to act jumpy. His ears pointed stiffly forward, and he slowed his pace as if he were listening for something. Suddenly he stopped altogether, and Pony could feel his body shaking slightly under the saddle. Little Vic, for the first time since he was a very young colt, was afraid! Pony peered into the shadowy spaces out before him. He listened with all his might. And after a moment or two he thought he heard the roar of thunder. Little Vic had begun to dance from side to side and to toss his head. Pony tried to talk to him, remembering that horses are often afraid of thunder. But Little Vic would not be quieted. He began to paw at the ground.

Now Pony heard what Little Vic had heard at the start. That roar was not thunder. It was the sound of racing water rolling down from the mountains with all the force of its quick drop to the valley floor below it. Pony waited only an instant before he turned Little Vic and began trotting back the way they had come. The horse was nearly wild now. He fought the bit and shook his head. Little Vic wanted to run. And then in a flash the whole world seemed to be caught up in one great roar as the water came racing toward them. How could such a flood come so fast, where only moments ago there had been a dry riverbed? No wonder they called them flash floods, Pony thought. And in the next instant he remembered the people camping in the draw. At the speed the water was coming, they could never get away in time. They might even be asleep by now and would never know about their danger until it was too late to do anything about it.

Thinking of those people, Pony quite forgot that he had been afraid ever to race again. He leaned forward over Little Vic's neck. Old habit was acting for him now, and without knowing that he did so, he gathered his horse for the start exactly as if he were in the stall of a starting gate. Then he gave the yell that had sent many a quarter horse leaping out ahead of the field and down the track and away. Little Vic needed no other urging. With a powerful spring he was off, and Pony's heart leaped with him. Now he remembered his old fear, but he was no longer afraid. This was the moment he had lived for, ever since the first moment he had looked at Little Vic. He knew that now. They had both been waiting for this moment because they had been meant for each other from the start.

Suddenly Pony began to talk to the horse, his small body bunched upon the horse's neck.

"This is the race you've been waiting for, fellow. This is the real thing. There isn't any money riding on you today. But the prize is the biggest one you'll ever win. It's the lives of all those people, Little Vic. If you aren't as good as I think you are, they won't have a chance. But you are. *You are!*"

The last two words were a yell, for Little Vic had settled into his speed. The roar was coming closer. Pony looked back once, as he might have done in a regular race to see how close the nearest horse was to him. But he could see nothing but the shadowy draw, and he began to wonder whether the sound he heard was the thunder of Little Vic's galloping feet or the sound of the flood.

He tried to remember the distance they had come. Was it a mile? Was it two miles? Could Little Vic, could *any* horse, keep this pace for a mile? Now another yell burst from Pony as he realized that they had drawn away

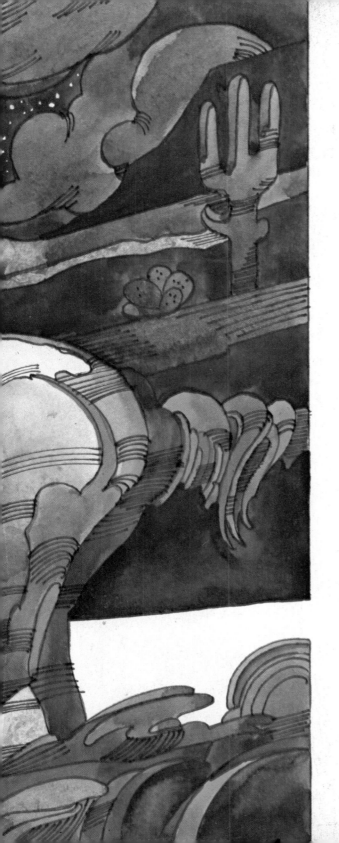

from the sound of water. Little Vic had gained! He might yet outrace the flood. Long legs were moving smoothly, strongly under him, never slowing in their pace, like a machine that could go on and on forever. But Pony knew that no horse could keep this pace for long. He drew him up a little, saving him for the stretch. In a moment the sound of the water again came to his ears.

All at once Pony caught sight of a small dot of light out ahead of them—the campfire. This was the stretch. He touched Little Vic with his whip, and the horse flew over the ground. As they came up to the fire, Pony fought to stop him. "Get out," he screamed to the campers. "The flood. It's coming! Don't stop for anything. Just get out!"

The astonished campers hardly believed him at first. Then they, too, caught the sound of the approaching thunder. Without waiting longer, they began to climb the bank of the draw, and they barely had time to get their breath before the flood had rolled over their campfire and swept their belongings away.

Now, at last, Little Vic stood in a winner's circle as the people he had saved closed round him in admiring wonder.

"He raced the flood and won," Pony told them simply. "There was no one to see, but he ran the greatest race of them all."

Like a great winner, Little Vic stood with head high, looking out past the people. In the moonlight his brown coat shone and the whites of his eyes flashed. Pony smiled and laid his hand upon the horse's neck.

Little Vic and Pony go on to make their bid in the big Handicap at Santa Anita, where they run against the greatest horses in the country. The exciting last chapter of the book LITTLE VIC *tells you how they do in that race.*

AUTHOR

When Doris Gates was a child in the Santa Clara Valley of California, she was given a little gray burro. She remembered the gift when she grew up, and the burro became an important part of her first book, *Sarah's Idea*. The next book Doris Gates wrote also came from her own experiences.

She knew about the many families in California that earned a living by working on the big farms in the San Joaquin Valley. As soon as the crop they worked on was picked, they had to move to another area and a different crop. These migrant families moved many times every year.

Doris Gates worked with the children from these families while she was the children's librarian in Fresno. Often she told stories at the camps where the migrant workers lived. Everyone enjoyed her story-telling, and she became well known. Her experiences with the migrant families taught her that what the children wanted most was a permanent home, so they would not have to move around. Her book *Blue Willow* is the story of a girl who wants her family to find a home.

Ms. Gates has written many books since she decided to give up her library career to have more time for writing. They include *Sensible Kate, The Elderberry Bush,* and *The Cat and Mrs. Cary*.

In 1969 the Fresno Free County Library opened a new children's room. It was named the Doris Gates Room in her honor.

Haiku

The crow flew, so fast
That he left his lonely caw
Behind in the fields.
                    Richard Wright

Well! Hello down there,
friend snail! When did you arrive
    in such a hurry?
                    Issa

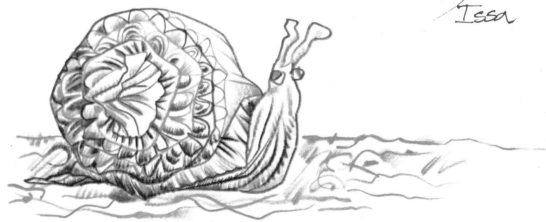

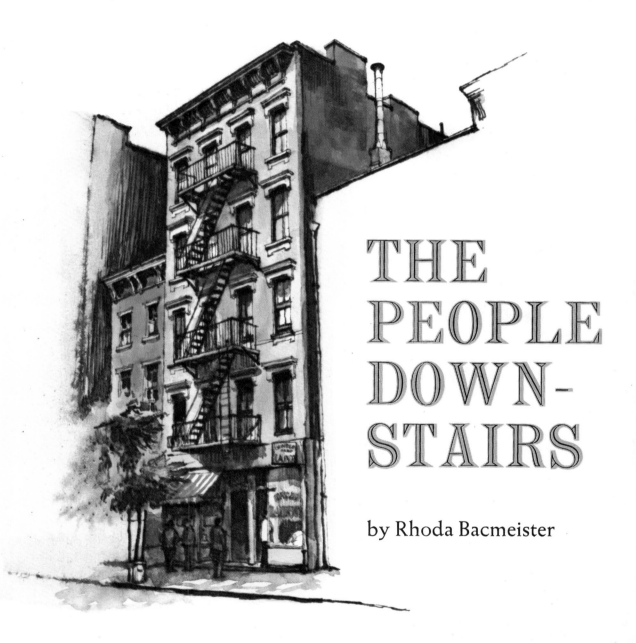

THE PEOPLE DOWN-STAIRS

by Rhoda Bacmeister

Cathy and Joey and George Sherrill lived on the top floor of an apartment house five stories high. There were lots of stairs to climb when they came in from outdoors, but from

the top floor, it was easy to go up to the roof. There was plenty of space to play up there, and their mother had a good place to hang the clothes to dry.

Cathy was nine and Georgie and Joey were seven and six. They had great fun playing together and with the Perez children, who lived on the fourth floor in the apartment right under the Sherrills.

Then one day the Perez family moved away and some new people moved in. Cathy didn't see any children, but one day she knocked on their door to ask if there was anyone she could play with.

The door opened just a crack, and a thin little woman looked out with a worried frown. Cathy started to speak, but before she could say a word, the woman whispered, "Shhh! Don't knock on this door, little girl. My man is asleep." She shut the door.

Cathy was so surprised that she just stood there. She

couldn't think why a grown-up man should be sleeping in the middle of the morning. She went up and told her mother about it.

Mrs. Sherrill seemed surprised, too. "Well, I suppose the poor man is sick today," she said. "We'll try to be extra quiet so we don't disturb him, and if I see her going out, I'll inquire. It would be only neighborly, since we've heard he's in bed."

The next day Cathy was looking out the window when she saw the lady downstairs. She told her mother, and right away Mrs. Sherrill whipped off her apron, took her purse and shopping bag, and started out.

"You stay and mind your brothers, Cathy," Mrs. Sherrill said. "I'll be back soon."

So Cathy set up a beanbag game she had made out of a carton, and they all played that. They had a fine time and didn't realize how loud they were laughing and shouting until their mother came back.

"Whisht!" she said the minute she came in the door. "No more of that! We have to keep quiet for a while, so off with you to the roof, and play there till I call you. Yes, you can take the game with you, and your tops and yo-yos, too, if you like."

The sun was bright on the roof and they had a good time. After lunch their mother took them for a walk, and when they got back, she sat down and read them stories. She hardly ever had time to spend the whole afternoon with them like that. The time just flew, and suddenly there was Father coming in.

They ran to meet him. He gave both Cathy and Georgie a scuffly kind of hug and tossed Joey up in the air. Joey shrieked with joy, and Mother said, "Shhhh!"

Father put his arm around her. "And how's my best girl been?" he asked.

Mother smiled at him but she still looked a little worried. "All right, but, Henry — it's the new people downstairs!"

"What's the matter with them?"

"Nothing, really," Mother answered. "Only the man works at night and needs to sleep almost all day. His wife wants us to keep the children quiet, because by the time her husband wakes up and has his breakfast in the middle of the afternoon, the baby has to have a nap."

"Hmmm, I see!" Father said. "Quite a lot of quiet they want!" Then he looked at his watch and grinned. "Hurrah!" he said in a very loud voice. "It's five-thirty and by now everybody must be *awake* downstairs. So we can have a little fun, can't we?" He began to tickle and tousle Georgie.

Mother laughed. "Oh, Henry! I guess so. I'll have dinner ready in no time, but you just don't know how careful I've had to be all day!"

Father cocked one eyebrow way up and made such a

solemn face that the children knew he was going to be silly. He began to chant:

> "Oh, the people downstairs
> Sleep longer than bears.
> We must walk on our toeses
> And not blow our noses
> Or we'll ruin the dozes
> Of the people downstairs!"

He shook out his big handkerchief and went around wiping everyone's nose, even Mother's, until they were all laughing.

They went on having a good time, but at seven o'clock Mother looked at the clock. "You'd better use your crayons until bedtime," she said. "The baby downstairs goes to bed at seven."

"More sleep downstairs?" Father asked.

"More sleep downstairs," Mother said, making a face.

The children sighed. "I wish the Perez family hadn't moved away!" exclaimed Cathy.

But the new people stayed on. Day after day Cathy and George and Joey had to try to be quiet. Sometimes they played on the roof and sometimes Mother found time to take them to the park to play, but whenever they were at home, it was, "Shhhh—the people downstairs!"

They got so tired of it that it made them cross, but if they did make noise, the thin little woman from downstairs would come up. "Please, could you keep the kids more quiet, ma'am?" she would say. "My husband does need his sleep."

Mother would sigh. "We will try." Then she would turn to the children. "Come now and I'll tell you a story." That helped, because Mother's stories were wonderful.

It got very tiring, though, trying to be quiet day after day. Mother sighed, Cathy pouted, Georgie said, "The people downstairs!" and stuck out his tongue, and Joey stamped his foot.

Then Father would try to cheer them up. He would tiptoe around with his finger on his lips, making such a game of it that everyone tiptoed around, quiet as mice, watching each other and giggling softly. Father's left eyebrow would go up, and he would make a bow and recite, just like somebody on a stage:

> "Oh, the people downstairs
> Can sleep very deep
> As buses go by
> Or jets in the sky.
> They continue to dream
> When fire sirens scream,
> But their lids fly apart
> And they wake with a start
> If we move the chairs—
> Do the people downstairs."

Then one day a moving van came and the people downstairs moved away.

"Hurrah!" cried Cathy and Georgie and Joey. Father and Mother looked happy, too. Nobody worried a bit about making noise that day. Mother let the pots and pans rattle and the dishes click as she washed them. Father led a march all around the apartment, and they sang songs as loud as they liked. They had a wonderful time for six days, and then — some new people moved into the apartment downstairs.

"Do they sleep all day?" Father asked when he came home.

Mother shook her head. "No, they're two old ladies. One looks sad and the other looks cross. The cross one says she has *very sensitive nerves,* and if she finds the noise up here too much, she'll just tap on the pipes to let us know."

"But she doesn't tap. She BANGS," Cathy said. "She has done it twice already."

Sure enough, when they all laughed at once over something, BANG-BANG went the pipes. Up went Father's left eyebrow, and his mouth had a funny quirk as he cried:

> *"Oh, the people downstairs*
> *Just hammer and pound*
> *If we make the least sound,*
> *So nobody dares*
> *Rouse the people downstairs!"*

So it began all over again. All day long it was, "Shhh—shhhhhh—shhhh! The people downstairs!" The weather was getting colder and the children couldn't play on the roof much. They got tired of stories and coloring and cutting things out, but if they made any noise, the lady downstairs would bang and whang. If they didn't stop at once, she got crosser, and the crosser she got, the louder she banged.

Then one day *those* people moved away and another family moved in. What a noise they made! The mother shouted at the movers. Flocks of children ran up and down the stairs, carrying bats, and dolls, and a drum, and a wiggling brown puppy, who barked "Yap-yap-yap!" Cathy and Georgie

and Joey hung over the stair rail watching. They could hardly wait to tell their father.

When he heard, he grabbed their hands and they all made a circle and danced around as he sang:

> *"Oh, the people downstairs*
> *Are an answer to prayers,*
> *For they've girls and they've boys*
> *And they simply love noise!*
> *Hurrah for the people downstairs!"*

"Can I go down and ask the kids to come up and play?" Cathy asked. "Can I?"

"You bet!" Father said, and Georgie and Joey shouted together, "Hurrah for the people downstairs!"

AUTHOR

The story you have just read is taken from the book *The People Downstairs* by Rhoda Bacmeister. The book is a collection of stories about families who live in apartment buildings in the city. In addition to children's books, she has also written many magazine articles and books for adults.

Mrs. Bacmeister was born in Northampton, Massachusetts. After attending college, she worked in various parts of the country, teaching almost every grade from nursery school through college. Her work and interests have always centered on children and often children who are poor.

Today Mrs. Bacmeister lives in a town near New York City, where she once lived and where she became friends with people who came from different countries. Mrs. Bacmeister has three children, five grandchildren, and one great-grandchild. She enjoys reading, swimming, growing flowers, weaving on her loom, and hearing from children who have enjoyed reading her stories. She is also called upon at times to give speeches and advice to groups of teachers.

Androclus and the Lion

Did you know that there once was a time when a man was made to fight a lion bare-handed if he broke certain laws? It's true. About two thousand years ago in the city of Rome, lawbreakers often were made to fight a hungry lion. These unfair contests were held in a large open-air arena where hundreds of people would come to watch.

In this story from James Baldwin's *Favorite Tales of Long Ago*, a terrified runaway slave is sent to the arena. What happens when he faces the lion amazes everyone.

In Rome there was once a poor slave whose name was Androclus. His master was a cruel man and so unkind to him that at last Androclus ran away.

He hid himself in a wild wood for many days; but there was no food to be found, and he grew so weak and sick that he thought he should die. So one day he crept into a cave and lay down, and soon he was fast asleep.

After a while a great noise woke him up. A lion had come into the cave and was roaring loudly. Androclus was very much afraid, for he felt sure that the beast would kill him. Soon, however, he saw that the lion was not angry but that he limped as though his foot hurt him.

Then Androclus grew so bold that he took hold of the lion's lame paw to see what was the matter. The lion stood quite still and rubbed his head against the man's shoulder. He seemed to say, "I know that you will help me."

Androclus lifted the paw from the ground and saw that it was a long, sharp thorn which hurt the lion so much. He took the end of the thorn in his fingers. Then he gave a strong, quick pull, and out it came. The lion was full of joy. He jumped about like a dog and licked the hands and feet of his new friend.

Androclus was not at all afraid after this, and when night came, he and the lion lay down and slept side by side.

For a long time, the lion brought food to Androclus every day. The two became such good friends that Androclus found his new life a very happy one.

One day some soldiers who were passing through the wood found Androclus in the cave. They knew who he was, and so took him back to Rome.

It was the law at that time that every slave who ran away from his master should be made to fight a hungry lion. So a fierce lion was shut up for a while without food, and a time was set for the fight.

When the day came, thousands of people crowded into a large arena to see the sport. They went to such places at that time very much as people nowadays go to see a circus show or a game of baseball.

The door opened and poor Androclus was brought in. He was almost dead with fear, for the roars of the lion could already be heard. He looked up and saw that there was no pity in the thousands of faces around him.

Then the hungry lion rushed in. With a single bound, he reached the poor slave. Androclus gave a great cry, not of fear, but of gladness. It was his old friend, the lion of the cave.

The people, who had expected to see the man killed by the lion, were filled with wonder. They saw Androclus put his arms around the lion's neck; they saw the lion lie down at his feet and lick them lovingly; they saw the great beast rub his head against the slave's face as though he wanted to be petted. They could not understand what it all meant.

After a while they asked Androclus to tell them about it. So he stood up before them, and with his arm around the lion's neck, told how he and the beast had lived together in the cave.

"I am a man," he said, "but no man has ever befriended me. This poor lion alone has been kind to me, and we love each other as brothers."

The people were not so bad that they could be cruel to the poor slave now. "Live and be free!" they cried. "Live and be free!"

Others cried, "Let the lion go free, too! Give both of them their liberty!"

And so Androclus was set free, and the lion was given to him for his own. And they lived together in Rome for many years.

AUTHOR

James Baldwin was born in a little town in Indiana and there spent his childhood. He liked to read so much that his mother said he was not born with a silver spoon in his mouth but rather with a book in his hand. Reading seemed to come to him as naturally as eating comes to others. His father had a small library, and James added books to this as often as he could. Certain understanding friends encouraged him in his reading and loaned books to him.

He became an editor of school books for a large publishing company, and at one time it was said that more than half the school readers used in the United States were either written or edited by him. He wrote more than fifty volumes, and his books were known and read in every part of the world. Mr. Baldwin died in 1925.

NOTES IN CODE

You can have fun sending your own notes in secret code. Here is one simple way of doing that. First, count the number of letters in your message. Then write the letters in two rows so that each row has the same number of letters.

For example, the message WAIT ON THE PLAYGROUND has nineteen letters, which is an uneven number. By adding an **X** at the end, you can divide the message into two rows of ten letters each.

W A I T O N T H E P
L A Y G R O U N D X

Spell out the message in code by writing the letters in the first column, then the letters in the second column, and so on, until you have written all the letters in the message.

W L A A I Y T G O R N O T U H N E D P X

To figure out this code note, write down every other letter, starting with **W**. Cross out each letter in the code after you have written it down. When you get to the end of the line, return to the beginning and start with the first unused letter. After you have written all the letters from the code, draw lines to separate the words in the message. Ignore the **X** at the end.

W A I T | O N | T H E | P L A Y G R O U N D | X

The code below was written in the same way as the code above. See if you can figure it out. If you need help, turn the book upside down for the answer.

Y D O W U R C I A T N E R I E N A C D O A D N E

Answer: You can read and write in code.

DECIDING ON PARAGRAPH TOPICS

Most of the pages which you study are printed in groups of sentences that are called paragraphs. It is easy to tell one paragraph from another because the first line of each paragraph begins a little farther to the right than the other lines do. But often the most important thing for you to figure out about a paragraph is the one thing which all its sentences are talking about.

Try now to think what each sentence in the following paragraph is talking about. The sentences are numbered so that you can think about them easily later.

1. An elephant's foot is almost round. 2. Elephants found in India have five nails on each front foot and four on each hind foot. 3. Those found in Africa have four nails on each front foot and five on each hind foot. 4. Under the bones of each foot is a pad that acts as a cushion. 5. An elephant's great weight of several tons makes its feet swell as it stands, but when it holds up a foot or lies down, the swelling goes down.

Sentence 1 tells the shape of *an elephant's foot*. Sentences 2 and 3 tell the number of nails on *an elephant's foot*. Sentence 4 tells that there is a pad on *an elephant's foot*. Sentence 5 tells what makes *an elephant's foot* swell and when that swelling goes down. You can see that every sentence in the paragraph tells something about *an elephant's foot.*

Most paragraphs that you study talk about only one thing. We call that one thing *the topic of the paragraph.* Every sentence in the paragraph tells or asks something about that topic. The topic of the paragraph you just read is *an elephant's foot.*

Sometimes right after you have read a paragraph only once, you will know quickly what its topic is. When that does not happen and you need to decide what the topic is, do these things:

1. Read the first sentence again and think what it is talking about. Write down a word or group of words that names what the sentence is talking about.

2. Do the same things for each of the other sentences in the paragraph.

3. Then look at the groups of words you have written and decide what one thing they all name. Usually that one thing will be the topic of the paragraph.

Can you decide what the topic of the following paragraph is?

To capture wild elephants, people often use tame elephants, horns, and a large pen made of heavy logs. After the pen is built, a tame elephant is placed inside to act as a lure to the wild beasts. Then some people called beaters, who are riding tame elephants, surround a wild herd. There the beaters set up a great racket by blowing horns and yelling. The frightened herd begins to move and is chased into the pen. When the wild elephants have quieted down, people enter the pen and tie stout ropes around each animal so that it is helpless.

Which of the following groups of words is the topic of the paragraph?

1. How elephants are tamed
2. The work that elephants do
3. How wild elephants are captured
4. The uses of tame elephants

Discussion

Help your class answer these questions:

1. What is meant by the topic of a paragraph? Why is *an elephant's foot* the topic of the paragraph that has five numbered sentences?
2. When you do not know what the topic of a paragraph is just by reading that paragraph once, what can you do to decide what the topic is?
3. You have read a paragraph in which one sentence says that beaters make a racket by blowing horns and yelling. Which of the four numbered groups of words listed after that paragraph is the topic? Why is each of the other three groups of words not the topic?

On Your Own

As you read the following paragraph to yourself, try to decide what the topic is. Then think of a good way to state that topic.

Traveling on our first steam trains was not comfortable. Because the seats in the passenger cars had no springs or cushions, people were tossed roughly up and down. When the brakes were put on, the train lurched and swayed and the passengers were jolted this way and that. Each time the train stopped, there was much clanking and bumping as each car slid against the one just ahead of it. Instead of glass, leather curtains were used on the windows and doors to keep out the rain, snow, and wind. One or two coal stoves were used in each car, but people who sat near them became too hot and those who sat farther away almost froze. After dark, the only light was that given by oil lamps.

Checking Your Work

If you are asked to do so, tell what you think the topic is. If the topic you name is not the right one, find out why it is not right.

Pepe GOES NORTH

by Doris Troutman Plenn

On the warm, sunny island of Puerto Rico, there live the tiny green tree frogs known as coquis (koh′kees). Each evening just after the sun goes down, the coquis begin to work. They call their work the Green Work, and to them it is the most important work in the whole world. Their work is singing the Green Song. It is the Green Song, they believe, that holds the stars in place and makes the moon shine.

The best singer and the smallest of the coquis was Pepe (peh′peh) Coqui. He lived in a sugar-cane field and often talked to the People who came there to work. One day Pepe was told that his field was not the whole world, and he heard about a wonderful city called New York, where many of the People from the Island had gone to live.

Pepe could hardly believe what he had heard, and he decided to see the world for himself. Of course, Pepe would have to learn many new words as he traveled, but he did not worry about that as he set out to find an airplane going to New York.

Pepe was happy. He waved back once to Coco, a friend of his, then set off briskly. By and by he came to the airport. He found the little window where a man was selling tickets. Suitcases and boxes were piled up like steps on one side of it, and Pepe climbed and hopped up over these until he reached the counter in front of the window. "I want to buy a ticket. I am going to New York," he said. "Now just what *is* a ticket?" he asked the man.

The ticket seller pushed his spectacles up on his forehead and looked at Pepe carefully. "A ticket," he said, "is a piece of paper that shows you have bought a seat on the plane."

"What can I do with the seat after I buy it?"

"You can sit on it."

"Oh, you mean a chair!" Pepe said. "How big is this chair?"

"It's a seat, and it's that big." The ticket seller pointed to a chair in the office where he stood.

"That chair is too big for me," said Pepe.

"Who cares?" The ticket seller began to shout.

Pepe was astonished. "Why, *I* do! What if I fell off? And then there is the matter of the cost."

"The cost is the same for every seat."

"Even if one sat only on a corner of it?"

"Nobody sits on a corner of it! A seat is for one person! It fits one person!"

"It doesn't fit *me*. Look!"

Pepe hopped down from the counter and sat on the seat inside the office. The ticket man had to put his spectacles back on to see him because he was so small and the chair was so big. The ticket man scratched his head. "How could we strap you in it?"

"Strap me?"

"Everyone must be strapped in for safety when the plane flies off the ground."

"In that case, I most certainly require a seat my size," Pepe told him with dignity.

"Just a minute," the ticket man said. "You wait here, and I will come back." He went out of his office, holding his head in his hands. He went to the office of his chief and threw himself into a chair. "I have a coqui in my office," he told the chief.

"Oh, that's all right," the chief answered. "They don't bite, you know, or sting, or anything ugly like that."

"But this one wants to buy a ticket to New York."

"Well, sell him one."

"He won't buy a regular one. He says the seat is too big."

"Hmmmmm," said the chief. "I'd better look into this. This is the first time a coqui has asked for a ticket. We'd better take good care of him."

The two went back to the ticket seller's office, where Pepe was waiting. He was still sitting in the middle of the big seat. "How do you do, sir?" the chief said.

"Very well, I thank you," Pepe replied. "Except in the matter of a seat for my visit to the world."

"Hmmm," said the chief. "It *is*

a little roomy, isn't it? Let's see what we can do about the proper seat for you."

The chief called his chief, and this chief called the first vice president, who called two more vice presidents who decided it was a matter for the traffic manager. The traffic manager thought it should be taken care of by the captain and officers of the plane. They talked a while and then the engineer said, "I think I will be able to fix it. Yes, indeed. How big is he?"

"He's not very big," the ticket seller said. "About this big." He measured a space in the air with his hands.

"Oh, no," said his chief. "He's *this* big." And he, too, measured the air with his hands.

"I will have to measure him myself," said the engineer. He took a ruler and went in where Pepe was still waiting. "Would you be good enough to sit on this ruler, please?"

"Why?"

"To see what your size is."

"I am the smallest of the coquis."

"But I must know your size exactly."

By now Pepe was expecting things to be strange, so although no one had ever before asked him to sit on a ruler, he hopped over and tried to sit on this one. It was not an easy thing to do because the ruler was made of shiny wood and was not only hard but slippery as well. Pepe slid down from it a few times, but finally he got a good grip on it with his feet and sat down. "Well, now, let me see," said the engineer. "It seems that you are almost an inch in size."

"I am?" Pepe was pleased. "That's a very fine size, I suppose?"

"Oh, yes, indeed. I think that now we can fix a seat that will be just right. Now, if you will excuse me," said the engineer, and he ran out of the office.

The ticket seller came back.

"Well, now that everything is settled, please make yourself comfortable. Your seat will be ready for the next plane, and they are having a talk about the price of your ticket."

"Will the price be according to size?" Pepe asked him.

"Well, yes."

"In that case," Pepe told him, "the price will be almost an inch."

"Almost an inch of what?"

"That is my size. I am almost an inch. I sat on the ruler."

"We don't sell tickets like that!"

"Like what?"

"By the inch!" the ticket seller shouted.

"You said it was according to size."

"It is—but not like that! Money doesn't come by inches!"

"Well, you said the ticket would be by size," Pepe said firmly, "and as I told you, *that* is almost an inch. Then I will measure the money to that."

Once again the ticket seller ran out of his office, holding his head in his hands. He went into the room where the two chiefs and the three vice presidents were holding their meeting. They looked at him, surprised.

"There is no reason for any of you to think about this problem any longer," he told them. "He"—and the ticket seller pointed to his office—"has got it all settled."

"Why, that's fine," said the first vice president.

"Just a minute. Who has got it all settled?" asked the second one, who had been dozing.

"The coqui! The one in my office! The ticket is to be according to size—his size—which, he says over and over, is almost an inch!"

"It may be the right answer, and again it may not be," said the first vice president. "Let's go in and talk to him."

When they came into the office, Pepe greeted them politely. "What can I do for you?" he asked.

"Well, it's about this ticket," the first vice president began.

"Didn't the ticket seller explain to you?" Pepe asked in surprise.

"Yes, but how, exactly, would it work?"

"That is what *I* would like to know," said Pepe. "Here is the ruler. Now you measure a ticket, almost an inch in size, you know."

The vice presidents nodded to

the ticket seller. His hands trembled as he put the ticket on the ruler. "I never thought I would be doing anything like this," he said. "Here, this is almost an inch."

"Well, cut that off," Pepe explained patiently.

The ticket seller cut off the ticket and gave it to Pepe. Pepe held up a dollar bill. He measured the bill to the ticket. "Almost an inch is not quite a quarter of a dollar," he said in a pleasant voice.

The ticket seller jumped. "It is not enough money!"

"It's according to size," Pepe told them all.

"I think," said the first vice president, "we had better let it go for the moment. Later, we can have many talks and decide about the regular price of coqui tickets."

The others thought the first vice president's words were very wise. They nodded to each other, and the ticket seller gave the ticket to Pepe. Pepe gave him the money. Then each of them bowed to Pepe.

In the plane, the carpenters worked on Pepe's seat. When it was all finished, the engineer went to the ticket office to tell Pepe that his plane was ready to go.

But just as he started to tell him, Pepe felt it in his bones that the sun had gone down some time ago and that it was time to begin the Green Work. So he raised his head and lifted his voice in the Green Song. Outside the ticket office Pepe could hear the other coquis singing.

Then, as suddenly as he had begun, Pepe stopped singing. He put his head on one side and listened. He heard the other coquis stop one by one. Everything was safe in the skies for the night, and he felt contented. He hopped up on the counter where the ticket seller was writing out tickets. "Well, I'm ready," he said. "The Green Song is over for tonight. I will go now. Good-by."

Pepe went through a big gate and hopped up the steps into the plane. All the other passengers were already seated, and the motor was humming.

"Here is your seat, sir," the

flight attendant said to Pepe. He saw his seat near the window.

Pepe hopped up and sat down.

"Adjust your belt, please."

"Do what to my belt?"

"Tighten it. We are taking off."

"Tighten it, or take it off — which do you mean?"

"Excuse me, sir," said the attendant. She leaned over and quickly bound the safety belt around Pepe.

"It's tight," he told her.

"It's supposed to be tight," she answered.

"I feel a little stuffed," Pepe told the attendant.

"You can unbuckle it as soon as we get aloft."

"As soon as we get where?" Pepe asked.

"As soon as we get up in the air. The plane is still climbing."

"It is? I am climbing with it. I am going on a visit to the world." Then he turned and looked out the window.

He was up among the stars. They were very close to him. They blinked at him as the plane sailed

159

by to show that they were his friends. "Hello, stars!" he called out.

The attendant came back quickly. "You mustn't talk to the stars," she said in a low voice.

"I mustn't?"

"No. It's late, and the passengers are trying to sleep." Then she went away.

"Are you trying to sleep?" Pepe asked his neighbor.

"Not very hard," the neighbor said, smiling.

"I am Pepe. Who are you?"

"I'm Alberto. I'm happy to know you."

"I am a coqui. I sing the Green Song."

"Yes, I know. I am a poet."

The attendant came with a little light and shone it on their faces. "Gentlemen," she said firmly, "your whispering is disturbing the other passengers. I must ask you to allow them to sleep." Then she went away.

Alberto nodded and shrugged his shoulders. Then he and Pepe both sighed.

"Good night, Alberto," said Pepe.

"Good night, Pepe," Alberto answered.

When Pepe and Alberto awoke, it was morning.

Soon the motor stopped roaring and became quieter and quieter until at last it was still. The plane had landed.

"Is New York out there all around us?" Pepe asked.

"No. We must take a bus into New York. Why don't you get up on my shoulder, and I'll give you a lift?" Pepe hopped from his seat up to Alberto's shoulder.

Alberto got up and walked toward the door of the plane. Suddenly he stopped. Then he stepped out of the aisle and sat down again on a seat.

"Pepe," he said, "there is something I must tell you. Right outside the door, Pepe, there is a new word. It's a falling kind of word. It's white."

"What is white?"

"White is the color of the new word. And it is cold, Pepe. Look out the window."

Pepe did. Snow was blowing everywhere. There was nothing else to see but snow. He trembled

Did you bring an overcoat?

and moved closer to Alberto's collar.

"Did you bring an overcoat, Pepe?"

"An overcoat?"

"A coat to put on to keep you warm."

"No."

"Well, let me see what I have." Alberto went through all his pockets. He took out a handkerchief and started to wrap it around Pepe. "No," he said, "it is not warm enough. Also, it is too big." Then he went through his pockets again and found a penwiper. "Now, this is what I use to keep my pens clean. It has a spot of ink on it, but it is a very little spot. The important thing is that it is made of wool and will be warm."

"Yes," Pepe agreed. Alberto wrapped it around him.

"It looks fine," Alberto said. "Here, just let me fold back a collar for you and pin it all together. Now we can go."

They started to walk to the door. At that moment the attendant came into the plane with two big men. She pointed to Alberto.

"There he is. He's the one you were asking about."

"Oh, no," said Alberto softly.

The big men stood on either side of Alberto. "The city's glad to see you. Let's go now," one of them said.

When they left the plane, the two big men walked very fast across the airfield. "Where are we going, Alberto?" cried Pepe. But Alberto only shook his head dismally. They came to a large automobile, and Alberto and Pepe got into the back seat. The two men sat in the front and drove the car away through the thick, falling snow. The car roared through the streets, going straight to the heart of the city.

Pepe shivered a little in his new overcoat.

"Are you cold, Pepe?"

"No. It's another kind of shivering. I don't know what it is."

"I do," Alberto told him. "It's because you feel that I am troubled. And you feel that we are together. Look now, Pepe. We are in New York."

Suddenly more People were

around them than Pepe had ever seen. The car stopped, and one of the men opened the door. "Here you are," he said. "Right this way." He took Alberto's arm and led him through all the People. Pepe held on tightly. They walked up many wooden steps and came to a wide place. There were only a few People here. Pepe looked around and saw that the great crowd of People was now below them. They were all looking up at the platform on which he was standing with Alberto. A man who had been talking to the People below came toward them. "Here he is, Your Honor," said the big man, leading Alberto forward. The new man now took Alberto's arm and began walking him to the front toward the People.

"You're just in time," he said. "We are ready for you. Stand right here beside me. I am the mayor. I'm delighted to know you."

"I am happy to know you," Alberto said, bowing gracefully.

The mayor turned and began talking to the People below. "And now," he said, "on this day, which has been set aside and called 'The Day of the Island,' we meet to celebrate the deeds of those of the Island's People who have come to live among us. On this day it gives me the greatest joy to tell you that the most distinguished Islander of them all, the Islander whose poems and songs are known the world over—"

"Pepe," Alberto whispered, "this is good. But I feel awful."

"Is the mayor talking about *you*, Alberto?"

Alberto tried to answer, but he choked. So he just nodded yes.

Pepe looked down and saw, beyond the whirling snow, hundreds and hundreds of faces that were like the faces of the People he knew on the Island. The mayor talked on.

"What does he want you to do, Alberto?"

"My throat won't work, Pepe," Alberto whispered.

"Does he want you to sing to the People?"

"In a manner of speaking, yes."

"Your throat must work to sing."

"You understand so well, Pepe. I always choke at times like this."

"Perhaps I could sing for you."

"Oh, Pepe! Would you? But it's not your time to sing! It's not evening, and it's cold! Do you think it might be wrong for you to try?"

"I don't think so. Of course, I could do only a little piece of the Green Song, not the real thing, you know."

They heard the mayor's voice: "Here he is! The poet whose songs are like a call from the Island itself! The man whose name the world honors!"

"Go ahead, Pepe," Alberto said with a choke in his voice.

Pepe hopped down on the table and opened his mouth. Snow fell into it. "Coqui, coqui," he sang. But he had swallowed the snow, and his notes went down his throat with it. The only sound Pepe made was a strange chirp.

"My word!" said the mayor. "A cricket!"

Pepe drew himself up proudly. "I am a coqui!" he announced in a strong voice that went straight into the microphone. When he said it, there was a great roar from the People below.

"A coqui!" they shouted.

"A coqui in New York!"

"Long live the coquis!"

They waved their handkerchiefs and laughed and clapped.

"Chirp some more, little cricket," the mayor told Pepe kindly.

Pepe opened his mouth again, and the snow fell in, but this time he swallowed it before his notes leaped out. "Coqui, coqui," he sang. Then he swallowed more snow and began again, singing part of the Green Song clearly and in tune. The People below were enchanted. They laughed and shouted and cried with joy.

But no coquis answered Pepe as he sang; only his own voice, made enormous by the microphone, came booming to his ears. It frightened Pepe, and he stopped. "Alberto!" he called suddenly.

But Alberto was nowhere to be seen. He had disappeared.

"That will do, friend," said the mayor. "We thank you. And now, my friends —" he began.

But the crowd shouted, "Long live the coquis! We want the coqui!" over and over. The mayor waved his arms up and down, and finally they were quiet. He looked at his watch. "We have only a few moments left in which to present the key to the city to—" He turned to the man beside him. "What *is* the name of that poet?"

"He's gone," the man answered in a sad voice. "Someone came up and pulled him down into the crowd."

"But what will I do with the key to the city?" the mayor cried. These words went into the microphone, and all the People heard them.

"Alberto!" Pepe yelled into the microphone. It seemed to him that he heard a small voice, far below, coming from somewhere in the heart of the crowd. It said, "Here I am, Pepe! I am coming!" But the crowd began roaring, "Give it to the coqui!" so loudly that Pepe could hear nothing else.

"And so," said the mayor, wiping his brow, "in token of our appreciation of your great gift of song, of the honor you have paid us all by coming here today, I wish to present to you—to you, that is, on behalf of the People—the key to the city of New York! I thank you one and all." The mayor put the key down beside Pepe and said to the gloomy man, "Come on, we must hurry. I never thought I'd live to see the day—giving the key to a cricket!"

The crowd clapped and hurrahed. They were still surprised by Pepe's visit and were happy that a coqui had been honored.

Pepe has just begun to see the whole world in New York. As he journeys on through the city, looking for Alberto, he has many exciting adventures. You can read about them in Doris Troutman Plenn's book THE GREEN SONG, *from which the story you have just read was taken.*

Doris Troutman Plenn was born in North Carolina. After she traveled a great deal in Europe and the United States, she decided to make her home in Puerto Rico.

Soon after she moved to Puerto Rico, she became very ill. While she was recovering, she began to look forward to the evening and the chirping of the little tree frogs, the *coquis*. They seemed to be singing as a celebration of sunset. Their song urged her to get well and to come out to see what was going on. She felt they were friendly and wanted to welcome her to the island.

When she was well again, she wanted to thank them somehow for the pleasure they had given her. She thought of the *coquis* again when she wanted to write a story to celebrate the birth of her newest niece. She says, "They were very little, and so was she, and the two seemed to suit each other." Ms. Plenn called her book *The Green Song.*

In This Quiet Hour

In this quiet hour
of the wide bay,
the afternoon is a peaceful port
of shadow and calm . . .
Night enters like a great ship
and throws upon the water
its first star
as an anchor.

Luis Palés Matos
Translated from the Spanish
by Ellen G. Matilla

CINDER ELLIE

by James S. Ayars

During the school year, Elinor Morgan was a runner on the girls' track team at her school in the city. Because she spent so much time running on cinder tracks, she was nicknamed Cinder Ellie.

Now the Morgans—Ellie, her brother, her parents, and her lively grandmother—were spending the summer at the beach at Lonesome Point. An all-day summer festival would be held at the old fairgrounds in a nearby town. The big day would include a hundred-yard dash for boys and a hundred-yard dash for girls. The boys on the Lonesome Point track team—Ray Olsen, Ernie Anderson, Tommy Tilbury, and others—would be there. Ellie wanted to be there, too, to run in the girls' race. When the day of the festival arrived, Grandma Morgan drove Ellie to the fairgrounds.

Ellie and Grandma Morgan arrived at the fairgrounds before any events had begun and before all the good seats in the grandstand had been taken. They sat down on a bench close to the exit. From there Ellie could slip out easily when the time came for her race.

The woodchopping contest began. Ellie wondered at the speed with which the yellow chips flew and seemed to fill the air.

Before the last panting woodchopper had cut through the last log and had his time announced by the judges, Ellie slipped out of the grandstand for her warm-up.

"The next event is the pie-eating contest," said the announcer. "After that, we'll have the hundred-yard dash for girls and the hundred-yard dash for boys. Following that is the tug of war. Pie eaters, report now to the platform across the track from the grandstand. Runners, report to the starter, the man with the white cap, on the track to the west of the grandstand."

As Ellie took her spiked shoes and starting blocks out of her grandmother's car, she saw boys running toward the starter from all directions. Boys, boys everywhere—some in track suits, some in blue jeans and blue shirts, some in blue jeans and no shirts. Some wore rubber-soled shoes, and a few wore spiked track shoes, but most were barefooted. A few carried starting blocks. Ellie joined the circle of boys crowded around the starter.

"The next event is the hundred-yard dash for girls," the starter said. "But where are the girls? Oh, yes, I see one." He had spotted Ellie at a far edge of the circle.

He spoke to the announcer, who put a megaphone to his lips and aimed it at the grandstand. Twice he shouted, "Last call for the hundred-yard dash for girls. Last call for the hundred-yard dash for girls."

The starter looked hopefully toward the grandstand and waited for half a minute, a minute, two minutes. Then, with a shrug of his shoulders, he turned toward the announcer.

"One girl. What'll we do? Doesn't seem right for her to come out here expecting to run and find no one to run against. Should we let her run with the boys if she wants to?"

"I don't know what people here will think about that," said the announcer. "Maybe it's all right. Why not ask her and then ask the boys?"

The starter looked at Ellie.

"There are no other girls to run the hundred," he said. "Should we just give you the blue ribbon to take home?"

Ellie shook her head.

"Not if I haven't earned it. I'd like to run."

"You mean run with the boys?" the starter asked.

"If there aren't any girls to run, I could run with the boys. I do at home."

The starter raised his voice enough to reach the whole group.

"We'll have to skip the hundred-yard dash for girls. The next event is the hundred-yard dash for boys. We'll start it as soon as we can after the pie-eating contest is over.

"We have about forty boys reporting for the hundred," he went on. "That's about three times as many as this track has room for. We'll have to run three heats and a final. The first four runners in each heat will qualify for the final."

He pointed at Ellie.

"This girl came to the meet prepared to run. No other girls have shown up, and we've had to cancel her event. She wants to run the hundred with you. What do you say?"

"Let her run," said half a dozen boys near the front of the group.

"No!" shouted three or four others. Ray Olsen's voice was the loudest.

"Sure! Let her run. We'll show her we can beat her," called a boy from the far edge of the circle.

The starter smiled.

"Let's settle it this way. The girl will run in the third heat. Any of you who don't want to run against her can go in the first or second heat. Then maybe you won't have to run against her at all."

The starter counted the boys—thirty-nine—and divided them into three groups: thirteen in each of the first two heats, thirteen and Ellie in the third.

"Most of you don't have starting blocks," he said. "So nobody will use them. You'll all take standing starts. Run in any shoes you choose—spiked shoes or rubber-soled shoes—or no shoes at all."

The starter blew his whistle.

"Runners in the first heat—" The starter waited while thirteen boys sorted themselves out of the group and lined up across the track. "Go to your marks. Get set." *Bang!*

In the ten minutes that had gone by since the end of the pie-eating contest, Grandma Morgan had been growing more impatient by the second. She had kept looking toward the starting line and trying to make out what was happening there. She had seen a man with a white cap surrounded by boys. Once she had seen Ellie. But where were the girls Ellie was supposed to run against?

Grandma Morgan was hardly aware of the sound of the gun or of the boys strung out across the track, kicking up soft, gray dust. She did not notice the cheers in the grandstand as the boys crossed the finish line. She didn't know—or care—which boy won.

"Well!" she exclaimed in an angry tone. She had come to watch Ellie run. And Ellie hadn't run at the time scheduled for her race.

Bang!

Grandma Morgan turned again toward the starting line. Again she saw boys strung out across the track and kicking up gray dust. Again she heard cheers as the boys crossed the finish line.

She wondered who was manager of this meet. She'd like to give him a piece of her mind. She shaded her eyes against the sun and again looked toward the starting line. More boys milling around and getting ready for the next race!

Where was that manager?

Grandma Morgan stood up.

"Down in front!" bellowed a man behind her.

Grandma Morgan turned to give the bellower a piece of her mind.

Bang!

The grandstand suddenly filled with a rushing sound like that of a strong gust of wind, the sound of many people rising to their feet.

"Run, girl! Run!" shouted the bellower.

"Yeah!" The crowd exploded in a great roar.

"Come on, girl! Run! Come on! Come on!" people shouted.

A fat man standing beside Grandma Morgan bent almost double as he slapped his legs and haw-hawed.

"Come on, girl! Come on! Beat 'em, girl! Beat 'em!" The shouts grew louder.

Grandma Morgan turned toward the track. Down there, right in front of the grandstand, was Ellie, running smoothly and at full speed. Ellie, with her brown hair streaming behind her, was leading a pack of boys, their feet digging the dust, their arms pumping, their heads bobbing, toward the finish line.

"Run, Cinder Ellie, run!" shouted Grandma Morgan.

"Run, Cinder Ellie, run!" The bellower took up the cry as Ellie broke the yarn stretched across the finish line.

"Ellie, Ellie, Cinder Ellie!" the people chanted as Ellie walked off the track.

Two minutes later, Ellie slid onto the bench beside Grandma Morgan.

"No other girls to run," she panted. "The starter was
awfully nice. He let me run with the boys. I'll have to run in
the final as soon as the tug of war is over."

"Where are your track shoes—your spikes?" asked
Grandma.

"I put them back in the car with the starting blocks. I
didn't use them, because only two boys in my heat had

spikes, and I didn't want an unfair advantage over the others. We couldn't use blocks. Had to use a standing start. I got a poor start. Guess I made up for it at about the twenty. I'm going down to get ready for the final.''

Ellie slid off the bench and disappeared as suddenly as she had appeared.

Ray Olsen had won the first heat. Ernie Andersen had placed fifth in the third heat and was not in the final.

''You'll have to run top speed all the way,'' Ernie told Ray as the two boys rested in the shade of a tree near the starting line. ''That girl can run! I saw her heels all the way down the track.''

''She shouldn't have run,'' Ray said angrily. ''She shouldn't have been allowed to run. She's a girl, and the race was for boys.''

''But her race was canceled,'' Ernie reminded him. ''It was only fair to let her run with us. Most of the boys agreed to let her run.''

''I didn't.''

''You were one of maybe three or four.''

Tommy Tilbury walked into the shade of the tree. He had a sheet of paper in one hand and a pencil in the other.

''You'll have to run the final faster than you ran your heat,'' he told Ray.

''I don't know why,'' said Ray. ''I ran faster in my heat than the boy who won the second heat.''

''The girl's the runner you'll have to beat,'' said Tommy. ''She won her heat by several yards.''

''I can beat her easily,'' said Ray.

''Maybe,'' said Tommy. ''But I think you ought to know what I've just discovered. I didn't believe my ears when I heard the times of the heats announced. I checked with the timers. That girl ran the hundred three-tenths of a second faster than you did and half a second faster than the winner of the second heat."

Tommy looked at the sheet of paper in his hand.

"According to my figures, if you and Ellie run the final in the times you ran the heats, Ellie will beat you by more than two yards."

"Something's wrong with those timers or their watches," Ray said. "That girl didn't run faster than I did. I watched her run."

"She runs so easily, she doesn't look as if she's running fast," said Ernie. "But I think you'd better not do any loafing after the gun is fired."

Ray didn't do any loafing after he heard the bang. But the final was like the third heat. The crowd shouted, "Ellie! Ellie! Cinder Ellie!" after their new hero had crossed the finish line more than two yards ahead of Ray, her nearest competitor.

Tommy and Ernie found Ray breathing hard and walking in small circles on a grassy spot behind the grandstand.

"Well, you said it. She can run," Ray admitted with a sad, crooked smile.

"You were ahead of her for the first fifteen or twenty yards," said Ernie.

"She got a poor start," said Ray. "I could see that. I was right next to her—on her left. She's not used to standing starts."

"You were awfully close to her when she passed you," said Tommy.

"I know," Ray said. "We were so close that we almost

bumped, but Ellie went right by me. I guess those timers were right about Ellie's speed. That girl can really run!''

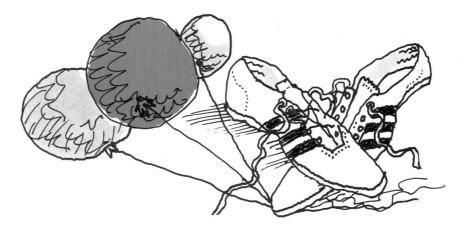

Cinder Ellie and the boys on the Lonesome Point track team go on to train for the big state meet in August. But this time Ellie and the boys are to run on the same team. You can find out what happens at the meet by reading the rest of the book TRACK COMES TO LONESOME POINT, by James S. Ayars.

AUTHOR

James S. Ayars has been writing about sports for many years. For a long time he worked for the *Athletic Journal* in Chicago, Illinois. One of his first books was *Basketball Comes to Lonesome Point.*

He says he wrote *Track Comes to Lonesome Point* for his daughter, Rebecca Jean, who was the original Cinder Ellie. Mr. Ayars and his wife drove Becky Jean to many track meets, where he learned about track. In 1956 Becky Jean was a member of the United States Olympic track team.

Mr. Ayars also likes to write about agriculture and the outdoors. One of his other books is called *John James Audubon: Bird Artist.* In addition to his interests in sports and the outdoors, Mr. Ayars enjoys gardening and photography. He and his wife live in Illinois.

I am running,
running, running.
I am running
just for fun.
Through the grass
and through the gravel
running faster
see me travel
past the people
staring, staring.
They are thinking
something's wrong.
I'm not looking.
I'm not caring.
I'm just running
hard and long.

Now my feet are
pounding pavement.
Now my heart is
pounding too.
I can feel the
sidewalk searing
through the bottom
of my shoe.
How the wind is
whipping past me.
How the trees are
whizzing by.
Rushing rivers
run forever.
Maybe *I* can
if I try.

Marci Ridlon

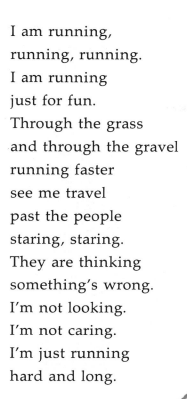

Running Song

Robert H. Goddard: Space Pioneer

by Milton Lomask

Bob Goddard, a shy, sickly child growing up in Massachusetts in the late 1800's, was always inventing something. By the time he was seventeen, he was dreaming of making a machine that could reach the moon. He overcame his childhood illnesses and finished his education with a Ph.D., or Doctor of Philosophy degree. After that, Dr. Goddard spent his time teaching and developing the science of rocketry. In 1930, Daniel Guggenheim, the son of a Jewish immigrant who had made a fortune in mining, gave Dr. Goddard the money he needed to go to New Mexico to go on with his experiments.

For two years Bob's "laboratory" was a sandy prairie in New Mexico called Eden Valley.

In the distance, mountains climbed to snowy peaks, but the valley itself was flat. Mesquite grew all over. In the spring this small tree put out pink and lavender blossoms. Esther, Bob's wife, had never seen anything as beautiful as the desert in bloom.

The Goddards lived in a clay-walled ranch house. Out back Bob built a shop. Here he worked long hours — too long, Esther thought. He was not a well man, and he never would be. His tuberculosis was no longer active, but it was still there. On some nights, fits of coughing kept him awake for hours. He often had colds.

Esther begged him to see a doctor.

"Soon," he promised, but it was months before he went.

"Well," said Esther when he returned, "what did the doctor say?"

"Nothing much."

Esther got in touch with the doctor herself. He told her what she expected to hear: Her husband needed more rest.

But she could keep him away from his work only on Sundays. Lately he had taken up painting pictures. Every Sunday morning he packed his brushes and paints into the family car. Then he and Esther drove far out into the desert.

All day Bob sat there in the sunshine, his easel before him. He painted pictures of the desert in bloom. Sometimes he chose a lonely cottonwood tree with the mountains behind it.

At his shop he invented new parts for his rockets. One was a cooling system. The flaming fuel often burned holes in the sides of the rocket motor. Bob arranged for the gasoline and liquid oxygen to enter the motor in a way that laid a film over the walls. As a rule, the film kept the fuel from burning through.

Bob also invented a system for steering the rocket. He told Esther, "To go high, a rocket must go straight. If it flops from side to side, it won't go very high. A gyroscope in the steering system helps. When the rocket flops over in one direction, the gyroscope spins in the opposite direction. As a result, the rocket straightens up."

Near his shop Bob put up an iron tower only twenty feet

high. Here he static-tested every new rocket by strapping the rocket to a steel rack. When he fired it, the rocket couldn't go anywhere, but he could see how it was doing. Then the crew loaded the rocket onto a trailer. A car towed it to a bigger launching tower ten miles away. Some rockets flew. Others blew up as soon as the fuel in them was lighted.

Bob learned from both his successes and his failures. When a rocket came down after a good flight, he called to his crew, "All right, let's look at it and see what we did right."

When a rocket exploded in the tower, he shouted, "All right, let's look at the pieces and see what we did wrong."

Early one morning Bob and his team prepared for a new shot. They meant to fire the rocket that afternoon, but they never did. They set the new rocket in the bottom of the tower. Five minutes later, however, a sudden windstorm ripped across the desert and smashed the rocket.

Cries arose from members of the crew. "The weather has done our Little Nell wrong," one of them wailed in a loud voice. After that, every rocket was called *Nell*.

Sad news arrived during the Goddards' first year in Eden Valley. Mr. Dan, the man who had helped Bob, was dead. The news came to Bob in a letter from Mr. Dan's son, Harry F. Guggenheim.

Harry Guggenheim told Bob to go on with his experiments. Daniel Guggenheim had given Bob fifty thousand dollars. When that was all gone, Harry Guggenheim would try to send more.

But the money ran out when America was in the middle of the Great Depression. Everywhere factories were closing, and people were losing their jobs. Even Harry Guggenheim could no longer afford to help.

The Goddards went home to Worcester, Massachusetts. "Just as we were really getting started," said Bob sadly.

"Cheer up," said Esther. "We'll return to New Mexico one of these days."

As usual, Esther was right. August, 1934, brought another letter from Mr. Guggenheim. Years before, his father had set up a foundation to help scientists. It now had enough money to finance Bob's experiments, so he and Esther could return to Eden Valley.

On a blustery March afternoon in 1937, a new rocket stood in the launching tower in Eden Valley. This *Nell* was the biggest yet. It was sixteen feet five inches tall.

Lately Bob's rockets had done well. One had gone seventy-five hundred feet into the air.

"This one should beat that," Bob said.

He pushed the starting button. The roar was deafening as the rocket went up.

The members of the crew followed its path with telescopes. They wrote down figures on paper pads, compared notes, and then made an announcement. *Nell* had risen nine thousand feet—almost two miles!

Cheers filled the air, and Esther had some trouble making herself heard.

"I suggest," she shouted, "that we call that rocket *Soaring Nell.*"

Bob joined in the laughter. "Okay, folks," he said, "we've had our fun. Now let's go back to the shop and start building the next *Nell.* Let's make it even bigger and better."

During the next two years Bob made many "bigger and better" rockets. His largest one was twenty-one feet eight inches tall and eighteen inches wide. Filled with fuel, it weighed five hundred pounds. When fired, it would give off as much energy as a train steam engine fifty times heavier.

"That much thrust," said Bob, "should send it pretty far up."

But Bob had put some new parts in this rocket, and some of these failed to work. As a result, his biggest rocket did not go as high as *Soaring Nell*. No other rocket made by Bob Goddard ever did.

Bob put new devices in every new rocket. He invented special pumps that made the rockets start faster, and he invented better steering and electrical systems.

All in all, he invented over two hundred rocket parts. Someday other scientists would use these parts in giant rockets that would rise hundreds of miles.

On August 10, 1945, Dr. Robert H. Goddard died at the age of sixty-two. But his dream did not die with him. It came true twenty-four years later, on the hot, bright morning of July 6, 1969. That morning a million people jammed the sandy beaches of Cape Kennedy, Florida.

On a steel launching pad at the Kennedy Space Center stood one of the biggest rockets ever built—the *Saturn 5*. It was as tall as a thirty-six-story building and was thirty-eight feet across at its widest point. Its cavernlike tanks held 6,484,000 pounds of liquid fuel.

At 9:38 A.M., a man sitting three and a half miles away pushed a button. The button started a computer. The computer fired the rocket. The earth shook as five giant engines burst into flaming life.

With others on a special platform, Esther Goddard watched the *Saturn 5* blast off. She remembered *Soaring Nell* and all the other *Nells*.

How small those rockets were compared to this one! Yet they had made this one possible. Bob had thought of most of the ideas that sent this gleaming monster into the sky. *Saturn 5* was really just a great big *Nell*.

Esther lifted her head to watch the swiftly rising giant. Her eyes misted as it poked a hole in a distant cloud and then disappeared into space.

In a cabin on top of the huge rocket rode three men in space suits.

Five days later two of them set foot on the dusty surface of the moon.

An odd-looking machine had brought them there. It was almost as odd looking as the moon-going machine Bob Goddard had dreamed of many years before.

AUGTHOR

The story you have just read is only part of Milton Lomask's book *Robert H. Goddard: Space Pioneer.* Mr. Lomask has written many books about famous people, including Presidents Andrew Johnson and John Quincy Adams. He has also written books about religious subjects. Most of Mr. Lomask's books have been written for adults and for children in the upper grades.

Before Mr. Lomask began to write books, he worked as a newspaper reporter in Iowa. Later he became an editor and worked in Missouri. Mr. Lomask has also been a teacher in a large university in New York.

Born in Fairmont, West Virginia, Mr. Lomask now makes his home in Washington, D. C.

SMORGASBORD

by Leone Adelson

Almost all of us can trace our family beginnings back to other countries. Think about your own ancestors. Where did they come from? When people came here, so did their customs—their food, language, holiday celebrations, and all their ways of living.

Who does not like to eat! Everyone does. That is why so many of the foreign words in the English language seem to stand for good things to eat. Many of the wonderful mouth-watering foods from Italy alone can make a delicious dinner.

First the *antipasto*—what you eat before the main meal—*pizza* and spicy sausages like *salami*, *bologna*, and *pepperoni*. And now the soup—*minestrone*, "the big soup," thick with beans and vegetables. Next comes the *pasta*. *Pasta* is nothing but a paste made of flour, eggs, and water, but to the Italians and now to Americans, it is *spaghetti*, *macaroni*, and *ravioli*. If you have room for dessert, have some Italian ice cream—*spumoni* or *tortoni*.

The Germans and the Dutch gave us *hamburgers* and *frankfurters*, from the German cities of Hamburg and Frankfurt. Our German and Dutch settlers brought us *sauerkraut* too, as well as *dumplings*, *cookies*, *crullers*, *pretzels*, *pumpernickel*, *seltzer*, *coleslaw*, *cranberries*, and last but not least, *noodles* and *strudels*.

Our close neighbors, the Spanish-speaking people of Mexico, have given us hot *tamales, chile con carne, tapioca, vanilla, bananas,* the *barbecue* way of cooking, and the *cafeteria.* The word *barbecue* is only slightly changed from the Spanish *barbacoa,* which is a little raised platform on which you build a fire to roast your meat.

Spanish was the first European language of our Southwest, just as cattle raising was the first business of the Southwest. Many of the Spanish words of the horse business and the cattle business are still with us. The movies and television have helped to make it so.

But long before the settlers from Europe came, bringing their languages with them, there were three hundred Indian languages being spoken by the Indians of North America and South America. We can thank the Aztec Indians for the words for two favorite foods, *chocolatl* and *tomatl.* It didn't take very long for the words *chocolate* and *tomato* to make their way around the world!

Indian words were hard to learn, since there were no books printed in Indian languages, so settlers wrote the words down as they thought they heard them. It is not surprising that *segankw* is our *skunk, arakun* is *raccoon, moos* is *moose,* and *chitmunk* is our little *chipmunk* friend.

If anyone asks you if you speak any other languages besides English, you may honestly say, "Yes, many!"

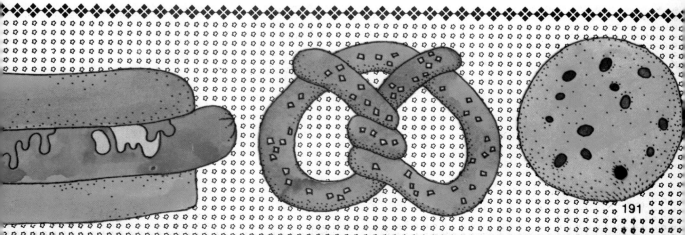

DRAWING CONCLUSIONS

Sometimes you need to be a kind of detective when you read. The reason for this is that writers may not always tell you directly everything they want you to know. They may expect you to use the information that they do give you to figure out some other things for yourself.

The following paragraphs tell about a game that Pam played in, but the writer does not say what kind of game it was. See if you can use the information that the writer does give to figure that out for yourself.

Pam was dirty but happy as she walked home from the park. She had just played in her first game with the big girls. They never would let her play before because they were afraid she might get hurt by the hard ball. Some even thought she wouldn't be able to swing the big bat that they used.

The big girls need not have worried. Pam caught every ball hit to her in right field and swung the bat well enough to get two hits.

Were you able to figure out that Pam played in a baseball game? Nowhere in those two paragraphs does the writer tell you outright that it was a baseball game. But you *are* told that the older girls were afraid Pam might get hurt by the hard ball. You are told that some of the girls thought Pam wouldn't be able to swing the big bat. You also are told that Pam caught every ball hit to her in right field and got two hits in the game. The writer expects you to use this information to figure out for yourself what kind of game it was.

If you think carefully about what you are reading, you can often use the information that a writer *does* tell you to find out things that he or she *does not* tell you. Thinking about what you read in this way is called **drawing conclusions.**

Whenever you draw a conclusion from your reading, make sure that it makes sense with what the writer has told you. If it does not make sense, your conclusion is an incorrect one.

The writer expects you to draw a conclusion from the following article. As you read it carefully, think about what the writer tells you.

In 1969, men traveled to the moon. We have set our sights next on the planet Mars. Scientists believe that in the near future we will successfully land on that planet. Many people wonder if at some time in the far-off future we will attempt to travel to the stars.

Stars are really huge hot suns. Some of the stars are larger and hotter than our own sun. Our sun looks larger because it is nearer to the earth than any other star is.

Our sun is about 93 million miles away. A rocket from the earth traveling at a speed of 25,000 miles an hour could reach our sun in about 155 days. A rocket from the earth traveling at the same speed would take about 115,000 years to reach the star nearest to our sun.

Will we ever travel to the stars?

Discussion

Help your class answer the following questions:

1. What does drawing a conclusion from your reading mean?
2. Why do you sometimes need to draw a conclusion from something you've read?
3. How can you help to make sure that a conclusion you have drawn from something you've read is a correct one?
4. What conclusion did you draw from the article you've just read? What information given in the article helped you to draw that conclusion?

On your own

As you read the following article carefully, think of a conclusion you could draw from it.

Thirteen

Many people today believe that certain numbers are lucky and that others are unlucky. For example, there are many who believe that 13 is an unlucky number. They may believe this so strongly that they will not take a room in a hotel if it has the number 13 in it.

Considering 13 to be an unlucky number may go back to the time when people first learned to count. By counting their ten fingers and two feet, people could use their fingers and feet to count to 12. Beyond that was the unknown — 13.

If you think that the number 13 is unlucky, look at the back of a dollar bill. There, you will see a picture of an eagle holding an olive branch with 13 leaves in one claw. In the other claw, the eagle is holding 13 arrows. Before you throw the dollar away, thinking it may be unlucky, you may be interested to know that each of those "13's" stands for the 13 colonies which first formed the United States. So 13 is a lucky number for millions of Americans.

Write and number your answers to the following questions on a sheet of paper.

1. Are there people today who are superstitious? What information given in the article led you to draw your conclusion?

2. Did the idea that 13 is unlucky begin recently or a long time ago? What information given in the article led you to draw your conclusion?

Checking your work

If you are asked to do so, read aloud your answers to one of the numbered questions. Check your paper as others read their answers.

from
...and now Miguel

by Joseph Krumgold

The trouble with Miguel Chavez (mee gel′ chah′ves) was that he was too young to do an adult's job and too old to enjoy children's play. He longed for a chance to prove to his father that he was ready to do the work of an adult on their New Mexico sheep ranch. When an unexpected storm scattered part of the flock, Miguel thought his chance had come at last. But his father would not let him take part in the search for the missing sheep. Disappointed, Miguel headed for school.

Juby is my oldest friend. He lives in Los Cordovas (lohs kor′doh vahs) where the schoolhouse is. Ever since I can remember doing anything, fishing or playing ball or just talking, most of these things I did with Juby. And as long as I can remember Juby, he's been wearing this same big black hat with a wide brim on it curved up on the sides like the wings on a buzzard when it circles around, taking things easy in the sky. By now the hat is pretty old and has some holes in it, but it still looks all right on Juby, because it would be hard to tell what Juby looked like without it.

He was playing basketball when I came to the yard of the schoolhouse, my sister Faustine and my younger brother Pedro after me. That is, Juby and some of the others were playing just shooting for baskets, and as soon as he saw me, he waved his hand and quit, and came over.

"How're you doing?" he asked me.

I said, "Pretty good," because what's the use telling everybody your troubles?

"D'you folks lose any sheep?" he asked me.

"What?" I made one grab at his arm and held tight.

"Sheep," he said. "What's the matter?"

"Now look, Juby," I said. "What's the use talking, you and me? How do you know we got missing sheep? What about them?"

"I saw them."

"What?"

"At least I think they're yours. From the shape of the numbers they look like yours."

We don't put our brand on the sheep until after we shear them. But our numbers have a different shape to them from any of the others in the neighborhood.

"Where?"

"Then you did lose some sheep?"

"Juby!" I was a little excited. "What's the use, Juby? Just to talk? Where did you see them?"

"Well, you know Carlotta?"

"Who?"

"Our milk cow."

"Cows? What about the sheep?"

"I'm telling you. She got loose last night, Carlotta, and when I went to herd her back, I saw these sheep."

"Where? Where? Where?"

"What's the matter with you, Mike? Something wrong?"

"Juby," I said. "You and me, you're my oldest friend, aren't you?"

"Sure."

"Then tell me, where are the sheep?"

"Give me a chance. I saw them across the river. Maybe fifteen, ewes and lambs. They were heading straight for Arroyo Hondo (uh roy′oh ohn′doh)." It was just in the opposite direction from where my older brother Blasito and the sheep wagon were, from where he had looked that morning. "Were they yours?"

"You don't know what this could mean, Juby. That is, for me."

But just then the bell started to ring, and Mrs. Mertian, who is the teacher of our school over there in Los Cordovas, she came to the door and told everybody to come in.

"Let's go." Juby went with the others into the class.

And that's the way things stood.

On one side, Mrs. Mertian with the bell ringing. And on the other side, the big mountains, looking very dark and a little mad, if you can think of mountains being mad. But that was the way they looked, and at that moment, there came thunder from behind them.

And in the middle, I stood. If it ever happened that I came home with the missing sheep? Could anything ever be better?

Mrs. Mertian said, "Miguel."

From the Sangre de Cristo (sahn′gree duh kris′toh) Mountains, there came thunder, very low.

I did not stand too long. Because there was no question about it! Nothing, that is to say, nothing at all could ever be better.

I headed straight for the boys on the other side of the yard.

"Miguel!" It was Mrs. Mertian yelling. I didn't even look back. I jumped into this whole bunch of bushes and started down the hill.

Big champion jumps, every one breaking a world's record: that's the way I came down that hill. With each jump, everything went flying. My books banging at the end of the rope in my hand, swinging all round. My arms, feeling like I had a dozen of them, each one going off by itself. My feet, like being on a bike, working away to keep my balance. But I couldn't balance. Except by jumping. I couldn't stop. Each jump bigger than the last. I cleared a bush, then a big cracked rock. Then, I wasn't going to make it but I did, a high cactus. Each jump I thought was the last. Each jump was going to end with a cracked head, a split rib, or maybe two broken legs. But it didn't. I don't know why. There was nothing I could do. I came down that hill like a boulder bumping in bigger and bigger bumps, bumping its way down a cliff. Straight for the river. Until I wasn't scared of falling anymore. I had to fall! Or land in the river. But how? I grabbed a bush. That didn't stop me. And then my books caught, between a couple of rocks. I slipped, grabbed at another bush. Slid a couple of feet, and then took off again. And then I landed. On my face. I landed in a whole piled-up bunch of mesquite. No one, I'm sure, ever since that hill was first there, ever came down it so fast.

I wasn't hurt. Except for a scratch stinging near my eye, I was all right. It didn't even bleed. All I needed was to catch my breath. I lay there in the bushes until I did. Breathing and listening for Mrs. Mertian, in case she came to the top of the hill and was yelling down at me. But I didn't hear any yelling. When I looked, she wasn't there. The school bell stopped, too. All there was to hear was the thunder, now and then, far off, and the wind blowing.

I got up, thinking I'd done it. After what Juby told me, there was only one thing to do, and now I'd done it. Here I was, just me, Miguel, getting the sheep that were lost, all alone. And there would be no one bringing them home but me. All I had to do was to get up there, on the mesa across the river, round up the bunch, and march them back to where everyone could see. It would be something worth watching, me herding the ewes and lambs that were lost back into the corral at home. My father would tell me how sorry he was about breakfast, the way he wouldn't let me go help. And I would tell my father, it was nothing, he didn't have to feel sorry.

I felt good. Looking at the mountains, and the mountains looking down at me as if to see what I was going to do next.

I hopped across the river. The easy place to cross was downstream a way, where there were more rocks to jump on. I didn't bother to go to the easy place. I could have made it even if the rocks were twice as far from each other, feeling good like I was, and all in practice from the way I'd come jumping down the hill. I only slipped into the water twice,

without much water getting into my shoes at all.

To get up the cliff on the other side was not easy. It was steep in this place and wet and slippery with the rain, the stones high and smooth with nothing to grab on to, except sometimes a juniper bush. And, besides, having the books in one hand. It would be better without the books. But I couldn't leave them around or hide them, seeing they might get wet. I made it all right, pulling and crawling my way up. Steep places and books, that wasn't too hard. Not to find a bunch of lost sheep, it wasn't.

When I got up to the top and looked, I didn't see them. I guess I did expect a little bit they'd be up there waiting for me. But they weren't. I didn't mind too much. The kind of thing I was doing had to be hard. Such a big thing couldn't be too easy. It'd be like cheating. I set out, walking to the north.

Up on the mesa, it looked empty. Like one of those pictures that Pedro draws. One straight line across the middle of the page and big zigzags off to one side for the mountains. Then dark on top for the clouds, which he makes by smudging up all the pencil lines. And dark on the bottom for the mesa, which he makes with a special black crayon. That's all there is in the picture. And that's why it's a good picture. Because that's all there is. Except for some little bushes, juniper and chaparral and sagebrush. With nothing sticking up, only a high soapweed or a crooked-looking cactus. Nothing else.

Especially, no sheep.

I walked from one rise to the next. Every three or four steps turning all around as I walked. And when I got near to the top of each rise, I had to run. Because I thought in the next ten, fifteen steps up top there, sure, I'd see them. The first few times I saw nothing, which I didn't mind too much. And the next few times, I saw nothing, too. Pretty soon I was getting ready to see them, because after an hour or so of walking and turning around and running, I figured it was hard enough. Even for something big.

Besides, I had a pebble in my left shoe. I felt it down there coming up the cliff. I didn't mind then, because it only made everything even harder. And that was all right with me. But now it was getting to

hurt good. And I couldn't sit down and take it out. That would be like giving up.

Besides, I didn't have any time to waste. The mesa spread out, as far as you could see, with many breaks—everywhere little canyons and washes. And it was sure that on top of the next canyon, maybe, I was going to see them, those sheep. If I didn't waste time getting up there. Which I didn't. But all I saw was the same kind of nothing that I saw from the last high place, just this wide straight line stretching right across the middle.

Walking down was harder than walking up. For one thing, walking down on my left heel made the pebble bigger. It was getting to feel like a rock. And for another, walking down, you've already seen what there is to see all around, and there's nothing to look forward to until you start to walk up again. It got so I was running more than I was walking. Running downhill because I wanted to get that part over with, and running up because I couldn't wait to get to the top. And all the time, turning around. I got pretty good at being able to turn around and keep running at the same time.

Except what good was it, getting pretty good at anything? When the only thing counted was to get one look, one quick look at those sheep.

All the turning around did was to get me so mixed up I didn't know whether I was going north, south, east, or west. Not that it made any difference, I guess. The sheep weren't particular which direction you went to find them. They weren't in any direction. There were just no sheep. There was all the dark sky, and all this straight flat plain you'd ever want to see. But no sheep.

And after a couple of hours of seeing no sheep, I would've been glad to see any sheep, even if they weren't ours. I kept trying to see sheep so hard, it was as if my eyes got dry and thirsty just to see sheep. To see nothing for two, three hours, especially sheep, it gets hard on your eyes.

It was getting hard on my left foot, too, with that big rock pressing in.

And it wasn't so easy on my hands, either, on account of the books. The books weren't very heavy, but when you keep that rope wrapped around your hand, it can pinch. And even if you take it off one hand and put it on the other, it isn't long before it's pinching that hand, too.

Another thing was, it got to be hard breathing. Because there was no time to stop and get a good breath. There was always somewhere to go take a look, and you couldn't stop because maybe that very second the sheep were moving away out of sight, and that very second if you were up on a top you'd see them.

After so many hours of it being so hard, I figured it was hard enough by then. It was getting long past the time I ought to find our sheep. Only it didn't make any difference how I figured. They weren't there to be found. Not anywhere.

And after a while, walking, walking, every place started to look as if you'd been there before. You'd see a piece of tumbleweed. And you were sure it was one you saw an hour before. It didn't help to think that maybe you were just walking up and around the same hill all the time.

Then looking, looking, I thought I heard a bell. I listened hard in the wind. One of the ewes that was lost might have a bell. In the flock, there are ten or a dozen sheep with bells. Each one is like the leader of a bunch. I stood still, listening. Then I heard it again, and it was for sure a bell. But it was the school bell, far away, back in Los Cordovas. It must've already become noon, and that was the bell for noontime. Soon the ringing far away stopped. And there was nothing to listen to again, except the quiet wind.

It was never the same, after I heard that bell. It made me feel hungry. Because the bell meant going home to eat. And feeling hungry, I got to feel not so good in the other parts of me. Like lonely. At the beginning, being alone was the best part of it, going off by myself to bring home the sheep. But now it was getting to look as if I wouldn't be bringing home any sheep. And that made a lot of difference about being alone, while everybody else was back there going home to eat. The only way I could go home was to find them. It wasn't only so I could bring the sheep back. I had to find them so I could go back, too.

From then on, I got very busy. I didn't stop to walk anymore. I ran. Everywhere I went, I kept up running, and I did most of my breathing going downhill when I didn't have to try so hard to keep running. There was hardly any breath left over to keep looking with. And that was the hardest part of all, the looking. Because there was never anything to see.

And after a long while, I heard the bell again. School was out for the day.

It was hard to figure out what to do next.

I could leave home. That's about all that was left. I couldn't go back without the sheep. Not after what my father said at breakfast, and especially not after the way he looked. And it was clear enough that, in all this whole empty place, I was never going to find them, those sheep. I could just as well stop, that's all. I could take some time and do a lot of breathing. I could bury my books under a bush. I could sit down and take off my shoe and get rid of that rock with all the sharp edges on it. Then I could go somewhere until I saw a lot of sheep and sit down and look at them, till I got enough again of looking at sheep. And then I could decide where I was leaving home to go to.

Maybe even to the Sangre de Cristo Mountains. On my own, by myself.

But when I looked at the mountains, I knew that was no good. It was impossible. There was only one way to go up into the Mountains of the Sangre de Cristo. And that was to make everyone see you were ready, and then you would go.

Indeed, in order that I should go this way, that's why I was looking for the sheep right now. And if I gave up looking for the sheep, then the idea of going up into the mountains, I had to give that up, too. I guess, if you are going to leave home, you just leave home, that's all, everything.

Except, it wasn't up to me anymore. It wasn't a question that I should give up looking for the sheep.

It was just no use.

I could keep running from the top of one rise up to the next, looking, looking with my eyes getting drier and drier, without any breath, and the bones in my hands like they were cracking, and the heel of my left foot like it was getting torn away, listening to nothing but the wind. I could keep on doing that forever. It wasn't a question of me giving up, it was a question that just everything had given up, me and everything.

So I sat down. I took a deep breath. And I started to untie the laces from my left shoe. And then — what do you think?

I smelled them.

It is not hard to know that what you're smelling is sheep. If only there are some sheep around to smell. They smell a little sweet and a little old, kind of like coffee that's been left over in a cup on the kitchen table for a very long time. That's sort of what they smell like.

So when there was this smell, I looked around. I found out from which direction was the wind. And in that direction I went to the top of the next rise, a dozen steps. And no farther away than you could throw a rock, there they were coming up the hill toward me, about fifteen ewes and their lambs, ambling along, having a good time eating, just taking a walk as if there were no trouble anywhere in all the world.

Wahoo! I took off. Around my head in a big circle, I swung my books like a rope. I was going to throw a loop on all fifteen at once. Wahoo! I took off down that hill as if I were a whole herd of buffalo and the sheep were somebody's chuck wagon that was going to get stampeded. Wahoo!

The sheep looked up, a little like a bunch of people in church interested to see who was coming through the door.

I showed them who was coming through the door. Before they knew what was happening, they were moving. *Whoosh*—I let my books swing out, and I hit one right in the rump. *Whish*—I kicked another one with my foot that had the rock, so that it hurt me more, I think, than the sheep. I picked up a stone and—*wango*—I let a third one have it in the rear. I got them running right in the opposite direction from the one they were going.

I kept them going at a gallop. Running first to the one side, then to the other, swinging the books around my head all the time. Yelling and hollering so they wouldn't even dare slow down. They looked scared, but I didn't care. I had waited too long for this. And now I wanted them to know that I was here. I ran them down the hill fast enough to be a stampede. And whichever one ran last was the unlucky one. There were a lot of rocks around, and I throw rocks good.

At the bottom of the hill, I quieted down. Why was I acting so mad? I had no reason to be mad at the sheep. It wasn't as if they started out to get me in trouble. Indeed, because of them, here I was doing a great thing. I was finding them and bringing them home. If they hadn't taken it into their heads to go out and get lost, I never would have this big chance.

I quieted down. I stopped and I breathed. The air was good. After the rain, it was clean and it smelled sweet, like a vanilla soda in Schaeffer's Drugstore in Taos (tah′ohs) before you start to drink it with the straw. I took in the air with deep breaths. I sat down and took off my shoe. I found the rock down near the heel. But my goodness, it wasn't any kind of rock at all. Just a little bit of a chip off a stone. In my foot it felt like a boulder. But in my hand it didn't look like anything at all.

I was quieted down. We started off. It was going to be a long drive home. I didn't mind. There were so many good things to think about. What my father would say to me, and my grandfather.

It is no great trouble to drive a small bunch of sheep. You just walk behind them, and if one begins to separate, you start in the same direction that it starts and that makes it turn back and bunch up again. It was very little work. So there was much time to think what my uncles would say, and

my big brothers. And how Pedro would watch me.

There was much time to look around. At the mountains, not so dark now and not so mad. There was much to see, walking along thinking, breathing, and looking around. How the clouds now were taking on new shapes, the dark ones separating and new big white ones coming up. And on the mesa everything looked fine. I saw flowers. Before, when I was looking, there were no flowers. Now, there they were. The little pink ones of the peyote plants. And there were flowers on the hedgehog cactus, too, kind of pinkish purple some, and others a real red.

After a little while, I had something else to do. One of the lambs lay down. Whether it was tired or why, I don't know. I picked it up, the lamb under my arm, and in the other hand the rope with my books. It was not so bad. Even the rope didn't pinch anymore. And when the lamb got heavy under one arm, I put it under the other.

I felt better, now, than in a long time.

Even when I had to pick up this second lamb, which was straggling

behind, I still felt good. It was harder this way because now I couldn't use one arm after the other when the lambs got heavy, and there were the books I had to carry in addition. By now, though, we were coming down the dry wash that led to the river. There was not much farther to go.

They were a good bunch of sheep, all of them. When I brought them to the place in the river that was not so deep, they waded right across without any trouble. As for me myself, I almost fell in, but all the way this time. I was balancing myself all right on the rocks going across when one of the lambs started to wriggle as if it wanted to shake itself apart. But I held on, and I kept my balance and didn't fall in. I wouldn't have minded, anyway, if I had. If I came to the house with all my clothes wet, that would make what I did look as if it was even harder than it was.

Blasito was the first one to see me.

He was walking across the top of the hill near the corral when I came around the bend from the river.

"Hey, Mickey," he yelled, "where you been? What's those sheep you got?"

"Yours," I shouted back.

"Mine? What do you mean mine? The lost ones?"

"That's what," I yelled. "The lost ones!"

"No! No fooling?" He turned away from me. *"Ai,* Grandpa. *Padre de Chavez. Mira!* Miguel's here, with the bunch of sheep that was lost!" He looked back to where I was coming up the hill. "Bravo, Miguelito (mee guh lee′ toh)! Where'd you find them? How did it happen?"

"I'll tell you." I needed my breath to get up the hill with those two lambs under my arms. "Wait'll I get there."

The two of them were waiting for me, Blasito and my grandfather. Grandpa took one of the lambs from my arms. I let the other one down. Blasito shooed the bunch into the corral. And all three of us talked at once.

"Where did you find them?" asked Blasito.

"How did this happen?" said Grandfather.

"I'll tell it to you all," I said, "from the beginning. On the way to school this morning, I started to think."

Blasito interrupted. "Can't you tell us where you found them?"

"But that's what I'm trying to do. It started on the way to school."

"Miguel!" Grandfather wouldn't let me talk. "That part, you can tell us later. Where were they, the sheep?"

"Well, I'll tell you that first, then. I found them on the way to Arroyo Hondo, about twenty or thirty miles from here. But the way it started——"

"How many miles?" My grandfather looked at me with a smile.

"Oh, many miles. Many, many. What happened was——"

"How come you went north?" asked Blas. "All morning we've been riding toward the Arroyo del Alamo. In just the other way."

"First comes the way I went down the hill," I tried to explain. "With world-record jumps."

"Why is it that you don't want to answer your big brother Blas?" asked Grandpa. "How did you know where to look?"

"But why can't I tell it the way it happened? There was much trouble and it's very interesting."

"Later," said Grandpa. "Now, how did you know?"

"Well, I figured it out, and then I kept my ears open to hear things."

"What things?" said Blasito.

"Things people say."

"Like who?"

"Like Juby."

"He told you?"

"Look," I said to Blasito. "If I can't tell you in my own way, then what's the use? The kind of questions you ask, it makes it all sound like nothing. If I have to tell it this way, just to answer a few little questions, then what's the use my going out and finding the sheep anyway?"

"Use?" Blasito started to laugh. He banged me on the back. "It's a great thing, finding those sheep. I mean it, Miguel. You did fine!"

"What did you say?"

"I said great, fine!"

Grandfather took me by the hand and shook it like two men shaking hands.

"It's the truth," he said. "This that you have done, it was good."

"What?" I asked my grandfather.

"It was good."

"Better than the rest of us could do," said Blasito.

"What?" I asked Blasito.

"Better than the rest of us!" Blasito shouted so I would hear.

Grandpa still held my hand, and he shook it again. "You brought them in all right, Miguel. Like a real pastor."

"What?" I asked my grandfather. I wanted to hear everything twice.

"A real pastor," Grandpa said again, and we all looked at each other and smiled.

"Anything else?" I asked.

Before anyone could answer, there was a great shout from the house. "Miguel!" It was my father. It was a shout that sounded like thunder. "Miguel, get over here!"

He stood, he and my mother both, they stood in front of the house. And with them was Mrs. Mertian, my schoolteacher. They stood with Mrs. Mertian, who had come from the school in Los Cordovas, and they talked together.

My father looked around at us once again. "Miguel!"

Grandpa nodded to me that I should go to my father. "Take off," said Blasito. "You'd better get going."

I went. What else? It was too bad, real bad, my teacher should talk to my father before I even got a chance. I knew now that the things I was thinking about on the way home, of what my father would say to me, I knew that these were probably not the things he was going to say to me now. I walked to the house, where they stood, and Mrs. Mertian smiled at my mother, and they shook hands. Then she smiled at my father and shook hands with him. Then everybody smiled at each other and she left. But when they turned to watch me coming up the path, my father and mother, nobody smiled.

"Where'd you go?" said my father.

"Up there to the Arroyo Hondo. Many miles."

"What's in Arroyo Hondo?"

I knew my father didn't want to know what's in Arroyo Hondo. He knew as well as I. Just a grocery store and some houses. If I told him that, then everything would get all mixed up.

"It was not for what's in Arroyo Hondo. It's that I went after the sheep that were lost."

"This morning at breakfast, didn't we talk about the lost sheep?"

"Yes." I knew what he meant. "And you told me to go to school. And I did, I went to school."

"That is true. But it is only one small piece of what is true. The rest is, you didn't go in."

"Because of Juby. He is my oldest friend."

"And why is it, Miguel, that you will obey your oldest friend? But your parents, who are friends to you even older than your oldest friend, what they say means nothing."

"But Juby told me where were the missing sheep. So I went. I got them. I brought them home."

This is not the way I wanted to tell it at all. It was worse than with Blasito and Grandpa. It didn't sound hard this way, or like a big thing. It was like going down to the spring for a pail of water, no more. But what else was there to do? If things kept up like they were, it could get bad.

"You brought what home?"

"The missing sheep. They are in the corral."

My father and mother looked. Blasito and my grandfather, who were watching us, they pointed out the bunch in the corral.

"Well!" My father, at least, he didn't sound so mad anymore when he looked back to me.

"That's why I didn't go to school."

"Well." My father put his hands in his back pockets and looked down at me. "That's different. But not so different to make too much difference, Miguel. The sheep are important. Sure! But you, too, that you go to school is important. Even more important. Always there has to be something done with the sheep. And if every time something had to be done, you stayed away from school, my goodness, you'd grow up to be a burro. And you tell me, do we need a burro around this place?"

"No. Only mules and horses."

"And even more, what we need is young men who are educated, who have learned to know what is the difference between what is right and what is wrong. Do you understand?"

"I understand. And I promise. I will never miss my school again."

"Good. Now get into the house. Mrs. Mertian brought the lessons from today. So go in and do them and write your homework for tomorrow."

My mother took me by the back of the head to go into the house with me. And then my father did a wonderful thing. He gave me one good spank. And when I looked around up at him, he was smiling.

"It would not be true," he told me, "if I didn't say also I am glad to have the sheep back. How you did it was wrong. But for what you did, I want to thank you."

And then he went off to go to Blas and Grandpa where they were working on the tractor. My mother took me with her into the house.

"Come, Miquito (mee kee′toh). That's enough for today. Good and bad, you've done enough."

How will Miguel Chavez finally prove that he can do an adult's job? You can find out by reading the rest of Joseph Krumgold's book . . . *and now Miguel.*

ABOUT THE AUTHOR

Joseph Krumgold was born in Jersey City, New Jersey, in 1908, and grew up near New York City. When he was young, his father owned and operated several movie theaters, so it was only natural that Joseph became interested in making movies. This interest eventually led him to Hollywood, California, where he began his career as a writer by writing stories for the movies. Mr. Krumgold says that his courses in chemistry and physics in high school and at New York University helped him learn about the technical production of movies, and his studies of English and history gave him ideas for stories.

Mr. Krumgold became interested in making documentaries, films that tell about real people and places. He left Hollywood and traveled and lived in many places, including France, Israel, and Italy, to make such films. His films won a number of prizes in the United States and abroad.

One of the films which Mr. Krumgold wrote and directed was made in New Mexico. It is about real people, the Chavez family, and was filmed while the story actually happened. Mr. Krumgold felt that he had more to say about Miguel Chavez than he could say in the movie, so he wrote the book . . . *and now Miguel.*

In 1954 . . . *and now Miguel* won the Newbery Medal, which is awarded each year to "the book which has made the most distinguished contribution to literature for children." The award encouraged Mr. Krumgold to write two other books on how a child grows up in different parts of the country. They are *Onion John,* awarded the Newbery Medal in 1959, and *Henry 3,* published in 1966.

Mr. Krumgold and his wife live with their one boy, Adam, on a farm near Hope, New Jersey, but a great deal of his time is spent abroad where he works on films and books.

BOOKS TO ENJOY

OPEN THE DOOR AND SEE ALL THE PEOPLE,
by Clyde Bulla

JoAnn and her little sister, Teeney, lose everything in the farmhouse fire. Then they get a chance to find out what city life is like when their mother finds a job there.

GREEDY MARIANI, *by Dorothy Sharp Carter*

These twenty tales from Puerto Rico, Cuba, Haiti, Jamaica, and other nearby islands are full of magic and spirits, as well as nonsense and humor.

GEORGINA AND THE DRAGON, *by Lee Kingman*

Lively Georgina is determined to get a job. That is where the "dragon," a fierce old lady, comes into the story.

RABBIT HILL, *by Robert Lawson*

The lives of the little country animals on Rabbit Hill are changed when people move into the house next to the hill.

MY DAD LIVES IN A DOWNTOWN HOTEL, *by Peggy Mann*

What is it like when parents get a divorce and Dad does not live at home anymore? Joey knows firsthand.

BABA AND MR. BIG, *by C. Everard Palmer*

In this story of present-day Jamaica, a boy and a lonely old man solve a mystery involving a hawk named Mr. Big.

51 SYCAMORE LANE, *by Marjorie Sharmat*

Who could have a short-wave radio, foreign mail, numerous notebooks, and a chicken named Miss America? Who else but a spy? Paul and his friends track down the new neighbor, with amusing results.

Symmetry

Symmetry

STORIES

ARTICLES

POEMS

JUST FOR FUN

SKILL LESSONS

Taken, in Part, from an Engraving by Paul Revere

PAUL REVERE'S BIG RIDE

by Jean Fritz

In 1735 there were in Boston 42 streets, 36 lanes, 22 alleys, 1,000 brick houses, 2,000 wooden houses, 12 churches, 4 schools, 418 horses (at the last count), and so many dogs that a law was passed prohibiting people from having dogs that were more than 10 inches high. But it was difficult to keep dogs from growing more than 10 inches, and few people cared to part with their 11- and 12-inch dogs, so they paid little attention to the law. In any case, there were too many dogs to count.

Along with the horses, streets, and alleys, there were, of course, people in Boston—more than 13,000. Four of them lived in a small wooden house on North Street near Love Lane. They were Mr. Revere, a goldsmith and silversmith; his wife, Deborah; their daughter, Deborah; and their young son, Paul Revere, born the first day of the new year.

Of all the busy people in Boston, Paul Revere would turn out to be one of the busiest. All his life he found that there was more to do, more to make, more to see, more to hear, more to say, more places to go, more to learn than there were hours in the day.

And there was plenty for Paul to do. When he was fifteen years old, his father died, and Paul took over the silversmithing business. He made beads, rings, lockets, bracelets, buttons, medals, pitchers, teapots, spoons, sugar baskets, cups, porringers, shoe buckles, and candlesticks. Once he made a silver collar for a man's pet squirrel.

To make extra money, he took a job ringing the bells in Christ Church. Sometimes at a moment's notice, word would come that the

bells were to be rung. Off Paul would run, his hat clapped to his head, his coattails flying.

In 1756, when Paul was twenty-one, he married Sarah Orne and began filling up the house with children. There were Deborah, Paul, Sarah, Mary, Frances, and Elizabeth (in addition to two babies who died young). Then Sarah died, and Paul married Rachel Walker, and along came Joshua, Joseph, Harriet, Maria, and John (in addition to three more babies who died young).

Paul kept putting up new chairs at the kitchen table, and now in addition to making buckles, spoons, cups, and all the other silver items, Paul had to find new ways to make money. So he engraved portraits, produced book-plates, sold pictures, made picture frames, brought out hymnbooks, and became a dentist. "Artificial Teeth. Paul Revere," he advertised. "He fixes them in such a Manner that they are not only an Ornament, but of real Use in Speaking and Eating."

You would think that with all Paul Revere did, he would make mistakes. But he always remembered to put spouts on his teapots and handles on his cups.

The false teeth that he whittled out of hippopotamus tusk looked just fine.

Generally when he did arithmetic in his daybook, he got the right answers.

Of course, sometimes there were so many different things to do that he forgot what he was doing. In the beginning of a new daybook, he wrote, "This is my book for me to—" But he never finished the sentence.

Sometimes he was in such a hurry that his writing looked sloppy. At the end of a letter he would write, "Pray excuse my scrawl."

Still, Paul Revere wasn't always at work. Occasionally he just dreamed. There was one page in his daybook that he used simply for doodling.

But beginning in 1765, there was no time for doodling. The English were causing trouble, telling the colonies they couldn't do this and couldn't do that, slapping on taxes, one after another. First there was a tax on printed matter. When this was withdrawn, there was a tax on tea, glass, printers' colors, and paper. The one tax that England would never give up was the tax on tea.

And what did Paul Revere do about it?

He became a leader of the Sons of Liberty, a secret club that found interesting ways to oppose the English.

One of Paul's busiest nights was December 16, 1773. He picked up his ax and joined other Sons of Liberty, all pretending to be Indians.

They were going to make sure that no one in Boston would pay taxes on the three shiploads of tea that had just arrived from England. So they marched on board the ships, hauled the chests of tea onto the decks, broke them open, and dumped the tea—10,000 pounds of it—into Boston Harbor. It was all done in an orderly fashion. No one was hurt; no other cargo was touched; the ships were unharmed. (There was only one minor incident, when a man found stuffing tea into the lining of his coat had to be punished.)

When the Sons of Liberty finished, they marched home,

washed their faces, and went to bed.

But not Paul Revere. Someone had to ride to New York and Philadelphia and spread the news. And Paul was picked to do it.

So off he galloped, his hat clapped to his head, his coattails flying. From Boston to Philadelphia he went. And back. Sixty-three miles a day.

He was back in Boston on the eleventh day, long before anyone expected him.

Paul Revere became Massachusetts' Number One express rider between Boston and Philadelphia. He also became a secret agent. In the winter of 1774 it looked more and more as if the English soldiers in Boston meant to make war on America, and Paul's job was to try to find out the English plans.

He patrolled the streets at night, delivered messages to Philadelphia, and kept himself ready at all times to warn the countryside.

But all his rides, Paul knew, were small compared to the Big Ride that lay ahead. Nothing should go wrong with this one. In the spring, everyone agreed, the English would march into the countryside and really start fighting. And when they did, Paul Revere would have to be ahead of them.

On Saturday, April 15, 1775, spring, it seemed, had arrived. Boats for moving troops had been seen on the Charles River. English scouts had been observed on the road to Lexington and Concord. A stableboy had overheard two officers making plans.

At 10:45 on Tuesday night, April 18, Dr. Joseph Warren, who was directing patriot activities in Boston, sent for Paul Revere. Other messengers had been dispatched for Lexington and Concord by longer routes. Paul was to go, as planned, the same way the English were going—across the Charles River. He was to alarm the citizens so they could arm themselves, and he was to inform John Hancock and Samuel Adams, Boston's two patriot leaders who were staying in Lexington. And Paul was to leave now.

He had already arranged a quick way of warning the people of Charlestown, across the river. Two lanterns were to be hung in the steeple of the North Church if the English were coming by water; one lantern if they were coming by land.

So Paul rushed to the North Church and gave directions. "Two lanterns," he said. "Now."

Then he ran home, flung open the door, pulled on his boots, grabbed his coat, kissed his wife, told the children to be good, and off he went—his hat clapped to his head, his coattails flying. He was in such a hurry that he left the door open, and his dog got out.

On the way to the river, Paul

picked up two friends who had promised to row him to the other side. Then all three ran to a dock near the Charlestown ferry, where Paul had kept a boat hidden during the winter. Paul's dog ran with them.

The night was pleasant, and the moon was bright. Too bright. In the path of moonlight across the river lay an armed English transport. Paul and his friends would have to row past it.

Then Paul realized his first mistake. He had meant to bring cloth to wrap around the oars so the sound would be muffled. He had left the cloth at home.

That wasn't all he had left behind. Paul Revere had started out for his Big Ride without his spurs.

Luckily, one of Paul's friends knew a lady who lived nearby. He ran to her house, called at her window, and asked for some cloth. This lady was not a time-waster. She stepped out of the petticoat she was wearing and threw it out the window.

Then for the spurs. Luckily,

Paul's dog was there, and luckily, he was well trained. Paul wrote a note to his wife, tied it around the dog's neck, and told the dog to go home. By the time Paul and his friends had ripped the petticoat in two, wrapped each half around an oar, and launched the boat, the dog was back with Paul's spurs around his neck.

Paul and his two friends rowed softly across the Charles River, they slipped carefully past the English transport with its sixty-four guns, and they landed in the

shadows on the other side. Safely. There a group of men from Charlestown who had seen the signal in the church steeple had a horse waiting for Paul.

And off Paul Revere rode on his Big Ride, beating on doors as he went, arousing the citizens. At Lexington he woke up John Hancock and Samuel Adams and advised them to leave town. He had a quick bite to eat, and then, in the company of two other riders, he continued to Concord, warning farmers along the way.

For a while all went well. And then suddenly from out of the shadows appeared six English officers. They rode up with their pistols in their hands and ordered Paul to stop. But Paul didn't stop immediately.

One of the officers shouted, "If you go an inch farther, you are a dead man."

Paul and his companions tried to ride through the group, but they were surrounded and ordered into a pasture at one side of the road.

In the pasture six other officers appeared with pistols in their hands.

One of them spoke like a gentleman. He took Paul's horse by the reins and asked Paul where he came from.

Paul told him, "Boston."

The officer asked what time he had left Boston.

Paul told him.

The officer said, "Sir, may I crave your name?"

Paul answered that his name was Revere.

"What! *Paul* Revere?"

Paul said, "Yes."

Now, the English officers certainly did not want to let Paul Revere loose, so they put him, along with other prisoners, at the center of their group, and they

rode off toward Lexington. As they approached town, they heard gunfire.

"What was that?" the officer asked.

Paul said it was a signal to alarm the countryside.

With this piece of news, the English decided they'd like to get back to their own troops in a hurry. Indeed, they were in such a hurry that they no longer wanted to be bothered with prisoners. So after relieving the prisoners of their horses, they set them free.

And then what happened?

Paul Revere felt bad, of course, to be on his Big Ride without a horse. He felt uneasy to be on a moonlit road on foot. So he struck out through the country, across stone walls, through pastures, over graveyards, back into Lexington to see if John Hancock and Samuel Adams were still there.

They were. They were just preparing to leave town in John Hancock's carriage. Paul and Hancock's clerk, John Lowell, went with them.

All went well. They rode about two miles into the countryside, and then suddenly John Hancock remembered that he had left a trunk full of important papers in a Lexington tavern. This was a mistake. He didn't want the English to find those papers.

So what happened?

Paul Revere and John Lowell got out of the carriage and walked back to Lexington.

It was morning now. From all over the area, farmers were gathering on Lexington Green. As Paul crossed the green to the tavern, there were between fifty and sixty armed men preparing to take a stand against the English. The troops were said to be near.

Paul went into the tavern, had a bite to eat, found the trunk, and carried it out, holding one end while John Lowell held the other. As they stepped on the green, the troops appeared.

And then what happened?

Paul and John held on to the

trunk. They walked right through the American lines, holding on to the trunk. They were still holding on when a gun was fired. Then there were two guns, then a succession of guns firing back and forth. Paul did not pay any attention to who was firing or who fired first. He did not stop to think that this might be the first battle of a war. His job was to move a trunk to safety, and that's what he did.

The battles of Lexington and Concord did, of course, begin the Revolutionary War. And Americans have talked ever since about Paul Revere's ride.

After the war, when Paul was forty-eight years old, he went back to silversmithing and opened a hardware store, too. Later he made bells—398 of them. Some still ring today. Paul Revere died in 1818, when he was eighty-three years old.

AUTHOR

When Jean Fritz remembers her childhood in Hankow, China, she thinks of the storybook characters who seemed to share the house. Peter Pan, the pirate Bluebeard, and Kipling's cat, who walked by itself, were all very real to her. Before long, she was writing her own stories. Although she still lived in China, her stories were always about people living in America. Since she had never been there, she had to imagine what it was like. She had heard about American holidays, so the characters in her first story celebrated both the Fourth of July and Thanksgiving. When she was thirteen, her family moved back to the United States.

Jean Fritz has written books for people of all ages, from young children to adults but she still writes mostly about Americans. She especially likes to write about people in American history. One of her books, *The Cabin Faced West*, was about pioneers. The Revolutionary War is her favorite time in history. In addition to *And Then What Happened, Paul Revere?* from which the story you have just read was taken, she has written two other books about that period—*Early Thunder* and *George Washington's Breakfast*.

Ms. Fritz now lives with her family in New York.

GARBAGE BOOM

by Francine Klagsbrun

It might surprise you to know that many valuable old objects you see in museums are really the junk and trash of ancient peoples. When the people of long ago wanted to throw something out, they simply dropped it on the ground or, in some cases, carried it off to a town dump. So broken pieces of pottery, used weapons, old tools, and bits of ornaments lay strewn about the settlements. Over the years, the settlements became covered by layers and layers of dirt and earth. When one group of people died out, other groups often took their places and added their junk to what was already there.

For the most part, ancient peoples were pretty messy house-keepers. Early peoples who lived near the Asian city of Troy, for example, dropped bones and all sorts of garbage on the floors of their homes. When the garbage piled up so high that the door would not open, they simply cut off the bottom of the door. Then it could slide open over all the trash, and they did not have to clean up the mess.

Today we all have many more things than people had in early days. And we throw away much more. Think of how many newspapers you and your family read and throw out every week. Think of the soda bottles and milk containers, the plastic bottles that hold soaps and cleansers and medicines, the cardboard boxes that hold games and toys, and the games and toys themselves.

While we have more trash than ever before, we have fewer places to get rid of it. Towns and cities have grown so big that there is little room left for old-fashioned garbage dumps. And the places that can be turned into landfills are being used up. Swamps and marshes are valuable spots for birds and fishes to live in or have their young and should not all be filled in.

So what do we do with our garbage? You might think the answer is simply to build more incinerators and burn all the trash. But tons of ashes remain after incinerators do their work. Where can we dump the ashes?

Sanitation workers and government officials are busy trying to find answers to this problem before the garbage boom makes life in the cities impossible.

Among the things sanitation people are working on are bigger and better incinerators. They hope to build incinerators that will burn everything, with little left over. They plan to make these incinerators in such a way that additional smoke does not poison the air.

Sanitation people also speak of great incinerator ships. The ships would carry garbage far out into the ocean. There trash would be burned and the ashes dumped at sea. Years ago, a great deal of garbage was actually dumped into the ocean. But even though laws said that the garbage had to be carried a long distance from shore, it often got washed up on the beaches. Many experts now feel that burning garbage on ships and dumping the ashes into the ocean would not harm our waterways or our beaches. Some experts, however, fear it might harm the life in the sea.

There are other ways by which sanitation workers hope to solve the garbage problem. They talk about carrying trash by train away from big cities to areas that do not have many people or buildings. The city of Philadelphia has already started to haul its garbage hundreds of miles to old mine pits that are no longer being used.

Another idea is to turn garbage into compost. This is a kind of fertilizer made of decayed plant and animal matter.

Still another thought is to use machines to press garbage into solid bricks that could be used for building.

Many people are thinking, "Let's cut down on the rubbish." Some containers, such as cans and bottles, are made of materials that could be used more than once. A number of manufacturing companies and some communities have now opened collection centers where people can turn in their old cans and bottles instead of throwing them into the trash can. The containers can be recycled, or used again to make new containers. Some companies are thinking of giving up containers such as plastic bottles, which are hard to get rid of. These companies plan, instead, to make containers of materials that can be recycled.

While all this thinking goes on, some experts have begun to look for ways of cleaning up the litter that has already been dumped in space and on the moon by our astronauts. This litter includes old instruments, used-up food packets, leftover clothing, and other space gear. Some people fear that space litter will grow into the great garbage problem of the future.

What do *you* think?

OUR COURT

We live right next
  To all our friends—
Five houses in a row;
  In every house
  A boy or girl—
We have not far to go.

  We like our court,
  It is the best—
We think of things to do;
  We laugh and play,
  We shout all day,
We fight and quarrel too.

  But when bad times
  And trouble come,
On neighbors we depend;
  We like to help
  Each other out—
We give and take and lend.

                    Lois Lenski

PECOS BILL
and the Mustang
by Harold W. Felton

Did you ever hear of Pecos Bill?

He was a cowboy. The first cowboy. He invented cowboys and everything about them, and he became the hero of all the other rootin'-tootin', high-falootin', straight-shootin' cowboys.

He could shoot a bumblebee in the eye at sixty paces, and he was a man who was not afraid to shake hands with lightning.

But before he became a man, he was a boy, and before he was a boy, he was a baby.

That seems only reasonable, doesn't it?

Bill was born a long time ago, away out in the wild and woolly west. It was so long ago the sun was only about the size of a dime. Of course, money went further in those days, so naturally a dime was bigger than it is now.

Bill always obeyed his parents. They used to say he was the best child they ever saw, and that was quite a compliment because he had seventeen brothers and sisters.

One day Bill's family saw smoke from a new neighbor's chimney. It was beyond the river and two hills, but Bill's paw allowed the country was getting too crowded. Bill's maw agreed. They liked plenty of elbow room, so they decided to move farther west.

So they loaded their wagon with all their household goods and their eighteen children, and off they went over the Texas plains, across the rivers, and over the mountains and the valleys.

They came to the Pecos River and crossed it. Then the left hind wheel hit a prairie-dog hole. The wagon lurched, and Bill fell out.

He landed headfirst on a rock. The rock broke into a thousand pieces, and Bill's head was bruised, a little.

The wagon juggled and rumbled away into the distance, toward the setting sun.

When Bill came to, he didn't know where he was or who he was. He didn't know what to do or how to do it. He didn't remember a single thing about his life, his maw and paw, or his seventeen brothers and sisters. He was all alone on the west bank of the Pecos River in West Texas. He didn't know his age, either, so no one knows exactly how old he was. But he was a little shaver, only about half as high as the withers of a pinto pony.

An old coyote rescued him. The coyote's name was El Viejo (ell vee-ay′hoh), which means *Old Man* in Spanish. El Viejo didn't know what the little boy's name was or what to call him. Finally he called him Pecos Bill, and took him to live with the coyotes.

So Pecos Bill grew up with the coyotes. He learned to walk like a coyote. He learned to talk like a coyote. He thought he *was* a coyote. That was only natural considering that he had lost his memory when he fell out of the wagon and broke the rock into a thousand pieces and bruised his head, a little.

His playmates were coyote pups. He wrestled with them and they yipped and yapped and growled playfully at him and nipped each other.

Bill learned to howl at the moon. He learned to scratch his ear with his foot, and he could run fast enough to catch a rabbit.

When he got older, he could run down an antelope without losing his breath.

Then, one day, Pecos Bill met a *man*. The man said, "Who are you?"

"I'm a coyote pup," Bill growled.

"You don't look like a coyote to me," said the man. "You look like a human."

"I am not a human," Bill snarled. "I'm a coyote and that's all there is to it!"

"If you're a coyote, where is your tail?" the man asked with a grin.

Bill looked over his shoulder. He couldn't see a tail. He must have a tail. All the coyotes Bill knew had long, bushy tails. He must have a tail. He must. After all, he was a coyote, wasn't he? At least he thought he was.

Bill looked around again, this time under his arm. He couldn't see a tail. Not even a little one. There must be some mistake!

He backed up to a stream and looked at his reflection in the water. It was true! He didn't have a tail! No tail at all! If he didn't have a tail, he couldn't be a coyote. If he wasn't a coyote, he must be a human.

And that is how Pecos Bill discovered he was a human and not a coyote.

Then he decided that if he wasn't a coyote, he shouldn't be living with coyotes. So he barked "good-bye" to El Viejo, and he yipped "so long, pals" to his coyote-pup friends, and started off with the man.

"As long as I'm a human, I'm going to be a cowboy," he said. "And if I'm going to be a *cowboy*, I'll need a horse."

"What's a cowboy?" the man asked.

"That's easy. He's a man who rounds up cattle," Bill answered.

"You won't need a horse," the man said. "We only have tame cows and you don't need a horse for tame cows."

"There are wild longhorn cattle around these parts," said Bill. "There are wild horses and other wild critters. No, sir! I'll need a horse because I aim to round up and catch those wild longhorns!"

But Pecos Bill was too big for an ordinary horse.

The biggest animal in that part of the country was a mountain lion. A long-haired, long-tailed, long-toothed mountain lion. Bill captured the mountain lion and broke him to ride.

The mountain lion didn't like it much, at first. He was quite peevish about it. He was as peevish as a bee with a boil. But he soon learned to like Pecos Bill and became quite friendly.

He liked to have Pecos scratch him behind the ears. That made him purr. When Bill's mountain lion purred, he sounded like a freight train rumbling by.

By this time, Bill was almost full-grown, and he was big. No one knows exactly *how* big, but he was big enough to chase bears with a switch.

Bill slept on a gravel bed, between sandpaper sheets. He used a soft rock for a pillow. On cold nights he pulled a blanket of fog over him.

He shaved with his bowie knife. Not with the knife itself—it was too sharp. He used its shadow to shave, as that was quite sharp enough.

One day a rattlesnake bit him. It was a tough, mean rattlesnake and challenged Bill to a fight. Pecos Bill was a gentle man. He didn't like to fight, but the rattler insisted.

Bill won that fight, too, and he used the rattlesnake for a *quirt*, or

riding whip. The rattler liked the job. It was something not every
rattlesnake got a chance to do.

It was quite a sight to see Pecos Bill riding his mountain lion on
a dead run, kicking up a cloud of dust and sandburrs and using the
rattler for a quirt.

But Pecos Bill wanted a horse. To be exact, he wanted the Famous
Pacing Mustang of the Prairies. No one had ever been able to catch
the mustang and ride him. They said even bullets could not stop him.
Few men had ever even seen him. Pecos Bill thought the Famous
Pacing Mustang of the Prairies was the horse for him.

He rode far out on the prairie until he found the herd of wild horses
led by the great Pacing Mustang. He gasped when he saw the horse.
He was a palomino. His shining coat was the color of a new
gold coin. His mane and tail were snowy white. He had four white
stockings and a white blaze between the eyes, and Bill made up his
mind to capture him that very day.

Bill mounted his mountain lion. He lifted his quirt and his rattlesnake rattled. The mountain lion roared and dug his claws into the ground. Cactus and tumbleweed swirled up in the dusty air as he shot forward like a bullet.

The Famous Pacing Mustang of the Prairies saw them coming and began to run away. But it was too late. Bill's galloping mountain lion rushed toward the mustang. They were running side by side. In another instant, the mustang would draw ahead. There was no time to lose. Bill had to act! At once!

The mountain lion roared. The rattlesnake rattled. Pecos Bill dropped his quirt and sprang from the mountain lion to the back of the Famous Pacing Mustang of the Prairies!

No one had ever been astride the mustang before. The mustang jumped and bucked and twisted and turned. But Pecos Bill kept his seat.

"Yippee!" Bill yelled. The mustang ran and kicked. Bill stayed on. The mustang reared and pawed the air. Bill could not be thrown off.

The horse covered the land from the Platte (plat) River in Nebraska to the Pecos River in Texas, from the Mississippi River to the Pacific Ocean. There was pinwheeling, high-diving, sunfishing, high-flying, and all the other tricks of a bucking bronco. But Bill stayed astride, waving his hat and shouting at the top of his voice, "Yippee-ee-ee!"

Pecos thought the mustang would never stop bucking, so he spoke to him. He told the horse how he wanted to be a cowboy and how he wanted to ride the range and lasso wild longhorn cattle and drive them to market. He told the mustang he needed a good horse to help him. If he didn't have a horse that was good enough, he might quit trying to be a cowboy and go back to being a coyote again. "I won't argue with you anymore," Pecos said. "I won't try to break you anymore. If you don't want to help me, you go your way, and I'll go mine."

Bill turned away and lay down to drink from the river. The Famous Pacing Mustang of the Prairies came to his side. He put his big nose in the water and he drank with Bill. It was a sign that the mustang wanted to belong to Pecos Bill. They both drank. They drank so much that the river went down three inches. Pecos Bill had a horse at last!

And that is how Pecos Bill got his first horse and became the first cowboy.

AUTHOR

The author of the tall tale you have just read, Harold Felton, was born in Neola, Iowa. His childhood was filled with enjoyable activities—reading, hunting, swimming, fishing, and camping. Although the family lived in town, they also owned a farm. Each evening after school, he and his brother would go to the farm, where they would work until dark. On the way back to town, Harold Felton's father used to tell them fables, tall tales, and cowboy stories, or recite poems for them. Sometimes the whole family would sing songs together.

In the summers during his college years, Mr. Felton worked as a driver of a mule team, as a farmer, and as an actor. After receiving his law degree, he was in dramatics and public speaking for a short time.

For many years Mr. Felton was a lawyer for the United States Government. Now retired, he still enjoys writing books for children. He writes about real people as well as about the make-believe characters of his tall tales. Two of his books are *Ely S. Parker, Spokesman for the Seneca* and *Gib Morgan, Oil Driller.*

Mary and the Monster

by Margaret J. Anderson

In the distant past, a huge reptile called an ichthyosaur (ik' thee uh sor') lived in the sea. It had the streamlined body of a fish and steered its way through the water with paddlelike flippers. It had a long snout and fierce-looking, sharp teeth. Great round eyes stared out from its smooth head.

Ichthyosaurs were so much like fish that it is hard to see why they all died out while fish have survived so well. Whatever the reason, the ichthyosaurs disappeared from the earth.

One of the last of the ichthyosaurs slumped down in some mud to die. There it lay, undisturbed, for a very long time, until — but that's our story.

The story begins over one hundred and fifty years ago beside the same seas where the ichthyosaurs had roamed. In the small town of Lyme Regis, on the southern coast of England, lived the Anning family. Mr. Anning had been a carpenter. Although they had never been rich, there had always been enough money to manage on. Since her husband had died the year before, Mrs. Anning had had a hard time supporting her two children, Mary and Joseph.

One day Mrs. Anning went to the door and called, "Mary, Mary."

There was no answer.

"Where is that girl?" she asked.

"I don't know," answered Joseph.

"She's down at the cliff, isn't she?" asked Mrs. Anning in an angry voice. "Haven't I said she's to waste no more time poking about those cliffs? She's twelve years old and does nothing around the house."

"We've found something good, Mama," said Joseph in a whisper.

"Something good, indeed!" Mrs. Anning answered angrily. "It will just be more rubbish and clutter like this!"

As she spoke, she threw a large shell fossil onto the flagstone floor. It broke, and part of it rolled under a chair. Joseph

dived after it and picked up the pieces. He tried to fit them together again.

"That's an ammonite (am′uh nite′), Mama," cried Joseph. "We could have sold it."

"Who'd pay money for a bit of worthless stone?" asked his mother crossly.

"Pa used to sell them for us in the shop," said Joseph.

"No one comes to the shop now," said his mother, and her mouth closed in a tight line.

When Mr. Anning was alive, he had encouraged the children to look for shells and bones along the gray cliffs overlooking the sea. Mary, with her sharp eyes and clever fingers, could pry ammonites right out of the rock. Mr. Anning told his customers about these curios from the distant past, and often they would toss Mary a penny or two in exchange for a fossil.

Now no one came to the empty shop, and the piles of fossils gathered dust. But Mary could not stay away from the cliffs. Finding pieces of history was all she wanted to do.

Mary didn't come home till after dark that night. She had been down on the shore since breakfast time, but she had not thought about food until she smelled the soup on the stove.

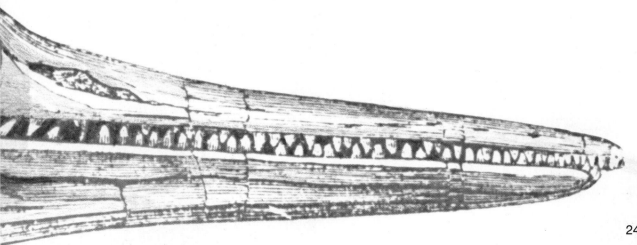

"Mary, how can you waste your days like this?" her mother asked.

"I've found something good, Mama," said Mary excitedly.

"That's just what Joseph said," answered her mother, a bit irritated.

"It's a monster, Mama. We're digging out a *monster*. It's as big as the house. It has eyes like dinner plates. Come and see it," Mary pleaded.

Mrs. Anning did not go to see it—not then. But she did let Joseph and Mary go down to the beach every day. Mary was so sure and so determined about her find that her mother didn't know how to argue with her.

One day, a week or two later, Mrs. Anning heard Mary and Joseph running on the cobbled street. She peered out the window and saw their beaming faces.

"We're rich, Mama!" cried Mary, jumping up and down. "I've sold the monster's bones to the Manor House. They gave me twenty-three pounds." Mary poured the money onto the table.

"Twenty-three pounds!" gasped Mrs. Anning. "Twenty-three pounds for some old *bones*!"

"It's because they *are* such old bones, Mama," said Mary. But she knew she'd never make her mother understand how important the bones were.

The ichthyosaur skeleton brought fame to Mary and to the little village of Lyme Regis. Scientists came from far away to see her fossils. Her collection grew. She found a plesiosaur (plee'see uh sor') and the first pterodactyl (tehr'uh dak'tihl) in Britain. Her discoveries gave her a chance to talk with scientists and with kings.

Today you can see that monster from the distant past. The ichthyosaur is on display in the British Museum of Natural History in London. And the little girl of one hundred and fifty years ago? Mary Anning is pictured in a stained-glass window in the Lyme Regis Parish Church.

AUTHOR

Margaret J. Anderson was born in Virginia, Minnesota, and went to Duluth Teacher's College. Her education didn't stop, however, when she received her teacher's certificate. She has taken many special courses since then, including one at the University of Oklahoma.

For a while she taught elementary school. Then she became a full-time writer. Many of her books are about religion.

Ms. Anderson enjoys sewing and photography as well as writing for young readers. She still lives in Minnesota.

Make a Fossil

by Aliki

How would you like to make a fossil? Not a one-million-year-old fossil but a one-minute-old "fossil."

Make a clay imprint of your hand, like this: Take some clay and flatten it out. Then press your hand into the clay and lift your hand away. Your hand is gone, but its shape is in the clay. You made an imprint. The imprint shows what your hand is like, the way a dinosaur's track shows us what its foot was like.

Suppose when it dried, you buried your clay imprint. Suppose a million years from now, someone found it. Your imprint would be as hard as stone. It would be a fossil of your hand. It would tell the finder something about you and something about life on earth a million years earlier.

Every time anyone finds a fossil, we learn more about life on earth long ago. Someday you may find a fossil, one that is millions and millions of years old. You may discover something that no one knows today.

How do we know about...

In the days when dinosaurs lived, there was no one who wrote about them. But some of these ancient animals left records of themselves in the earth. Not written records, of course, but they can be read just the same if you know how.

Some of these records, such as teeth and bones, have been dug up and studied. Dinosaurs left their footprints, too, which scientists have found and studied.

The footprints or bones that sometimes remain of these animals are called fossils. This word comes from the Latin word *fossilis*, meaning "dug up." Women and men who study fossils are called paleontologists.

dinosaurs?

by Glenn O. Blough

Fossils were made in many different ways. When dinosaurs died, they were often washed into lakes or oceans. They were heavy and sank to the bottom. Mud and clay and sand in the water settled on the bottom, too, and covered the animals. The soft parts of the animals rotted, but the bones did not. They stayed in the mud and clay and sand, which pressed down on them. A long, long time passed. The bones lay pressed into the mud and clay and sand, which slowly turned into rock. Then, of course, the fossils were in the rock.

More time passed. Many of the lakes and oceans dried up, leaving the fossils on dry land where scientists could dig them up.

Dinosaur bones also became fossils when they turned into stone. This happened very, very slowly, a little bit at a time. Lime or some other hard material in the water entered the bone and took the place of the material in the bone. When this happens, we say that a bone becomes petrified, or turns into stone.

Fossils were made in other ways, too. Sometimes hard parts of the animals were imprinted in soft mud. A dinosaur may have walked in mud and left its tracks. Then sand and mud filled the footprints and kept them from being washed away. Slowly the sand and mud hardened into rock, making a fossil of the track.

But no matter how a fossil was made, it took a long, long time to make it.

Of course, of all the dinosaurs that were once alive, the bones of only a few remain. Many died on land, rotted, and disappeared. They did not become fossils. But enough bones remained to tell us about these animals.

SKILL LESSON

USING AN INDEX

When you want to find the information that a book has on a certain subject, or on a question you want answered, how do you try to find it? Do you open the book just anywhere and start turning the pages, hoping that you will come to the information you want? Some people may do this, but there is a much quicker and easier way to find just which pages give the information you want. You can use the **index** at the back of the book. The index is a list of the topics which the book tells about.

It is not hard to learn to use the index of a book, and using it can save you a great deal of time. With a little practice, you can learn to find out quickly which pages in a book give information on any topic that the book tells about.

On the next page is part of the index of a book. The words which are printed in heavy black letters and begin farthest to the left in each column are called **main topics.** They name people, places, and things that the book tells about, and they are arranged in alphabetical order. You can see that **Alaska** is the first main topic on that page. What are some of the other main topics listed?

The main topics in an index are arranged in alphabetical order, just as the words in a dictionary list are arranged. Topics that begin with *a* come first. Then come those that begin with *b*.

The topics that begin with *c* come next, and so on through the topics that begin with *z*. Whenever you need to find a main topic in the index of a book, use alphabetical order just as you do when you look up a word in a dictionary list.

When you use the index of a book to help you find information that will help you answer a question, you must decide what word to look for among the main topics. We call that word the **key word.** Try to choose as a key word one that names what the question asks about.

Often a key word for a question is one of the words in that question. Which word would you use as a key word for each of the following questions:

1. Who invented the telephone?
2. What do squirrels eat?
3. What are the different kinds of bears?

In some questions there may be more than one word that should be used as a key word. For example, take the question:

What work do elephants do in a circus?

If you use only the word *elephants* as a key word, you may find only part of the information that the book gives on the question. You may need to use the word *circus* as a key word also in order to find the rest of the information that the book gives.

In each of the following questions, there are two words that might be used as key words. What are they?

4. Is Mars the smallest planet?
5. Are whales the largest of mammals?
6. Were fireworks first used in China?

In the part of an index shown on page 253, find the main topic **Bats.** After it you can see these three groups of words: *food of, kinds of, superstitions about.* Each of these groups of words is called a **subtopic.** The three subtopics show what the book tells about the main topic **Bats.**

When you read a subtopic in an index, always think of the main topic. When you read *kinds of* after **Bats,** think *kinds of bats.* When you read *cities* after **Alaska,** think *cities in Alaska.*

In most indexes, subtopics are arranged in alphabetical order. After each subtopic you will find one or more numbers. Each of those numbers is the number of a page on which information is given about the subtopic. A dash between two numbers, such as 70-74, means that information is given not only on pages 70 and 74, but also on the pages between 70 and 74. When no subtopics are given after a main topic, the numbers listed are the numbers of the pages on which information is given about the main topic. For example, notice that in the part of an index on page 253, no subtopics are listed after **Alaska Highway.**

Discussion

Help your class answer these questions:

1. What is an index? Where will you usually find the index of a book?
2. What are main topics in an index? What are subtopics? How are they arranged?
3. What subtopics are given after the main topic **Arizona?** After the main topic **Bananas?**
4. What is the key word for each of the first three numbered questions on page 254?
5. Why will you sometimes need to use more than one word as a key word for a question? What words should be used as key words for each of questions 4, 5, and 6?
6. What does the dash between two page numbers tell you?

On your own

On what pages listed in the part of an index on page 253 would you expect to find information on the following questions. Write and number your answers on a sheet of paper.

1. When was the Alaska Highway built?
2. What national parks are located in Arkansas?
3. Is Boston the largest fishing port in the United States?
4. Is baseball the most popular sport in Japan?
5. What is the largest city in Australia?
6. What is the largest Indian tribe in Arizona?
7. For what purposes can atomic power be used?
8. Is the Amazon River the longest river in Brazil?

Checking your work

If you are asked to do so, read aloud one or more of your answers. If you made a mistake in any, find out why it is a mistake.

The Mystery of the Moon Guitar

by Marie Niemeyer

Su-Lin Lee had heard the story of the moon guitar from Grandfather. Very lovely and shaped like the moon, the guitar was a family treasure that Great-grandfather had brought from China when he came to San Francisco. But the guitar had not been seen since it disappeared at the time of the San Francisco earthquake in 1906, over sixty years ago.

One day Grandfather told the story of the moon guitar to Tracy, Su-Lin's new friend, and the girls decided to do a little detective work. In Great-grandfather's old school books they found the address of the mansion in which he had lived as a servant. From an old note they discovered, they guessed the guitar might be hidden in a wall of Great-grandfather's room.

Finding the mansion empty and about to be torn down, the girls decided that they must begin their search at once. But first Tracy told someone else the secrets she and Su-Lin had uncovered. That someone was Grandfather's friend Mr. Wu, an art dealer interested in old Chinese treasures.

In this story from the book *The Moon Guitar*, Su-Lin tells about the exciting treasure hunt and lively chase through the narrow streets of San Francisco's Chinatown.

The next day was Saturday. Tracy waited for me on our usual corner, holding an old flight bag that looked pretty heavy.

"What's that?" I asked. I heard the clank of metal as she gave it a shake.

"Tools I borrowed from my brother," she said. "Hammer, chisel, saw, and my big flashlight." She opened the bag and held it up to show me.

"I can see you're planning to get a head start on those wreckers," I said.

"Well, who knows what we might have to take apart? I don't feel like using my fingernails."

The bus trip to Sacramento Street was too short for comfort. The sight of Tracy's tools had made this whole crazy plot unpleasantly real. I would have liked to have more time to think about it—like maybe a year.

Tracy bounded off the bus in high good humor. I followed her. She was feeling great. I was not.

The quiet street was empty. The lonesome houses seemed to stare at us as we walked down the street. I had the queerest notion that they didn't want us here. Another strange feeling was growing on me, too—the feeling of eyes, somewhere, looking at me. Once I turned around quickly, but I saw nobody.

The big iron gate and the door with the broken glass looked exactly as we had left them. We squeezed by the gate and pushed at the door. It opened slowly with an awful creak.

"*Ee-ee*, what a welcome," said Tracy nervously.

"If there's anybody in the house, they now know we're here, too," I said.

"Never mind the happy thoughts." Tracy's voice sounded shaky. "Let's pretend it's a treasure hunt. Where do you guess we should start looking?"

I looked down the little hall. A steep and narrow flight of stairs went up from where we stood to the first floor of the house. Ahead to the left I saw the open door of a big room that was evidently the front half of the basement. Straight on to the back, the hall opened out into another big room.

"Down here," I said and led the way. Two old laundry tubs, a little sink, and a place for a stove showed that this had been a kitchen.

"Do you know what Grandfather told me about Chinese servants in big old mansions like this?" I asked Tracy. "He said that they always lived in a little room off the kitchen."

Tracy looked around and went quickly to a door across the room. "It's here," she cried triumphantly. I came over and looked in. My own great-grandfather had lived here. Here, in this dark little room, with its one narrow window, he had lived and worked and raised his son.

For the first time, I began to wonder about him. He had had the courage to break the tie that held him to his family in China. He had made his way in a strange, new world. He, out of all my family, might have understood my longing to get free of the old ways. "We would have liked each other, my great-grandfather and I," I told Tracy.

"I hope he doesn't mind if we look for his moon guitar," she said. "Now, you said the word *north* was in that note. Sacramento Street runs east and west, so . . ." She walked over and put her hand on one of the blank walls. "This must be the north wall."

"Right," I agreed. "But now what?"

Tracy put her satchel down next to her, took out the chisel, and began, in a very businesslike way, to thump the cracked walls with the handle. Clouds of dust billowed out at every bang, and shreds of old wallpaper fluttered to the floor.

I just stared at her.

"I'm trying to find out if there's a hollow place in the wall," she said. "This is the back wall of the house, so it's pretty solid. If there's a little empty spot like a hiding place, it should sound different when I hit it."

"Then you'd better pound a lot softer," I whispered. "If anybody's looking for us, you'll lead them right here." I was beginning to get that unhealthy "followed" feeling again, right between the shoulder blades.

Tracy didn't answer. She had stopped at one particular place in the wall and had put one ear against it while she tapped very gently. I held my breath.

"This sounds different!" Her voice was excited. She pulled off a big piece of the tattered wallpaper. Even to my eyes, the part of the wall underneath looked different from the surrounding area. It was patched-looking and rough, as if some inexpert person had tried to even out the plaster.

"And there are fingerprints in it," Tracy cried. She attacked the wall with hammer and chisel. Within seconds, she had made a tiny hole. Then she gave the wall an enormous whack. A big piece of the plaster fell out, exposing a hole in the wall behind it. Tracy put her hand into the hole and felt around in it. "There's something here!" she exclaimed. "I can feel it, but I can't get a grip on it."

I went over to her and held out my hand for the tools. This

was the moment we'd been waiting for, and I wanted to finish our search with my own hands. "It's my turn now," I said.

She stepped back and put the hammer and chisel into my hands. "Give it a good sock," she said, with a huge grin.

I hit the wall a good one with the hammer. The whole center of the patched place shattered and fell away. Inside the hiding place lay a package. It looked like a bundle of nothing at all. Silently, I reached in and took it out. It was something large and hard, wrapped in cloth that must have been white once but now was yellow with age.

Gently, I unwrapped the layers of silk. There before me lay the moon guitar. It was as Grandfather had described it—shiny black lacquer, inlaid with jade and mother-of-pearl, and trimmed with tassels of gold. It looked as perfect as it must have the last time a Lee had touched it, sixty years ago.

Tracy now touched it with one careful finger. "It's the most beautiful thing I ever saw," she breathed.

I smoothed the lacquer. "I can't believe we've really done it," I said. I felt very close to the man who had lived in this room. We had found his treasure, and now it would go back to his family where it belonged. I had a lovely warm feeling of satisfaction as I carefully rewrapped the guitar in its yellowed cloth.

Suddenly Tracy froze. She was looking toward the window. "Did you see something out there?" she asked in a whisper.

I went over to the window and tried to look through the dirty glass. I could see nothing at all, but I went back and picked up the guitar. "Let's leave," I said to Tracy. I couldn't prove it, but I still had the sensation that we were being watched. I wanted to get away quickly from this silent old house.

Then we heard a creak and another creak from the stairs.

Someone was coming downstairs. I put my finger to my lips and pointed to the front room. If we could get in there without the intruder seeing us, we could get out the basement door and out of the house. We tiptoed across the kitchen. I heard the footsteps coming closer and closer.

"Now run!" I yelled. We tore across the front room, into the tiny hall, and out the basement door.

Down the street, the bus had let off one lone passenger, and the doors were already closing. We began to yell as we ran. The driver looked around, opened the doors again, and then shut them quickly behind us. We staggered up the aisle and found seats.

After a few minutes, Tracy got her voice back and asked, "Did anyone follow us, do you think?" She craned her neck, trying to see back along the street.

"I don't know," I said. "Anyway, nobody else made the bus." I looked out of the window at a little red sports car waiting next to the bus at the stoplight and immediately got an unpleasant shock. The driver was staring up at me in a very meaningful way. As I looked, the light changed and he shot ahead.

Rapidly, I told Tracy what I had seen. "I've never seen him before," I said, "but he looked as if he knew me. We'd better get off the bus at Powell. We may surprise him by getting off there, and he probably won't be able to park his car at a moment's notice and follow us."

As we hurried off the bus at Powell Street, Tracy clutched at my arm. Of all the luck—the little red sports car was sliding into a parking place at the corner. Out jumped the man I had seen. He came up to us in two long steps.

Without a word he snatched the wrapped moon guitar from under my arm and gave me a push that sent me flying. Then he disappeared around the corner into Powell Street. Tracy darted after him and came running back in a few moments.

"I saw where he went," she reported breathlessly.

I picked myself up and brushed off my skirt angrily. "I don't know what we can do, but I'm not going to give up now." I said. "Come on!"

We rounded the corner on the run. Tracy pointed out the shop she had seen him go into. It was on the street level of an old gray stone building, just a little hole-in-the-wall shop, with a narrow door and one small display window. The gilt letters on the window, with Chinese characters below—all dull and blurry with age—said WU AND SON, CHINESE ART.

I crept up to the front door and listened. Not a sound. Then I risked a look. The faded curtains were drawn over the door and window. There was no sign of life inside.

Tracy beckoned to me eagerly. She was standing at the head of the tiny alley that ran alongside the building. Partway up was another door.

"Bet it's their back door," she whispered. She tiptoed up to it, stood close, then frowned and shook her head. "I hear voices, but I can't understand what they're saying. You try."

I put my ear to the door. For a few seconds I could hear nothing at all. Then came a man's voice, speaking in Chinese.

"Yes," he said clearly, "this is the moon guitar. You have done well, my son. It is indeed a treasure. You are sure you were not followed? Good. Then leave me alone with my treasure."

I heard the movement of chairs inside the room, then footsteps coming toward the door. I grabbed Tracy's hand, looking around wildly. Farther up the alley a flight of basement steps offered our only chance. We jumped down them, landing in a confused heap at the bottom. The back door of Mr. Wu's shop opened, and I heard footsteps come out into the alley. They stopped. There was a frightening silence, then a rapid tap-tap-tap receding toward the street.

I dared a glance down the alley. It was the man from the red sports car. He went out of the alley without looking back, and I began to breathe again.

My head was in a whirl. Mr. Wu was nothing but an old pirate! And his son was another. I told Tracy what I had heard.

"This whole mess is my fault," she whispered. "If I hadn't told him everything I know, he wouldn't have the guitar now."

I patted her consolingly. I was beginning to have the ghost of an idea. Fortunately, it looked as though Mr. Wu would stay put for a while. I wouldn't need more than a half-hour to get my plan going.

"I think I know how we can get it back," I said in a low voice. "But I have to get to my house right away. You stay here on the stairs and watch that door. If he leaves with the guitar, follow him, and call me when you can. I'll go home again if you're gone when I get back."

Tracy clutched my hand as I got up. "But what are you going to do?"

"No time to explain now. You'll see!"

I tiptoed up the steps. The alley was empty. A quick inspection showed me that no one was lurking on the street outside, so I headed for home fast. I was hoping that Grandfather and my brother, Chickie, would be out.

They were out, luckily. It took me five minutes to collect

what I needed and get back downstairs. I had almost reached the door when a boy loomed up in the opening. We were saved from a head-on collision only by his neat side step. It was Tracy's brother, Scott.

"Hi," he greeted me cheerfully. "Where's Tracy?"

I tucked my big cardboard box under my arm and grasped his hand. "Come on," I panted, dragging him after me. As we ran down the street, dodging the slow-moving Saturday strollers, I managed to gasp out most of the story.

"Boy!" His voice was excited. "Sounds as if you two could use some help." Even in my panicky condition, that was enough to slow me down to a fast walk.

"Help!" I retorted. "We've been doing just fine by ourselves, I'd say."

"Okay, okay," Scott said soothingly. "But what are you going to do now?"

"You'll see," was all I would say. I hitched the box up under my arm and went right on.

When we got to where I had left Tracy on guard, it looked as though she hadn't moved an inch since I'd left. Huddled against the wall, she gave me an accusing look. "What did you bring *him* for?" she demanded. "And why did you take so long? I never was so scared in my life!"

Well, I didn't blame her for that. This dim, quiet place gave me the creeps, too. "I found him on my doorstep," I told her, "and I brought him because I thought we might need him."

Scott folded his arms and plopped down on a step. "I don't move another inch until I find out what's on your minds," he said firmly.

I put the cardboard box down on the step next to Tracy and opened it. In the box lay all of Chickie's fireworks, the treasure he had been saving for Chinese New Year. Stacks of red-wrapped firecrackers and sinister-looking red cylinders made a gorgeous display.

Scott gave a long, low whistle. "I'm beginning to see your idea," he said, "and I don't believe it. Have you got rocks in your head? Why don't you get the police?"

I gave him a scornful look. "And how do we convince them we're the real owners of the moon guitar?" I asked belligerently.

Scott shook his head. "I suppose you're right," he admitted. "But if you're thinking what I think you're thinking, it's absolutely nutty. It'll never work."

I took a big cannon cracker out of the box and waved it under his nose. "We've got to get him to open the door, and I think this ought to do it."

I couldn't help laughing. I personally thought it was a pretty good idea. I had seen something like it in one of those spy shows on TV, and I had been dying to try it ever since. So I picked up the box of fireworks and started up the steps.

Tracy stood up, brushed off her clothes, and followed. "After all the work we did to get that guitar," she said to her brother, "I'm not going to let that man beat us out. So there!"

I felt like a general as I set up my army. Scott took his position at the far end of the alley, with the box of firecrackers at his feet. Tracy and I stood at the corner of the shop, where the alley met the street and where we could see both front and back doors.

I took one quick look in both directions. Then I lifted my hand and made a huge, dramatic, downsweeping gesture. Scott lit one of Mother's big kitchen matches and dropped it into the box of firecrackers. Then he ran like crazy for the head of the alley.

There was a breathless moment of silence, and then the firecrackers let go. Little ones popped and big ones banged. A package of sparklers blossomed all at once, while a big Roman candle sprayed a rain of colored sparks at the sky. In the narrow alley, the noise was sensational.

Mr. Wu's back door opened in the middle of the commotion, and he scuttled out into the alley. He threw up his hands at the sight of the smoke and sparks and began to shout in Chinese. As if bewildered, he took a few steps forward, then turned to run down the alley, waving his hands frantically over his head.

That was our signal. Scott and Tracy and I raced to the front door of the shop. Mr. Wu was standing in the street, still yelling in Chinese as we piled into the tiny room.

It was dim and dusty, its walls lined with ceiling-high cabinets of dark wood. The one long counter was bare. I made for the swaying bead curtain that separated the front part of the room from the back.

There it was — the moon guitar! Lying on a small table, it looked unexpectedly beautiful in the dingy room. I rushed over and picked it up. Then Scott grabbed me and whirled me around.

"Out, quick!" he shouted. We ran back to the front door, stepping on each other's toes as we pushed through. Out in the street, a crowd had gathered around Mr. Wu. They were all yelling at once, pushing and shoving and pointing up the alley.

Then a man spotted us. He burst into a flood of Chinese and pulled at Mr. Wu's arm. Mr. Wu spun around, screeching at us angrily as he started toward us.

I looked up and down the street desperately. We were standing a few steps from the Powell Street entrance of the YWCA. Here was a chance. If we could get through the "Y" and out the back way, maybe we could lose him.

"Run through the 'Y'!" I screamed. We took off down the street at a mad pace. Mr. Wu was almost at our heels as we reached the entrance and plunged through the door.

We ran across the lobby, making for the stairs that led to the lower level. We were down the first flight before the startled-looking woman at the desk could do more than reach out a hand to stop us.

On the first landing, I stopped to listen. I heard the quick tap of heels across the lobby, a sharp question, a soft answer, and then the tap of heels again running toward the stairs.

On we went, down the stairs and out the door that led to the garden in back.

We ran headlong across the garden toward the little gate in the wall. I reached it first and gave the handle a twist. Nothing happened. Scott pushed me aside and heaved at it. Again, nothing.

Now I turned to look back. A crowd of people appeared on the other side of the garden, headed by Mr. Wu and the building's janitor. They hurried toward us. Desperately, I turned back to Scott. One more mighty heave, and with a rusty creak, the gate swung open and we were safely through.

Su-Lin, Tracy, and Scott manage to escape the crowd and return the moon guitar safely to Grandfather Lee. But the story does not end here, for the moon guitar holds a secret yet to be discovered. You can find out what that secret is by reading Marie Niemeyer's book *The Moon Guitar*.

AUTHOR

Marie Niemeyer, a native of New York, now lives in California. She has worked as a writer, but *The Moon Guitar* is her first book for young people.

Many Chinese-American families live in the area where she and her family now make their home. She says getting to know some of them is "one of the nice things about living on the West Coast."

The Moon Guitar is set in San Francisco, which is only a few miles north of Ms. Niemeyer's home. She wanted to make certain that all the events in the story were possible and that the setting was accurate. She spent a lot of time in San Francisco walking through the area and looking carefully at the stores, streets, and alleys, as well as the people.

Trip: San Francisco

I went to San Francisco.
I saw the bridges high
Spun across the water
Like cobwebs in the sky.
                    Langston Hughes

TAKING AWAY AND PUTTING INTO

by Louisa Shotwell

Roosevelt Grady wished that he and his family could stay and live in one place, but they had to keep moving from one place to another in order to make a living. This story from the book *Roosevelt Grady* tells about one of his reasons for wanting to stay in one spot.

The Opportunity Class. That's where the bean-pickers got put.

Roosevelt Grady wondered what it meant.

Roosevelt knew about schools. Third grade, fourth grade, things like that. He knew about schools from experience: three weeks here, six weeks there, a day or two somewhere else. But Opportunity Class. This was something new.

Looking around the schoolroom, he decided that Opportunity Class must mean mixing up the little children and the big boys and girls in the same room. But why? Opportunity for what?

The teacher was Miss Gladys. She wore a black dress all wrinkles and chalk dust. She was skin and bones strung together; no soft fat places anywhere. She had a voice like the horn on Cap Jackson's beat-up truck, trembly but plenty loud. She taught with a stick.

The children sang. You couldn't hear anybody but Miss Gladys. Her horn-like voice drowned out the sound of everybody else. Roosevelt couldn't even hear himself, but he kept on singing anyway.

The stick jerked back and forth on each beat.

"Look away" (*jerk jerk*)
"Look away" (*jerk jerk*)
"Look away" (*jerk jerk*)
"Dixie Land" (*jerk jerk*)

In oral reading, *tap tap tap* went the stick on the blackboard, three taps for every word.

Two girls fell to laughing. Miss Gladys held the stick straight up in the air and high. It worked like

magic. The room got still as a piney wood. One thing was plain. Nobody wanted trouble.

Time came for figures.

Roosevelt looked at his work sheet. A whole page full of nothing but taking away.

Take 12 from 17. A cinch. He licked his stubby pencil and in the answer space he wrote a nice fat 5.

Take 28 from 33. Same old answer. He began to get bored. He made another fat 5 and this time he put a curly tail on it.

Take 29 from 84. Here was a mean one, but it didn't catch Roosevelt. He knew all about taking away. This answer had to be 55.

Miss Gladys must be crazy about 5's.

Roosevelt was sick and tired of 5's.

He was sick and tired of taking away. He wanted to learn about putting into.

At the last school where he'd been, they'd finished taking away and begun on putting into. That he liked. Being there when they began on something new made him feel regular, as though he belonged.

Besides, putting into had one special thing about it he had to find out.

So here he was in a new school, all ready to learn more about putting into, and not a thing to work on but the same old taking away.

He sighed. He went back and

added curly tails to the 55, bottom and top.

The boy behind him tapped on his shoulder and whispered, "What's that you're making?"

Roosevelt covered his paper with both hands and didn't answer.

The boy made a dive for the paper. In nothing flat the two of them were in the aisle, wrestling.

Crack! Smack down on some-one's desk came Miss Gladys's stick.

"We don't have nonsense here," she announced.

The boys slunk back into their seats.

Miss Gladys went on. "Here we never forget," she said. "We are the Opportunity Class."

That was when Roosevelt said it. He had no idea he was going to speak, but he did.

"Please, ma'am," he asked, "opportunity for what?"

Silence.

Somebody tittered and all at once the whole class burst out laughing. They roared and they rocked in their seats. The boys thumped each other. The girls poked their elbows into their neighbors' ribs and laughed with delight.

Shame burned inside Roosevelt's head, and his eyes smarted. He hadn't meant to be funny or fresh or anything. He simply wanted to know.

Up in the air went the stick and they all got quiet.

"Exactly what, young man," said Miss Gladys, "do you want opportunity for?"

Roosevelt felt miserable but he couldn't see any way to back down. "For putting into," he said. "Please, ma'am, I want opportunity to learn about putting into."

Miss Gladys stared at him.

He plunged on. "I'm tired of taking away," he explained desperately. "There's a thing I need to know about putting into."

Another silence.

Then came the surprise of the day. Roosevelt couldn't believe his ears. Miss Gladys giggled. And then she began laughing so hard she dropped the stick. She had to go and sit down behind her desk. She opened a drawer and took out a white handkerchief. She wiped her eyes and then she blew her nose, loud.

"Hands up," she said, "all those who are tired of taking away."

All over the room hands shot up.

"Hands up," she said, "all those who want to learn about putting into."

Again the air shivered with waving hands.

"Very well. Tomorrow," she said, "tomorrow all the big boys and girls will study putting into. That's a promise."

Roosevelt felt good. As if he belonged.

That afternoon, as the school bus rolled along beside the irrigation ditch, Roosevelt sank down into the cushy seat low on his spine and shut his eyes. He thought about putting into. About that special thing he wanted to know. Tomorrow he'd find out. Miss Gladys would explain it. Maybe she wasn't such a bad teacher, after all, even if she did have a voice like a trembly truck horn. Even if she did teach with a stick. Maybe the Opportunity Class was a good place for bean-pickers. A place where they could find out things. If they asked.

Back home in camp came the second surprise of the day, and this was not a good surprise. The Grady family was packing up.

"Beans all run out," said his father. "Nothing more to pick here. We'll pull out early in the morning. Head north."

Roosevelt's heart dropped. Here it was happening all over again. Not ever, probably, would he get to stay put in a school long enough so he'd really belong.

Too soon the Gradys were on their way, riding away from Roosevelt's chance to learn that thing about putting into. Roosevelt bunched his sweater underneath him to soften the jouncing

floor of the moving truck. He leaned his head back against his mother's arm. If the air got any chillier, he'd have to take his sweater out from under him and put it on to keep warm, but it wasn't quite that cold. Not yet.

Along with three other families, the Gradys rode in the back of the truck. All but Papa, who sat up front to spell Cap Jackson. Cap was the regular driver and he was the crew leader, too. He owned the truck, and in it he carried the people to places where crops were ready for picking.

"We're heading for beans and cucumbers," Cap Jackson said.

Roosevelt's mother sat straight up on the flat side of the family suitcase. It was made of metal and it was slippery, so she had her feet planted wide apart and flat on the floor to brace herself. On her lap she held the baby, Princess Anne.

Between Mamma's feet lay Sister. She was seven years old and dainty, with dimples. Her smile, Papa always said, could charm a snake out of a tree.

"Honest, could it?" Roosevelt had asked his father one time.

"Well, I tell you, Roosevelt," Papa said, "the first time we find a snake in a tree, we'll get Sister to smile at him and we'll see what happens." So far they hadn't found a tree with a snake in it.

On the other side of Mamma slumped Matthew, who was only five and chubby. Matthew had a lame foot, but that didn't keep him from enjoying life. He was great on making jokes, and he didn't miss a thing.

The truck had a canvas roof. The roof sloped up on each side to a peak like the top of a barn, and it kept you from seeing the sky. There wasn't enough light outside to see, anyway.

Between sleeping and waking, Roosevelt thought about putting into. He thought about that special thing he wanted to know. The question kept running around his head the way a mosquito teases you in the dark.

This was his question: When you put something into something else and it doesn't come out even, what do you do with what's left over?

What happened yesterday was exactly what had happened at the school where he'd first heard about putting into. The teacher came to where it seemed she must explain it the very next day. And then what? That time it wasn't beans that ran out. It was celery, but it didn't matter what the crop was. If it ran out, it ran out, and that was the end. The whole family packed up and piled into Cap Jackson's sputtery old truck and away they went to find a place where onions or tomatoes or some old thing was coming along ready to harvest. And same as yesterday, Roosevelt never got back to school to hear what the teacher had to say.

Some places there wouldn't be any school at all. Or else there'd be a school and the bean-picker boys and girls didn't get to go to it. The school would be for residents, and bean-picker families weren't residents. They didn't belong.

Once there was a school and it was closed when they got there. It was closed because the crop was ripe. A crop vacation, folks called this, and everybody picked, young ones and grown-ups and old people. Everybody except, of course, Princess Anne. Over in Louisiana she sat by herself in a fruit crate at the end of the strawberry rows and sucked her thumb, cute as a bug.

Roosevelt rubbed his eyes, leaned his head against Mamma's knee, and tried hard to go to sleep. He'd almost made it when buzz went that mosquito again, nagging at him about putting into. Like 3 into 17. You can't say 17's got six 3's in it, because six 3's need 18. So the answer has to be five 3's. But that's only 15. So what do you do with the poor little 2 that gets left over?

Roosevelt liked to have things come out even. He liked to have a place to put every piece of whatever it was he had. He liked to pick all the ripe beans quick and clean off one plant and then move along that row to the next. He liked to fill his basket just full enough so it was even across the top. If one bean stuck up in the air, he'd pull it out and make a little hole among the other beans and poke it carefully down in. He liked to make a pan of corn bread and cut it into exactly enough squares to make one piece for everybody in the family. Except Princess Anne. Her teeth hadn't come through far enough yet to chew anything crusty. Sometimes Mamma would break off a little of her piece of corn bread and dunk it in her coffee to soften it. Then she gave that to Princess Anne.

Bouncing along in the back of

the truck, Roosevelt got to thinking some more about numbers. Take nine. Right now nine was an important number in his life. He was nine years old. His birthday was the ninth day of September, and if you began to count the months with January one and February two and so on, what did September turn out to be? Why, nine!

To be perfectly sure, he whispered the months over to himself, counting on his fingers. Sure enough, nine came out to be September.

How many different schools had he been to in his lifetime? He counted to himself. Six, seven, eight . . . and nine. There was that nine again. Different schools, that is. If you counted twice the schools he'd been to and then gone back to, they made thirteen, but Roosevelt didn't want to count that way. He didn't like the number thirteen. Papa said thirteen was unlucky. Mamma said she didn't believe in lucky or unlucky.

One day a while back, Roosevelt had asked Papa about putting into and the poor little leftover number. He had laughed and said, "Just throw it away."

But Roosevelt couldn't feel right doing that. What would become of it?

Another day he had asked Mamma. She said, "Save it till you need it."

"What do you do with it," Roosevelt wanted to know, "while you're waiting to need it?"

Mamma didn't laugh nearly so often as Papa did, but she laughed that time.

"Put it in your pocket," she said, "and go fetch me a bucket of water."

The story you have just read is only the beginning of Louisa Shotwell's book about Roosevelt and his family. To find out how Roosevelt solved the problem of the poor little leftover number and how he tried to find a way for his family to stay in one place, read the rest of the book *Roosevelt Grady.*

A few years ago, Louisa Shotwell wrote a book for grown-ups about the problems of families like the Gradys—families who move around the country harvesting crops and who don't really have a home anywhere. While she was writing that book, she began thinking of a story she could also write about a boy who wished his family could find a place where they could "stay put." The boy turned out to be Roosevelt Grady, the hero of Miss Shotwell's first book for children.

Since then, she has written three other books for boys and girls. Her book *Beyond the Sugar Cane Field* tells about some of the children she met on her travels in India, Thailand, and Indonesia. Her other books, *Adam Bookout* and *Magdalena,* take place in Brooklyn, New York, where Miss Shotwell lives in the wintertime.

Although Miss Shotwell was born in Chicago and has lived in a number of different places, she regards her summer cottage on Skaneateles Lake in New York State as her favorite place to "stay put."

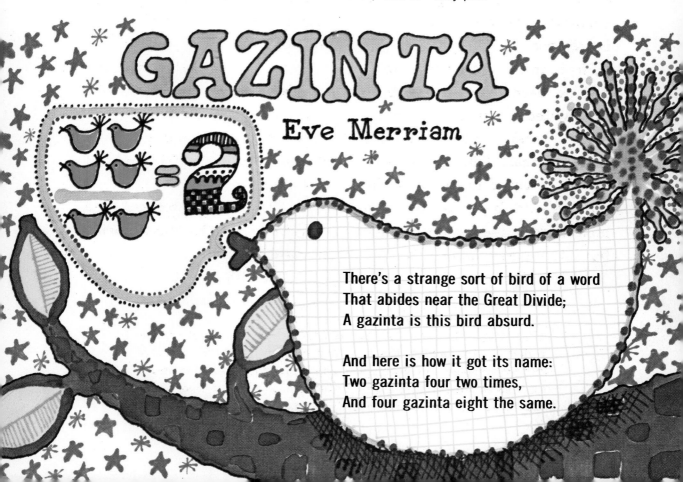

GAZINTA

Eve Merriam

There's a strange sort of bird of a word
That abides near the Great Divide;
A gazinta is this bird absurd.

And here is how it got its name:
Two gazinta four two times,
And four gazinta eight the same.

Bicycle racing can be fun. Here are some races you and your friends might like to try.

RACES ON WHEELS

by Jane Sarnoff

Snail Race

All racers line up with their bikes at the starting line. On the signal, the racers go as slowly as possible to the finish line. The rider who gets there last wins. Anyone who puts a foot on the ground before the finish line is out.

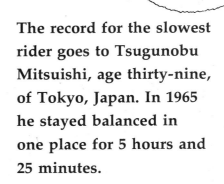

The record for the slowest rider goes to Tsugunobu Mitsuishi, age thirty-nine, of Tokyo, Japan. In 1965 he stayed balanced in one place for 5 hours and 25 minutes.

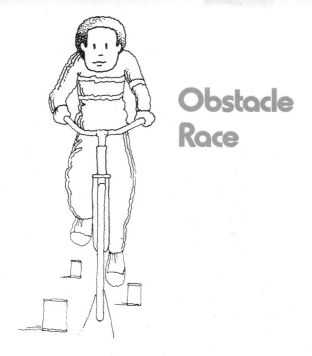

Obstacle Race

Set up a path about 5 inches wide and 45 feet long. Every 6 feet, first on one side and then on the other, put a large tin can or stone—no glass! One at a time, riders go down the middle of the path. Points are given each time the rider goes off the path or touches an obstacle. The rider who makes the best time and has the least points wins.

Coasting Race

The racers line up with their bikes twenty feet from the starting line. The starter stands by the line. On the signal, the racers pedal as hard as possible toward the line. At the line they stop pedaling and coast. The racer who coasts the farthest wins.

←———— 20´ ————→

about 20 feet

Slalom Race

Use the obstacle race-course. The riders, one at a time, weave in and out of the obstacles. Points are given for touching an obstacle or putting a foot on the ground. The rider who makes the best time and has the least points wins. The closer you ride to an obstacle, the more chance you have of touching it—but riding close will also get you to the finish line faster.

Quick-Stop Race

All racers start about twenty-five feet back from the finish line and on a signal ride as fast as possible toward it. The winner must get to the finish line first and must also stop the closest to it without touching or going over it and (the hard part) without skidding the wheels. One way to avoid skidding is to shift your weight to the rear as you start to apply the brakes.

THE SEA TURTLE

by Keith G. Hay

Roaming the oceans are the largest turtles in the world. These giant reptiles are called sea turtles.

If you and your whole family could get on the bathroom scales at one time, your combined weight would not equal that of the leatherback.

The leatherback is the largest of five different kinds of sea turtles found along our Atlantic and Gulf coasts. Some weigh more than 1500 pounds! The four other kinds are the hawksbill, ridley, loggerhead, and green turtle. This last one is not the tiny green turtle you can buy in the pet store, although it is a distant cousin.

Sea turtles have been swimming the open seas and coastal bays throughout the world for millions of years. They are powerfully built for their life in the ocean, with strong flippers for swimming and the ability to stay underwater for over an hour with only one breath of air.

Their huge, hard shells protect them against most enemies. But to a hungry shark, even a tough turtle looks good. When attacked, a sea turtle may raise its body and slap the water with its flippers to frighten away the attacker.

Turtles travel together through the open seas. A group may travel more than a thousand miles during one year. Much of their time

Turtles being fed by a diver at an aquarium.

clams, oysters, sponges, shrimp—even jellyfish.

We know very little about these giants of the sea. They are rarely seen except in zoos or large aquariums near the ocean.

We do know that they journey great distances at sea, but they return during late spring and summer to the same area every year to mate and lay eggs. In the United States, their nesting areas are mainly along the coasts from North Carolina to Texas.

During the summer nights when the tide is in, the big mother turtles swim ashore to build a nest and lay eggs. Each one wanders about the beach until she finds just the right spot for her nest. She digs a shallow pit in the sand with all four flippers. Then she begins to carve a round hole in the sand, using her hind flippers only. Very carefully she moves her body from side to side, cupping her flippers one at a time, neatly removing the sand. When the hole is as deep as she can reach—usually about two feet deep and ten inches wide—

is spent floating on the surface just sleeping. Sometimes they will wander up rivers that flow into oceans and get hooked by someone fishing. But not for long, for one swish from a huge flipper and the fishing line is broken. Many a fisher would be surprised to know that the "big one that got away" was really a very large sea turtle.

In the sea the turtles find many different kinds of food. They often dine on fish only, but sometimes eat sea plants, crabs,

A mother green turtle digs a hole in the sand.

She deposits her eggs in the hole.

she stops and begins to lay her eggs.

Once the eggs start to fall, she pays no attention to onlookers. Large "tears" stream down her face. But she is not really crying. Her eyes water constantly so that they will be kept clear of loose sand.

It takes the female turtle about twenty minutes to lay from 100 to 150 eggs. They are perfectly round, about the size of golf balls, and have thick shells which prevent their breaking as they fall into the nest. She immediately covers the hole with sand, packing it down with her flippers, and throws sand about to hide the nest.

After resting a few minutes, she turns toward the dark ocean, wearily walks into the surf, and swims out to sea. She leaves her eggs to hatch with the heat of

The mother turtle crawls back to the sea.

Tides have washed away one side of a nest, revealing the eggs.

Baby turtles hatch and crawl toward the sea.

A sand crab catches a baby turtle.

the sun, and her young to face the world alone.

During the summer, a mother sea turtle may "nest" several times. After each nesting, she rejoins her mate offshore. The father turtles never leave the sea, but wait until the end of summer when the group is once again free to travel.

The baby turtles hatch in about sixty days. Their size varies from one to four inches, depending upon the kind of sea turtle. Together they slowly dig and wiggle up through the sand. They wait until nightfall and then suddenly burst out of the nest to be welcomed by enemies eager to destroy them. On the shore are raccoons, wild dogs, hogs, and other enemies searching for a meal. In the sea wait large fish. No one knows what happens to the young turtles once they enter the ocean. They just disappear and are seen again only after they have grown up.

Few of the babies live to be adults. It's a good thing the

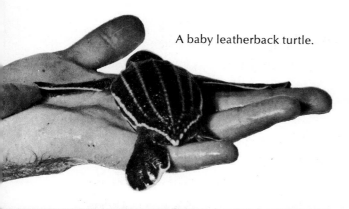

A baby leatherback turtle.

An adult leatherback turtle.

mother lays so many eggs because so few of her young do survive. But, even so, there has been a decline in the number of sea turtles.

Turtle eggs were once gathered and sold by the thousands in marketplaces. The meat of some sea turtles is very tasty, and many have been caught and used in soup or "turtleburgers." Few

beaches are left that sea turtles can use for nesting, and even these are slowly being taken over by people.

The United States government protects many wild animals by setting aside for them large areas of land called wildlife refuges. There they can live without being disturbed by people. Two of the refuges where sea turtles nest are Cape Romain in the state of South Carolina and Blackbeard Island, which is off the coast of the state of Georgia.

There are now laws, too, that help to protect sea turtles. It is illegal to hunt them at sea, and people are not allowed to take their eggs or to disturb the adults or young on land.

All these protections are necessary in order that these interesting and ancient reptiles may continue to live.

A young ridley turtle.

DISTINGUISHING BETWEEN FACT AND OPINION

The boys and girls in Mrs. Smith's class decided to put out a newspaper. They wanted to make it as much like a real newspaper as they could and planned to have many news articles in it. These would be factual reports of events that had actually taken place or that were going to take place. In addition, one page of the paper would be made up entirely of editorials. In the articles written for this particular page, individual pupils would express their opinions about different topics of interest to the class.

Tommy was chosen as one of the news reporters. He was supposed to turn in factual articles. For his first assignment, this is what he wrote:

> For the past five years, our school has had a Pet Day. This is a day when everyone may bring a pet to show to the class.
>
> On Pet Day last Friday, some cats and dogs got into fights. They even knocked over a bookcase in one room.
>
> Because of the fights, we probably won't be able to have Pet Day next year. I think there wouldn't have been any trouble if pupils hadn't brought cats.

When Tommy read over what he had written, he realized that two of his statements would have to be left out if the article was to appear in the class paper as a news story. He knew that a news story should give nothing but facts, but now he noticed that instead of keeping to facts, he had included some of his own opinions. Which of Tommy's statements do you think were statements given as fact? Which were opinions?

In the first two paragraphs, Tommy gave only statements of fact. Each of his four statements could be checked and proved true or false. But in his third paragraph he stopped giving facts and started giving opinions, telling what he himself thought. Can you pick out the words in Tommy's last two sentences which are signals that he was giving an opinion? Why wouldn't words like *probably* and *I think* be used in statements given as fact?

News reporters like Tommy are not the only ones who need to know the difference between statements given as fact and statements of opinion. You and everyone else who reads books, magazines, and newspapers should be able to distinguish between the two. You'll find that, once you have mastered this skill, it is easier for you to understand and make judgments about the statements you read for school work as well as for pleasure.

For instance, suppose you have always believed that the American space program and the accomplishments of the astronauts are extremely important and worthwhile. One day, however, as you are reading a magazine article about space travel, you come across the sentence: "America's space flights have been great achievements, but they have not been of any real value and should not be continued."

If you take this as a statement of fact, won't you have to change your thinking about the astronauts and the Apollo flights? Won't you have to question their importance? But changing your thinking because of that one statement would be both unfortunate and unnecessary, for the sentence quoted is not a statement of fact at all. It is a statement of the author's opinion and merely expresses his or her personal belief.

You can see why you need to be able to distinguish fact from opinion, but how good are you at telling the difference between the two? The first thing you should keep in mind is that statements given as fact can be tested to determine whether or not they are true. Such statements are usually made about objects, situations, or events whose actual existence or occurrence can be proved. If the author of the article about space travel had written, "Yuri Gagarin (yoo'ree gah gah'reen), a Russian cosmonaut, was the first man in space," that would be a statement of fact. You could test it by checking it in an encyclopedia or other reference book. Sometimes it is your own knowledge and experience that can be used to test a statement. Here are three more simple statements of fact:

My father's picture was in the newspaper yesterday.
Ms. Perez is in charge of the school science fair.
In 1985, Christmas will fall on a Thursday.

Statements of opinion, on the other hand, tell what one individual or group thinks, feels, or believes to be true. Often, such statements are easily recognized because they contain words like *probably* and *I think*—which Tommy used in the third paragraph of his newspaper article—or *possibly, apparently, It seems that,* and *In the author's judgment.* Here are some statements of opinion:

That chocolate pudding was much too sweet.

Lew seems nervous about the game with Westwood.

This picnic will be the best one we've had.

Whenever you have difficulty distinguishing between fact and opinion, ask yourself, "Can this statement be tested to find out whether it is true or false?" If it is, it is a statement given as fact. But if it tells what the writer believes to be true or how he or she feels about something, it is a statement of opinion. The examples and explanations given in the next three paragraphs will provide you with further help on recognizing the difference between the two kinds of statements.

"It is snowing outside" is a statement of fact. You could look outside and actually see for yourself whether it is snowing or not. But "It is a nice day outside" is a statement of opinion. It is based, not on fact, but on one person's belief or feeling about what makes a day "nice." You might think it is *not* a nice day outside because it is either warmer or colder than you like.

"Bill weighs ninety pounds" is a statement of fact. If Bill stood on some scales, it would be possible to determine just how much he weighs. But "Bill is a big boy" is a statement of opinion. It is based on someone's idea of how big a boy must be in order to be called "big."

"The Empire State Building is 1,250 feet tall" is a statement of fact. Although you couldn't measure the building yourself, you could look in a book and find out exactly how high the building is and whether the statement is true or false. But the statement "The Empire State Building is a beautiful building" is a statement of opinion. The person making the statement thinks the building is beautiful, but many other people might not agree.

Which of the following sentences are statements of fact? Which are statements of opinion?

1. I think our team will win the game easily.
2. His father is six feet tall.
3. It looks as though it will rain this afternoon.
4. She is a very good basketball player.
5. Ben's new bicycle has a flat tire.

Discussion

Help your class answer the following questions:

1. How does a statement given as fact differ from a statement of opinion?
2. Why wouldn't words like *probably* and *I think* be used in statements given as fact?

3. What two sentences can you think up as examples of statements given as fact?
4. What are two examples of statements of opinion?
5. Which of the five numbered sentences on the opposite page are statements given as fact, and which are statements of opinion? On what did you base your decisions?

On your own

Some of the following sentences are statements of fact and some are statements of opinion. Number a piece of paper from 1 to 10. After each number, write the letter *F* if that sentence is a statement of fact or write the letter *O* if it is a statement of opinion.

1. The average January temperature in Florida is higher than the average January temperature in Michigan.
2. Skating is more fun than swimming.
3. Alaska is the largest of our fifty states, but it has the smallest population.
4. No tennis player was ever better than Hazel Wightman.
5. *Treasure Island* is an unusually interesting book.
6. John Glenn was the first American to orbit the earth.
7. Watching football is as exciting as playing it.
8. A football field is three hundred and sixty feet long.
9. The world's highest mountains are in northern India.
10. Red is the best color for a bicycle.

Checking your work

If you are asked to do so, tell whether you wrote *F* or *O* for one of the ten sentences listed and explain why you answered as you did.

from

LITTLE HOUSE ON THE PRAIRIE
by
Laura Ingalls Wilder

The book *Little House on the Prairie* tells about the adventures of a pioneer family who traveled west in a covered wagon and settled on the grassy prairie of Kansas, which was Indian country in those days. The author, Laura Ingalls Wilder, really is the little Laura in the story. In addition to her mother and father, Laura's family included her two sisters, Mary and Baby Carrie, and their dog, Jack.

After traveling for many days across the prairie, Laura's father finally found a good spot near a creek to build their new home. Mr. Edwards, who lived two miles away and was their nearest neighbor, helped her father build a log cabin. The cabin wasn't completely finished right away because a stable had to be built for their horses, Pet and Patty. But even though the cabin was without a fireplace, had no door or windows, and had only the bare ground for a floor, Laura and her family felt snug and safe inside its stout walls.

The story you are about to read is only a part of the book. In it, Mrs. Wilder tells about an exciting time when she and her family were especially grateful for the safety that their little house on the prairie provided.

The Wolf Pack

All in one day, Pa and Mr. Edwards built the stable for Pet and Patty. They even put the roof on, working so late that Ma had to keep supper waiting for them.

There was no stable door, but in the moonlight Pa drove two stout posts well into the ground, one on either side of the doorway. He put Pet and Patty inside the stable, and then he laid small split logs one above another, across the door space. The posts held them, and they made a solid wall.

"Now!" said Pa. "Let those wolves howl! I'll sleep tonight."

In the morning, when he lifted the split logs from behind the posts, Laura was amazed. Beside Pet stood a long-legged, long-eared, wobbly little colt.

When Laura ran toward it, gentle Pet laid back her ears and snapped her teeth at Laura.

"Keep back, Laura!" Pa said, sharply. He said to Pet, "Now, Pet, you know we won't hurt your little colt." Pet answered him with a soft whinny. She would let Pa stroke her colt, but she would not let Laura or Mary come near it. When they even peeked at it through the cracks in the stable wall, Pet rolled the whites of her eyes at them and showed

them her teeth. They had never seen a colt with ears so long. Pa said it was a little mule, but Laura said it looked like a jack rabbit. So they named the little colt Bunny.

When Pet was on the picket line, with Bunny frisking around her and wondering at the big world, Laura must watch Baby Carrie carefully. If anyone but Pa came near Bunny, Pet squealed with rage and dashed to bite that little girl.

Early that Sunday afternoon, Pa rode Patty away across the prairie to see what he should see. There was plenty of meat in the house, so he did not take his gun.

He rode away through the tall grass, along the rim of the creek bluffs. Birds flew up before him and circled and sank into the grasses. Pa was looking down into the creek bottoms as he rode; perhaps he was watching deer browsing there. Then Patty broke into a gallop, and swiftly she and Pa grew smaller. Soon there was only waving grass where they had been.

Late that afternoon Pa had not come home. Ma stirred the coals of the fire and laid chips on them, and began to get supper. Mary was in the house, minding the baby, and Laura asked Ma, "What's the matter with Jack?"

Jack was walking up and down, looking worried. He wrinkled his nose at the wind, and the hair rose up on his

neck and lay down, and then rose up again. Pet's hoofs suddenly thudded. She ran around the circle of her picket rope and stood still, whickering a low whicker. Bunny came close to her.

"What's the matter, Jack?" Ma asked. He looked up at her, but he couldn't say anything. Ma gazed around the whole circle of earth and sky. She could not see anything unusual.

"Likely it isn't anything, Laura," she said. She raked coals around the coffeepot and the spider and onto the top of the bake oven. The prairie hen sizzled in the spider and the corn cakes began to smell good. But all the time, Ma kept glancing at the prairie all around. Jack walked about restlessly, and Pet did not graze. She faced the northwest, where Pa had gone, and kept her colt close beside her.

All at once Patty came running across the prairie. She was stretched out, running with all her might, and Pa was leaning almost flat on her neck.

She ran right past the stable before Pa could stop her. He stopped her so hard that she almost sat down. She was trembling all over and her black coat was streaked with sweat and foam. Pa swung off her. He was breathing hard, too.

"What is the matter, Charles?" Ma asked him.

Pa was looking toward the creek, so Ma and Laura looked at it, too. But they could see only the space above the bottom-lands, with a few treetops in it, and the distant tops of the earthen bluffs under the High Prairie's grasses.

"What is it?" Ma asked again. "Why did you ride Patty like that?"

Pa breathed a long breath. "I was afraid the wolves would beat me here. But I see everything's all right."

"Wolves!" she cried. "What wolves?"

"Everything's all right, Caroline," said Pa. "Let a fellow get his breath."

When he had got some breath, he said, "I didn't ride Patty like that. It was all I could do to hold her at all. Fifty wolves, Caroline, the biggest wolves I ever saw. I wouldn't go through such a thing again, not for a mint of money."

A shadow came over the prairie just then because the sun had gone down, and Pa said, "I'll tell you about it later."

"We'll eat supper in the house," said Ma.

"No need of that," he told her. "Jack will give us warning in plenty of time."

He brought Pet and her colt from the picket line. He didn't take them and Patty to drink from the creek, as he usually did. He gave them the water in Ma's washtub, which was standing full, ready for the washing next morning. He rubbed down Patty's sweaty sides and legs and put her in the barn with Pet and Bunny.

Supper was ready. The campfire made a circle of light in the dark. Laura and Mary stayed close to the fire and kept Baby Carrie with them. They could feel the dark all around them, and they kept looking behind them at the place where the dark mixed with the edge of the firelight. Shadows moved there, as if they were alive.

Jack sat on his haunches beside Laura. The edges of his ears were lifted, listening to the dark. Now and then he walked a little way into it. He walked all around the campfire, and came back to sit beside Laura. The hair lay flat on his thick neck and he did not growl. His teeth showed a little, but that was because he was a bulldog.

Laura and Mary ate their corn cakes and the prairie hen's drumsticks, and they listened to Pa while he told Ma about the wolves.

He had found some more neighbors. Settlers were coming in and settling along both sides of the creek. Less than three miles away, in a hollow on the High Prairie, a man and his wife were building a house. Their name was Scott, and Pa said they were nice folks. Six miles beyond them, two bachelors were living in one house. They had taken two farms and built the house on the line between them. One man's bunk was against one wall of the house, and the other man's bunk was against the other wall. So each man slept on his own farm, although they were in the same house and the house was only eight feet wide. They cooked and ate together in the middle of the house.

Pa had not said anything about the wolves yet. Laura wished he would. But she knew that she must not interrupt when Pa was talking.

He said that these bachelors did not know that other settlers were in the country. They had seen only Indians. So they were glad to see Pa, and he stayed there longer than he had meant to.

Then he rode on, and from a little rise in the prairie, he saw a white speck down in the creek bottoms. He thought it was a covered wagon, and it was. When he came to it, he found a man and his wife and five children. They had come from Iowa, and they had camped in the bottoms because one of their horses was sick. The horse was better now, but the bad night air so near the creek had given them fever 'n' ague. The man and his wife and the three oldest children were too sick to stand up. The little boy and girl, no bigger than Mary and Laura, were taking care of them.

So Pa did what he could for them, and then he rode back to tell the bachelors about them. One of them rode right away to fetch that family up onto the High Prairie, where they would soon get well in the good air.

One thing had led to another, until Pa was starting home later than he had meant. He took a shortcut across the prairie, and as he was loping along on Patty, suddenly out of a little draw came a pack of wolves. They were all around Pa in a moment.

"It was a big pack," Pa said. "All of fifty wolves, and the biggest wolves I ever saw in my life. Must be what they call buffalo wolves. Their leader's a big gray brute that stands three feet at the shoulder, if an inch. I tell you my hair stood straight on end."

"And you didn't have your gun," said Ma.

"I thought of that. But my gun would have been no use if I'd had it. You can't fight fifty wolves with one gun. And Patty couldn't outrun them."

"What did you do?" Ma asked.

"Nothing," said Pa. "Patty tried to run. I never wanted anything worse than I wanted to get away from there. But I knew if Patty even started, those wolves would be on us in a minute, pulling us down. So I held Patty to a walk."

"Goodness, Charles!" Ma said under her breath.

"Yes. I wouldn't go through such a thing again for any money. Caroline, I never saw such wolves. One big fellow trotted along, right by my stirrup. I could have kicked him in the ribs. They didn't pay any attention to me at all. They must have just made a kill and eaten all they could.

"I tell you, Caroline, those wolves just closed in around Patty and me and trotted along with us. In broad daylight.

For all the world like a pack of dogs going along with a horse. They were all around us, trotting along, and jumping and playing and snapping at each other, just like dogs.''

"Goodness, Charles!" Ma said again. Laura's heart was thumping fast, and her mouth and her eyes were wide open, staring at Pa.

"Patty was shaking all over and fighting the bit," said Pa. "Sweat ran off her, she was so scared. I was sweating, too. But I held her down to a walk, and we went walking along among those wolves. They came right along with us, a quarter of a mile or more. That big fellow trotted by my stirrup as if he were there to stay.

"Then we came to the head of a draw, running down into the creek bottoms. The big gray leader went down it, and all the rest of the pack trotted down into it behind him. As soon as the last one was in the draw, I let Patty go.

"She headed straight for home, across the prairie. And she couldn't have run faster if I'd been cutting into her with a rawhide whip. I was scared the whole way. I thought the wolves might be coming this way and they might be making better time than I was. I was glad you had the gun, Caroline. And glad the house is built. I knew you could keep the wolves out of the house with the gun. But Pet and the colt were outside.''

"You need not have worried, Charles," Ma said. "I guess I would manage to save our horses."

"I was not fully reasonable at the time," said Pa. "I know you would save the horses, Caroline. Those wolves wouldn't bother you, anyway. If they had been hungry, I wouldn't be here to —— ''

"Little pitchers have big ears," Ma said. She meant that he must not frighten Mary and Laura.

"Well, all's well that ends well," Pa replied. "And those wolves are miles from here by now."

"What made them act like that?" Laura asked him.

"I don't know, Laura," he said. "I guess they had just eaten all they could hold, and they were on their way to the creek to get a drink. Or perhaps they were out playing on the prairie, and not paying any attention to anything but their play, like little girls do sometimes. Perhaps they saw that I didn't have my gun and couldn't do them any harm. Or perhaps they had never seen a man before and didn't know that men can do them any harm. So they didn't think about me at all."

Pet and Patty were restlessly walking around and around, inside the barn. Jack walked around the campfire. When he stood still to smell the air and listen, the hair lifted on his neck.

"Bedtime for little girls!" Ma said cheerfully. Not even Baby Carrie was sleepy yet, but Ma took them all into the house. She told Mary and Laura to go to bed, and she put Baby Carrie's little nightgown on and laid her in the big bed. Then she went outdoors to do the dishes. Laura wanted Pa and Ma in the house. They seemed so far away outside.

Mary and Laura were good and lay still, but Carrie sat up and played by herself in the dark. In the dark Pa's arm came from behind the quilt in the doorway and quietly took away his gun. Out by the campfire, the tin plates rattled. Then a knife scraped the spider. Ma and Pa were talking together and Laura smelled tobacco smoke.

The house was safe, but it did not feel safe because Pa's gun was not over the door and there was no door; there was only the quilt.

After a long time, Ma lifted the quilt. Baby Carrie was asleep then. Ma and Pa came in very quietly, and very quietly went to bed. Jack lay across the doorway, but his chin was not on his paws. His head was up, listening. Ma breathed softly, Pa breathed heavily, and Mary was asleep, too. But Laura strained her eyes in the dark to watch Jack. She could not tell whether the hair was standing up on his neck.

Suddenly she was sitting straight up in bed. She had been asleep. The dark was gone. Moonlight streamed through the window hole and streaks of moonlight came through every crack in that wall. Pa stood black in the moonlight at the window. He had his gun.

Right in Laura's ear a wolf howled.

She scringed away from the wall. The wolf was on the other side of it. Laura was too scared to make a sound. The cold was not in her backbone only; it was all through her. Mary pulled the quilt over her head. Jack growled and showed his teeth at the quilt in the doorway.

"Be still, Jack," Pa said.

Terrible howls curled all around inside the house, and Laura rose out of bed. She wanted to go to Pa, but she knew better than to bother him now. He turned his head and saw her standing in her nightgown.

"Want to see them, Laura?" he asked softly. Laura couldn't say anything, but she nodded and padded across the ground to him. He stood his gun against the wall and lifted her up to the window hole.

There in the moonlight sat half a circle of wolves. They sat on their haunches and looked at Laura in the window, and she looked at them. She had never seen such big wolves. The biggest one was taller than Laura. He was taller even than Mary. He sat in the middle, exactly opposite Laura. Everything about him was big—his pointed ears, and his pointed mouth with the tongue hanging out, and his strong shoulders and legs, and his two paws side by side, and his tail curled around the squatting haunch. His coat was shaggy gray and his eyes were glittering green.

Laura clutched her toes into a crack of the wall and she folded her arms on the window slab, and she looked and looked at that wolf. But she did not put her head through the empty window space into the outdoors where all those wolves sat so near her, shifting their paws and licking their chops. Pa stood firm against her back and kept his arm tight around her middle.

"He's awful big," Laura whispered.

"Yes, and see how his coat shines," Pa whispered into her hair. The moonlight made little glitters in the edges of the shaggy fur, all around the big wolf.

"They are in a ring clear around the house," Pa whispered. Laura pattered beside him to the other window. He leaned his gun against that wall and lifted her up again. There, sure enough, was the other half of the circle of wolves. All their eyes glittered green in the shadow of the house. Laura could hear their breathing. When they saw Pa and Laura looking out, the middle of the circle moved back a little way.

Pet and Patty were squealing and running inside the barn. Their hoofs pounded the ground and crashed against the walls.

After a moment Pa went back to the other window and Laura went, too. They were just in time to see the big wolf lift his nose till it pointed straight at the sky. His mouth opened, and a long howl rose toward the moon.

Then all around the house, the circle of wolves pointed their noses toward the sky and answered him. Their howls shuddered through the house and filled the moonlight and quavered away across the vast silence of the prairie.

"Now go back to bed, little half-pint," Pa said. "Go to sleep. Jack and I will take care of you all."

So Laura went back to bed. But for a long time, she did not sleep. She lay and listened to the breathing of the wolves on the other side of the log wall. She heard the scratch of their claws on the ground, and the snuffling of a nose at a crack. She heard the big gray leader howl again, and all the others answering him.

But Pa was walking quietly from one window hole to the other, and Jack did not stop pacing up and down before the quilt that hung in the doorway. The wolves might howl, but they could not get in while Pa and Jack were there. So at last Laura fell asleep.

Laura felt a soft warmth on her face and opened her eyes into morning sunshine. Mary was talking to Ma by the campfire. Laura ran outdoors, all bare inside her nightgown. There were no wolves to be seen; only their tracks were thick around the house and the stable.

Pa came whistling up the creek road. He put his gun on its pegs and led Pet and Patty to the creek to drink as usual. He had followed the wolf tracks so far that he knew they were far away now, following a herd of deer.

The mustangs shied at the wolves' tracks and pricked their ears nervously, and Pet kept her colt close at her side. But they went willingly with Pa, who knew there was nothing to fear.

Breakfast was ready. When Pa came back from the creek, they all sat by the fire and ate fried mush and prairie-chicken hash. Pa said he would make a door that very day. He wanted more than a quilt between them and the wolves next time.

ABOUT THE AUTHOR

Laura Ingalls Wilder was born in 1867 in a log cabin on the edge of a Wisconsin forest. From there, with her parents and sisters, she traveled in a covered wagon across Minnesota, Iowa, and Missouri, to Kansas, where the family built a cabin on the prairie. Because they had settled on unfriendly Indian territory, they had to move on again. This time they moved to Minnesota, where they lived for several years on a farm on the banks of a creek. Then, when Laura was thirteen, they went west again to the shores of a lake in Dakota Territory. During the extremely cold winters, they lived in the little town of De Smet. At the age of fifteen, Laura began to teach school, and three years later she married Almanzo Wilder.

The books in which Mrs. Wilder told the story of her own childhood and young womanhood in the pioneer West are *Little House in the Big Woods, Little House on the Prairie, On the Banks of Plum Creek, By the Shores of Silver Lake, The Long Winter, Little Town on the Prairie,* and *These Happy Golden Years.* In *Farmer Boy* she wrote about the childhood of the farm boy, Almanzo, whom she later married.

After their marriage the Wilders lived, with their little daughter, Rose, on a farm in Mansfield, Missouri. At the age of sixty-five, Mrs. Wilder wrote the first of her "Little House" books. Her last one was published when she was seventy-six. Laura Ingalls Wilder died in 1957.

BOOKS TO ENJOY

THE BIG JOKE GAME, *by Scott Corbett*

Ozzie likes games and jokes more than anything in the world, but he learns that there is a time and place for being funny.

HUGO, *by Maria Gripe*

Hugo gets involved in schemes for earning money, along with Josephine and the mysterious new girl, Miriam. This is the third book in a popular series about Hugo.

THE TIME-AGO TALES OF JAHDU, *by Virginia Hamilton*

"In a fine, good place called Harlem," Mama Luka takes care of Lee Edward after school and tells him stories about an imaginary, mischievous boy named Jahdu.

TONKA THE CAVE BOY, *by Ross Hutchins*

The story of Tonka, a boy who lived very long ago in what is now Alabama, is based on recent discoveries unearthed from the floor of an ancient cave.

ME AND WILLIE AND PA, *by Ferdinand N. Monjo*

Tad, the youngest son of Abraham Lincoln, tells what it was like during the four years his father was president.

RICE CAKES AND PAPER DRAGONS, *by Seymour Reit*

Meet Marie Chan, a Chinese-American girl who lives in an unusual neighborhood in the middle of New York City.

THINK ABOUT IT, YOU MIGHT LEARN SOMETHING,
by Robyn Supraner

This is Jennifer's journal. In it she describes some of the wonderful and painful events in the life of a fourth-grader—all with a real sense of humor.

Crescendo

Crescendo

STORIES

PLAY

ARTICLES

POEMS

JUST FOR FUN

SKILL LESSONS

ALONG SANDY TRAILS

Ann Nolan Clark

My grandmother tells me,
 "Small Papago Indian,
 girl of the Desert People,
 for two summer moons
 I will walk with you
 across the sand patches,
 by the rock ridges
 and the cacti,
 through the dry washes
 and along the sandy trails
 that you may know the desert
 and hold its beauty
 in your heart forever."

I walk with my grandmother
  along a sandy trail.
The sand beneath my feet
  is damp and cool
  because, last night
  while I was sleeping,

clouds rained down
  upon our thirsty land.
Rain washed the flowers
  of all the cacti,
  the pincushion and the cholla,
  the hedgehog and the prickly pear.

The ocotillo branches
are tipped
with torches
of fire.

We sit by the trail to rest.
Nearby a giant cactus lifts
   its many arms
   to hold its flower crown
   against the sky's bright blue.
Beside me a lizard's track
   is penciled lightly
   on the sand.
I touch it with my fingers.

A cobweb hangs between two leaves
   like a lace mantilla
   spun of starlight thread.

A paloverde tree
    waves its golden flowers
    above my head.
Each flower has one white petal
    and four of yellow-gold.
I ask my grandmother, "Why?"
She says, "There are some things
    no one knows."

I see a gila woodpecker
  pecking the trunk
  of a giant cactus.
If I listen . . . listen . . . listen,
  I will hear him pecking.

Along the trail
  a roadrunner runs
  all stretched out
  as if he cannot get
  to where he is going
  fast enough, soon enough.
I look and see. I listen and hear.
There are so many things
  in this quiet land.

But I like best the quail.
I watch them walking,
  their black plumes bobbing
  from their red bonnets.
They walk across the trail
  near my grandmother and me,
  so busy talking together
  they do not see us.

Above us in the sky
  a hawk soars
  in slow, wide circles.
My grandmother whispers,
  "Watch. Be still.
  See the guard quail
  sitting on the cholla,
  not eating,
  not talking,
  just sitting.
  Listen. He is calling
  cra-er, cra-er, cra-er,
  warning his covey
  of the enemy hawk."

My grandmother knows so much.
I ask her, "Is this because
   you are Indian?"
She answers me, "Perhaps,
   but also I am old,
   and with years
   comes the knowing
   of many things."

Then my grandmother says,
   "Down the trail a little distance
   I will show you something
   to remember always."
We walk along and come
   to a spreading creosote.
Under its branches, on the ground,
   in a round place
   lined with desert grass,
   is a quail's nest.

In the nest are many eggs.
One is broken.
I count them
   but do not touch them
   or make a noise of any kind.
The eggs are pinkish in color
   with brown patches,
   purple spots,
   and dots of lavender.
Mother quail must love her babies,
   she makes so beautiful
   the eggs that hold them.

When quail eggs are hatched,
  the babies look
  like little round balls.
I have seen baby quail
  rolling along on the sand,
  their tiny plumes bobbing
  from their red topknots.
I wish I could see these babies
  rolling along.

I feel that I know them,
  having seen the eggs.
I like best the quail.
But my grandmother likes
  the giant cactus,
  standing tall and stark
  against the sky.

Giant cactus gives us
    many important things.
When it lies, a fallen giant
    on the sun-baked sand,
    its trunk withers and dies.
Then we use its bare, dry ribs
    to make our house walls
    and our fences.

The rainwater stored
   in its pleated trunk
   stays our thirst
   when the winds
   of the dry moon
   sweep across our land.
Its white and yellow flower-crowns
   ripen slowly to scarlet fruit
   that we gather
   and store as food
   for the time
   of the hunger moon.

Our baskets are filled
   with the ripe fruit
   of the giant cactus
   that we have gathered,
   my grandmother and I,
   and that now we take
   to my mother's house.
The sand beneath our feet
   is deep and shifting.
The way seems long
   and our baskets heavy.
We walk and rest.
We walk and rest.

After a time of just resting,
   happy and quiet,
   Grandmother says, "Come,
   little Indian granddaughter,
   the sun travels westward
   to make the day's ending.
   Your father has worked
   his fields.
   Your mother has woven
   her baskets.
   Nighttime is waiting."

"Your father has brought firewood
  for our supper fire
  and to light the evening shadows
  that come to bring
  the dark of night."

When we have eaten supper
  and the silver moon
  shines down
  on the ashes
  of the supper fire,
  I go into my mother's house
  and light a store-bought candle
  to remember
  all our walks
  these moons of summer
  along the sandy trails.

AUTHOR

Ann Nolan Clark was born in Las Vegas, New Mexico. Although she has spent most of her life in the Southwest, she has traveled and worked in other parts of the world as well.

In the southwestern United States there are many children who speak Spanish or an Indian language. They do not learn English until they come to school. Mrs. Clark was a teacher in the Southwest, and she wanted these children to have books to read before they knew English. She knew that children often like to read about things they know, as well as about new things. There were not any good books for these children who did not yet speak English, so she began to write books for them herself.

Many stories had been written *about* Indian children, but Mrs. Clark wrote stories *for* them. Indians translated them into their own languages and also drew the illustrations for them. These books were also published in English. Although the stories were written for Indian children, they are enjoyed by young readers all over North America and South America.

Because her books were enjoyed so much by Indian- and Spanish-speaking children in the United States, she was asked to work on books and other materials for children of Central America and South America.

In 1953 Mrs. Clark was awarded the Newbery Medal for her book *Secret of the Andes.* She now lives in New Mexico.

The Wise People of Gotham

by Eleanor D. Leuser

Characters

HERALD

JOHN
RICHARD
HARRY
TIMOTHY
ROBERT
GAVIN
MARTIN
FAIR ELLEN — *Townspeople*
MARY
BETSY
ELIZA
ALICE
JOAN

LORD HIGH CHANCELLOR
STRANGER

SCENE 1

TIME: *A long time ago in England.*

SETTING: *A square in the town of Gotham.*

(HERALD *is standing on a stone or a small platform as* JOHN, RICHARD, HARRY, TIMOTHY, ROBERT, GAVIN, MARTIN, *and* FAIR ELLEN *enter and gather about him, talking among themselves.*)

THE WISE PEOPLE OF GOTHAM by Eleanor D. Leuser is reprinted from *Dramatized Folk Tales of the World*, Sylvia E. Kamerman, Editor, Plays, Inc., Publishers, Boston, Mass. 02116. Copyright © 1966 by Plays, Inc.

HERALD: Come ye! Come ye! All good people of Gotham, I have a message from your King. (*Townspeople grow quiet as* HERALD *continues.*) The new King of England has just learned of your fair village of Gotham. He has also learned that never in the last one hundred years has Gotham been visited by royalty. He feels that this has been a grievous wrong that should be righted. Therefore, he is sending his Lord High Chancellor to Gotham to make arrangements for a royal visit and bids you welcome him. That is all. (HERALD *turns and exits.*)

JOHN: This is not good.

RICHARD: If the King comes, he will not be satisfied just to *see* our town. He will want to raise our taxes.

HARRY: He will probably plan to make public roads out of our farm lands.

TIMOTHY: He will take our best people to Court with him to act as his advisers. Our town will suffer.

ROBERT: It would be better if no outsider came for another hundred years, especially one from the Court.

GAVIN: And most especially the King.

MARTIN: But what can we do about it?

JOHN: There must be something.

FAIR ELLEN (*Jumping up onto the stone*): Listen, good people, all of you. I have an idea!

ALL (*Crowding around her; ad lib*): What is it? How? Tell us please!

FAIR ELLEN: When the King's Lord High Chancellor arrives, let all our townspeople pretend to be foolish and act half-witted. The Lord High Chancellor will be amazed and return to the King. His Majesty, hearing such a tale, will never wish to visit such a town.

JOHN (*Doubtfully*): But the King might punish *us*, the people of Gotham.

FAIR ELLEN: He would never punish us, for he would think we knew no better.

RICHARD (*Hesitating*): I do not know. I am afraid it might not work.

FAIR ELLEN (*Coaxingly*): But if the King does not come, he will forget about us. Then there will be no tax. Everything will be as it has been for another hundred years.

HARRY: It might be worth trying.

TIMOTHY: How would we go about it?

FAIR ELLEN: Let me talk to the women of the town. We will make the plans, if you will go along with us. Everything will be in readiness when the Lord High Chancellor appears.

ROBERT: Anything will be better than having the King come—

GAVIN: And tax us and upset all our lives.

MARTIN: I say Fair Ellen should do as she sees best.

RICHARD: Yes, yes, go ahead. Plan for us all to be exceedingly crazy.

FAIR ELLEN: I promise, you'll never be sorry. I shall gather together the women of Gotham, and we shall make our plans. (FAIR ELLEN *exits as the curtain falls.*)

SCENE 2

TIME: *Two weeks later.*

SETTING: *The same as Scene 1.*

(*The* LORD HIGH CHANCELLOR *enters.*)

LORD HIGH CHANCELLOR (*Looking all around*): I wonder where everyone is. (*Calling*) Ho, good people of Gotham! Come hither. I come from your King. Ho, there, I say! (TOWNSPEOPLE *peer out briefly from behind tree, bench, and platform, then draw back as* JOHN *enters. He is pushing a wheelbarrow upside down.* LORD HIGH CHANCELLOR *looks surprised.*) Fellow, what on earth are you doing with your wheelbarrow upside down?

JOHN (*Looking stupid*): Why, good sir, 'tis to make sure that no one will put anything in it. (*He laughs foolishly and wheels wheelbarrow off stage.*)

LORD HIGH CHANCELLOR: Methinks I never saw one so foolish in my life. (*Looking off stage*) Aha, here come some village women. (BETSY, MARY, ELIZA, *and* ALICE *enter, carrying boxes, pans, and butterfly nets. They chase each other about the stage.*)

BETSY (*Almost knocking down* LORD HIGH CHANCELLOR *as she pretends to catch something in net, just above his head*): Oh, I beg pardon, sir. I thought I had it.

MARY (*Approaching* LORD HIGH CHANCELLOR): It's there! It's there! (*She almost knocks his hat off.*)

LORD HIGH CHANCELLOR (*Crossly*): My good ladies, what *are* you doing?

ELIZA: We are trying to catch the sunshine, sir.

LORD HIGH CHANCELLOR (*Astounded*): Catch the sunshine! Are you crazy?

ALICE (*Winking at others*): Of course not, good sir. (*Gesturing toward backdrop or toward wings*) You see, our houses have become so overshadowed by these large trees that they are quite dark inside.

BETSY: We are trying to catch the sunlight to put inside our houses. Then they will be light as day.

LORD HIGH CHANCELLOR: 'Tis a witless idea. Catch sunlight, indeed!

MARY (*Looking sad*): Oh, what a pity. We thought it would work.

RICHARD (*Entering*): I've been listening to you women, and I have a better idea.

WOMEN (*Excitedly, ad lib*): What? How? Tell us!

RICHARD: I'll get the other men of Gotham to help me take the roofs off the houses. Then the sunlight will pour in.

WOMEN (*Ad lib*): Wonderful! Wonderful! A fine idea!

LORD HIGH CHANCELLOR: You numskull! The rain and the wind will come in, too. Leave the roofs alone and cut down some of the trees.

ALL (*Ad lib*): Why didn't we think of that? Naturally. Of course! (JOAN *enters, carrying a large feather.*)

JOAN (*Upset*): Oh, dear! Oh, dear!

LORD HIGH CHANCELLOR: Now, what is the matter with you, my woman? Why are you upset?

JOAN: Oh, good sir, this feather has lost its bird, and it is feeling so sad about it.

LORD HIGH CHANCELLOR: It would be more to the point if the *bird* were feeling sad about losing its feather. Is there no one with any sense in this town?

JOAN (*Hesitating*): Why, there is one person—

LORD HIGH CHANCELLOR: Go and fetch that person immediately, whoever it is.

JOAN: It's Mistress Ellen, sir. She's the brightest of us all.

LORD HIGH CHANCELLOR: Bring her here immediately. I cannot stand one more of these half-wits. (JOAN *exits briefly and returns with* FAIR ELLEN, *who comes dancing in and curtsies to the* LORD HIGH CHANCELLOR. *He addresses* ELLEN *severely.*) The townspeople say you have good sense. Well, you'd better try to give some of it to your neighbors. They don't seem to have any at all.

FAIR ELLEN: Oh, yes, sir!

LORD HIGH CHANCELLOR: Now, listen. Tell these people of Gotham that before the King comes to visit them, he must receive the first installment of their taxes. It seems they have never paid any taxes at all. When your people have proved their good faith in this matter, then the King will be pleased to visit Gotham. Now I must be gone. (*He leaves, muttering to himself and shaking his head.*)

FAIR ELLEN (*Standing on the stone as the townspeople gather round her*): Good people, you were all most beautifully mad. Yet, we must all be even more foolish than before if any other nobleman from the Court comes to visit us. Now, I have an idea about the taxes—(*All gather still closer about* FAIR ELLEN, *and as she begins to whisper her plan, the curtain falls.*)

Scene 3

Time: *Two months later.*

Setting: *The same.*

(John *is mending a net.* Betsy, Alice, Mary, *and* Eliza *each have a mirror into which they are gazing.* Martin *has a huge sieve into which he is trying to pour water.* Joan *is running about wildly.* Gavin *and* Harry *are holding a white rabbit.* Fair Ellen *enters and all stop their activities.*)

Fair Ellen (*Out of breath*): 'Tis good you are practicing your madness, for I have come to tell you that a stranger is coming down the road. I feel sure by his dress that he is from the King. Now, you each know what you are to say and do?

All (*Ad lib*): Yes, yes, we know. We are ready. (Fair Ellen *runs from one to the other, whispering into their ears, as they resume their activities.* Stranger *enters and watches them quietly for a moment before he speaks.*)

Stranger: Good day, my good people. You all look very busy. (*He goes up to* John, *who works intently on his net.*) What are you doing, my man?

John (*Making an O of his thumb and forefinger and holding it up in the air*): I'm taking holes out of the air and sewing them together to make a net. (*He smiles foolishly.*)

Stranger: Marry, good man, you are cleverer than I. (*He goes up to the women, who immediately close their eyes and hold up their mirrors as if to look into them.*) Good women, are you looking into your mirrors to see how fair you are?

Betsy (*Laughing*): Oh, no, good sir.

Alice: We are just trying to find out how we look when we're asleep.

ELIZA: That's why our eyes are closed.

MARY: Isn't it a good idea, sir?

STRANGER: Hm-m. A clever idea—or is it a foolish one? I begin to wonder. (JOAN, *who has started to run around again, bumps into him.*)

JOAN: I'm sorry, good master. I was just trying to catch something very important.

STRANGER (*Curiously*): And what is that?

JOAN: My shadow!

STRANGER: Why on earth would you want to catch your shadow?

JOAN: Then it could help me in my work. At present, it does nothing but follow me around.

STRANGER: I'll wager if you catch it, it will be the first shadow in captivity. (*He goes up to* MARTIN, *who is trying vainly to pour water into his sieve.*) What is your trouble, good fellow?

MARTIN: I do not know what is the matter, sir. This sieve will not hold a drop of water.

STRANGER: I cannot believe what I see or hear. No people can be as witless as these. (*Raising his voice*) Good people of Gotham, you have not yet sent your yearly taxes to the King. I have come to see what is the matter. (GAVIN *and* HARRY *come forward.* HARRY *carries white rabbit.*)

GAVIN: Oh, but we did, my lord.

HARRY: We tied the money around the neck of our pet hare and sent the hare on its way to the King.

GAVIN (*Pointing to the rabbit*): And here it is. It came back without the money, so it must have reached there.

STRANGER (*Groaning*): But don't you know that London, where the King is, is a good fifty miles from here? How much money did you send with this hare?

HARRY: We put a thousand gold pieces in a purse and tied it around the hare's neck.

STRANGER: A pox on such stupid fellows to waste so much money in such a stupid way. I cannot understand this situation at all. Methinks there is something strange going on. Begone, all of you, while I think this through. (*As all start to leave, he speaks to* FAIR ELLEN.) Wait, woman! You stay. You look as if you had some wits. I would talk with you. (*All but* FAIR ELLEN *exit.*) What is your name, good woman?

FAIR ELLEN (*Curtsying*): I am called Fair Ellen.

STRANGER: Perhaps, Fair Ellen, you can tell me what is happening in this town. Perhaps the King can help—

FAIR ELLEN: Why doesn't the King leave our people alone? He must know that we are poor and witless.

STRANGER: I have a feeling that those townsfolk are too witless to be true. I noticed you flitting from one to the other and whispering in their ears. I feel that some trickery is being played upon the King.

FAIR ELLEN: Oh, sir! Why would the people of Gotham do such a thing?

STRANGER: That's what I want to know. Tell me, Fair Ellen, and I will try to understand.

FAIR ELLEN: But will the King understand also?

STRANGER: I, personally, will see to it that the King does understand.

FAIR ELLEN: Then I shall tell you. We feared that if the King came to visit us, he would demand more taxes from us, take away our farm lands for roads, and send our best people to his Court.

STRANGER: You have an unfortunate opinion of your King. What then?

FAIR ELLEN: We thought that if we pretended to be mad, his messengers would go back and report that the whole village was crazy. Then the King would never bother to come here, and we would be forgotten.

STRANGER: I have the feeling that you were the one who invented this scheme to keep your village of Gotham safe. Is that not so?

FAIR ELLEN (*Smiling*): I had some small hand in it.

STRANGER: I thought so.

FAIR ELLEN: If the King were only like you, he might understand us.

STRANGER (*Taking off his cape and revealing royal emblem on his coat*): I *am* the King!

FAIR ELLEN (*Startled, then curtsying low*): Oh, Your Majesty, what have I done?

KING: Do not be alarmed, Fair Ellen. You have done nothing but good.

FAIR ELLEN: I am not certain whether I have been more wise or more foolish. I thought I was fooling both *thee* and the King.

KING: Your game has ended better than you think. All of you have made both wise and foolish things seem the same. It was a merry foolery, and it would have been a wise device if your King had turned out to be as stupid as you thought. I will leave your town of Gotham to its own manner of living. (*Calling*) Good people of Gotham! Good people of Gotham! I have good news for you! (*They enter, crowding around.* KING *mounts platform.*) I am your King.

TOWNSPEOPLE (*Ad lib*): The King! He is the King!

KING: I proclaim the village of Gotham to be free from taxes forever, and the town shall be under my personal protection. You have shown yourselves to be more clever than mad, and I have great need of such people as you.

TOWNSPEOPLE (*Ad lib*): Hurrah! Hurrah for the King! (*Curtain*)

UNDERSEA PARKS—
A New Wave in Hawaii
by Lorraine M. Ruff

What is there about Hanauma Bay in Hawaii that makes it such an exciting place to visit? Beautiful weather and quiet blue water are two very good reasons. But the things that make Hanauma Bay a *really* special place are the many kinds of brightly colored fish, unusual seashells, and napping turtles and the wonderful display of coral.

Thousands of years ago, a crater stood in the place of Hanauma Bay. The crater was part of a chain of volcanoes that ran along Oahu Island's eastern shore. During one of many volcanic eruptions, the side of the crater that faced the sea opened up. The sea rushed in, forming what is now Hanauma Bay. Over the next thousand years or so, tiny animals went about building the beautiful coral reefs that can be seen in the glasslike waters of the bay. But let's take a look for ourselves.

Imagine that you have just put on your mask, snorkel, and flippers and that you are sinking into the warm, clear waters of Hanauma Bay. What do you think you will see first as you glide over the coral seascape? You may see a moray eel wriggling out of its rocky den. You will almost be sure to see parrot fishes, surgeonfishes, and mullets. If you are a very good diver, you will be able to see the *humu-humu-nuku-nuku-apuaa,* or triggerfish. Giant stingrays will seem to fly just above the sandy bottom, throwing dark shadows over the small fish and plant life below. A short distance ahead may be a sleepy turtle resting on a coral bed. These large sea turtles often weigh as much as 150 pounds and are sometimes found snoozing in caves and under ledges.

But life in Hanauma Bay was not always this plentiful. About twelve years ago, hobbyists and collectors came to the bay and took away tropical fish, coral, and shells. Concerned divers and people living on Oahu loved their bay. They were afraid that maybe all would be lost if the plundering did not stop at once.

Parrot fish

Surgeonfishes

Triggerfish

A group of divers got together and looked over the bay. In their report to the government of Hawaii, they said that the bay should be set aside as a state park and that no collecting of any kind should be allowed. But picture taking was encouraged. Soon, the motto of Hanauma Bay became "Take beautiful pictures home instead of living animals so that others can enjoy."

Besides Hanauma Bay, the Hawaiian government has also set aside another offshore spot to protect it from collectors. Kealakekua Bay is the second undersea park in the state. There are no roads leading to the park, but there *are* boat trips that carry visitors there.

Why are the people of Hawaii setting aside offshore places? They are beginning to see that the sea is not an endless reservoir to use as a dump for people's wastes.

Perhaps if people see how beautiful the sea can be by visiting an undersea park like Hanauma Bay, they will think before they pollute the sea or carry home coral, seashells, or starfish.

Words in a Circle

You'll be going around in circles to find these hidden words! The arrow shows the direction you must go. For example, start with the letter N, and follow the direction of the arrow. You will find NEST. Then go back to a letter to spell another word. Did you go back to S and spell STAB? There are many other words in the circle. See how many you can find. At the bottom of the page are twenty-two of the words that are hidden in the circle.

	HONEST	ARE	LEAF	AS
NO	EACH	FARE	ALE	EAST	TABLE
ONE	REACH	FAR	TALE	LEAST	TAB
HONE	AREA	AFAR	STALE	ABLE	STABLE

355

SKILL LESSON

USING AN ENCYCLOPEDIA

You have learned that a dictionary contains thousands of words and that it is helpful to you in checking the spelling, pronunciation, and meaning of any word you're not sure about. But because a dictionary does give this information about so many words, there is no room in it for other kinds of information that you will often want to find.

Suppose you have been asked to tell your class about an important crop grown in this country, and you have chosen corn. You already know most of what a dictionary would tell you if you looked up the word *corn:* how to spell and pronounce it and that it is a grain or seed. To locate such information as how and where corn is raised, what products are made from it, and how valuable a crop it is, you can turn to an **encyclopedia.**

Because an encyclopedia is usually made up of many books, called **volumes,** it has space enough—unlike a dictionary of one volume—for long articles on nearly every subject, with maps, photographs, and other useful illustrations. While a dictionary explains in only a few words what an airplane, a horse, or an ocean is, in an encyclopedia you may find ten or fifteen pages of detailed information about each of those topics. An encyclopedia helps answer questions like these: How are astronauts trained? What causes lightning? When was baseball first played? Who discovered electricity?

The topics in an encyclopedia are usually arranged alphabetically. In the picture below, notice the letter or letters on each of the volumes. They are called **guide letters,** and they tell you the beginning letters of all the main topics listed in that volume.

All the topics that start with the letter *a* come first, followed by those starting with *b,* and so on. By using the letters printed on the spine (the narrow back edge) of the books, you can quickly find the volume you need. The numbers on the books make it easy for you to put back a volume you have used or to speak about one of the volumes by number.

In the encyclopedia shown, so many topics start with *C* and *S* that there are two volumes for each of those letters. To know whether you should look in volume 3 or in volume 4 for the topic *coal,* for example, you would have to think about the second letter of *coal.* Because *co* comes between *ci* and *cz* in alphabetical order, you would chose volume 4.

The letters on volume 11 shown on page 357 tell you that you would find in it any topic beginning with either *J* or *K.*

In order to find what you want to know in an encyclopedia, you must first decide on a key word to look for, just as you do when you are using an index. Suppose you are trying to answer this question: How did we make the discovery of the atom? The words *we* and *discovery* are too broad to be used as key words. That is, articles about those two topics would give so much general information that you would probably find nothing in them about the atom. And it is the atom, after all, that you're really concerned with. That is why *atom* should be your key word.

Often it is important to use more than one key word. To learn all you could about the mining done in New Mexico, for instance, you would look up both *mining* and *New Mexico.*

Except for the names of people, topics having more than one word are alphabetized by the first word. You would find **New Mexico** under *N,* **Space Travel** under *S,* and **Mount Whitney** under *M.* But to locate information about a person, you should use the person's last name as your key word.

To locate the key word *atom* in the encyclopedia shown on the opposite page, you would select volume **A.** But because all the topics in that book begin with *A,* you would have to think about the second letter of your key word in order to know where to start looking for *atom.* Since *t* comes toward the end of the alphabet, you would open the volume near the back.

CATBIRD is a North American songbird that is related to the mockingbird. The catbird is about 9 inches long and is slate gray in color. The top of its head is black, and it has a brick-red patch beneath the base of its long tail feathers. Catbirds breed in the United States and southern Canada, as far west as the Rocky Mountains. They fly south in the fall, and winter in the Gulf States, West Indies, Mexico, and Central America.

The catbird hides its loosely made nest of twigs and rootlets in tangled thickets and thick brush. Catbirds lay three to five bluish-green eggs. They sometimes eat strawberries, raspberries, blackberries, and cherries. But they help man by eating beetles, ants, crickets, and other harmful insects.

The catbird is an excellent singer, and has a delightful song. It can imitate the songs of other birds almost as well as the mockingbird can. The catbird gets its name from one of its mewing call notes, which sounds like a cat. The catbird sometimes sings for hours on warm, moonlit nights.

Scientific Classification. The catbird belongs to the mockingbird and thrasher family, *Mimidae.* It is genus *Dumetella,* species *D. carolinensis.* ALBERT WOLFSON

See also BIRD (color pictures: Other Bird Favorites, Birds' Eggs); MOCKINGBIRD.

CATBOAT. See SAILING (Kinds of Sailboats).

CATCHUP is a spiced sauce made from tomatoes. The name originated in the Orient from a word pronounced like "Kaychup." It is often spelled *catsup, katchup,* or *ketchup.* Catchup consists of tomato pulp, sugar, salt, mustard, vinegar, and spices. There is no standard formula for its manufacture. The U.S. Food and Drug Administration has established a "Standard of Identity" for catchup. This standard specifies what optional ingredients may be included in catchup. It also specifies, for some ingredients such as dextrose, the maximum amount that may be used. RICHARD A. HAVENS

CATECHISM, *KAT ee kiz'm,* is a system of questions and answers used for religious instruction in Christian churches. The first regular catechisms were compiled in the 700's and 800's.

Among the chief catechisms are the Lutheran, published by Martin Luther (1529); the Genevan, the work of John Calvin (1537); the Heidelberg or Palatinate Catechism (1563), used in the Dutch Reformed Church; the Anglican (1549-1661), found in the Book of Common Prayer; the Tridentine (1566), prepared at the Council of Trent, and of high authority in the Roman Catholic Church; the Shorter (1647) and Larger (1648) Catechisms, used in the Presbyterian Church; and the Methodist Catechism. FULTON J. SHEEN

CATECHU, *KAT ee choo,* is a brown, sticky substance obtained chiefly from the wood of tropical trees called acacias. *Cutch* is another name for catechu. This material is used in dyeing and tanning, and in medicines. The heartwood of the acacia is cut into pieces and boiled in water until a substance like tar or resin is produced. When catechu is partly hardened, it is formed into rough blocks or balls and wrapped in large leaves. It is marketed in this form. Catechu makes rich brown dyes used in coloring leather. It is also used to dye and print cotton cloth such as calico. FRED FORTESS

See also ACACIA.

CATERING is the preparation and provision of refreshments, service, and supplies. Catering services are often used for social events and in public eating places. The service ranges from an individual caterer who furnishes food and drink for a small party, to a catering company that provides everything daily for a large eating establishment. Typical events at which a catering service might be used include birthday parties, wedding receptions, cocktail parties, banquets, and conventions. Catering also is provided for use in hotels, restaurants, clubs, and cafeterias, and on steamships, railroads, and airplanes. T. KENT MORRIS

CATERPILLAR is a wormlike creature that is the second, or *larval,* stage in the life history of butterflies and moths. When a butterfly egg hatches, a tiny caterpillar crawls out and begins to eat. The caterpillar grows, but its skin does not grow with it as does the

Lee Smiley

The Caterpillar has strong, biting jaws. Its ravenous appetite makes it one of the greatest enemies of plants.

skin of most animals. Soon the skin becomes too tight, and the caterpillar prepares to throw it off. A split appears on the upper part, near the head end, and the caterpillar wriggles out. It appears in a new soft skin formed under the old one. In a few days this, too, is outgrown, and the process is repeated a number of times. In the temperate regions, most species remain in the caterpillar stage from two to four weeks. In very cold climates, some species take from two to three years to pass from the egg to the butterfly stage.

Appearance. A caterpillar usually has 12 rings or segments, not including the head. To each of the first three segments is attached a pair of five-jointed legs. These develop later into the legs of the adult insect. But the leg-like *prolegs* on the abdomen are not really legs, and are shed with the last skin. Occasionally, as in the so-called measuring worms, there are two pairs

of prolegs on the abdomen, and the larva moves by drawing these hind legs up to the front pair.

The head has six simple eyes on each side. The caterpillar guides itself by a pair of short, jointed feelers. Its strong, biting jaws differ from the sucking mouth parts of the butterfly. The body may be naked or covered with hairs, bristles, or spines.

Some caterpillars have glands that secrete an unpleasant fluid. Others have a sickening taste which saves them from being eaten by birds and other animals. False eyespots help frighten away attackers of some caterpillars, while long, whiplike appendages on the backs of other larvae are lashed about as a means of defense. But, in spite of these devices, very few caterpillars that are hatched ever reach the adult stage. Larger animals eat them, and parasites burrow into their bodies and kill them.

Habits. Caterpillars are heavy eaters. A butterfly or moth does all its growing during the caterpillar stage. The larva stores up the tissues that later are transformed into the adult insect. The adult grows no more after it grows wings. A few larvae, such as the silkworms, are valuable, but most are not. Sometimes, in years when caterpillars are numerous, fields are made bare of vegetation, and trees are stripped of their leaves. The cabbage worm, the cotton worm, the army worm, and the cutworms are especially troublesome. E. GORTON LINSLEY

Related Articles in WORLD BOOK include:

Army Worm	Larva
Butterfly	Measuring Worm
Cankerworm	Moth
Cutworm	Rotenone
Jumping Bean	Silk (Raising Silkworms)

CATFISH is the name of a large group of fish that have sharp spikes or spines on their breast and back fins. In some of the smaller species, these spines are poisonous and can give a fisherman a painful injury. Catfish also have *barbels,* or whiskers, around their mouths. Most catfish have no scales, but some of the South American kinds have bony plates over their skin. They are good to eat. The *channel catfish,* which lives in the Mississippi Valley and the Great Lakes, sometimes weighs as much as 42 pounds. Both the *blue catfish* and the channel catfish have tail fins that divide into a fork. The *brown bullhead,* or *horned pout,* and the *black bullhead* have square-cut tails.

Catfish make their nests in sheltered places. Some fishermen consider them a favorite because they bite at any kind of bait. They also eat waste matter that might spoil the water for other fish. A small species of catfish can be raised along with other varieties of fish in an aquarium. Its diet should include tropical fish food, earthworms, and raw meat.

Scientific Classification. The catfish belongs to the family *Ameiuridae.* The blue catfish is genus *Ictalurus,* species *I. furcatus.* The black bullhead is genus *Ameiurus,* species *A. melas.* CARL L. HUBBS

See also BULLHEAD; FISH (color picture, Fresh-Water Fishes); FISHING (table, Game-Fishing World Records).

CATGUT is a tough cord made from the intestines of certain animals and used mainly for the strings of musical instruments and for sewing up wounds. The word catgut probably came originally from *kit,* an old English term for violin. The strings of these instruments probably were first called *kit gut.* There is no evidence that the intestines of cats were ever used for violin strings. Most catgut is made from the intestines of hogs or sheep. The intestine casings are split into ribbons that are cleaned, cured, and spun into string. The string is dried and polished. Catgut is also used for stringing tennis rackets, on looms, in the controls of artificial limbs, and in the mechanisms of clocks and typewriters.

CATHARINE. See CATHERINE.

CATHARSIS, *kuh THAHR sihs,* literally means a *cleaning out.* In psychoanalysis, the term signifies the healing process by which the mind is cleansed of factors that tend to disrupt mental functioning and cause a person a great deal of anguish, anxiety, or unhappiness. These factors, mostly unconscious, include early harmful experiences, threatening impulses, and disturbing complexes. Psychoanalysts do not now use the term as often as they did in the early days of psychoanalysis. See also PSYCHOANALYSIS; PSYCHOTHERAPY. ALEXANDER A. SCHNEIDERS

CATHAY, *kuh THAY,* is the name Europeans once gave to China, especially the part north of the Yangtze River. From the early A.D. 700's to the early 1100's, a pre-Mongol people called *Khitan* controlled parts of China. The term *Cathay* came into the English language when it was used in a report by William of Rubruck in 1253. Marco Polo also called the country Khitai, or Cathay, in his account of his travels to the land of Kublai Khan. H. F. SCHURMANN

See also KUBLAI KHAN; POLO, MARCO.

The Channel Catfish lives in fresh waters of North America. It has a deeply forked tail and slender body. This species prefers clear, moving water, and is rarely found in muddy rivers.

The Blue Catfish, abundant in the waters of the Mississippi Valley, weighs up to 100 pounds. It is an excellent game fish, because it gives fishermen a hard fight when hooked.

Chicago Natural History Museum

William M. Harlow

Tall, Graceful Lombardy Poplars make excellent windbreaks in open areas. They grow much faster than most other trees.

POPLAR is any one of a group of fast-growing trees found throughout the Northern Hemisphere. Aspens and cottonwoods are poplars. About 10 of the 35 species in the group are native to North America. These trees have pointed leaves with wavy, toothed edges. Many kinds of poplars have such flat leafstalks that even a slight breeze will cause the leaves to flutter. Early in spring, before the leaves appear, small greenish flowers form in drooping clusters called *catkins.* Tiny seeds are hidden in fluffy cottony hairs that make it easy for the wind to carry them through the air.

Poplars grow best in moist places. They grow easily from *cuttings,* or cut twigs. People often plant poplars for shade trees because they grow fast. But they do not live long. Also, their roots tend to clog underground drainpipes and sewers. For this reason, some cities forbid planting poplars along streets. Poplar wood is whitish or light brown. It is also soft, light, and weak. Manufacturers use it to make boxes and crates. Papermakers use it for paper pulp and excelsior.

Balsam poplar, or *tacamahac,* is widely distributed across Canada. It lives as far north as trees will grow and south to the northern United States. The sticky buds and young leaves have an odor of balsam. Honeybees use the fragrant gummy substance to waterproof their hives. *Balm of Gilead* is a cultivated variety with heart-shaped leaves.

The *white poplar* has leaves that are silvery white beneath and have three or five lobes like a maple leaf. The bark on the branches is white. The *Lombardy poplar* looks like an exclamation point. It has diamond-shaped leaves and a tall, narrow shape. Its upright branches press toward the trunk. People often plant these poplars in rows in formal gardens, for roadside landscaping, and to shelter other plants from winds. These trees do not produce seeds.

The *Carolina poplar* is a hybrid derived from the native eastern cottonwood and the black poplar from Europe (see HYBRID). It has triangle-shaped leaves. This tree probably originated first in France about 1750. It can endure city smoke and dust and often is seen growing in large cities. All Carolina poplar trees are male and do not produce the cottony seeds.

Scientific Classification. Poplar trees belong to the willow family, *Salicaceae.* Balsam poplar is genus *Populus,* species *balsamifera;* white poplar is *P. alba,* Lombardy poplar is *P. nigra,* var. *italica.* Carolina poplar is *P. canadensis.* ELBERT L. LITTLE, JR.

See also ASPEN; BALM OF GILEAD; COTTONWOOD; TREE (color picture, Autumn Colors).

William M. Harlow

Lombardy Poplar Leaves flutter with a clattering sound in the faintest breeze. The triangular leaves are light green.

The Bark of Lombardy and other black poplars is darker and much rougher than that of white poplar varieties.

William M. Harlow

Omar Marcus

Snow-Capped Popocatepetl stands out boldly above the plateau of central Mexico. Many old fortresses and historic churches and cathedrals lie in view of the majestic sleeping volcano. Popocatepetl is one of the highest peaks in North America.

POPLIN is a ribbed fabric. It can be made of wool, cotton, rayon, silk, synthetics, or a mixture of these. The ribs run across the fabric. They are formed by using coarse filling yarns in a plain weave. The name *poplin* comes from *papeline,* a fabric woven of silk at Avignon, France, in the 1400's. The new fabric was named in honor of the papal residence at Avignon. The first poplin was made from silk. KENNETH R. FOX

POPOCATEPETL, *poh POH kah TAY pet'l,* is a volcano about 40 miles southeast of Mexico City. For location, see MEXICO (physical map). It is one of the highest peaks in North America. Its altitude (17,887 feet) is only 2,433 feet less than that of Mount McKinley, the highest peak on the continent. Its Aztec name means *smoking mountain.* Popocatepetl is often called simply "Popo." The top of Popocatepetl is always covered with snow. Banana, palm, and orange trees grow at its base. In the clear Mexican air, the mountain appears closer to Mexico City than it really is. Popocatepetl has not erupted violently in years, but clouds of smoke and gas, and sometimes stones and ashes, pour from its mouth. A small eruption of ash took place in the crater in 1943. The last major eruption of Popocatepetl occurred in 1702. Sulfur inside the crater has been mined from time to time, although transportation is difficult in the region.

The mountain can be climbed fairly easily. A member of Hernando Cortes' group which conquered Mexico in the 1520's was probably the first white man to climb it. GORDON A. MACDONALD

POPOVICH, PAVEL R. See ASTRONAUT.

POPPAEA SABINA. See NERO.

POPPY is the common name for several related groups of flowers. The most important member is the white opium poppy of China, India, and Iran. It has been raised in the Orient since ancient times.

The flowers of poppies are admired for their delicate beauty and gracefulness. Breeders have produced many variations in the size and form of the blossom. The plants are hardy and easy to cultivate. The tiny seeds have no narcotic properties, and are sold for bird food. They also yield an oil used in preparing some foods. The oil cake remaining is a valuable cattle food. Poppy seeds are also used as flavoring. They may be sprinkled on bread and rolls, or used in filling for cakes.

The common corn poppy grows wild in the grain fields and grassy meadows of Europe. Many varieties of the poppy, including the *Shirley poppy,* are grown from seed in flower gardens. The *Iceland poppy* grows as far south as Colorado. Its long-lasting flowers are various shades of yellow, rose-pink, and scarlet. The California poppy, or "cup of gold," grows wild in the "Golden State." The most showy of all poppies is the large-flowered Oriental poppy, whose red, orange, white, or salmon blossoms often have blackish-purple centers.

Many poppies are annual plants that can be grown from seed. But the Oriental poppy is a perennial, best transplanted by root sections in late summer. The poppy is one of the flowers of the month of August.

Opium comes from the young capsule of the poppy

As you will see from the first illustration on page 359, guide words similar to those in a dictionary appear at the top of most encyclopedia pages. Often they are the names of people or places. Once you have decided on a key word and selected the correct volume, the guide words will help you to find your key word quickly. If you open the **A** volume near the back to look for *atom* and find that there are many pages having guide words which begin with **at,** use the third letter of *atom* in order to narrow your search to the few pages that have guide words starting with **ato.**

Sometimes the title of an article, appearing in large type as the heading on a page, serves as the guide word. If there are pictures at the top of two facing pages, as in the bottom illustration on page 359, guide words are often omitted. In that case, use as your guide words the first main topic, printed in heavy black type, on the left-hand page and the last main topic on the right-hand page.

Discussion

Help your class answer these questions:

1. What are some topics you might look up in an encyclopedia to help you in work you are now doing in geography, science, or other school subjects?
2. How are topics in an encyclopedia arranged? What do the guide letters on the volumes tell you?
3. What is a key word? How do guide words in an encyclopedia help you to locate a key word? If you were trying to find the key word *Panama* in the **P** volume, would you start looking for it near the pages shown in the bottom illustration on page 359? Why or why not?

4. What is the number of the volume pictured on page 357 in which you would find each of these topics?

snow   Los Angeles   knights   Kit Carson

On your own

Answer the following questions on a sheet of paper. Write the number and letter of each part of a question first (1a, 1b, and so on) and then your answer to it.

1. What is the number of the volume shown on page 357 in which you would look for each of the following topics?

   a. New York City
   b. cameras
   c. Benjamin Banneker
   d. steamships
   e. Canary Islands
   f. Harriet Tubman

2. What key word or key words would you use to find information to answer each of these questions?

   a. How do helicopters stay in the air?
   b. What section of the United States produces the most lumber?
   c. What is the size of a football field?
   d. What famous clipper ships did Donald McKay build?

3. What are the guide words on the encyclopedia pages shown in the picture at the top of page 359?

4. What would you use as guide words for the two pages shown in the bottom picture on page 359?

Checking your work

If you are asked to do so, read aloud one or more of your answers. Then tell why you answered each question as you did. Listen while other boys and girls read their answers, and compare your answers with theirs. If you made a mistake in any of your answers, find out why it was a mistake.

The Train That Never Came Back

by Freeman Hubbard

Everybody knows that when a railroad train pulls out of a station at one end of the line, it runs to a station at the other end, and then it turns around and runs back again.

But there was a train once, many years ago, that never came back. And it never even reached the other end of the line!

The story takes us back a good many years to a hot September day in 1894. A thin, bluish-gray haze drifted in from the big woods of Minnesota. It filled the railroad station, the whole city of Duluth (duh-looth′), and the Duluth Limited, a crack train waiting at the depot.

Old Jim Root, engineer on the St. Paul & Duluth Railroad, wiped the sweat off his brow and climbed into the wooden cab of his engine, Number 39. His young fireman, Jack McGowan, stood in the tender breaking up huge chunks of coal with a pick. Ahead of them was the long ride to St. Paul.

"The woods must be burning pretty badly," said Mr. Root. "I've seen plenty of brush fires, but this smoke has 'em all beat."

Jack laid aside his pick. "I'm not surprised. We haven't had any rain worth speaking of since way back in April."

Mr. Root leaned out of his cab window, waiting. He watched the passengers pile into the three wooden coaches. Then he heard Tom Sullivan, the conductor, call out "A-a-all aboard!" and saw him raise his arm in the go-ahead signal that railroaders call the "highball." Mr. Root glanced at his watch.

"Two o'clock! Let's go!"

It was then that Jack asked, "Mr. Root, do you think it's safe to make this trip? Suppose a forest fire——"

The old man rested his hand on the throttle. He had known danger since he first went railroading at fourteen, and he wasn't afraid of anything. He'd been under fire in the Civil War and had seen wrecks and floods and snowbound trains and forest fires. And he felt sure that Number 39 —"old faithful" he called it—

would bring them through anything. But he knew that Jack was
young.

"You don't have to go out today," said Mr. Root. "Say the
word and I'll find another fireman for this run."

Jack flushed. He wasn't a quit-
ter. His only answer was to yank
the whistle cord and hold it down
for two long, ear-splitting wails.
That meant, in whistle talk,
"We're leaving town!"

Mr. Root grinned. His right
hand opened the throttle while
his left eased the brake. Jack
rang the engine bell, and they
rolled out into the smoky sunlight.

Heat waves filled the air. The
bluish-gray smoke from the big
woods grew thicker and thicker.
The red glare of the sun changed
to a strange lemon color. By the
middle of the afternoon, the sky
had become so dark that Jack had
to light the lamps in the engine
cab. When they stopped at the
next station, he got off to light
the headlight up front.

There were more than a hundred and forty passengers on
board the Limited that day, and
not one of them felt at ease. Some
were leaning back in their seats
trying to sleep. Others coughed
and fidgeted. Small children kept
digging into lunch baskets and
fussing for drinks of water. By
and by, the brakeman and the
porter went through the cars
lighting the gas lamps.

Conductor Sullivan calmly told
the people not to worry. "We'll
be all right as soon as we get past
the smoke area," he said.

After a while he called out,
"Next stop, Hinckley!"

Hinckley was a clearing in the
forest that consisted of about two
hundred houses, three churches
and a school, a few stores and
hotels, one restaurant, and a
roundhouse where four steam
engines could be kept. All the
buildings except the roundhouse
were made of wood.

Engineer Root stopped beside
the Grindstone River. This was
a shallow creek on the edge of
town, near the Brennan lumber
mill. He had to stop because the

bridge just ahead of him was full of people running toward the train. Some were carrying babies, but most of them were empty-handed.

Mr. Root shouted to his fireman, "You stay here, Jack! Don't let anyone get on board the engine! I'll go see what's wrong."

He swung down from the cab and walked quickly up to the bridge. Men, women, and children crowded around him. Their faces were grim and sad.

"You've got to save us, Mister!" they cried. "The whole town is burning up!"

For the first time, he took a good look and saw that it was true. Flames were sweeping across the big woods into Hinckley. Fire blew from the top of one tall tree to another, dropping great showers of sparks on the ground beneath. Flames kept shooting up on all sides.

For hours the Hinckley Volunteer Fire Department had fought to save the town, the people told Mr. Root. Just about every person in Hinckley had been carrying pails of water. But nothing could stop the fire, and it burned up one house after another. People choked as the air filled with smoke and sparks and gray, powdery ashes. The fire chief had sent to another town for more hose, but he couldn't even wait until it came. He saw that the fire had them beaten.

Mounting a horse, the fire chief galloped down the main street, shouting, "We can't save the town! It's burning on three sides! Run to the gravel pit!"

The gravel pit was a large shallow pool near the center of town. Many of the frightened people rushed there to safety. Others lay down on patches of cleared field, covering themselves with wet quilts, and a few found shelter in barrels of water until the danger passed.

Other men, women, and children ran wildly toward the Duluth Limited. About two hundred of them crowded into the three coaches and the baggage car with the passengers who had come down from Duluth.

Mr. Root talked it over quickly with Mr. Sullivan. "What do you say, Tom? Can we run them back to Skunk Lake?"

The conductor nodded. "Sure thing! It's the only safe place around here now. I reckon we can make it."

"We'll try!" the old engineer said firmly.

Skunk Lake was just a marshy pond about sixty feet wide that lay on both sides of the track, six miles north of town. Bullfrogs and dragonflies lived there, and sometimes a few wild ducks. Mr. Root had seen the muddy green water hundreds of times from his engine cab window.

He knew that the forest fire, fanned by the high wind, was headed that way. He knew, too, that Number 39 was a good engine and would run as long as it had coal in its firebox and steel rails under its eight wheels.

The old man climbed into his cab. Stragglers were still running through the woods to board the Limited. He waited for them as long as he dared. Then a low whine warned him that the onrushing flames were very near. He couldn't risk a moment's delay!

Mr. Root released his brakes, opened the throttle, and moved the reverse lever. Jack pulled the whistle cord. "Waa-hoo-oo! Waa-hoo-oo! Waa-hoo-oo!" Old Number 39 started backing up on the six-mile trip to Skunk Lake, pushing the cars behind it.

A sea of flame swirled up from the creek. Even the air seemed to be burning. The engineer took his overcoat out from under his seat and put it on as a protection against the sparks that blew into his cab. The overcoat itself caught fire.

His face was red and blistered. He grew dizzy and felt as if he couldn't last much longer. He did not see Jack but realized that he must be in the water tank on the tender. Now the engineer was too weak to shout for help. Pretty soon he toppled over.

Five, maybe ten, minutes later, he became conscious again. He struggled back into his seat and looked around. The train was still going — even with no hand on the throttle!

The engine cab was blazing. So were the roofs of all four cars. The last car — which had become the head of the train because it was running backward — was burning both inside and out. Frantic passengers pushed their way into the already crowded cars behind. Time was running out. Unless they could reach Skunk Lake very, very soon, it would be too late!

Mr. Root kept straining his smoke-filled eyes until at last he caught the glint of water beside the track.

"Skunk Lake!" he shouted. "We're safe!"

He brought the fiery train to a stop. Then he fell over again to the floor of his cab. Jack McGowan tried to lift him up.

"Get the passengers off!" gasped the old man. "Help them off! Come back for me later!"

So Jack led the frightened people through the heavy smoke to the water. Many of them lay down in the shallow water. Others sat in it, splashing their heads and shoulders. In all, some three hundred and forty men, women, and children found safety in Skunk Lake—and all because of Jim Root and Jack McGowan.

But the people weren't alone. They shared the pond with animals—horses, cows, and a pig.

Even deer, timber wolves, a large black bear, and ducks were seeking shelter there.

Jack and the conductor helped their engineer out of his cab and into the water. There the old man soon revived. He sat beside Jack, watching sadly as the train kept burning.

"Can't we save any of the cars?" he asked.

The fireman shook his head. "Not a chance."

"But what about my engine?" pleaded the engineer. "Its wooden cab is done for, but the rest is still good. Let's try to move it to a safe place. The cab fire will soon burn itself out, but that awful heat from the burning coal

369

in the tender is likely to melt it."

"All right, Mr. Root, I'll go. But you stay here."

"No," answered the engineer. "I've got to try to save it."

Carefully they made their way through the shower of sparks till they came to the engine. Jack managed to pull out the coupling pin from in front of the tender. Then the engineer got into his cab and stayed there just long enough to run old 39 a short distance from the rest of the train. It was safe at last.

"Now I feel better," said Mr. Root.

Then they both rushed back into the water. There the people and the animals stayed for most of the night. As the forest fire burned itself out, the wild beasts crept away one by one. About three o'clock the next morning, a rescue party arrived.

Some time afterward, Jim Root and Jack McGowan were each given a fine gold watch, engraved with the story of their heroism in the big fire. Both men returned to work. Old 39 was rebuilt with a new cab, and Mr. Root drove it again—but nothing else was saved from the train that never came back.

AUTHOR

Freeman Hubbard was born and raised in Philadelphia, Pennsylvania. Because his father was a railroad man, Mr. Hubbard became interested in railroads at an early age.

After graduating from high school, he attended art school with the intention of becoming a professional artist. He later changed his mind, however, and decided on a career as a writer. At first, he worked for newspapers in Philadelphia and New York. His continued interest in railroads eventually brought him to his present position, which is editor of the *Railroad Magazine.*

Mr. Hubbard has written hundreds of magazine articles and stories, both for children and adults. Most of them are about the railroads. Many of his best stories can be found in the book *The Roundhouse Cat and Other Railroad Stories.*

What Is the Last Number?

by Mary Elting

Suppose you were to start counting and did nothing but count, day and night, for the rest of your life. Would you get to the last number? The answer is *no*, because there is no last number. People who study mathematics tell us that we can never get to the end of numbers by counting. No matter how big a number we think of, there is always a bigger number. This idea is a very important one in science, and it has a name—the idea of infinity. Scientists write infinity this way: ∞

A million is a large number. A billion is larger. From there on, we don't very often use names for numbers, and some of them don't even have names. One of the largest numbers that has a name is a *googol*. It is a 1 with 100 zeros after it.

10,000,000,000,
000,000,000,000,
000,000,000,000,000,
000,000,000,000,000,
000,000,000,000,000,000
000,000,000,000,000,
000,000,000,000,000

Arap Sang and the Cranes

Hundreds of years ago, people in different lands believed that many powerful gods ruled over them. Many stories, called myths, were made up and told about the deeds of these imaginary beings.

This story, retold by Humphrey Harman in his book TALES TOLD NEAR A CROCODILE, *is a myth from Africa. It tells about Arap Sang, a great chief and part god, and the strange magic that he works.*

Some people of Africa believe that before you give anything to anyone you should first think out what your gift will mean to the person. They are often shocked at the way some people give things, anything—tractors and trousers, pets and radios—showering them down on people's heads with no kind of thought about what they will *mean* to the people who get the presents. Like being given a camera when you can't afford to buy film. That's worse than not having a camera.

A gift is a great responsibility to the giver, they say, and after they have said that, they may tell you the story of *Arap Sang and the Cranes.*

Arap Sang was a great chief and more than half a god, for in the days when he lived, great chiefs were always a little mixed up with the gods. One day he was walking on the plain, admiring the cattle.

It was hot. The rains had not yet come; the ground was almost bare of grass and as hard as stone; the thorn trees gave no shade, for they were just made of long spines and thin twigs and tiny leaves, and the sun went straight through them.

It was hot. Only the black ants didn't feel it and they would be happy in a furnace.

Arap Sang was getting old and the sun beat down on his bald head (he was sensitive about this and didn't like it mentioned) and he thought, "I'm feeling things more than I used to."

And then he came across a vulture sitting in the crotch of a tree, his wings hanging down and his eyes on the lookout.

"Vulture," said Arap Sang, "I'm hot and the sun is making my head ache. You have there a fine pair of broad wings. I'd be most grateful if you'd spread them out and let an old man enjoy a patch of shade."

"Why?" croaked Vulture. He had indigestion. Vultures usually have indigestion; it's the things they eat.

"Why?" said Arap Sang mildly.

"Now that's a question to which I'm not certain that I've got the answer. Why? Why, I suppose, because I ask you. Because I'm an old man and entitled to a little assistance and respect. Because it wouldn't be much trouble to you. Because it's pleasant and good to help people."

"Bah!" said Vulture.

"What's that?"

"Oh, go home, Baldy, and stop bothering people; it's hot."

Arap Sang straightened himself up and his eyes flashed. He wasn't half a god for nothing, and when he was angry, he could be rather a terrible old person. And he was very angry now. It was that remark about his lack of hair.

The really terrifying thing was that when he spoke, he didn't shout. He spoke quietly and the words were clear and cold and hard. And all separate like hailstones.

"Vulture," he said, "you're cruel and you're selfish. I shan't forget what you've said and you won't either. NOW GET OUT!"

Arap Sang was so impressive that Vulture got up awkwardly and flapped off.

"Silly old fool," he said uncomfortably.

Presently he met an acquaintance of his (vultures don't have friends; they just have acquaintances) and they perched together on the same bough. Vulture took a close look at his companion and then another, and what he saw was so funny that it cheered him up.

"Hee-hee!" he giggled. "What's happened to you? Met with an accident? You're *bald*."

The other vulture looked sour, but at the same time you felt he might be pleased about something.

"That's good, coming from you," he said. "What have you been up to? You haven't got a feather on you above the shoulders."

Then they both felt their heads with consternation. It was quite true. They were bald, both of them, and so was every other vulture, the whole family, right down to this very day.

Which goes to show that if you can't be ordinarily pleasant to people, at least it's not wise to go insulting great chiefs who are half gods.

I said that he was rather a terrible old person.

Arap Sang walked on. He was feeling shaky. Losing his temper always upset him afterward, and doing the sort of magic that makes every vulture in the world bald in the wink of an eye takes it out of you if you aren't as young as you used to be.

And he *did* want a bit of shade.

Presently he met an elephant. Elephant was panting across the plain in a tearing hurry and was most reluctant to stop when Arap Sang called to him.

"Elephant," said Arap Sang

weakly. "I'm tired and I'm dizzy. I want to get to the forest and into a bit of shade but it's a long way."

"It *is* hot, isn't it?" said Elephant. "I'm off to the forest myself."

"Would you spread out your great ears and let me walk along under them?" asked Arap Sang.

"I'm sorry," said Elephant, "but you'd make my journey so slow. I must get to the forest. I've got the most terrible headache."

"Well, I've got a headache, too," protested the old man.

"I'm sure," said Elephant, "and no one could be sorrier about that than I am. Is it a very big headache?"

"Shocking big," said Arap Sang.

"There, now," said Elephant. "Consider how big I am compared

to you and what the size of *my* headache must be."

That's elephants all over, always so logical. Arap Sang felt that there was something wrong with this argument but he couldn't just see where. Also he had become a little uncomfortable about all those bald vultures and he didn't want to lose his temper with anyone else. You have to be careful what you do when you're half a god. It's so dreadfully final.

"Oh, all right," he muttered.

"Knew you'd see it that way," said Elephant. "It's just what I was saying about you the other day. You can always rely on Arap Sang, I said, to behave reasonably. Well, good-by and good luck."

And he hurried off in the direction of the distant forest and was soon out of sight.

Poor Arap Sang was now feeling very ill indeed. He sat on the ground and he thought to himself, "I can't go another step unless I get some shade, and if I don't get some soon, I'm done for."

And there he was found by a flock of cranes.

They came dancing through the white grass, stamping their long delicate legs so that the insects flew up in alarm and were at once snapped up in the cranes' beaks. They gathered round Arap Sang sitting on the ground, and he looked so old and distressed that they hopped up and down with embarrassment, first on one leg, then the other. "Korong! Korong!" they called softly, and this happens to be their name as well.

"Good birds," whispered Arap Sang, "you must help me. If I don't reach shade soon, I'll die. Help me to the forest."

"But, of course," said the cranes, and they spread their great handsome black and white wings to shade him and helped him to his feet, and together, slowly, they all crossed the plain into the trees.

Then Arap Sang sat in the shade of a fine cotton tree and felt very much better. The birds gathered round him and he looked at them and thought that he had never seen more beautiful creatures in the whole world.

"And kind. Kind as well as

beautiful," he muttered. "The two don't always go together. I must reward them."

"I shan't forget your kindness," he said, "and I'll see that no one else does. Now I want each one of you to come here."

Then the cranes came one after another and bowed before him, and Arap Sang stretched out his kindly old hand and gently touched each beautiful sleek head. And where he did this, a golden crown appeared, and after the birds had gravely bowed their thanks, they all flew off to the lake, their new crowns glittering in the evening sun.

Arap Sang felt quite recovered.

He was very much pleased with his gift to the cranes.

Weeks later a crane dragged himself to the door of Arap Sang's house. It was a pitiful sight, thin with hunger, feathers broken and muddy from hiding in the reeds, eyes red with lack of sleep.

Arap Sang exclaimed in pity and horror.

"Great Chief," said the crane, "we beg you to take back your gift. If you don't, there'll soon be not one crane left alive, for we are hunted day and night for the sake of our golden crowns."

Arap Sang listened and nodded his head in sorrow.

"I'm old and I'm foolish," he said, "and I harm my friends. I had forgotten that people can be greedy and selfish and that they'll do anything for gold. Let me undo the wrong I have done by giving without thought. I'll make one more magic but that'll be the last."

Then he took their golden crowns, and in their place he put a wonderful halo of feathers which they have until this day.

But they still are called Crowned Cranes.

AUTHOR

Humphrey Harman first went to Africa in World War II. He spent most of his time with African soldiers in Africa, Madagascar, and the Far East. After the war was over, Mr. Harman decided to go back to Africa because he liked the people and felt that it would be a good place to live, so he became a schoolteacher and went to the African country of Kenya. He spent more than ten years there, working in the area of Lake Victoria as a trainer of Kenyan teachers.

Tales Told near a Crocodile, the book from which "Arap Sang and the Cranes" was taken, is a collection of stories told by the various people who live around Lake Victoria. The stories are tales, legends, and fables that had never been put into writing but had been handed down orally for hundreds of years. Mr. Harman wrote them down just as they were told to him by these skillful storytellers.

Askia the Great

My grandmother tells me
True stories of Africa
In the early centuries.
I like to hear about Askia the Great
Wealthy black ruler of the kingdom of Songhay
On his royal pilgrimage
To the holy place of Mecca
With a retinue of some two thousand men.
I also like to hear how Askia the Great
Encouraged learning
At the University of Sankore in Timbuktu
Where brilliant scholars black and white
Gathered to study.
My grandmother says
The children of black America do not know
That some of their ancestors
Rank among the greatest kings.

Ruth Duckett Gibbs

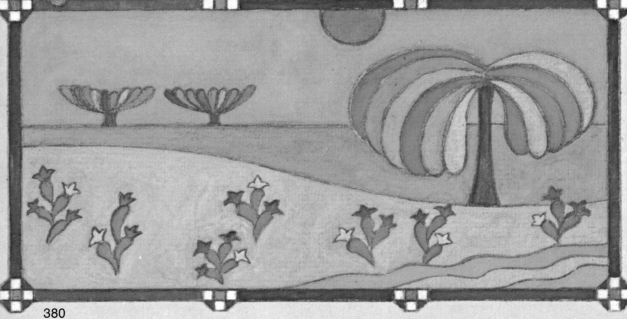

He Reached for the Stars

by *Lavinia Dobler and Edgar A. Toppin*

Young Benjamin Banneker sat on the doorstep of his grandmother's house in Maryland, looking at the night sky with all its stars. His grandmother sat beside him. Suddenly a sparkling white object shot across the heavens. Seconds later it was gone.

"Where did it go?" he asked, puzzled. The boy leaned his head back as far as he could, searching eagerly for the mysterious star. But his sharp black eyes could not find it.

"Grandma, where *did* the star go?" he asked. Benjamin often asked his grandmother questions about things that he did not understand.

"I do not know," she answered, shaking her head. "Maybe the Book can tell us," she added as she got up from the wooden step.

Together they went inside the weather-beaten cabin. His grandmother lighted a candle, and Benjamin, standing on his bare toes, reached for the Bible on the shelf. He carried the heavy book to the table.

Mrs. Banneker had taught Benjamin his letters. On Sunday mornings Benjamin used to read the Bible to her. She hoped he would grow up to be a religious man.

His grandmother, who had learned to read as a girl, turned the pages and searched for passages about the stars and the heavens. But she could not find the answer about the shooting star.

"You are a bright boy and you can read," she said proudly. "Someday you will find the answer to your question."

Benjamin was born on November 9, 1731, three and one-half months before George Washington. His birthplace was his grandparents' farm near the Patapsco River, about ten miles from Baltimore. When Benjamin Banneker was growing up, Maryland was a colony belonging to England.

One spring morning in 1737, six-year-old Benjamin woke up and scrambled into his clothes. All he could think of was "This is the day!" Today his parents and his grandparents were going to deliver several thousand pounds of fine tobacco to Richard Gist. The tobacco had been grown on his grandparents' farm.

His parents, Robert and Mary Banneker, had waited many years for this chance. Now, with the earnings from the tobacco, they were going to buy land. They knew that they were taking on a big responsibility. It would mean putting in longer hours each day than they were now doing. But both were hard workers and liked to be outdoors, and their children were old enough to help them.

There were few free blacks at that time in Maryland who owned big farms. But the younger Bannekers were eager to own their own land. The grandparents had done well, and they also hoped to succeed. And they did succeed. People often talked about the fine crops the Banneker family produced.

Benjamin started to school that year. He could hardly wait. At last he would have many books to read. Then, too, he had so many questions he wanted to ask. If the teacher didn't know all the answers, then he surely could find them in the books.

The school was a short way from the farm, and Benjamin ran

all the way, clutching a slate in his hand. But when he reached the schoolhouse, he straightened his tie and brushed his white shirt and walked slowly up the steps. The Quaker schoolmaster was at the desk, talking to several white and black children.

Until he was sent to school, the only book Benjamin knew was the Bible. But now that he was going to school, he was fascinated by the books his teacher showed him.

Every school day was a new adventure for Benjamin. He listened carefully to every word the teacher said. Benjamin repeated the words to himself so that his way of saying them would be the way his teacher spoke.

But it was arithmetic that he liked best of all. He quickly learned how to add and subtract, and he liked to multiply and divide.

The first time the teacher gave the students problems to figure out, Benjamin had the answers in no time at all. He raised his hand to let the teacher know that he was finished with his work.

"Have you worked all the problems?" the teacher asked, as he peered over his eyeglasses.

"Yes, sir," Benjamin answered.

"Have you checked them? You know you must prove them."

Benjamin nodded.

"Bring your slate to my desk," the teacher said.

Benjamin walked proudly to the front of the room and placed the slate on the big oak desk.

"The answers are correct," the teacher said a few minutes later. "I shall have to give you much more difficult problems."

In 1746, when he was fifteen, his nine years of schooling were over. Benjamin missed going to school, especially because there were so few books at home. He continued to be a careful observer of nature and listened closely to anyone who could give information to him.

As a young man, Benjamin Banneker did not seem to have any desire to leave his family or the farm. He seemed to prefer to remain at home, for there was a close family tie.

Benjamin was twenty-eight when his father died. Seventy-two acres of farmland were left to Benjamin, the only son, and to his mother, as joint heirs. The rest was left to Benjamin's three sisters.

Since Benjamin had worked with his father, he was able to go on living comfortably from the produce grown on the farm, including the fruit, vegetables, and honey. His mother did most of the selling of the farm products. Benjamin plowed and hoed the fields, planted crops, and cared for the bees, but he also found time to study mathematics.

People who knew Benjamin Banneker often spoke about his keen mind and the ease with which he solved difficult mathematical problems. When he built a wooden clock in 1753, his fame spread far beyond Baltimore County. At that time Benjamin was twenty-two years old.

Banneker had never seen a clock, but he had a pocket watch, which served as his model. Probably there was not a clock within fifty miles of the farm. He worked a long time on his clock. He had few of the right tools that would have made the work easier, but he did have the watch, which he took apart. The clock he made was much larger than the watch.

In 1853 an article in the *Atlantic Monthly* described the wooden clock: "It is probable that this was the first clock of which every portion was made in America. It is certain that it was as purely his own invention as if none had ever been made before."

Word got around that a black with little education had made a clock with wooden parts that worked. Visitors came for miles around to the Banneker farm.

As the days went by, people became more aware of Banneker's unusual memory and his mathematical ability. He was now known as one of the best mathematicians, for he was very rapid

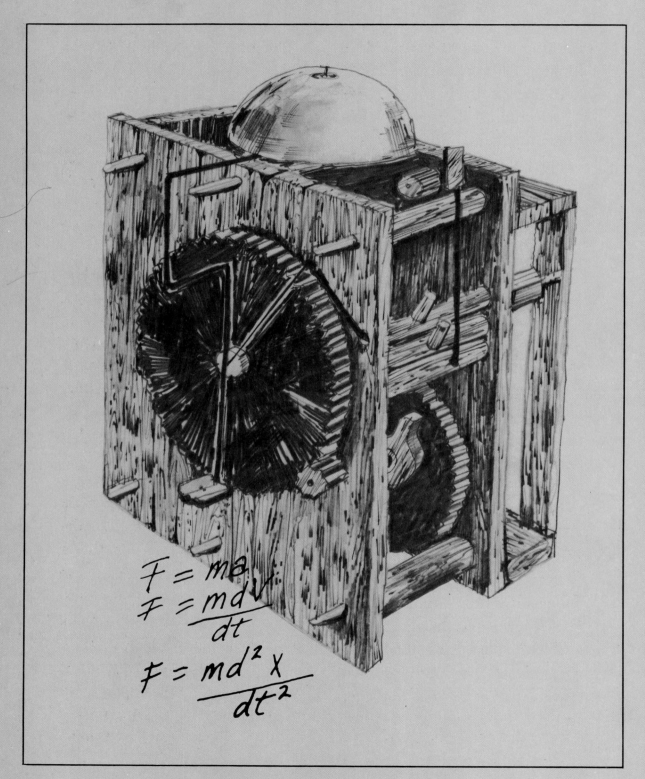

$$F = ma$$
$$F = m\frac{dv}{dt}$$
$$F = m\frac{d^2x}{dt^2}$$

in figuring out problems. People from other sections of the thirteen colonies sent him puzzles to test him. As soon as he received them, he would sit down at his table and start figuring them out. With his quick mind, he would have the correct answers in no time at all.

Banneker found that he liked figuring out and making up problems much more than he liked working on the farm. But in order to have food, he had to plant crops and hoe the fields.

Finally he got tenants for most of the farm, keeping a small part for himself. But the tenants wouldn't pay him, and they stole his fruit and goods.

Banneker's responsibilities for the family farm troubled him a great deal. He had fine orchards that produced sweet, juicy pears and cherries. The boys in the neighborhood knew about the Banneker orchards. They would knock at his door and ask permission to pick some of his fruit. Banneker would agree. Then, after he closed his door and went back to his studies, the boys would take most of the fruit, sometimes even before it was ripe.

Even though Banneker was becoming well known, he was very lonely. He had never married, so he did not have a wife or children to talk to. There was no one in his neighborhood who could talk with him about mathematical and scientific problems. Then something wonderful happened.

In 1772, when Banneker was forty-one, the Ellicott brothers, Joseph, Andrew III, and Nathaniel, moved to Patapsco Valley. They were millers. Joseph, like Banneker, had made a clock that had received much attention.

While the Ellicott mills were being built, the Ellicotts bought food for their workers from the Banneker farm. Banneker's mother always selected for them the largest and freshest vegetables and fruits, the fattest chickens, and the best grade of honey.

What interested Banneker most about the mills was the machinery that ground the wheat into flour. He studied the big rollers.

The Ellicotts were impressed with this fine man who came often to the mills. They entertained him in their home and visited him at his farm. George Ellicott, son of Andrew, became Banneker's closest friend.

One day in 1787, when Banneker was visiting at his friend's home, George Ellicott offered to lend him some books on astronomy. Banneker was delighted. When he was ready to return to his farm with the books, George Ellicott said, "I'll be over soon to help you."

"I shall appreciate that very much," Banneker said.

But George Ellicott was called away on business. When he came back, he went over to visit Banneker, expecting to explain certain ideas. To his surprise, he found that Banneker had already understood them and was studying them. At this time Banneker was about fifty-six years old.

From that time on, astronomy became very important to Benjamin Banneker. As a boy, he had been fascinated with the stars that shone so brightly, but up to now he had never had the good fortune to see any books on the subject.

During the last twenty years of his life, Banneker spent most of his time with scientific studies. Every night as soon as it was dark, Banneker would leave his log cabin. A blanket over his arm, he would walk over to a certain tree. He would carefully spread the blanket on the ground and then lie on his back so that he could watch the stars. Until they disappeared in the early dawn, Banneker would still be there, his hands under his head, his black eyes studying the heavens.

As soon as the sun rose, he would get up, stretch, and go inside his house to sleep.

His neighbors, who did not understand Banneker's odd habits, would shake their heads.

"He is a lazy old man," they would say. "When he was young, he was a hard worker and was proud of his fine crops."

What his neighbors said about him did not seem to bother Banneker. He was too busy with his scientific observations. Through his study of astronomy, Banneker predicted an eclipse of the sun in 1789. Because of his mathematical training, he even found mistakes in the works of famous astronomers.

Banneker also was still keenly aware of nature. He noted that some locusts seemed to come out every seventeen years, and then he explained how they lay eggs. He also observed that a stronger hive of bees seemed to have taken the honey of a weaker hive and then killed the bees when they tried to get their honey back.

After hearing gunfire, he wrote the following: "Standing at my door, I heard the discharge of a gun; and in four or five seconds after the discharge, the small shot came rattling around me, one or two of which struck the house, which plainly demonstrates that the velocity of sound is greater than that of a cannon bullet."

Until the 1790's, Banneker's fame was still mostly local. Then in the next ten years he received

national and world recognition in two ways.

The Congress of the United States, in 1790, passed a law to set up a capital on the Potomac River. The President, George Washington, decided just where on the river the capital city would be built.

Seven months later, in February 1791, President Washington sent Andrew Ellicott IV to survey the land. The plan for the city was to be made by the Frenchman Pierre Charles L'Enfant.

At the request of Mr. Ellicott and Thomas Jefferson, then Secretary of State, Benjamin Banneker was named to help Ellicott survey the land. Banneker worked ably, serving from 1791 to 1793. George Ellicott encouraged

Banneker to put some of his figuring into an almanac. Almanacs then were one of the best examples of scientific learning. Many people read them for news of the weather and the tides, and also for entertainment. Banneker worked on his almanac while helping to lay out the nation's capital.

Banneker was sixty years old when his first almanac was

published. He continued to publish almanacs until 1802, when he was seventy-one.

On Sunday, October 19, 1806, Banneker took a walk. He admired the beauty of the gold, bronze, and red leaves that covered the ground. Suddenly he fell to the ground. Friends carried him into the log cabin where his wooden clock still ticked. Then he died. He was almost seventy-five years old.

So outstanding was Banneker that Marcus Conway, in an article printed during the Civil War, long after Banneker's death, wrote: "History must record that the most original scientific mind which the South has yet produced was that of . . . Benjamin Banneker."

The story you have just read told about some of the important things Benjamin Banneker did. But he did still more: In 1791 he wrote a letter to Thomas Jefferson, then Secretary of State. In that letter he told about his hope for both a new attitude towards black people and an end to slavery. Benjamin Banneker cared about the moon and the stars and the tides, but he cared also about the way in which people were treated.

AUTHORS

Lavinia Dobler was born in Wyoming and went to college in California and also in New York, where she now lives. She has written many books and stories for young readers. She especially likes to write about American history and about people around the world. Some of her books are set in Puerto Rico, where she once lived.

Edgar A. Toppin was born in New York and went to Howard University in Washington, D.C., and to Northwestern University in Chicago. He has written several books about black history in addition to *Pioneers and Patriots: The Lives of Six Negroes of the Revolutionary Era*, which he and Lavinia Dobler wrote together. Mr. Toppin and his family now live in Virginia.

HUGHBERT AND THE GLUE

Hughbert had a jar of glue.
From Hugh the glue could not be parted,
At least could not be parted far,
For Hugh was glued to Hughbert's jar.
But that is where it all had started.
The glue upon the shoe of Hugh
Attached him to the floor.
The glue on Hughbert's gluey hand
Was fastened to the door,
While two of Hughbert's relatives
Were glued against each other.
His mother, I believe, was one.
The other was his brother.
The dog and cat stood quite nearby.
They could not move from there.
The bird was glued securely
Into Hughbert's mother's hair.

Hughbert's father hurried home
And loudly said to Hugh:
"From now on I would rather
That you did not play with glue."
Karla Kuskin

WEB WEAVERS
by RUTH FAGEN

You have probably run headfirst into a spider web at one time or another. Did you stop to notice how neatly it had been put together? Because its web is both home and trapping ground to the spider, it works very carefully, often producing a web as beautiful as it is useful.

Of all the different kinds of spider webs, the orb web is probably the most beautiful. It is called an orb web, and its owner an orb weaver, because the lines of the web go around and around in circles. All the lines are made of a very strong silk, the finest thread to be found in nature. It

is so strong that if you were to make a rope of it one inch thick, it would be stronger than a one-inch-thick rope made of *iron*! The orb web usually hangs straight up and down so that flying insects will be caught in it. The circling lines of the web stretch and are very sticky. The spider waits in the center or along the side. When an insect gets caught on the sticky lines, the spider moves along one of the cross-lines, which look like the spokes of a wheel. These are not sticky.

If you look out your window on a dewy morning, you will

sometimes see your yard carpeted with grass-spider webs. The grass spider weaves this web in almost the same way we weave a piece of cloth. It crosses back and forth from side to side and from top to bottom until a very firm silk sheet is formed. The spider attaches this sheet to blades of grass and little plants nearby. Then it waits for flies and other small insects to get caught in the web.

Many people are afraid of spiders and would like to kill every one they see. What they do not realize is that spiders are among our best friends because they eat thousands of harmful insects every year.

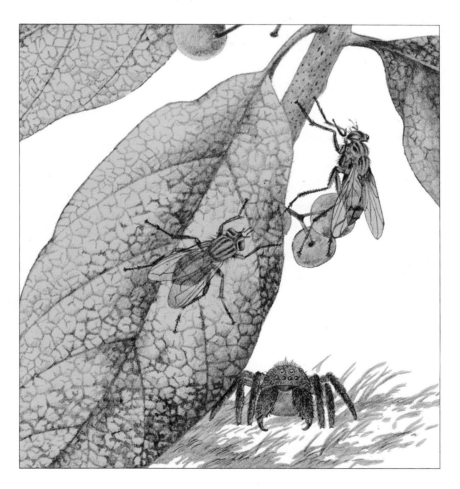

MAKING AN OUTLINE

Sometimes you need to study carefully a group of two or more paragraphs which we can call an article and which has a title. To do that studying, you can make an outline of important points which the article gives about the title. Doing this can help you understand and remember just what the article says.

The first thing to do in making such an outline is to read the title and think what it means. Then think of a question which you expect the article to answer. Your question may ask *How, What, When, Where, Which, Who,* or *Why.* If you saw an article that had the title *Some Kinds of Seeds We Use as Food,* what question would you expect the article to answer?

The next thing to do in making the outline is to read the article itself so that you get answers to your question. Do that now with the article that follows. Use the question *What are those kinds of seeds?*

Some Kinds of Seeds We Use as Food

Most of the seeds we eat are grains. Often we boil and season rice as a vegetable or use it in making desserts. Corn is also cooked as a vegetable, on or off the cob. Many breakfast cereals are made of rice, corn, or wheat. Much wheat and some rice are ground separately to make wheat flour and rice flour, and corn is ground to make cornmeal. We use this flour and meal in making many kinds of bread and cake.

Peas and beans are vegetable seeds. Usually we boil and season peas without the pods in which they grow. Some beans are boiled or baked without the pods. Others are cooked and eaten along with their pods.

The nuts we eat are seeds. Often pecans, almonds, and walnuts are eaten raw. Sometimes we use them in making salads, candy, cakes, and other desserts.

What answers did you get to the question *What are those kinds of seeds?* Your answers should be (1) grains, (2) vegetable seeds, (3) nuts. These three ideas are the main points in the article. When we put them into an outline, we call them **main topics,** and they look like this:

Some Kinds of Seeds We Use as Food
I. Grains
II. Vegetable seeds
III. Nuts

Notice these things about the part of an outline above:
1. The first word, the last word, and each important word in the title begin with a capital letter.
2. To number the main topics correctly, the right Roman numeral and a period are placed before each one. Each main topic begins with a capital letter, but there is no period at the end.

You already know how to decide what the topic of a paragraph is. Often a part or all of the topic of a paragraph will be a main topic in an outline you are making. The topic of the paragraph you read about grains can be stated as *Some grains we eat.* Is the first main topic in the outline all, or just part of, that paragraph topic?

You can check to see whether the points you have chosen for main topics in an outline you are making are the right points. To do that, try to make for each main topic a statement which makes sense and which includes that main topic and the *same word or words* from the title of the article. For example, you could make these statements for the outline on page 397.

1. Grains are *seeds we use as food.*
2. Vegetable seeds are *seeds we use as food.*
3. Nuts are *seeds we use as food.*

Usually you will need to put into an outline points that the article gives about each main topic. To find out what these points are for each main topic, think of a question which you expect the article to answer about that topic. Then read all or part of the article to get all the answers it gives to your question. Do these things now as you look again at the article about seeds to get points for *Grains,* the first main topic in the outline. Use the question *What are these grains?*

What answers did you get to the question about grains? They should be (1) rice, (2) corn, (3) wheat. When we put these points into the outline, we call them **subtopics,** and they look like this:

Some Kinds of Seeds We Use as Food
  I. Grains
   A. Rice
   B. Corn
   C. Wheat
  II. Vegetable seeds
 III. Nuts

Notice that each subtopic is indented under the main topic to which it belongs. The correct capital letter and a period come before each subtopic. Each subtopic begins with a capital letter, but there is no period at the end.

You can check to see if points you have chosen for subtopics in an outline you are making are the right points. To do that, try to make for each subtopic a statement which makes sense and which includes that subtopic and the *same word or words* in the main topic. For example, you could make these statements for the subtopics in the outline above: (1) Rice is a *grain,* (2) Corn is a *grain,* (3) Wheat is a *grain.*

What points in the article about seeds would you choose for subtopics to put under the second main topic? Under the third main topic?

You can use a good outline you make of an article to review quickly the important points the article gives about its subject. Read the outline as many times as you must to see how points in the article are related to one another and to fix those points in your mind.

Discussion

Help your class answer these questions:

1. What subtopics would you put under the second main topic in the outline about seeds? Under the third main topic?

2. How can making an outline help you study an article? How can you use that outline?

3. What is the first thing to do when you begin to make an outline of an article? What is the next thing to do?

4. What do the main topics in a good outline tell about? What do the subtopics tell about?

5. Why is it a good thing to have a question in mind when you read an article to choose points to use as main topics in an outline? To choose points for subtopics?

6. How can you check to see whether points you have chosen for main topics in an outline you are making are the right points? How can you check points you have chosen for subtopics?

7. Where are capital letters, Roman numerals, and periods used in an outline? Where should the subtopics be written?

On your own

On a sheet of paper, make an outline of important points in the article that follows. Use main topics and subtopics, and follow suggestions that this lesson has given you. Be sure to leave space between the main topics so that you can write the subtopics where they belong.

Some Cuts of Meat People Eat

Many of the cuts of meat we eat are called roasts. Among the most popular of these are a rump roast and a chuck roast. Often, but not always, vegetables are cooked along with either of these roasts and served with it on one large plate. A favorite roast for some people is a pork loin.

Some cuts of meat are steaks. Perhaps you like a piece of round steak, flank steak, or sirloin steak. The commonest ways of cooking steaks are broiling and frying. Often in the summertime, people broil steaks over charcoal outside the house.

Many people are quite fond of chops, broiled or fried. These may be pork, lamb, or veal. Sometimes thick pork chops are stuffed and baked.

Ground meat may be hamburger or sausage. Often you have seen hamburger made into patties and broiled or fried to use in sandwiches. Sausage is made into patties or links that we fry and sometimes eat with eggs.

Checking your work

If you are asked to do so, read part of your outline aloud. Find out why any mistake you may have made in choosing a point for a main topic or a subtopic is a mistake.

A STORY TREASURE

From *Charlotte's Web*

by E. B. WHITE

When Wilbur was born, he was a small, sickly pig who needed special care. Fern, his owner's eight-year-old daughter, took care of him until he was big enough to be sold to Mr. Zuckerman.

At Mr. Zuckerman's farm, Wilbur lived in a nice barn with many other animals for neighbors. Lurvy, the hired man, fed him regularly, and Fern came to visit him almost every day. Wilbur would have been really happy except for one thing — he didn't have a real friend among all his neighbors in the barn.

The following two chapters are only a small part of a complete story for children titled CHARLOTTE'S WEB, *by E. B. White, with illustrations by Garth Williams.*

Loneliness

The next day was rainy and dark. Rain fell on the roof of the barn and dripped steadily from the eaves. Rain fell in the barnyard and ran in crooked courses down into the lane where thistles and pigweed grew. Rain spattered against the Zuckermans' kitchen windows and came gushing out of the downspouts. Rain fell on the backs of the sheep as they grazed in the meadow. When the sheep tired of standing in the rain, they walked slowly up the lane and into the fold.

Rain upset Wilbur's plans. Wilbur had planned to go out, this day, and dig a new hole in his yard. He had other plans, too. His plans for the day went something like this:

Breakfast at six-thirty. Skim milk, crusts, middlings, bits of doughnuts, wheat cakes with drops of maple syrup sticking to them, potato skins, leftover custard pudding with raisins, and bits of shredded wheat.

Breakfast would be finished at seven.

From seven to eight, Wilbur planned to have a talk with Templeton, the rat that lived under his trough. Talking with Templeton was not the most interesting occupation in the world but it was better than nothing.

From eight to nine, Wilbur planned to take a nap outdoors in the sun.

From nine to eleven, he planned to dig a hole, or trench, and possibly find something good to eat buried in the dirt.

From eleven to twelve, he planned to stand still and watch flies on the boards, watch bees in the clover, and watch swallows in the air.

Twelve o'clock—lunchtime. Middlings, warm water, apple parings, meat gravy, carrot scrapings, meat scraps, stale hominy, and the wrapper off a package of cheese. Lunch would be over at one.

From one to two, Wilbur planned to sleep.

From two to three, he planned to scratch itchy places by rubbing against the fence.

From three to four, he planned to stand perfectly still and think of what it was like to be alive, and to wait for Fern.

At four would come supper. Skim milk, provender, leftover sandwich from Lurvy's lunch box, prune skins, a morsel of this, a bit of that, fried potatoes, marmalade drippings, a little more of this, a little more of that, a piece of baked apple, a scrap of upside-down cake.

Wilbur had gone to sleep thinking about these plans. He awoke at six and saw the rain, and it seemed as though he couldn't bear it.

"I get everything all beautifully planned out and it has to go and rain," he said.

For a while he stood gloomily indoors. Then he walked to the door and looked out. Drops of rain struck his face. His yard was cold and wet. His trough had an inch of rainwater in it. Templeton was nowhere to be seen.

"Are you out there, Templeton?" called Wilbur. There was no answer. Suddenly Wilbur felt lonely and friendless.

"One day just like another," he groaned. "I'm very young, I have no real friend here in the barn, it's going to rain all morning and all afternoon, and Fern won't come in such bad weather. Oh, *honestly!*" And Wilbur was crying again, for the second time in two days.

At six-thirty Wilbur heard the banging of a pail. Lurvy was standing outside in the rain, stirring up breakfast.

"C'mon, pig!" said Lurvy.

Wilbur did not budge. Lurvy dumped the slops, scraped the pail, and walked away. He noticed that something was wrong with the pig.

Wilbur didn't want food, he wanted love. He wanted a friend—someone who would play with him. He mentioned this to the goose, who was sitting quietly in a corner of the sheep-fold.

"Will you come over and play with me?" he asked.

"Sorry, sonny, sorry," said the goose. "I'm sitting-sitting on my eggs. Eight of them. Got to keep them toasty-oasty-oasty warm. I have to stay right here, I'm no flibberty-ibberty-gibbet. I do not play when there are eggs to hatch. I'm expecting goslings."

"Well, I didn't think you were expecting woodpeckers," said Wilbur, bitterly.

Wilbur next tried one of the lambs.

"Will you please play with me?" he asked.

"Certainly not," said the lamb. "In the first place, I cannot get into your pen, as I am not old enough to jump over the fence. In the second place, I am not interested in pigs. Pigs mean less than nothing to me."

"What do you mean, *less* than nothing?" replied Wilbur. "I don't think there is any such thing as *less* than nothing. Nothing is absolutely the limit of nothingness. It's the lowest you can go. It's the end of the line. How can something be less than nothing? If there were something that was less than nothing, then nothing would not be nothing, it would be something — even though it's just a very little bit of something. But if nothing is *nothing*, then nothing has nothing that is less than *it* is."

"Oh, be quiet!" said the lamb. "Go play by yourself! I don't play with pigs."

Sadly, Wilbur lay down and listened to the rain. Soon he saw the rat climbing down a slanting board that he used as a stairway.

"Will you play with me, Templeton?" asked Wilbur.

"Play?" said Templeton, twirling his whiskers. "Play? I hardly know the meaning of the word."

"Well," said Wilbur, "it means to have fun, to frolic, to run and skip and make merry."

"I never do those things if I can avoid them," replied the rat, sourly. "I prefer to spend my time eating, gnawing, spying, and hiding. I am a glutton but not a merrymaker. Right now I am on my way to your trough to eat your breakfast, since you haven't got sense enough to eat it yourself." And Templeton, the rat, crept stealthily along the wall and disappeared into a private tunnel that he had dug between the door and the trough in Wilbur's yard. Templeton was a crafty rat, and he had things pretty much his own way. The tunnel was an example of his skill and cunning. The tunnel enabled him to get from the barn to his hiding place under the pig trough without coming out into the open. He had tunnels and runways all over Mr. Zuckerman's farm and could get from one place to another without being seen. Usually he slept during the daytime and was abroad only after dark.

Wilbur watched him disappear into his tunnel. In a moment he saw the rat's sharp nose poke out from underneath the wooden trough. Cautiously Templeton pulled himself up over the edge of the trough. This was almost more than Wilbur could stand: on this dreary, rainy day to see his breakfast being eaten by somebody else. He knew Templeton was getting soaked, out there in the pouring rain, but even that didn't comfort him. Friendless, dejected, and hungry, he threw himself down in the manure and sobbed.

Late that afternoon, Lurvy went to Mr. Zuckerman. "I think there's something wrong with that pig of yours. He hasn't touched his food."

"Give him two spoonfuls of sulphur and a little molasses," said Mr. Zuckerman.

Wilbur couldn't believe what was happening to him when Lurvy caught him and forced the medicine down his throat. This was certainly the worst day of his life. He didn't know whether he could endure the awful loneliness any more.

Darkness settled over everything. Soon there were only shadows and the noises of the sheep chewing their cuds, and occasionally the rattle of a cow chain up overhead. You can imagine Wilbur's surprise when, out of the darkness, came a small voice he had never heard before. It sounded rather thin, but pleasant. "Do you want a friend, Wilbur?" it said. "I'll be a friend to you. I've watched you all day and I like you."

"But I can't see you," said Wilbur, jumping to his feet. "Where are you? And *who* are you?"

"I'm right up here," said the voice. "Go to sleep. You'll see me in the morning."

Charlotte

The night seemed long. Wilbur's stomach was empty and his mind was full. And when your stomach is empty and your mind is full, it's always hard to sleep.

A dozen times during the night, Wilbur woke and stared into the blackness, listening to the sounds and trying to figure out what time it was. A barn is never perfectly quiet. Even at midnight there is usually something stirring.

The first time he woke, he heard Templeton gnawing a hole

in the grain bin. Templeton's teeth scraped loudly against the wood and made quite a racket. "That crazy rat!" thought Wilbur. "Why does he have to stay up all night, grinding his clashers and destroying people's property? Why can't he go to sleep, like any decent animal?"

The second time Wilbur woke, he heard the goose turning on her nest and chuckling to herself.

"What time is it?" whispered Wilbur to the goose.

"Probably-obably-obably about half-past eleven," said the goose. "Why aren't you asleep, Wilbur?"

"Too many things on my mind," said Wilbur.

"Well," said the goose, "that's not *my* trouble. I have nothing at all on my mind, but I've too many things under my behind. Have you ever tried to sleep while sitting on eight eggs?"

"No," replied Wilbur. "I suppose it *is* uncomfortable. How long does it take a goose egg to hatch?"

"Approximately-oximately thirty days, all told," answered the goose. "But I cheat a little. On warm afternoons, I just pull a little straw over the eggs and go out for a walk."

Wilbur yawned and went back to sleep. In his dreams he heard again the voice saying, "I'll be a friend to you. Go to sleep — you'll see me in the morning."

About half an hour before dawn, Wilbur woke and listened. The barn was still dark. The sheep lay motionless. Even the goose was quiet. Overhead, on the main floor, nothing stirred: the cows were resting, the horses dozed. Templeton had quit work and gone off somewhere on an errand. The only sound was a slight scraping noise from the rooftop, where the weather vane swung back and forth. Wilbur loved the barn when it was like this — calm and quiet, waiting for light.

"Day is almost here," he thought.

Through a small window, a faint gleam appeared. One by one the stars went out. Wilbur could see the goose a few feet away. She sat with head tucked under a wing. Then he could see the sheep and the lambs. The sky lightened.

"Oh, beautiful day, it is here at last! Today I shall find my friend."

Wilbur looked everywhere. He searched his pen thoroughly. He examined the window ledge, stared up at the ceiling. But he saw nothing new. Finally he decided he would have to speak up. He hated to break the lovely stillness of dawn by using his voice, but he couldn't think of any other way to locate the mysterious new friend who was nowhere to be seen. So Wilbur cleared his throat.

"Attention, please!" he said in a loud, firm voice. "Will the party who addressed me at bedtime last night kindly make himself or herself known by giving an appropriate sign or signal!"

Wilbur paused and listened. All the other animals lifted their heads and stared at him. Wilbur blushed. But he was determined to get in touch with his unknown friend.

"Attention, please!" he said. "I will repeat the message. Will the party who addressed me at bedtime last night kindly speak up. Please tell me where you are, if you are my friend!"

The sheep looked at each other in disgust.

"Stop your nonsense, Wilbur!" said the oldest sheep. "If you have a new friend here, you are probably disturbing his rest; and the quickest way to spoil a friendship is to wake somebody up in the morning before he is ready. How can you be sure your friend is an early riser?"

"I beg everyone's pardon," whispered Wilbur. "I didn't mean to be objectionable."

He lay down meekly in the manure, facing the door. He did not know it, but his friend was very near. And the old sheep was right—the friend was still asleep.

Soon Lurvy appeared with slops for breakfast. Wilbur rushed out, ate everything in a hurry, and licked the trough. The sheep moved off down the lane, the gander waddled along behind them, pulling grass. And then, just as Wilbur was settling down for his morning nap, he heard again the thin voice that had addressed him the night before.

"Salutations!" said the voice.

Wilbur jumped to his feet. "Salu-*what?*" he cried.

"Salutations!" repeated the voice.

"What are *they*, and where are *you?*" screamed Wilbur. "Please, *please*, tell me where you are. And what are salutations?"

"Salutations are greetings," said the voice. "When I say 'salutations,' it's just my fancy way of saying hello or good morning. Actually, it's a silly expression, and I am surprised that I used it at all. As for my whereabouts, that's easy. Look up here in the corner of the doorway! Here I am. Look, I'm waving!"

At last Wilbur saw the creature that had spoken to him in such a kindly way. Stretched across the upper part of the doorway was a big spider web, and hanging from the top of the web, head down, was a large grey spider. She was about the size of a gumdrop. She had eight legs, and she was waving one of them at Wilbur in friendly greeting. "See me now?" she asked.

"Oh, yes indeed," said Wilbur. "Yes indeed! How are you? Good morning! Salutations! Very pleased to meet you. What is your name, please? May I have your name?"

"My name," said the spider, "is Charlotte."

"Charlotte what?" asked Wilbur, eagerly.

"Charlotte A. Cavatica. But just call me Charlotte."

"I think you're beautiful," said Wilbur.

"Well, I *am* pretty," replied Charlotte. "There's no denying that. Almost all spiders are rather nice-looking. I'm not as flashy as some, but I'll do. I wish I could see you, Wilbur, as clearly as you can see me."

"Why can't you?" asked the pig. "I'm right here."

"Yes, but I'm nearsighted," replied Charlotte. "I've always been dreadfully nearsighted. It's good in some ways, not so good in others. Watch me wrap up this fly."

A fly that had been crawling along Wilbur's trough had flown up and blundered into the lower part of Charlotte's web and was tangled in the sticky threads. The fly was beating its wings furiously, trying to break loose and free itself.

"First," said Charlotte, "I dive at him." She plunged head-first toward the fly. As she dropped, a tiny silken thread unwound from her rear end.

"Next, I wrap him up." She grabbed the fly, threw a few jets of silk around it, and rolled it over and over, wrapping it so that it couldn't move. Wilbur watched in horror. He could hardly believe what he was seeing, and although he detested flies, he was sorry for this one.

"There!" said Charlotte. "Now I knock him out, so he'll be more comfortable." She bit the fly. "He can't feel a thing now," she remarked. "He'll make a perfect breakfast for me."

"You mean you *eat* flies?" gasped Wilbur.

"Certainly. Flies, bugs, grasshoppers, choice beetles, moths, butterflies, tasty cockroaches, gnats, midges, daddy longlegs, centipedes, mosquitoes, crickets—anything that is careless enough to get caught in my web. I have to live, don't I?"

"Why, yes, of course," said Wilbur. "Do they taste good?"

"Delicious. Of course, I don't really eat them. I drink them —drink their blood. I love blood," said Charlotte, and her pleasant, thin voice grew even thinner and more pleasant.

"Don't say that!" groaned Wilbur. "Please don't say things like that!"

"Why not? It's true, and I have to say what is true. I am not entirely happy about my diet of flies and bugs, but it's the way I'm made. A spider has to pick up a living somehow or other, and I happen to be a trapper. I just naturally build a web and trap flies and other insects. My mother was a trapper before me. Her mother was a trapper before her. All our family have been trappers. Way back for thousands and thousands of years, we spiders have been laying for flies and bugs."

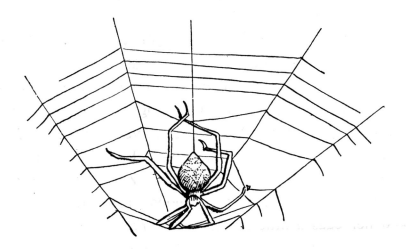

"It's a miserable inheritance," said Wilbur, gloomily. He was sad because his new friend was so bloodthirsty.

"Yes, it is," agreed Charlotte. "But I can't help it. I don't know how the first spider in the early days of the world happened to think up this fancy idea of spinning a web, but she did, and it was clever of her, too. And since then, all of us spiders have had to work the same trick. It's not a bad pitch, on the whole."

"It's cruel," replied Wilbur, who did not intend to be argued out of his position.

"Well, *you* can't talk," said Charlotte. "*You* have your meals brought to you in a pail. Nobody feeds me. I have to get my own living. I live by my wits. I have to be sharp and clever, lest I go hungry. I have to think things out, catch what I can, take what comes. And it just so happens, my friend, that what comes is flies and insects and bugs. And *further*more," said Charlotte, shaking one of her legs, "do you realize that if I didn't catch bugs and eat them, bugs would increase and multiply and get so numerous that they'd destroy the earth, wipe out everything?"

"Really?" said Wilbur. "I wouldn't want *that* to happen. Perhaps your web is a good thing after all."

The goose had been listening to this conversation and chuckling to herself. "There are a lot of things Wilbur doesn't know about life," she thought. "He's really a very innocent little pig. He doesn't even know what's going to happen to him around Christmastime; he has no idea that Mr. Zuckerman and Lurvy are plotting to kill him." And the goose raised herself a bit and poked her eggs a little further under her so that they would receive the full heat from her warm body and soft feathers.

Charlotte stood quietly over the fly, preparing to eat it. Wilbur lay down and closed his eyes. He was tired from his wakeful night and from the excitement of meeting someone for the first time. A breeze brought him the smell of clover—the sweet-smelling world beyond his fence. "Well," he thought,

"I've got a new friend, all right. But what a gamble friendship is! Charlotte is fierce, brutal, scheming, bloodthirsty—everything I don't like. How can I learn to like her, even though she is pretty and, of course, clever?"

Wilbur was merely suffering the doubts and fears that often go with finding a new friend. In good time he was to discover that he was mistaken about Charlotte. Underneath her rather bold and cruel exterior, she had a kind heart, and she was to prove loyal and true to the very end.

Wilbur and Charlotte become very good friends and live happily together in Mr. Zuckerman's barn. The day comes when Charlotte becomes a true "lifesaver" to Wilbur. The whole story is told in the book CHARLOTTE'S WEB.

ABOUT THE AUTHOR

E. B. White was born in Mount Vernon, New York, but has lived on a farm in Maine since 1938. For nearly fifty years, he has been a contributing editor and writer for a well-known national magazine. He is the author of many books for adults, and his three books for children are regarded as modern classics. One is *Charlotte's Web,* two chapters of which you have just read. The others are *Stuart Little,* a story about a boy only two inches tall who looks just like a mouse, and *The Trumpet of the Swan.*

Young people often ask Mr. White where he got the ideas for his children's books. A dream he had one night was the start of *Stuart Little,* and Mr. White gives this explanation of how he happened to write *Charlotte's Web:*

"I like animals, and my barn is a very pleasant place to be, at all hours. One day when I was on my way to feed the pig, I began feeling sorry for the pig because, like most pigs, he was doomed to die. This made me sad. So I started thinking of ways to save a pig's life. I had been watching a big gray spider at her work and was impressed by how clever she was at weaving. Gradually I worked the spider into the story, a story of friendship and salvation on a farm. . . .

"Are my stories true, you ask? No, they are imaginary tales, containing fantastic characters and events. In *real* life, a family doesn't have a child who looks like a mouse; in *real* life, a spider doesn't spin words in her web. But real life is only one kind of life—there is also the life of the imagination. And although my stories are imaginary, I like to think that there is some truth in them, too—truth about the way people and animals feel and think and act."

BOOKS TO ENJOY

THE OX OF THE WONDERFUL HORNS, *by Ashley Bryan*
Here are five African folktales that are full of fun and that capture the feeling of Africa.

HELEN KELLER, *by Margaret Davidson*
This biography tells about the early years and the unusual education of a remarkable woman.

MUNGO, *by Rosalie Fry*
Strange things happen when Richie discovers an alarmingly long creature, the last and gentlest of the ancient sea monsters.

ISABELLE THE ITCH, *by Constance C. Greene*
When Isabelle gets the chance to take over her brother's paper route, her extra energy is finally put to good use.

RAY CHARLES, *by Sharon Bell Mathis*
This short biography of a popular musician describes how he got his start and became successful in spite of his handicaps.

THE TOOTHPASTE MILLIONAIRE, *by Jean Merrill*
Can a couple of kids make a million dollars by inventing a toothpaste that tastes terrific and sells for almost nothing? Kate and Rufus try to find out.

HIGH ELK'S TREASURE, *by Virginia Driving Hawk Sneve*
In a present-day Sioux adventure story, Joe High Elk stumbles onto hidden treasure while searching for his lost horse.

Encore

Encore

STORIES

ARTICLES

POEMS

JUST FOR FUN

SKILL LESSONS

Three Strong Women by Claus Stamm

Long ago in Japan, there lived a famous wrestler, and he was on his way to the capital city to wrestle before the Emperor.

He strode down the road on legs thick as the trunks of small trees. He had been walking for seven hours and could walk for seven more without getting tired.

The time was autumn; the sky was a cold blue, the air chilly. In the small bright sun, the trees along the roadside glowed red and orange.

The wrestler hummed to himself in time with the long swing of his legs. Wind blew through his thin brown robe, and he wore no sword at his side. He felt proud that he needed no sword, even in the darkest and loneliest places. The icy air on his body only reminded him that few tailors would have been able to make warm clothes for a man so broad and tall. He felt much as a wrestler should—strong, healthy, and rather conceited.

A soft roar of fast-moving water beyond the trees told him that he was passing above a river bank. He hummed louder; he loved the sound of his voice and wanted it to sound clearly above the rushing water.

He thought, "They call me Forever-Mountain because I am such a good, strong wrestler—big, too. I'm a fine, brave man and far too modest ever to say so. . . ."

Just then he saw a girl who must have come up from the river, for she carried a bucket on her head.

Her hands on the bucket were small, and there was a dimple on each thumb, just below the knuckle. She was a round little girl with red cheeks and a nose like a friendly button. Her eyes looked as though she were thinking of ten thousand funny stories at once. She climbed up onto the road and walked ahead of the wrestler, jolly and bounceful.

"If I don't tickle that girl, I shall be sorry all my life," said the wrestler under his breath. "She's sure to go 'squeak,' and I shall laugh and laugh. If she drops her bucket, that will be even funnier—and I can always run and fill it again and even carry it home for her."

He tiptoed up and poked her lightly in the ribs with one huge finger.

The girl gave a squeal, giggled, and brought one arm down so that the wrestler's hand was caught between it and her body.

"Ho-ho-ho! You've caught me! I can't move at all!" said the wrestler, laughing.

"I know," said the jolly girl.

He felt that it was very good-tempered of her to take a joke so well, and he started to pull his hand free. Somehow, he could not.

He tried again, using a little more strength. "Now, now—let me go, little girl," he said. "I am a very powerful man. If I pull too hard, I might hurt you."

"Pull," said the girl. "You won't hurt me."

She began to walk, and though the wrestler tugged and pulled until his feet dug great furrows in the ground, he had to follow.

Ten minutes later, still tugging while following helplessly after her, he was glad that the road was lonely and that no one was there to see.

"Please let me go," he begged. "I am the famous wrestler Forever-Mountain. I must go and show my strength before the Emperor"—he burst out weeping from shame—"and you're hurting my hand!"

The girl steadied the bucket on her head with her free hand and looked over her shoulder. "You poor, sweet little Forever-Mountain," she said. "Are you tired? Shall I carry you? I can leave the water here and come back for it later."

"I do not want you to carry me. I want you to let me go, and then I want to forget I ever saw you. What do you want with me?" moaned the pitiful wrestler.

"I only want to help you," said the girl, now pulling him up and up a narrow mountain path. "Oh, I am sure you'll have no more trouble than anyone else when you come up against the other wrestlers. You'll win, or else you'll lose, and you won't be too badly hurt either way. But aren't you afraid you might meet a really *strong* man someday?"

Forever-Mountain turned white. He stumbled. He was imagining being laughed at throughout Japan as "Hardly-Ever-Mountain."

She glanced back.

"You see? Tired already," she said. "I'll walk more slowly. Why don't you come along to my mother's house and let us make a strong man of you? The wrestling in the capital isn't due to begin for three months."

"All right. Three months. I'll come along," said the wrestler.

"Fine," she said happily. "We are almost there."

She freed his hand. "But if you break your promise and run off, I shall have to chase you and carry you back."

Soon they arrived in a small valley. A simple farmhouse stood in the middle.

"Grandmother is at home, but she is an old lady and she's probably sleeping." The girl shaded her eyes with one hand. "But Mother should be bringing our cow back from the field. Oh, there's Mother now!"

She waved. The woman coming around the corner of the house put down the cow she was carrying and waved back.

She smiled and came across the grass, walking with a lively bounce like her daughter's.

"Excuse me," she said, brushing some cow hair from her dress. "These mountain paths are full of stones. They hurt the cow's feet. And who is the nice young man you've brought, Maru-me?"

The girl explained. "And we have only three months!" she finished.

"Well, it's not long enough to do much, but it's not so short a time that we can't do something," said her mother, looking thoughtful. "But he does look very weak. He'll need a lot of good things to eat. Maybe when he gets stronger, he can help Grandmother with some of the easy work about the house."

"That will be fine!" said the girl, and she called her grandmother—loudly, for the old woman was a little deaf.

"I'm coming!" came a creaky voice from inside the house, and a little old woman leaning on a stick and looking very sleepy tottered out the door. As she came toward them, she tripped over the roots of a great oak tree.

"Heh! My eyes aren't what they used to be. That's the fourth time this month I've tripped over that tree," she said, and wrapping her skinny arms about its trunk, pulled it out of the ground.

"Oh, Grandmother! You should have let me pull it up for you," said Maru-me.

"Hm. I hope I didn't hurt my poor old back," muttered the old lady. She called out, "Daughter! Throw that tree away, so no one will fall over it. But please make sure it doesn't hit anybody."

Maru-me's mother went to the tree, picked it up in her two hands, and threw it. Up went the tree, sailing end over end, growing smaller and smaller as it flew. It landed with a faint crash far up the mountainside.

"Ah, how clumsy," she said. "I meant to throw it *over* the mountain. It's probably blocking the path now, and I'll have to get up early tomorrow to move it."

The wrestler was not listening. He had very quietly fainted.

"Oh! We must put him to bed," said Maru-me.

"Poor, feeble young man," said her mother.

"I hope we can do something for him. Here, let me carry him; he's light," said the grandmother. She slung him over her shoulder and carried him into the house, creaking along with her cane.

The next day they began the work of making Forever-Mountain over into what they thought a strong man should be. They gave him the simplest food to eat, and the toughest. Day by day they prepared his rice with less and less water, until no ordinary man could have chewed it.

Every day he was made to do the work of five men, and every evening he wrestled with Grandmother. Maru-me and her mother agreed that Grandmother, being old and feeble, was the least likely to hurt him.

He grew stronger and stronger but hardly knew it. Grandmother could still throw him easily into the air—and catch him again—without ever changing her sweet old smile.

He quite forgot that outside this valley he was one of the greatest wrestlers in Japan and was called Forever-Mountain. His legs had been like logs; now they were like pillars. His big hands were hard as stones, and when he cracked his knuckles, the sound was like trees splitting on a cold night.

Sometimes he did an exercise that wrestlers do in Japan—raising one foot high above the ground and bringing it down with a crash. Then people in nearby villages looked up at the winter sky and told one another that it was very late in the year for thunder.

Soon he could pull up a tree as well as the grandmother could. He could even throw one—but only a short distance. One evening, near the end of his third month, he wrestled with Grandmother and won.

"Heh-heh!" she laughed. "I would never have believed it!"

Maru-me squealed with joy.

"Very good, very good! What a strong man," said her mother, who had just come home from the fields, carrying, as usual, the cow. She put the cow down and patted the wrestler on the back.

They agreed that he was now ready to show some *real* strength before the Emperor.

The next morning, Forever-Mountain tied his hair up in the topknot that all Japanese wrestlers wear and got ready to leave. He thanked Maru-me and her mother and bowed very low to the grandmother, since she was the oldest and had been a fine wrestling partner.

When Forever-Mountain reached the palace grounds, many of the other wrestlers were already there, sitting about eating great bowls of rice, comparing one another's weight, and telling stories. They paid little attention to Forever-Mountain, except to wonder why he had arrived so late this year. Some of them noticed that he had grown very quiet and that he took no part at all in their boasting.

All the ladies and gentlemen of the court were waiting in a special courtyard for the wrestling to begin. Behind a screen sat the Emperor—by himself, because he was too noble for ordinary people to look at.

The first two wrestlers chosen to fight were Forever-Mountain and a wrestler who was said to have the biggest stomach in the country. He and Forever-Mountain both threw some salt into the ring. It was understood that this drove away evil spirits.

Then the other wrestler, moving his stomach somewhat out of the way, raised his foot and brought it down with a fearful stamp. He glared at Forever-Mountain as if to say, "Now *you* stamp, you poor frightened man!"

Forever-Mountain raised his foot. He brought it down.

There was a sound like thunder; the earth shook, and the other wrestler bounced into the air and out of the ring, as gracefully as any soap bubble.

He picked himself up and bowed to the Emperor's screen.

"The earth-god is angry. Possibly there is something the matter with the salt," he said. "I do not think I shall wrestle this season." And he walked out, looking over one shoulder at Forever-Mountain.

Five other wrestlers then and there decided that they were not wrestling this season either. They all looked annoyed with Forever-Mountain.

From then on, Forever-Mountain brought his foot down lightly. As each wrestler came into the ring, Forever-Mountain picked him up very gently, carried him out, and placed him before the Emperor's screen, bowing most politely every time.

The court ladies and gentlemen looked troubled and a little afraid. They loved to see fierce, strong men tugging and grunting at each other, but Forever-Mountain was a little too much for them. Only the Emperor was happy behind his screen. He ordered all of the prize money handed over to Forever-Mountain. "But," he said, "you had better not wrestle anymore."

Forever-Mountain promised not to wrestle again. Everybody looked happier.

"I think I shall become a farmer," Forever-Mountain said, and he left at once to go back to Maru-me.

When Maru-me saw him coming, she ran down the mountain, picked him up, together with the heavy bags of prize money, and carried him halfway up the mountainside. Then she put him down. The rest of the way he carried her.

Forever-Mountain kept his promise to the Emperor and never fought in public again. But up in the mountains, sometimes, the earth shakes and rumbles, and they say then that Forever-Mountain and Maru-me's grandmother are practicing wrestling in the hidden valley.

AUGHOR

AUTHOR

Claus Stamm has lived in Japan, where he found the ideas for stories he has written. The story you have just read, taken from the book *Three Strong Women*, is a tall tale that Mr. Stamm heard in Japan. He liked the story so much that he decided to retell it in English. *Three Strong Women* has recently been published in paperback.

Esmé on Her Brother's Bicycle

One foot on, one foot pushing, Esmé starting off beside
Wheels too tall to mount astride,
Swings the off leg forward featly,
Clears the high bar nimbly, neatly,
With a concentrated frown
Bears the upper pedal down
As the lower rises, then
Brings her whole weight round again,
Leaning forward, gripping tight,
With her knuckles showing white,
Down the road goes, fast and small,
Never sitting down at all.

Russell Hoban

Chinese New Year

by Betty Lee Sung

Zzzz. . . . Boom! Bang! Boom boom! Bang bang! Firecrackers exploded everywhere. The noise split the air and bounced off the tall buildings surrounding Chinatown. String after string of firecrackers went off in front of stores and homes. Firecrackers are an important part of any Chinese celebration. The noise adds to the joy and is supposed to scare away the evil spirits.

Down the street, the dragon pranced and danced to the clang of cymbals and the beat of drums. The huge dragon head, held high by the lead dancer, was richly decorated with many-colored frills and tassels and bells.

The dragon stopped in front of a store, where the dancers saw a long cord. From it dangled a head of lettuce, a tangerine, a piece of coconut, and money wrapped in red paper.

The dragon bowed. He shook his head, and with a low swoop,

went into his routine. The long line of dancers holding the dragon tail twisted and turned like a snake.

The drums and cymbals beat louder and louder. The dragon reached for the lettuce on the cord. He tore it to shreds and scattered the leaves. He grabbed the tangerine and the coconut. Next came the money wrapped in red paper. Someone from the store pulled the cord up, and the dragon had to stretch higher. Still he could not reach it.

A dancer from the tail moved in under the dragon head. The head dancer leaped onto the shoulders of the tail dancer, keeping time to the beat of the drums. This time, the dragon reached the packet of money. He snapped the cord, made another bow before the store, and moved on down the street. This store was now protected by the dragon for the new year. The evil spirits no longer dared lurk.

The occasion was Chinese New Year, and Chinatown was celebrating the first day of the first moon of the lunar calendar. The Chinese base their calendar on the moon, not the sun. The beginning of the year may fall anywhere between January 20

437

and February 20. The years are figured in cycles of twelve, and each year is identified by the name of an animal. The twelve animals are the rat, ox, tiger, rabbit, dragon, snake, horse, sheep, monkey, chicken, dog, and pig. The Chinese government now uses the Western calendar. But the people still observe the holidays according to the lunar calendar.

Chinese New Year is the most important event of the year. For everyone, it not only marks renewed hopes for a better year, but it is also everyone's birthday. When the clock strikes midnight on the first day of the first moon, everyone is a year older.

Chinese New Year's celebrations last a long time. Weeks before the first day of the first moon, the house is cleaned from top to bottom. The rooms are filled with potted plants and sweet-smelling flowers such as chrysanthemums and miniature kumquat trees. Happy sayings or good wishes are written with a brush on red paper and are pasted over the doorways.

In the living room, a table is arranged with tangerines, oranges, and pomelos. The word for these fruits has the same sound as the word for good luck, so they are traditional foods for joyous times. Special treats are pastries and sweets — red melon seeds, sugared coconut strips, preserved fruits, and candies.

The last meal of the year is the most elaborate and the most important. It is called *tuan-yuan,* meaning "group around." New Year's Eve is a family festival, and everyone stays home instead of going out.

New Year's Day is a day for visiting and feasting. The children pay their respects to their elders and receive gifts of money wrapped in red paper. Everyone wishes one another best wishes for a happy and prosperous New Year. Everyone is careful to say and do the right thing, for superstition has it that whatever happens on New Year's Day determines the events for the coming year.

Certain things are forbidden on the first day of the New Year. These are spanking, crying, sweeping the floor, or washing the hair. If the floor is swept, the family luck may be swept away.

To the Chinese, the New Year is a time to begin a new slate. This means finishing chores left undone, settling disagreements, and most important, paying off all debts by the end of the old year.

In China, the New Year's celebration lasts at least seven days. In the United States, Chinese-American families do not have time to observe the New Year for a week or more. Different families follow those customs that have meaning and memories for them. They may just go to Chinatown to watch the fireworks and dragon dance. Or they may eat the traditional foods and visit their families.

The family groups, however, take this time to have banquets or get-togethers. Restaurants in Chinatown are sometimes booked solid through March for these festive events.

Even if Chinese Americans do not observe any of the other Chinese holidays, they like to celebrate the New Year. It is full of joy, fun, tradition, and ritual.

AUTHOR

The article you have just read is part of Betty Lee Sung's book *The Chinese in America*. In writing that book, Ms. Sung drew upon her own experiences. She herself is a Chinese American and lived for many years in China.

Once an editor and a librarian, Ms. Sung now teaches courses in Chinese-American heritage in a college in New York City.

Treasure Island, USA

by Rafe Gibbs

"May we come aboard, Captain Burnside?"

"Permission granted. Pipe our visitors aboard, Jason."

Jason, a fat, green parrot, was perched on top of a coat rack. He croaked anything but a piping note. Then two girls and two boys came aboard the screened front porch of Captain Otis Burnside, their good friend.

The captain's home on Sanibel Island, off the west coast of Florida, faced the Gulf of Mexico. His home was now his ship—his last command. Captain Burnside had been born in Bangor, Maine. There he grew up watching ships being built. He had first gone to sea as a cabin boy, and a ship had been his home most of his life. Now in his eighties, with his hair and beard turned a salty white, he spent his days and years with Jason, watching the sea.

Motels had been built on both sides of his old white frame home. People had tried to buy his beautiful beach with its giant royal palm trees. The captain would not allow the would-be buyers aboard even his front porch. However, the neighborhood children, who came to hear his stories of the Seven Seas, were always welcome.

Eleven-year-old Mary Scoggins was the oldest of the four who had just arrived. Her eyes always reminded the captain of the deep blue waters of the Bay of Bengal. Little Susan Sokolov, with her freckles, pigtails, and big smile,

was the youngest. In between were David Jenkins, who for his ten years was quite a business-man, and Freddie Newburg. Freddie had come visiting from New York only a few weeks before. Already he thought of Sanibel as his second home.

The children sat down on the floor around Captain Burnside's chair. The captain sighted along his gold-headed cane as if it were a telescope. "Where shall we sail to today?" he asked.

"We don't want to sail any-where today, Captain," said Mary. "We've got a problem."

"Tell me about it. Maybe I can help."

"You know about the money that's being raised to send little Marjorie Cook to Miami for op-erations—so she'll be able to walk again after her car accident? Well, the people at the chamber of com-merce just figured out a way the children on the island could help. They offered to give ten cents to the fund for every can or bottle we find on the beach or roadside."

"Well, what's wrong with that?"

"Nothing," said David. "But I guess people today aren't the litterbugs they used to be. We found only ninety dollars and forty cents' worth on the whole island."

"Ninety dollars and forty cents isn't to be sneezed at," said the captain. "You don't want people to get careless again with their bottles and cans, do you?"

"Gosh, no!" exclaimed Freddie.

"We just want to know how we can earn some more money to help get Marjorie to the hospital. They need twenty thousand dollars to cover hospital expenses, and they've collected only about six thousand, so we've come to you. You always seem to have an answer for everything."

Captain Burnside blushed.

"Hurump-ph! The answer to this question will take some thinking," he said.

Four eager faces watched hopefully as the captain thought and thought. Finally his eyes began to twinkle.

"How about digging for pirate treasure?"

"Pirate treasure! Where?" cried David. Before he tried anything, David always wanted to know exactly how it could be done.

So did Jason, the captain's parrot, because he echoed, "Where? Where?"

"Well, now, I guess I've never told you about the pirate José Gaspar, or Gasparilla, as he was better known. Many years ago,

he lived with his crew on the island north of us now called Gasparilla Island. From time to time he visited Captiva."

"You mean he was on the island right next door to us?" asked Susan.

"That's right, Susan—next door on Captiva. There was no bridge between Sanibel and Captiva then, of course. Now, I have reason to think that Gasparilla got over to Sanibel. I'll come to that in a minute.

"For years Gasparilla attacked ships sailing the Gulf of Mexico. He was a cruel man, killing the men on the ships he captured and looted. One day in 1821, he sighted a ship with what appeared to be cargo stacked on its decks. This, he thought, would be a rich prize.

"Off the pirates went in their ship, preparing to fire the cannons as they neared their victim. But the ship Gasparilla had sighted was not a trading vessel; it was the U.S.S. *Enterprise*. Quickly the American sailors

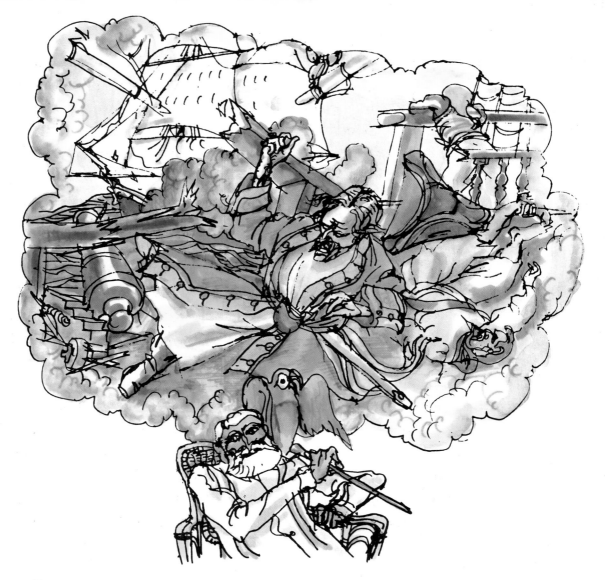

pulled the covering from their big guns and put an end to Gasparilla and his whole band of evil men.

"Captiva folk felt sure Gasparilla had left some of his treasure buried on Captiva, but they never found it. My idea is that Gasparilla figured people would look for it there. To fool them, he may have sailed across the channel on dark nights and buried his loot on Sanibel."

"But where?" repeated David.

"Yeah—where, where?" cawed Jason.

"Right on my beach!" replied Captain Burnside. "The palm trees on my land are very old and are the tallest on the island. They would have made good markers. Also, years ago I found this on my beach."

The captain dug into his pocket and pulled out a worn gold coin.

"This is an old Spanish doubloon. It used to be worth five to fifteen dollars, but it's worth much more now."

"That's great, Captain!" cried Mary. "Let's get digging!"

"Just a minute, Captain." Freddie held up his hand. "How come you never went digging yourself?"

The old man smiled gently.

"Jason and I have so few needs. My sailor's pension takes care of all of them. And I didn't want the land dug up. But this is a special case. Mrs. Cook has a hard time as a waitress bringing up four children. She could never pay big hospital bills for Marjorie. So I think it's time to start digging, with just one reminder. Every night all holes must be filled. I can't have people stepping into them in the dark."

"Let's go!" shouted four voices.

"Go! Go!" repeated Jason.

So the digging for pirate treasure on Sanibel Island began.

That night, as he did almost every night, Mr. Gabriel O'Toole arrived at Captain Burnside's house to play chess. Mr. O'Toole was a shell dealer. He bought and sold the many kinds of beautiful and interesting sea shells for which Sanibel is noted, such as Lion's Paw, Jewel Box, Junonia, Bleeding Tooth, Scotch Bonnet, and Turkey Wing. Mr. O'Toole was almost always a jolly man. Now, as he thought over a chess move, he seemed troubled, and not about the game.

"What's bothering you, Gabe?" asked the captain.

"You," answered Mr. O'Toole. "You've got everybody on the island talking about putting those youngsters to work looking for buried treasure."

"The children aren't complaining. They're having a lot of fun. And did you notice how nicely they covered up the holes they dug today?"

"Yes, but folks think it's going to be an awful letdown for those boys and girls when they don't find any treasure."

"Don't you fret, Gabe. You never know when and where in life you'll strike it rich. You just have to keep digging. And I feel it in my bones that those youngsters will come up with treasure of some sort."

"What sort?"

"Never you mind, Gabe. Uh— it's your move."

"Yeah, man, move . . . move," croaked Jason.

The next day, there were two major happenings. First, there was the trouble about the lemonade stand. The stand was the idea of David's in order to make money for the fund. He had gotten a table, a chair, an umbrella, lemons, sugar, ice, and paper cups from his family. He was doing a good business selling the lemonade to beach strollers who had stopped to watch the digging. But the diggers weren't buying— or digging. They were just sitting on the sand and glaring at David. They had decided he had a good thing going—in the shade.

Captain Burnside came out with cane in hand and Jason on shoulder. He pushed back his gold-braided cap and fixed his eyes on David, not saying a word. Jason started to sound off, but the captain lifted his shoulder, and the parrot stopped talking with a weak "caw-aw."

David became so upset that he spilled the lemonade he was pouring for a customer.

"Captain," he said, "we weren't making any money digging, and I thought . . ."

"Good idea, David, good idea," said Captain Burnside. "There's just one thing wrong. This try at hunting treasure is share and share alike. How about that, David?"

"That's easy, Captain," said

David, smiling. "I'll get back to digging, and everybody can take turns selling lemonade in the shade."

"Hurray for David!" cheered the sitters, ready to dig again—or sell lemonade.

"For he's a jolly good fellow . . ." squawked Jason.

Lemonade sales that day came to $40.80—all profit, thanks to David's family. What really boosted sales was the second big event of the day. Reporters from newspapers, radio, and television arrived from the mainland. Children digging for pirate treasure to help a child walk again made a good story. The reporters even wanted a picture of the lemonade stand. Susan was minding it at the time. She graciously said that David should be handing out the lemonade while the pictures were being taken. Not to be outdone, David asked Susan to pose with him.

Then Captain Burnside came out again to see what all the excitement was about. Before long,

he was being photographed showing the Spanish doubloon he had found on the beach. As he was holding it out, Jason flopped down out of a palm tree, landed on the captain's head, and got his share of attention.

Finally, Marjorie Cook was brought down to the beach in her wheelchair to be interviewed and photographed as she watched the digging.

"I want to thank my friends for what they're doing," she said.

"And I just wish that I could help them dig."

"Hey," said a TV reporter. "I'll bet this makes the national news. That ought to help."

She was right. The story was told on TV, on the radio, and in newspapers all over the country. The Sanibel Chamber of Commerce began to get telephone calls from people in different parts of the United States who said they were sending checks to help Marjorie. Some of the checks were small, but there was a really big one—for five thousand dollars—from a woman in Pittsburgh.

The next day the chamber of commerce put a huge chart in front of the building. The figures on it were changed daily to show the total amount in the Marjorie Cook Fund. Everybody on the island began to watch the chart.

Captain Burnside was afraid the children would toss away their shovels as the money poured in, but the rising figures on the chart seemed to make the diggers work even harder. David arranged

to borrow an electronic metal detector, a machine that looked something like a vacuum cleaner. Soon all the treasure seekers were taking turns passing it over the sand.

The detector helped turn up

449

all sorts of things: some small change and even an old silver dollar, an earring, two pocket-knives, a table fork, and a wedding ring. Mrs. Robardo, who lived nearby, was delighted to get back the ring she had lost seven years before.

Money continued to come in, and the fund climbed to $16,037. Then, for two days, the total didn't change except for $43.70, which had been collected from the lemonade sales.

That evening the four diggers visited Captain Burnside. They told him that they had dug in every possible spot on his land, and in a lot of other places as well, without finding any treasure. They were ready to give up.

"You've worked hard, and what you've done has added thousands of dollars to the fund," the captain said. "But the goal of twenty thousand hasn't quite been reached. It's too bad to give up now. When you're sailing a ship, you don't stop out in the ocean. You keep going until you get to shore. Also, I noticed that there's a spot on my land that you missed. Do you think you'd like to do a bit more digging there tomorrow?"

"Sure . . . sure . . ." chorused the four.

"Should I bring the detector?" asked David.

"Perhaps you'd better," said the captain.

The next morning the treasure hunters were at Captain Burnside's house before the captain and Jason had finished their breakfasts. The captain took one more bite of toast, then picked up his cane and went outside with the children. Jason waddled after them.

"David, bring the detector over here by the side of the house," said the captain.

David swung the detector back and forth, back and forth over the spot the captain pointed to.

"Nothing, Captain. There's not a thing."

"Keep moving it, David," said Susan.

Suddenly David stopped and stepped back.

"Captain, this thing's going wild!"

"Well, why are we just standing here?" cried Mary. "Let's shovel!"

And four shovels went into action. Down a foot—nothing. Down two feet—nothing. Then the point of Freddie's shovel struck something.

"Easy now . . . easy," warned the captain. "You don't want to damage whatever it is you've found."

Minutes later, Freddie and Mary lifted out of the hole an old metal box. The lid was stuck, but Captain Burnside pried it open with his pocketknife.

The children held their breath. All they could see were folds of

dark green velvet. The captain lifted up the cloth. Beneath it were shells—gorgeous seashells.

"Oh, no," said David, "not shells! We thought we had found real treasure."

"Ah, but you have!" declared Captain Burnside. "These are specimens of some rare shells of the world. Look at that Glory-of-the-Seas Cone—a beauty! And this Golden Cowry!" As he held the shells in his hand, they seemed to light up with color.

"You mean these shells are worth a lot of money, and we can turn it over to the fund?" asked Mary.

"The answer is yes to both questions. I'm the only one who has ever lived on this land. How these shells came to be buried here will probably always be a mystery. We'll have to see what Gabe O'Toole will give for this find."

At Mr. O'Toole's shop, the children again held their breath. The shell dealer first admired and then examined each of the

shells. When he finished, he did some figuring. Then he said, "I'll give thirty-five hundred — uh, thirty-seven hundred — for the whole collection."

The children started to shout, but Captain Burnside stopped them.

"Gabe," he said, "it will take just four thousand dollars to put the Marjorie Cook Fund over the top. Take another look at that Golden Cowry. I'm sure there's not another in the world that can match it. See if you can't raise your offer just a little bit more."

"Four thousand dollars!" agreed Mr. O'Toole.

The cheering that followed was heard over a good part of the island. Jason, on the captain's shoulder, began to flap his wings and screech loudly. Marjorie Cook and her mother were not long in getting the word.

That night as Captain Burnside and Mr. O'Toole sat before the chessboard on the captain's porch, Mr. O'Toole remarked, "I've wondered, Captain, when

I would get those shells of yours. I suppose you buried them out in your yard last night."

The captain chuckled.

"That I did, Gabe. Sometime, somewhere on either Sanibel or Captiva, somebody may find some of what Gasparilla left behind. But the children were getting tired, and treasure had to be found. So last night I got busy digging and shoveling and covering up my tracks . . . wound up with an aching back."

The captain was silent for a moment. Then he said, "I used to enjoy getting out those shells and looking at them. Collecting them took me a lifetime of wandering around the world. But, you know, I'll enjoy seeing Marjorie walk again a lot more."

Jason croaked from the coatrack, "You can say that again!"

AUTHOR

Rafe Gibbs decided to be a writer when he was about eleven years old. At thirteen, he wrote and sold his first short story for thirty-five dollars. He wrote his stories while sitting between boxes of canned goods in the storeroom of his father's grocery store in Yakima, Washington.

Mr. Gibbs studied writing at the University of Idaho. While in college, he had many articles published in magazines. He paid for much of his college education with the money that he earned.

After graduating with honors, Mr. Gibbs worked for five years for a newspaper in Milwaukee, Wisconsin. During World War II, he became a colonel in the United States Air Force. From 1946 to 1970 he was Director of Information and also taught a course in magazine writing at the University of Idaho. In 1970 he helped start Florida International University in Miami, Florida, where he was Dean of University Relations for three years. Recently he worked with the Idaho Historical Society, writing a history of the state.

New Hope for the Whooping Crane

by J. M. Roever

A strange noise sounds across the salt marshes like the notes of a toy horn. This call is the voice of one of the rarest birds in the United States — the whooping crane.

If bothered or angered, the whooping crane makes a loud call that can be heard more than a mile away. The call comes through a hollow neck passage called a windpipe. The crane's windpipe is longer than its whole neck. Part of the windpipe is coiled like a French horn, deep inside the crane's breast.

The life of a whooping crane begins deep in the wilderness of Canada's Northwest Territories. In late May or June the adult cranes build a nest in a clump of protected marsh grass. Normally two eggs are laid in the nest. For about thirty-four days the parents take turns sitting on the eggs to keep them warm.

The newly hatched chicks are covered with soft reddish down. As the young cranes grow, new feathers replace the soft baby down. These new feathers have a mixed color of grayish white and brownish red. Sometimes the young cranes look almost pink.

When whooping cranes are about four months old, the summer in Canada ends, and the young birds fly south with their parents. Whooping cranes fly with their long necks stretched out in front of them and their long black legs stretched out behind. Sometimes, when the winds are right, the whooping cranes join in a breathtaking show. Circling and diving, they swoop back and forth in the sky, and their majestic white wings flash and sparkle.

One by one the whooping crane families arrive at their winter feeding grounds on the coast of Texas. Each family group quickly selects a home territory. The area occupied by one whooping crane family often covers four hundred acres of marshland and water.

When the warm winds of spring blow over the Texas marshlands, the whooping cranes become restless. They sense that winter is ending in their nesting grounds in Canada. The young cranes lose their early feathers. Their new feathers are white, like those of their parents. Suddenly, the parent whooping cranes chase their full-grown offspring away.

As the time for spring migration nears, the adult birds do their courtship dance. Nodding his head and flapping his wings, the male crane struts toward his mate. He skips back and forth before the female crane and then leaps high into the air. His legs are stiff, his neck is bent over his back, and his bill is pointed toward the sky. The female crane suddenly joins him, and the birds do the dance together. Soon they will return to Canada to raise a new family.

Long ago, when large areas of water covered North America, great flocks of whooping cranes stalked through the marshes. As the years passed, the marshes began to dry up, and forests grew in their places. The flocks of whooping cranes slowly grew smaller. Most of the great birds settled in the marshes on the coasts of Texas and Louisiana.

The Louisiana whooping cranes did not migrate. The rest of the cranes migrated inland every spring to the wide prairie marshes. There they built their nests and raised their young.

When the pioneers, trappers, farmers, and hunters settled North America, the whooping cranes rapidly disappeared. The great prairie marshes were drained to make wheat fields and grazing lands. The marshy grasslands of Louisiana were changed into rice fields.

Looking for a safe place to raise their chicks, the cranes flew off to northern Canada. For more than thirty years no one knew where the great birds were hiding their nests. Still, every winter the whooping cranes flew south to the marshes of Louisiana and Texas. Sometimes they brought a few offspring with them. But often they returned fewer in number than before.

In 1940 a terrible storm blew the Louisiana cranes out of their marsh. A few years later the wild Louisiana cranes were gone forever. When all the wild whooping cranes of Texas and Louisiana were counted in 1941, only fifteen of them were left. The whooping cranes had almost disappeared from the earth.

Even before the storm of 1940, people were taking steps to save the wild whoopers. In 1916 the governments of the United States and Great Britain signed the Migratory Bird Treaty. The treaty made it illegal to kill whooping cranes and certain other birds in the United States and Canada. Later, the United States government bought a part of the Texas marshland as a safe winter home for the whooping cranes. Today this place is called the Aransas National Wildlife Refuge.

Even at Aransas the whooping cranes were not safe from the things people did. A deep channel for boats was made through the once-quiet salt marshes. Soon people were traveling by water into the whooping cranes' feeding grounds to hunt, to fish, and to see the sights. The noise from private planes broke the stillness of the wildlife refuge.

The greatest danger to the whooping cranes has always come from people. Today the overuse of chemicals and poisons threatens the cranes. Sea animals such as the blue crab, on which the

cranes feed, are always the first to die when poisons are washed into the water. Deadly DDT, a poison used to kill insects, has been found in the bodies and eggs of the unlucky cranes.

Because most people did not have a chance to see the few wild cranes that were still living, they gave all their attention to the only cranes they could visit—the cranes in captivity. The most famous of all captive whooping cranes was Josephine, "Queen of the Cranes." Josephine had been found in Louisiana by a farmer after the storm in 1940. She was the only one of her flock that had survived. For twenty-four years Josephine lived at the Audubon Park Zoo in New Orleans.

Josephine and Crip, a captive male whooping crane, raised four chicks. Their offspring live in the Audubon Park Zoo.

In April, 1956, a female whooping crane flew into a high wire in Texas and damaged her wing. She was rescued by a rancher and was sent to the San Antonio Zoo. There she was nicknamed Rosie. After Josephine's death, Rosie became Crip's new mate. In 1967 Rosie and Crip raised a male whooping crane named Tex.

The births of the baby cranes at the zoos showed that whooping cranes could be raised in captivity. Many people hoped that the offspring of captive cranes could be set free.

A plan was drawn up by the Canadian Wildlife Service and the United States Department of the Interior. In 1967 biologists flew to Wood Buffalo National Park, in Canada. They took six eggs from different whooping cranes' nests.

The Canadian biologists carried each egg in a wool sock to a waiting helicopter. They placed the eggs in incubators to keep them safe and warm. Then the American biologists lifted the incubators into a jet plane, which rushed them to their new home in the United States. The whooping cranes' eggs were finally put into special incubators at the Patuxent Wildlife Research Center in Maryland.

When the eggs hatched, the chicks received as much attention as human babies. Their food was specially prepared, and their pens were carefully warmed.

Two other whooping cranes were brought to live at Patuxent. One was Tex, the offspring of Rosie and Crip. The other was Canus, who was found hurt on the nesting grounds in Canada. His name is formed from the names of his two countries — Canada and the United States.

The experiment in Canada did not stop the wild cranes from hatching the eggs remaining in their nests. In 1967 they brought nine new offspring with them to the Aransas Refuge in Texas.

Today there is a new hope for the wild whooping cranes. They have grown in number from only fifteen birds in 1941 to about seventy-five birds in 1974. The strange call of the whooping crane still drifts across the marshes as it did many years ago.

Angry

Sometimes when the day is bad
And someone's made me very mad
Or I've been given angry stares,
I go behind the front porch stairs.

There, curled up with chin on knee,
I like to be alone with me
And listen to the people talk
And hurry by me on the walk.

There I sit, without a sound,
And draw stick pictures on the ground.
If I should tire of it all,
I throw some pebbles at the wall.

After I've been there awhile
And find that I can almost smile,
I brush me off and count to ten
And try to start the day again.

Marci Ridlon

RECOGNIZING IMPORTANT
STORY ELEMENTS

No matter what your favorite pastime is, the more you know about it, the more you can enjoy it. Playing or watching football or softball is more fun if you understand the rules. If you like to walk in the woods, knowing some wild flowers, trees, and birds to look for will make your walk more enjoyable. Reading a good story is more entertaining, too, if you know a few things to look for.

When authors write stories, they try to make them as interesting for their readers as they can. Before they even begin to write, they think about three important things that every story must have: characters, setting, and plot. If you think about these same things as you read a story, you will understand it better and enjoy it more.

The **characters** are the people or animals that are in the story. In the story from . . . *and now Miguel*, the characters are Miguel, his friend Juby, Mrs. Mertian, and Miguel's family, because they are the people who are in the story. The main character is the person who has the most important part in the story. In this story, Miguel is the main character, because the story is about an adventure of his. Sometimes a story has

more than one main character. Who are the main characters in "Chester Makes Some New Friends"? Are they both people? The other characters in a story are called minor characters, and often one of them is as interesting as a main character. Who is the minor character in "Chester Makes Some New Friends"? Do you think he is as interesting as Chester?

Every story happens in some place and at some time. The **setting** of a story is the combination of the place and time in which the events occur. The setting of "The Mystery of the

Moon Guitar" is San Francisco in the present day. Do you remember what the setting of "Androclus and the Lion" is? Often an author does not state a setting directly, as the author of "Androclus and the Lion" does. Instead, you may learn about the setting through the actions of the characters. What do the actions of the characters tell you about the setting of "The Spider, the Cave, and the Pottery Bowl"?

The **plot** of a story is the plan for the things that happen in the story. Usually, early in a good story, an author tries to get you interested in the plot. Some parts of the plan may be left in doubt, so you will want to read on to find out how they come out. One or more characters may have a problem, making you want to read on to find out how this problem is solved.

In "Treasure Island, USA," for example, you learn early in the story that the children are depending on Captain Burnside to help them find a way to earn money for a friend's medical bills. You want to keep reading to find out what he will suggest and whether or not his ideas will be successful.

Often you find that the plot shows characters having difficulties, some of them unexpected, in solving their problems. As you read along, you may find hints about how the characters are going to solve their problems in the story. For instance,

if you keep in mind that Captain Burnside's friend buys valuable seashells, you may not be surprised when the children's treasure turns out to be a box full of shells that are worth a great deal of money.

Sometimes, though, an author keeps you guessing about some things until the very end of the story. In "Treasure Island, USA," when did you learn that the captain had buried the seashells himself for the children to find?

A deeper feeling for the characters, setting, and plot can help you enjoy a story more. Make pictures in your mind of the characters and imagine how they would sound if you could hear them. As the author tells you more and more about the setting, use what you are told to picture in your mind the time and place, too. As the author develops the plot, notice the questions to be answered or problems to be solved. Then, notice the hints and clues that the author gives to help you guess how things are going to turn out.

If you remember to look for these three things in a story—characters, setting, and plot—you will find that you understand the story better and that you enjoy it more.

Discussion

Help your class answer each of the following questions:

1. What three important things must authors think about before they begin to write a story?
2. Who is the main character in "Arap Sang and the Cranes"? Who are the minor characters?
3. What is the setting of "Meet Delilah"?
4. Briefly explain the plot of "Androclus and the Lion."

On your own

On a sheet of paper, write the number of each question that follows and then your answer to it. If you cannot remember enough about any one of the stories, you may look at it again to refresh your memory.

1. Who are the main characters and who are the minor characters in "Little Vic's Greatest Race"?
2. Is the main character of "Pepe Goes North" a person or an animal?
3. What is the setting of "The Wolf Pack"?
4. What is the plot of the story "Three Strong Women"?

Checking your work

If you are asked to do so, read aloud one or more of your answers. Listen while other boys and girls read their answers, and compare your answers with theirs. If you made a mistake in any of your answers, find out why it is a mistake.

ERNESTINE ROSE

by Johanna Johnston

People have long believed that women should stay at home keeping house and caring for their families. But despite this unfair belief, many women have set out to do other kinds of important work. Ernestine Rose, who lived about one hundred years ago, was one of these women.

Every day Ernestine listened to her father say his prayers. Every day she heard him give thanks that he had not been born a woman. One day, she had to ask, "Why? What is wrong with being a woman?"

Her father was angry that she dared to question a prayer that Jewish men had said for hundreds of years. "Nothing is wrong with being a woman," he said. "It is just better to be a man."

Ernestine said, "But that doesn't seem fair."

Her father said, "Be quiet. Who are you to say what is fair or what is unfair?"

Who was she, indeed? She was Ernestine Potowski, the young daughter of a rabbi in a little town in Poland. But it seemed she was also a person who could not keep still when anything seemed wrong or unfair to her. She grew older and kept asking questions.

Finally, after her mother died, her father decided that Ernestine needed a husband. One day he told Ernestine that he had arranged a marriage for her.

Ernestine asked the man's name and then said, "Father, I'm sorry, but you must tell the man I cannot marry him. I don't love him."

Her father said, "I'll do no such

thing. The contract is already signed, the dowry promised."

Ernestine said, "I didn't sign any contract. If you won't tell him that there will be no marriage, then *I* will."

Ernestine went to the man's house and did so.

He said, "You are breaking the contract, so I will still claim the dowry that your father promised me."

Ernestine thought about this for a while. Then she decided to take the matter to court and speak as her own lawyer. For a young Jewish woman in Poland to do such a thing was unheard of. But Ernestine Potowski made it so clear that it would be unfair for the man to keep her dowry that the court ruled in her favor. She could keep her dowry and did not have to marry a man she did not love.

Before long, Ernestine left her father's house and went to live in Berlin, Germany. But she was soon traveling on—to England. Here she met a group of people who were giving their lives to

speaking out against laws and customs that seemed unfair. Suddenly, Ernestine knew that this was what she wanted to do with her life also.

She fell in love with a man, William Rose, who thought just as she did. Soon they were married. Together they decided that the United States might be the best place to speak out for the changes that were needed in the world, so they sailed for America.

They were excited by New York City. It was so big and colorful and busy. It happened that just then a New York senator was trying to pass a bill in the legislature to provide that when women were married, they could keep control of any money or property they owned. So Ernestine Rose began her life in America going from door to door, asking women to sign a paper saying that they were in favor of the bill. Ernestine was surprised that so few women were interested. She asked them if they liked having so few rights before the law.

Finally, because Ernestine and other workers would not give up,

the bill was passed. But it had taken years. By that time, Ernestine had begun to give lectures in public. This was something few women dared to do. When Ernestine came out on a platform, the men in the audience booed and jeered. Ernestine waited until they were quiet and then began to talk.

Sometimes she spoke about the unfair way women were treated. Sometimes she spoke about the unfairness of slavery. Very few people wanted to hear such talk, but Ernestine was such a good speaker that they listened in spite of themselves.

The years passed by, and as

Ernestine Rose traveled back and forth across the country, giving speeches, people began to feel that women — well, some women, anyway — could speak in public without shame. They also began thinking more seriously about some of the laws and customs in America that kept it from truly being "the land of the free."

Ernestine Rose spent thirty-three years traveling and speaking in the United States. Then she and her husband went back to England to live. But the woman who could not help speaking out against anything that seemed unfair had left a lasting mark on her adopted country.

AUTHOR

Johanna Johnston and her husband live in New York. She has written for radio and has worked for a broadcasting network. One of her many books for young readers is called *Great Gravity the Cat*. The ideas for it came from her own cat, Taffy. Another of her books is *Who Found America?*

The Bronze Hippo

by Shay Rieger

The first time I saw sculpture, I was seven years old. A teacher took our class to a museum. We saw beautiful Italian figures in marble. They were life-size, with every detail of their features and their clothes carved perfectly. Most of the sculptures were roped off from us, while others were enclosed in dusty glass cases. The teacher kept telling us, "Don't touch!" and the museum guards stood by to make sure that we didn't.

The only outdoor sculptures I saw as a child were those in the park. They were usually huge bronze statues of some general on horseback. They looked even more immense and distant because they stood on high pedestals. For a long time sculpture seemed to me to be a thing out of reach that had nothing to do with our daily lives.

Maybe it was because of that first museum that I was particularly happy when I was asked to

473

I often do quick pen-and-ink sketches, using just a few lines to suggest the forms and features I want to remember later.

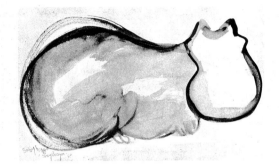

do bronze sculptures for a garden in Harlem, in New York City. The site chosen for the sculpture in the city was perfect—right in front of the entrance to a community center, where hundreds of children would pass each day and be able to reach and touch the sculptures.

Before starting the sculptures, I visited the zoo. I was planning to make a hippopotamus, a camel, and an elephant for the city garden in Harlem.

This is the beautiful young hippo I used as one of my models. The hippo is two years old and weighs six hundred pounds— and poses very nicely.

Later, in the studio, I began the sculpture. With the moist clay I molded the hippo, keeping the sketches nearby. While I was working on the clay, I kept in mind that the final form would be bronze. I wanted the finished bronze to express my sense of the hippo as a heavy, earthbound creature.

It took four weeks to finish the clay hippo and many more weeks to do the camel and elephant.

This is a foundry, where clay models are cast into bronze. Since this is done by a very special technique, most sculptors do not do this work themselves. It is done by trained workers at a foundry.

Making a clay sculpture into bronze involves many stages. One of the most important steps is making a wax reproduction of the clay model.

First, a rubber mold is made by pouring liquid rubber over the clay. When the rubber sets, it hardens into the exact form of the clay hippo.

The next step is to remove the

rubber mold and pour hot wax into it. The workers pour off the extra wax, leaving a thin layer inside that will harden into the shape of the clay model.

The men then pull the rubber mold off the hardened layer of wax. The wax hippo is just like the clay hippo except that it is hollow inside. Wax tubing is set into the form to make gates and air vents. The air vents allow air and gases to escape when the hot, molten bronze is poured. The gates allow the bronze to run into the mold.

The tubing in the mouth will be the opening for the pouring of the metal. The toothpicks are put in to make still more air vents, and the nails hold the mold together.

After it is sprayed with a solvent, the wax hippo is ready to be given a covering of plaster and silica. This mixture can withstand heat and will not burn away when the wax hippo is later put into an oven. The spray helps the mixture stick to the wax model.

A foundry worker begins to throw the mixture. It looks and feels like heavy cream and hardens quickly. It is also put inside the wax hippo to act as a core so that the bronze cast will be hollow. The wax hippo is encased in a block and is now nearly all covered except for the opening on top for pouring the bronze.

This oven is called a kiln. The wax hippo—in the plaster mold—is placed inside the kiln at a 1,000 degree temperature. The heat melts the wax, which runs out, leaving a space in the mold that is the exact shape of the hippo. It is into this space that the bronze will be poured.

Into the top opening of the mold the men are pouring the hot, molten bronze. The liquid metal will cool and harden in a few hours. Then a foundry worker will break the mold to free the bronze inside. The plaster core will also be broken and shaken out to make the sculpture hollow.

The bronze hippo emerges, but with some rough spots. A worker removes them with an electric file. This is called chasing. After the final touches—a bit of color and a coat of wax—the hippo is ready to be sent to the Harlem garden. Along with the hippo will go the camel and the elephant, which were also cast in bronze at the foundry.

At a dedication ceremony the animals are welcomed to the community. Here the camel, the elephant, and the hippo have been set in a cement base and become a permanent part of the garden.

There was a young lady of Niger
Who smiled as she rode on a tiger;
They returned from the ride
With the lady inside,
And the smile on the face of the tiger.

Anonymous

LIMERICKS

There was an old man in a barge,
Whose nose was exceedingly large;
But in fishing at night,
It supported a light,
Which helped that old man in a barge.

Edward Lear

480

Old Bessie, a brown speckled cow,
Tried to swim, but she didn't know how.
So she stitched up a sail,
Hitched it fast to her tail,
And you ought to see Bessie go now!

Edward Mullins

A TAME BEAR? by Walt Morey

Karl and Ellen Andersen and their son, Mark, lived in a small fishing village in Alaska. Mark was lonely there until he got to know Ben, a five-year-old Alaskan brown bear. Ben's owner had kept him in chains in a dark shed since he was a cub, and until Mark started visiting Ben on his way home from school, no one realized that the huge brownie had grown up to be a tame, gentle animal. In a short time, the two became good friends.

When Ben's owner decided to have him killed, Mark pleaded with his father to buy Ben and save his life. Mr. Andersen was reluctant at first. Alaskan brown bears are meat-eating animals and can be dangerous. Ellen Andersen, however, had seen Ben and her son together, and knew that the bear would never harm the boy. After seeing Mark and Ben together for himself, Mr. Andersen finally gave in, but he couldn't help wondering if he had made the right decision.

As this story from the book *Gentle Ben* begins, Mark and his mother have made plans to take Ben down to the creek with them while they gather grass to make him a bed of hay. Mr. Andersen has insisted that his fishing partner, Clearwater, take a rifle and go along to protect them—just in case.

When Mark came hurrying down the trail and into the kitchen after school, Clearwater was sitting at the table, finishing a cup of coffee. He was short and broad, with a deep chest and powerful shoulders. "Clearwater should have been at least a six-footer," his father often said, "but his legs quit growing too soon." His face was round and full and deeply tanned. His bullet head held only a fringe of gray hair around the ears. Winter and summer he wore a black knit beret. In summer it protected his bald head from the sun and in winter kept it warm. He had merry gray eyes and a ready smile, but neither were in evidence today.

He finished his coffee, and rose. "All right. Let's get goin'," he said, and reached for the rifle.

Mark and Clearwater led the way up the trail to Ben's shed. Mark's mother followed them, carrying the new scythe. She was dressed in jeans and a man's light shirt, the sleeves rolled above her round, lightly tanned arms.

At the shed Clearwater said, "Your dad tells me you can handle this brute. All right, bring 'im out. But don't get in my way. Understand?"

"There won't be any trouble with Ben," Mark's mother said.

"Course not." Clearwater's voice was unusually harsh. "He's just a five-year-old brownie! As gentle as a day-old kitten."

When Mark brought Ben into the sunlight, Clearwater stepped back and studied Ben as the bear stood blinking in the bright sunlight, swinging his head and sampling the breeze. "All right," he said finally. "Take off, Mark."

Clearwater made Mark and Ben walk ahead. He came a few feet behind, rifle cradled in his arms, finger on the trigger.

Mark's mother came last. The scythe was slung across her shoulder, and a small smile lifted her lips.

They crossed the soft, sun-warmed tundra with Ben lumbering along at his pigeon-toed gait, first behind, then beside Mark. Every few feet he stopped and thrust his inquisitive black nose into the tundra moss. Mark pulled at him, urging and scolding: "Come on. You know what that smells like. You don't eat tundra moss. We're going down to the creek where you can get grass and roots and things like that. Now, quit fooling around and come on." Ben seemed to understand, or else he decided there was nothing in the tundra moss to eat. He finally fell in beside Mark, and padded steadily along with no more stops to sniff and investigate.

They dropped over the rim of the tundra into the small valley where the creek ran and the long grass grew. Mark's mother said, "This is fine. This grass will make good hay."

Mark unsnapped the chain, and Clearwater said sharply, "You're not turnin' him loose?"

"He won't go far," Mark said.

"Well, why not?" Clearwater said grimly. "It'd take a dozen men to hold th' brute anyway."

Ben padded off a few feet, blew loudly into a tempting clump of grass, ripped it out, and began chewing with a great smacking of lips.

Clearwater stationed himself on guard on a small hump of ground, prepared to watch his three charges.

Mark and his mother paid no further attention to Ben or Clearwater. Ellen said, "This is the way you scythe grass, Mark. I did it often as a girl at home. The scythe is one of the oldest farm tools known. For thousands of years it was the only way people had to cut grass and grain." She gripped the stubby handles and swung the scythe with a smooth, full-armed sweep. There was a sound like ripping cloth, and a narrow half-moon of grass fell smoothly before the flashing blade. She stepped forward, set her feet, and the scythe flashed again. There was the ripping sound, and the half-moon had doubled in size.

Mark watched for several minutes. Then she stopped and held out the scythe to him. "Don't try to use the full length of the blade. Cut with the last six inches or so. Try it."

Mark set himself, and swung. The point dug into the soft earth. He reached too far, took too wide a cut, and got less than half the grass. He swung too high, and the grass bent before the blade. It took some minutes to get the feel, for the timing and rhythm to come. Finally he laid down his first half-moon of grass. It was not as smooth as his mother's or as neat, but it was cut.

Scything, Mark discovered, was hard work. He soon tired. Then his mother took the scythe and cut grass while he rested. They took turns cutting for some time, and the field of mown grass grew rapidly.

They had stopped once to rest and survey their work when Clearwater left his mound and came over to them. "Feel kind of silly standin' there with a rifle, doin' nothin' while you two do all th' work," he explained.

"You're the guard," Mark's mother explained.

"Guard from what?" Clearwater asked. "Look over there."

A short way off, Ben had just finished a particularly succulent patch of grass and now gave every indication he was ready for his afternoon nap in the shade of a willow bush.

"You've decided he's tame and not dangerous?" Mark's mother asked.

"Nope," Clearwater said promptly. "Brownies're untamable, unpredictable, and dangerous. But he's gonna take a nap for an hour at least, and he's right in plain sight where I can peek at him every few minutes. So I might as well make myself useful." He laid down the rifle and said, "Gimme that grass cutter. You two take it easy while I do some mowin'."

At first Clearwater did not do much better than Mark had done. But he concentrated on the job, and soon, because of his greater strength, the cut was smooth and even. He became fascinated watching the grass fall in a clean sweep before the blade. A drop of sweat formed at the band of his beret and tracked down his leather-brown cheek. He was smiling, enjoying himself, ripping the scythe through with mighty strokes, when there was an explosive "Whoof!" at his very heels. He had heard that sound many times before, and knew exactly what it meant. He dropped the scythe and dived for the rifle. His feet tangled in the long grass and he sprawled full length. The beret bounced from his head and landed a few feet off. He rolled over frantically, gathered himself to spring erect—and froze.

Ben towered over him, his huge head bent down not more than a yard away. In all his years in the North, Clearwater had never looked into the face of a brownie this close, or looked up at one from a prone position. Ben looked immense, a veritable mountain of bone, muscle, and fur. Clearwater could see the black nostrils expand and contract as they sucked in the man scent. The big head stretched closer, and Ben's little eyes studied Clearwater.

Clearwater darted a glance at the rifle twenty feet away. He thought of springing to his feet and dashing for it, but he knew he'd never make it. Clearwater decided that his only chance was to lie perfectly still. In his sixty years in the North, he had come through many tight spots by refusing to panic.

He lay still and taut, staring back into Ben's eyes, his fingers digging into the soft earth while he waited. He waited for Ben's curiosity to be satisfied, for the bear to turn away, or for his nearness and the man scent to arouse the killing lust within him.

Then he heard Ellen's clear laugh and Mark's too, high and gleeful. The boy came running through the grass, threw an arm around Ben's neck, and stood laughing down at Clearwater. "He likes you. Ben likes you, Clearwater."

"He does?" Clearwater asked skeptically. "You can tell?"

"Of course." Mark was still laughing. "Just look at him."

Clearwater had every opportunity. The bear's lips were not drawn back to disclose long ugly teeth ready to rip and tear. He saw only the brownie's insatiable curiosity, and an apparent lack of fear of human scent.

"Pet him," Mark said, suiting the action by banging Ben solidly between the eyes with his hand. "Go ahead, Clearwater; scratch his ears, like this. He likes it."

Clearwater was no coward. And here a slip of a boy with an arm about the brute's neck was urging him on confidently. And behind them stood Ellen, hands on hips, smiling. Clearwater carefully stretched forth a hand and touched Ben's ear. Nothing happened. He scratched tentatively. Ben rolled his big head, so that Clearwater automatically scratched first one ear, then the other.

"He likes being scratched under the chin most," Mark volunteered. "Scratch him under the chin, Clearwater."

More confident, Clearwater thrust his hand under the massive chin and raked his stubby fingers through the coarse hair.

"Harder, scratch harder," Mark urged.

Ben flattened his head, stretched his neck, and moved closer until his black nose was no more than a foot from Clearwater's chest. He closed his eyes blissfully and began grunting like a pig, with pure delight. Clearwater looked at Mark and at Ellen. He began to grin. He scratched harder. Then he suddenly laughed outright. His other hand came forward and patted Ben between the eyes as he'd seen Mark do. "Benjamin"—he laughed delightedly—"you're quite a boy. Yes, siree, so help me Hannah! You're quite a boy!" He gave Ben a final pat, a final scratch, and scrambled up.

Ben thrust his nose up at Clearwater, sucked in a single explosive sniff, then turned and padded off. Clearwater retrieved his beret and the scythe, and stood watching Ben, who had stopped to dig up a skunk-cabbage root.

Ellen asked quietly, "A tame brownie, Clearwater?"

"What else?" Clearwater agreed. He punched the beret back on his head. "Forty years I been around these brutes, and now I find I don't know a thing about 'em. How about that?"

They worked another hour, the three of them taking turns scything. Ben wandered among them, hunting tender shoots and digging roots.

Finally Mark's mother stopped and wearily surveyed the field of cut grass. "We've got enough," she said. "Tomorrow we can gather it into piles."

When they were ready to leave, Clearwater could not find the rifle. They hunted about, kicking through the mown grass. Ben finally found it. Some faint aroma of burned powder or gun oil touched his delicate nostrils, and curiosity sent him digging through layers of fresh-cut grass. Clearwater saw him pawing and sniffing at the muzzle of the rifle. "Fine guard," he grumbled to Mark's mother. "Can't even keep track of th' rifle." He patted Ben, and said, "Nice goin', pal."

Mark put the chain on Ben, and they trudged off across the tundra toward home. This time Clearwater carried both the rifle and the scythe.

Mark and Ben have many adventures together. You can read about them in Walt Morey's book *Gentle Ben.*

AUGHOR

Walt Morey has lived in the American Northwest for most of his life. Following World War II, he went to Alaska where he was an inspector of fish traps. Today Mr. Morey and his wife operate a sixty-acre filbert farm located a few miles outside Portland, Oregon. Because of his fondness for the wilderness areas in Alaska, however, Mr. Morey hopes to go back to Alaska someday.

Toad's Tongue Twister

A tree toad loved a she-toad
That lived up in a tree.
He was a two-toed tree toad,
While a three-toed tree toad was she.
The he-toad tree toad tried to gain
The she-toad's friendly nod,
For the two-toed tree toad loved the ground
That the three-toed tree toad trod.
The two-toed tree toad tried in vain
But couldn't please her whim,
For from her tree toad bower
With her she-toad power
The three-toed tree toad vetoed him.

American folk rhyme

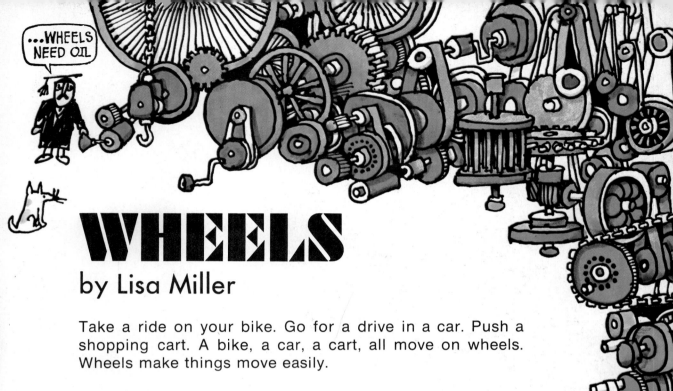

WHEELS

by Lisa Miller

Take a ride on your bike. Go for a drive in a car. Push a shopping cart. A bike, a car, a cart, all move on wheels. Wheels make things move easily.

Wheels help us to move things because they cut down *friction.* Friction is the force that makes objects hard to move when they rub against each other.

Little, highly polished balls called ball bearings, or roller bearings, help to reduce friction in many wheels. Instead of the wheel rubbing against its axle, it slides around smoothly on the roller bearings. Both the wheel and the axle touch only a tiny part of each ball. And the balls touch only a tiny part of each other. There is very little friction. That is why you can skate faster on ball-bearing roller skates than on learners' skates.

DAM TO STORE WATER...

WATER MILL

GRAIN IS GROUND INTO FLOUR BETWEEN THE TURNING MILL-STONES...

MILLSTONES

AXLE

GEAR

FALLING WATER TURNS THE WATERWHEEL ...

Oil and grease help reduce friction, too. The wheel joints on a car are greased regularly. The grease makes the wheel spin easily on the axle instead of rubbing on it and wearing it down. The wheels on a locomotive are greased. So are the wheels on a lawn mower. And even a Ferris wheel needs grease!

Wheels are used for more than moving people and goods. A wheel and its axle is a *simple machine.* A machine is any device that helps us to do work. Wheels help us to do many different kinds of work. They make things move more easily, or faster — or both.

A doorknob is a wheel. If you had to open a door *without* a knob to turn, you would have a very hard time. A doorknob is a wheel you can easily grasp in your hand. It is easier to turn a large wheel than a small one.

A different kind of wheel is a waterwheel. A waterwheel is turned by water instead of your hand. As the wheel turns, it moves other wheels that grind grain. A paddle wheel is also a waterwheel. It is used to move a boat.

COG

BIG GEAR

LITTLE GEAR

STEAM ENGINE DRIVES PADDLE WHEEL...

494

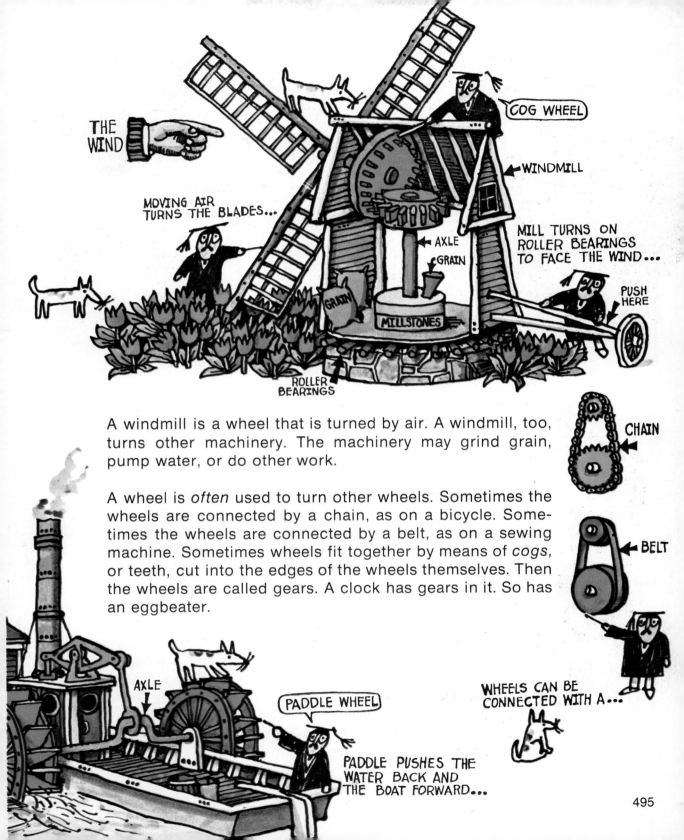

THE WIND

COG WHEEL

WINDMILL

MOVING AIR TURNS THE BLADES...

MILL TURNS ON ROLLER BEARINGS TO FACE THE WIND...

AXLE

GRAIN

GRAIN

MILLSTONES

PUSH HERE

ROLLER BEARINGS

A windmill is a wheel that is turned by air. A windmill, too, turns other machinery. The machinery may grind grain, pump water, or do other work.

A wheel is *often* used to turn other wheels. Sometimes the wheels are connected by a chain, as on a bicycle. Sometimes the wheels are connected by a belt, as on a sewing machine. Sometimes wheels fit together by means of *cogs,* or teeth, cut into the edges of the wheels themselves. Then the wheels are called gears. A clock has gears in it. So has an eggbeater.

CHAIN

BELT

AXLE

PADDLE WHEEL

WHEELS CAN BE CONNECTED WITH A...

PADDLE PUSHES THE WATER BACK AND THE BOAT FORWARD...

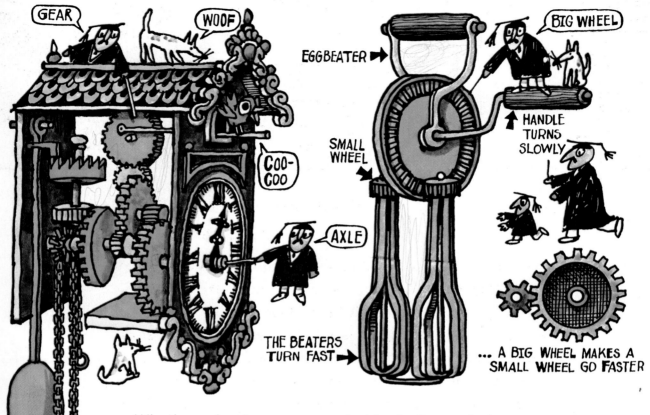

Whether wheels are connected by belts or chains or gears, a large wheel always makes a small wheel turn faster. The handle on an eggbeater is a large wheel, and it is easy to turn. It drives a small wheel that makes the beaters go. No matter how fast you turn the big wheel, the small wheel goes much faster. That is why the beater can always turn faster than your hand.

If you look around your house, you will find many wheels. The dial on your telephone is a wheel. The knobs on your television set are wheels. And so are the knobs on your stove. The turntable of your record player is a wheel. So is a fan. There are even wheels in the washing machine and in the refrigerator.

Wheels are everywhere. See how many you can find.

RECOGNIZING ELEMENTS
OF AUTHOR'S STYLE

You already know that authors use the important story elements of character, setting, and plot to make their stories as
interesting as possible. You know that keeping these story
elements in mind as you read will help you to enjoy a story.
You can also learn to recognize other ways by which authors
make their stories interesting and enjoyable.

Reread the first paragraph of the story from *Charlotte's Web*
on page 403 to see which word is repeated several times. Does
the repetition of the word *rain* help you to feel how dreary the
day was? Continue reading until you come to the picture on
page 404. Most of the paragraphs about Wilbur's plans for
the day begin in the same way, although the exact words are
not repeated. What is similar about the way these paragraphs
begin? The **repetition** produces an orderly sound that helps
you to realize how much Wilbur liked to get everything "all
beautifully planned out."

Repetition may be part of an author's **style,** or the individual
way an author writes. Although every author has a style of
his or her own, some elements of style are used by many
authors. The author of "Jack and the Three Sillies" also uses
repetition, but he uses it in a different way. In the story, the

man with the pig sees Jack and his *unruly* cow and asks, "You havin' a little trouble?" Then an old woman with a goose sees Jack with the *unruly* pig and asks, "Havin' trouble, Jack?" When the goose becomes *unruly* and Jack meets a girl with a cat, you are ready for her question. What does she ask? Repetition of the same or almost the same question and repetition of the word *unruly* to describe the cow, the pig, and the goose help to make this part of the story funny.

An author's **choice of descriptive words** is another element of style. Authors use descriptive words to help you picture what is happening in a story. The author of "The Train That Never Came Back" helps you picture the day of the forest fire by writing about the "smoky sunlight," "the bluish-gray smoke," and the "great showers of sparks." What other words help you picture the events in the story?

There are spider webs in three selections in *Medley,* and each one is described in a different way for a different purpose. E. B. White wants to go on to tell you a great deal about Charlotte, so all he wants you to know about the web is where it is and how large it is. He writes, "Stretched across the upper part of the doorway was a big spider web." Eleanor Clymer wants you to know why Kate, in "The Spider, the Cave, and the Pottery Bowl," noticed the web. She writes, ". . . drops of water on the threads sparkled in the light." Each author chose a different way to call your attention to the web.

The third spider web is in "Along Sandy Trails." Ann Nolan Clark wants you to imagine what the web looked like, and she uses a **comparison** to help you. She writes, "A cobweb hangs between two leaves like a lace mantilla spun of starlight thread." Here is another comparison from the same poem: "The ocotillo branches are tipped with torches of fire." Do these comparisons make it easier for you to picture the spider web and the ocotillo branches? Can you find other comparisons in the poem?

Authors use other elements of style as well as repetition, choice of descriptive words, and comparison to make their stories interesting. The next time you read something that particularly pleases you, take the time to reread it, paying attention to the way the author has written it. Doing this will help you become aware of the care good authors take in their writing and the beauty they can create for a careful reader.

Discussion

Help your class answer each of the following questions:
1. What is meant by an author's style?

2. What are some elements of an author's style?

3. Why do authors use descriptive words and comparisons in stories?

4. An author may use repetition in a story to make more clear a character's feelings about something. What else can repetition be used for?

On your own

On a sheet of paper, write the number of each question that follows and then your answer to it.

1. On pages 405–406 of the story from *Charlotte's Web*, Wilbur is looking for a friend. He asks three different animals the same, or nearly the same, question. What is his question?

2. In the first paragraph on page 205, what does Miguel say that sheep smell like? What element of style is used to tell you that?

3. In the first three lines on page 309 of "The Wolf Pack," Pa repeats the same comparison twice to tell how the wolves behaved. What does he compare them to?

4. In the first complete paragraph on page 379 of "Arap Sang and the Cranes," a sentence tells how the unfortunate crane looked. Find that sentence, and write down the descriptive words that help you picture how the crane looked.

Checking your work

If you are asked to do so, read aloud one or more of your answers. Listen while other boys and girls read their answers, and compare your answers with theirs. If you made a mistake in any of your answers, find out why it is a mistake.

from UNDERSTOOD BETSY

by Dorothy Canfield Fisher

Betsy Has a Birthday

Betsy was a shy, nervous little girl who had lived with two of her aunts in a city in the middle of the United States. Her aunts understood her, or so they thought, and gave her the very best care. They insisted on doing everything for her, so that she never had to think for herself. But when one of her aunts became ill, Betsy had to be sent to stay with her relatives in Vermont. Life at Putney Farm with Aunt Abigail, Uncle Henry, and Cousin Ann was a new experience for Betsy. Here a little girl was expected to know how to do and think for herself.

This story from the well-loved book UNDERSTOOD BETSY *tells about Betsy's visit to the county fair with Molly, a little six-year-old who also was living at Putney Farm. When a problem occurred at the fair that day, Betsy solved it in a way that showed she had learned to do her own thinking very well.*

Betsy's birthday was the ninth day of September, and the Necronsett Valley Fair is always held from the eighth to the twelfth. So it was decided that Betsy should celebrate her birthday by going up to Woodford, where the fair was held. The Putneys weren't going that year, but the people on the next farm, the Wendells, said they could make room in their surrey for the two little girls; for, of course, Molly was going, too.

When the great day arrived and the surrey drove away from the Wendells' gate, Betsy, because it was her birthday, sat on the front seat with Mr. Wendell. Part of the time, when there were not too many teams on the road, she herself drove. Mrs. Wendell and her sister filled the back seat solidly full from side to side and made one continuous lap on which Molly happily perched, her eyes shining, her round cheeks red with joyful excitement.

The two little girls were thrilled by the sights and sounds and smells of their first county fair. They were allowed to wander about as they pleased until noon, when they were to meet the Wendells in the shadow of Industrial Hall and eat their picnic lunches together. The two parties arrived from different directions, having seen very different sides of the fair. The children were full of the merry-go-rounds, the balloon seller, the toy-venders, and the popcorn stands, while the Wendells exchanged views on the shortness of a hog's legs, the dip in a cow's back, and the thickness of a sheep's wool. The Wendells, it seemed, had met some cousins they hadn't expected to see, who, not knowing about Betsy and Molly, had hoped that they might ride home with the Wendells.

"Don't you suppose," Mrs. Wendell asked Betsy, "that you and Molly could go home with the Vaughans? They're here in their big wagon. You could sit on the floor with the Vaughan children."

Betsy and Molly thought this would be fun and agreed enthusiastically.

"All right, then," said Mrs. Wendell. She called to a young man who stood inside the building, near an open window, "Oh, Frank, Will Vaughan is going to be in your booth this afternoon, isn't he?"

"Yes, Ma'am," said the young man. "His turn is from two to four."

"Well, you tell him, will you, that the two little girls who live at Putney Farm are going to go home with them. They can sit on the bottom of the wagon with the Vaughan young ones."

"Yes, Ma'am," said the young man, with a noticeable lack of interest in how Betsy and Molly got home.

"Now, Betsy," said Mrs. Wendell, "you go round to that booth at two and ask Will Vaughan what time they're going to start for home and where their wagon is. Then you be sure not to keep them waiting a minute."

"No, I won't," said Betsy. "I'll be sure to be there on time."

She and Molly still had twenty cents to spend out of forty they had brought with them, twenty-five earned by berry-picking, and fifteen a present from Uncle Henry. They now put their heads together to see how they could make the best possible use of their four nickels. Betsy was for merry-go-rounds, but Molly yearned for a big red balloon; and while they were buying that, a man came by with toy dogs. He called out that they would bark when you pulled their tails, and seeing the little girls looking at him, he pulled the tail of the one he held. It gave forth a fine loud yelp. Betsy bought one all done up neatly in a box tied with blue string. She thought it a great bargain to get a dog that would bark for five cents. (Later, when they undid the string and opened the box, they found the dog had one leg broken off and wouldn't make the faintest squeak when its tail was pulled.)

Now they had ten cents left, and they decided to have a ride apiece on the merry-go-round. But, glancing up at the clock-face in the tower over Agricultural Hall, Betsy noticed it was half-past two. She decided to go first to the booth where Will Vaughan was to be and find out what time they would start for home. She found the booth with no difficulty, but William Vaughan was not in it, nor was the young man she had seen before. There was a new one, a strange one, a careless, whistling young man, with very bright socks and striped cuffs. He said, in answer to Betsy's inquiry, "Vaughan? Will Vaughan?

Never heard the name." Immediately he went on whistling and looking up and down the aisle over the heads of the little girls, who stood gazing up at him with very wide, startled eyes.

An older man leaned over from the next booth and said, "Will Vaughan? He from Hillsboro? Well, I heard somebody say those Hillsboro Vaughans had word one of their cows was sick, and they had to start right home that minute."

Betsy came to herself out of her momentary daze and snatched Molly's hand. "Hurry! Quick! We must find the Wendells before they get away!"

In her alarm (for she was really very much frightened) she forgot how easily terrified little Molly was. Her alarm instantly sent the child into a panic. "Oh, Betsy! Betsy! What will we do!" she gasped as Betsy pulled her along the aisle and out the door.

"Oh, the Wendells can't be gone yet," said Betsy, though she was not at all sure she was telling the truth. She ran as fast as she could drag Molly's fat legs, to the horse shed where Mr. Wendell had tied his horses and left the surrey. The horse shed was empty, quite empty.

Betsy stopped short and stood still, her heart seeming to be up in her throat so that she could hardly breathe. After all, she was only ten that day, you must remember. Molly began to cry loudly, hiding her weeping face in Betsy's dress. "What will we do, Betsy! What can we *do*!" she wailed.

Betsy did not answer. She did not know what they *would* do! They were eight miles from Putney Farm, far too much for Molly to walk, and anyway, neither of them knew the way. They had only ten cents left, and nothing to eat. And the only people they knew in all that throng of strangers had gone back to Hillsboro.

"What will we do, Betsy?" Molly kept on crying out, horrified by Betsy's silence.

The other child's head swam. She asked herself, desperately, "What would Cousin Ann do if she were here?" But that did not help her much because she could not possibly imagine what Cousin Ann would do under such circumstances. Yes, one thing Cousin Ann would be sure to do, of course: She would quiet Molly first of all.

At this thought, Betsy sat down on the ground and took the panic-stricken little girl into her lap, wiping away the tears and saying, "Now, Molly, stop crying this minute. I'll take care of you, of course. I'll get you home all right."

"How'll you ever do it?" sobbed Molly. "Everybody's gone and left us. We can't walk!"

"Never you mind how," said Betsy, trying to be brave, though her own underlip was quivering a little. "That's my surprise for you. Just you wait. Now come on back to that booth. Maybe Will Vaughan didn't go home with his folks."

She had very little hope of this and went back there only because it seemed to her a little less strange than every other spot in the howling wilderness about her. All at once the fair, which had seemed so lively and cheerful and gay before, seemed a frightening, noisy place, full of hurried strangers who came and went their own ways, with not a glance for two little girls stranded far from home.

The young man in bright colors was no better when they found him again. He stopped his whistling only long enough to say, "Nope, no Will Vaughan anywhere around here yet."

"We were going home with the Vaughans," murmured Betsy, hoping for some help from him.

"Looks as though you'd better go home on the cars," advised the young man casually. He smoothed his black hair back straighter than ever and looked over their heads.

"How much does it cost to go to Hillsboro on the cars?" asked Betsy with a sinking heart.

"You'll have to ask somebody else about that," said the young man. "I don't know anything about this state. I never was in it before."

Betsy turned and went over to the older man who had told them about the Vaughans.

Molly trotted at her heels, quite comforted now that Betsy was talking so competently to grownups. She did not hear what they said, nor try to. Now that Betsy's voice sounded all right, she had no more fears. Betsy would manage somehow. Then Betsy led her away again out-of-doors, where everybody was walking back and forth under the bright September sky, blowing on horns and eating popcorn and candy out of paper bags.

That reminded Molly that they had ten cents yet. "Oh, Betsy," she proposed, "let's take a nickel of our money for some popcorn."

She was startled by Betsy's fierce, sudden clutch at their little purse as she answered, "No. No, Molly. We've got to save every cent of that. I've found out it costs thirty cents for us both to go home to Hillsboro on the train. The last one goes at six o'clock."

"We haven't got but ten," said Molly.

Betsy looked at her silently for a moment and then burst out, "I'll earn the rest! I'll earn it somehow! I'll have to! There isn't any other way!"

"All right," said Molly, not seeing anything unusual in this. "You can, if you want to. I'll wait for you here."

"No, you won't!" cried Betsy, who had quite enough of trying to meet people in a crowd. "No, you won't! You just follow me every minute! I don't want you out of my sight!"

They began to move forward now, Betsy's eyes wildly roving from one place to another. How *could* a little girl earn money at a county fair! She was horribly afraid to go up and speak to a stranger, and yet how else could she begin?

The man who was selling lemonade answered Betsy's shy question with a stare and a curt "Of course not! What could a young one like you do for me?"

The little girls wandered on, Molly calm and confident in Betsy, Betsy with a dry mouth and a gone feeling. They were passing by a big building now, where a large sign proclaimed that the Woodford Ladies' Aid Society would serve a hot chicken dinner for thirty-five cents. Of course, at half-past three, almost four, the chicken dinner had long ago been eaten. In place of the diners was a group of weary women standing by a great table piled with dirty dishes. Betsy paused here, thought a moment, and went in rapidly so that her courage would not evaporate.

A woman with gray hair looked down at her a little impatiently and said, "Dinner's all over."

"I didn't come for dinner," said Betsy, swallowing hard. "I came to see if you wouldn't hire me to wash your dishes. I'll do them for twenty-five cents."

The woman laughed, looked from little Betsy to the great pile of dishes, and said, turning away, "Mercy, child, if you washed from now till morning, you wouldn't make a hole in what we've got to do."

Betsy heard her say to the other women, "Some young one wanting more money for the side shows."

Now, now was the moment to remember what Cousin Ann would have done. She would certainly not have shaken all over with hurt feelings nor have allowed the tears to come stingingly to her eyes. So Betsy sternly made herself stop doing these things. And Cousin Ann wouldn't have given way to the dreadful sinking feeling of discouragement but would have gone right on to the next place. So, although Betsy felt like nothing so much as crooking her elbow over her face and crying as hard as she could cry, she stiffened her back, took Molly's hand again, and stepped out, heartsick within but very steady (although rather pale) without.

She and Molly walked along in the crowd again, Molly laughing and pointing out the pranks and antics of the young people, who were feeling livelier than ever as the afternoon wore on. Betsy looked at them grimly with unseeing eyes. It was four o'clock. The last train for Hillsboro left in two hours, and she was no nearer having the price of the tickets. She stopped for a moment to get her breath, for although they were walking slowly, she kept feeling breathless and choked. It occurred to her that if ever a little girl had had a more horrible birthday, she had never heard of one!

"Oh, I wish I could, Dan!" said a young voice near her. "But honest, Momma'd just eat me up alive if I left the booth for a minute!"

Betsy turned quickly. A very pretty girl with yellow hair and blue eyes was leaning over the edge of a little canvas-covered booth, the sign of which announced that homemade doughnuts and soft drinks were for sale there. A young man, flushed and lively, was pulling at the girl's blue gingham sleeve. "Oh, come on, Annie. Just one turn! The floor's just right. You can keep an eye on the booth from the hall! Nobody's going to run away with the old thing anyhow!"

"Honest, I'd love to! But I've got a lot of dishes to wash, too!" She looked longingly toward the open-air dance floor, from which just then floated a burst of music.

"Oh, *please*!" said a small voice. "I'll do it for twenty cents."

"Do what, kiddie?" asked the girl in good-natured surprise.

"Everything!" said Betsy. "Wash the dishes, tend the booth; *you* can go dance! I'll do it for twenty cents."

The eyes of the girl and the man met. "My! Aren't we up and coming!" said the man. "You're almost as big as a pint cup, aren't you?" he said to Betsy.

The little girl flushed—she hated being laughed at—but she looked straight into the laughing eyes. "I'm ten years old today," she said, "and I can wash dishes as well as anybody." She spoke with dignity.

The young man burst into a great laugh.

"Some ten-year-old—what?" he said to the girl, and then, "Say, Annie, why not?"

The girl laughed too, out of high spirits. "Here, you cute little thing," she said. "Here's my apron." She took off her long apron and tied it around Betsy's neck. "There's the soap. Stack the dishes up on that counter."

She was out the little gate in the counter in a twinkling

just as Molly, in answer to a beckoning gesture from Betsy, came in. "Hello! There's another one!" said the lively fellow. "Hello, button! What are you going to do? I suppose when they try to crack the safe, you'll run at them and yell and drive them away!"

Molly opened her sweet, blue eyes wide, not understanding a single word. The girl laughed, swooped back, gave Molly a kiss, and disappeared, running side by side with the young man toward the dance hall.

Betsy stood upon a soap box and began joyfully to wash the dishes. She had never thought that ever in her life would she simply *love* to wash dishes! But it was so. Her relief was so great that she could have kissed the coarse, thick plates and glasses as she washed them.

"It's all right, Molly, it's all right!" she said to Molly over her shoulder. Molly only nodded and asked if she might sit up on a barrel, where she could watch the crowd go by.

"Two doughnuts, please," said a man's voice behind Betsy.

Oh, mercy, there was somebody come to buy! Whatever should she do? She came forward, intending to say that the owner of the booth was away and that she didn't know anything about . . . but the man laid down a nickel, took two doughnuts, and turned away. Betsy gasped and looked at the homemade sign stuck into the big pan of doughnuts. Sure enough, it read "2 for 5." She put the nickel up on a shelf and went back to her dishwashing. Selling things wasn't so hard, she decided.

Now that she saw a way out, she began to find some fun being behind a counter instead of in front. When a woman with two little boys approached, she came forward to wait on her, feeling important. "Two for five," she said in a business-like tone. The woman put down a dime, took up four dough-nuts, divided them between her sons, and departed.

"My!" said Molly, looking admiringly at Betsy's coolness. Betsy went back to her dishes, stepping high.

But she looked anxiously at the clock. It was nearing five. Oh, suppose the girl forgot and danced too long!

"Two bottles of ginger ale and half a dozen doughnuts," said a man with a woman and three children.

Betsy looked feverishly among the bottles ranged on the counter and selected two marked *ginger ale*. How *did* you get them open?

"Here's your opener," said the man, "if that's what you're looking for. You get the glasses and I'll open the bottles. We're in a hurry. Have to catch a train."

"Well, they were not the only ones who had to catch a train," Betsy thought sadly. They drank in gulps and departed, cramming doughnuts into their mouths. Betsy wished that the girl would come back. She was now almost sure that she had forgotten and would dance till nightfall. But there, there she came, running along, as light-footed after an hour's dancing as when she had left the booth.

"Here you are," said the young man, producing a quarter. "We've had the time of our young lives, thanks to you."

Betsy gave him back one of her remaining nickels, but he refused it.

"No, keep the change," he said. "It was worth it."

"Then I'll buy two doughnuts with that nickel," said Betsy.

"No, you won't," said the girl. "You'll take all you want for nothing. What we sell here has got to be fresh every day anyhow. Here, hold out your hands, both of you."

"Some people came and bought things," said Betsy, happening to remember as she and Molly turned away. "The money is on that shelf."

"Well, now," said the girl, "if she didn't take hold and sell things! Say . . ." She ran after Betsy and gave her a hug. "You smart young one, I wish I had a little sister just like you!"

Molly and Betsy hurried along out the gate into the main street of the town and down to the station. Molly was eating doughnuts as she went, but Betsy could not think of eating till she had those tickets in her hand.

She pushed her quarter and a nickel under the ticket seller's window and said "Hillsboro" in as confident a tone as she could; but when the precious bits of paper were pushed out at her and she actually held them, her knees shook under her, and she had to go and sit down on the bench.

"My! Aren't these doughnuts good?" said Molly. "I never in my life had *enough* doughnuts before!"

Betsy drew a long breath and began to eat one herself. She felt, all of a sudden, very, very tired.

She was more tired still when they got out of the train at Hillsboro Station and started wearily up the road toward Putney Farm. Two miles lay before them, two miles which they had often walked before, but never after such a day as now lay behind them. Molly dragged her feet as she walked and hung heavily on Betsy's hand. Betsy plodded along, her head hanging, her eyes gritty with sleepiness. A buggy spun round the turn of the road, the horse trotting fast as though the driver were in a hurry. The little girls drew to one side and stood waiting till the road would be free again. When he saw them, the driver pulled the horse back so quickly it stood almost straight up. He peered at them through the twilight and then with a loud shout sprang over the side of the buggy.

It was Uncle Henry! Oh, goody, it was Uncle Henry come to meet them! They wouldn't have to walk any farther!

But what was the matter with Uncle Henry? He ran up to them, exclaiming, "Are ye all right? Are ye all right?" He stooped over and felt over them desperately, as though he expected them to be broken somewhere. And Betsy could feel that his old hands were shaking. When she said, "Why, yes, we're all right, Uncle Henry. We came home on the cars," Uncle Henry leaned up against the fence as though he couldn't stand up. He took off his hat and wiped his forehead, and he said — it didn't seem as though it could be Uncle Henry talking, he sounded so excited — "Well, well, well! My! And so here ye are! And you're all right! *Well!*"

After they all got into the buggy, he quieted down a little

and said, "Thunderation! But we've had a scare! When the Wendells came back with their cousins early this afternoon, they said you were coming with the Vaughans. And then when you didn't come and *didn't* come, I hitched up Jessie and went over to the Vaughans. They said they hadn't seen hide nor hair of ye, and didn't even know you were *at* the fair at all! I tell you, your Aunt Abigail and I had an awful turn! Ann set right out with Prince up toward Woodford and I took Jessie down this way; thought maybe I'd get trace of ye somewhere here. Well, land!" He wiped his forehead again. "Wasn't I glad to see you standing there. . . . Get along, Jess! I want to get the news to Abigail soon as I can! Now tell me what in thunder *did* happen to you!"

Betsy began at the beginning and told it straight through. Now that it was all safely over, Betsy thought her story quite an interesting one. She omitted no detail, although she wondered once or twice if Uncle Henry were listening to her, he kept so still.

They turned into the Putney yard now and saw Aunt Abigail's bulky form on the porch.

"Got 'em, Abby! All right! No harm done!" shouted Uncle Henry.

Aunt Abigail turned without a word and went back into the house. When the little girls dragged their weary legs in, they found her quietly setting out some supper for them on the table, but she was wiping away with her apron the joyful tears that ran down her cheeks, such pale cheeks! It seemed so strange to see rosy Aunt Abigail with a face as white as paper.

"Well, I'm glad to see ye," she told them soberly. "Sit right down and have some hot milk. I had some all ready."

The little girls ate their supper in a tired daze, not paying any attention to what the grownups were saying, until rapid hoofs clicked on the stones outside and Cousin Ann came in quickly. Her eyes brightened when she saw the children.

"For mercy's sake, tell me what happened," she said.

Uncle Henry broke in, "*I'm* going to tell what happened. You and Mother just listen, just sit right down and listen." He went on and told of Betsy's afternoon, her fright, her confusion, her forming the plan of coming home on the train, and her earning the money for the tickets.

When Uncle Henry came to the part where she went on asking for employment after one and then another refusal, Cousin Ann reached out her arms and gathered Betsy up on her lap, holding her close as she listened.

And when Uncle Henry finished—he had not forgotten a single thing Betsy had told him—he asked, "What do you think of *that* for a little girl ten years old today?"

Cousin Ann burst out, "I think I never heard of a child's doing a smarter, grittier thing!"

Betsy, enthroned on those strong knees, wondered if any little girl had ever had such a beautiful birthday.

ABOUT THE AUTHOR

Dorothy Canfield was born in Kansas in 1879 and spent most of her childhood there and in Nebraska. She enjoyed long vacations, however, with her relatives in Vermont, where she always felt at home. Later, she lived there on a mountainside farm with her husband and two children, Jimmy and Sally.

When Dorothy was nine years old, she went to Europe with her mother, who was an artist. While in France, Dorothy learned French so quickly that she soon became her mother's interpreter. Later, she learned other languages and earned a Ph.D. degree in French. She also began writing articles and stories for magazines. Although she had planned to become a professor of languages, she decided instead to make her living as a writer.

In 1907 Dorothy Canfield married James Fisher, who also was a writer. Both of them were interested in education and young people. Mrs. Fisher wrote about raising children in some of her books for adults, and during World War I and World War II, she helped children who had lost their homes and families.

Mrs. Fisher wanted to share with children some of her own memories and some of the things she had learned, so she wrote *Understood Betsy,* from which the story you have just read was taken. Mrs. Fisher thought that self-reliance was one of the most important things that girls and boys could learn. Mrs. Fisher used her maiden name, Dorothy Canfield, for *Understood Betsy,* although most of her other books were published under her married name, Dorothy Canfield Fisher.

Mrs. Fisher died in 1958, at the age of seventy-nine.

BOOKS TO ENJOY

A BOOK OF FLYING SAUCERS FOR YOU,
by Franklyn M. Branley

Here is everything you have always wanted to know about UFO's, or unidentified flying objects.

THE KID WHO ONLY HIT HOMERS, *by Matt Christopher*

With the help of a mysterious visitor, Sylvester suddenly becomes a great baseball hitter.

OH, THAT'S RIDICULOUS! *by William Cole*

Some are foolish; all are fun!
These are poems for everyone.

FISH HEADS AND FIRE ANTS, *by George Cook*

At a survival camp, two boys with opposite personalities must struggle through three days on an island, using only the few supplies they bring with them.

HALF MAGIC, *by Edward Eager*

Jane finds a magic charm that takes her and her sisters and brother on strange and exciting adventures.

RACHEL CARSON: WHO LOVED THE SEA,
by Jean Lee Latham

The subject of this biography is Rachel Carson, a scientist who loved nature and wrote about it. She was one of the first people to make others care about their environment.

GOING TO SCHOOL IN 1776, *by John Loeper*

What was it like going to school two hundred years ago? What did children learn? What games did they play? This book gives the answers.

GLOSSARY

Some of the words in this book may have pronunciations or meanings you do not know. This glossary can help you by telling you how to pronounce those words and by telling you the meanings with which those words are used in this book.

You can find out the correct pronunciation of any glossary word by using the special spelling after the word and the pronunciation key at the bottom of each left-hand page.

The pronunciation key below is a full one that shows how to pronounce each consonant and vowel in a special spelling. The pronunciation key at the bottom of each left-hand page is a shortened form of the full key.

FULL PRONUNCIATION KEY

CONSONANT SOUNDS

b	bib	k	cat, kick, pique	t	tight
ch	church	l	lid, needle	th	path, thin
d	deed	m	am, man, mum	*th*	bathe, this
f	fast, fife, off,	n	no, sudden	v	cave, valve, vine
	phase, rough	ng	thing	w	with
g	gag	p	pop	y	yes
h	hat	r	roar	z	rose, size,
hw	which	s	miss, sauce, see		xylophone, zebra
j	judge	sh	dish, ship	zh	garage, pleasure,
					vision

VOWEL SOUNDS

ă	pat	ī	by, guy, pie	ōō	boot, fruit
ā	aid, they, pay	î	dear, deer,	ou	cow, out
â	air, care, wear		fierce, mere	ŭ	cut, rough
ä	father	ŏ	pot, sorry	û	firm, heard, term,
ĕ	pet, pleasure	ō	go, row, toe		turn, word
ē	be, bee, easy,	ô	alter, caught,	yōō	abuse, use
	leisure		for, paw	ə	about, silent, pencil,
ĭ	pit	oi	boy, noise, oil		lemon, circus
		ōō	book	ər	butter

STRESS MARKS

Primary Stress ′   *Secondary Stress* ′
bi•ol′o•gy (bī ŏl′ə jē)   **bi′o•log′i•cal** (bī′ə lŏj′ĭ kəl)

Pronunciation key and word meanings adapted from *The American Heritage School Dictionary*, published by American Heritage Publishing Co., Inc., and Houghton Mifflin Company.

a•bly (ā′blē) *adv.* In a capable manner.

a•broad (ə brôd′) *adv. & adj.* **1.** In or to foreign places: *going abroad.* **2.** Outdoors and about: *There were people abroad in spite of the rain.*

ab•sorb (ăb sôrb′) *or* (-zôrb′) *v.* **1.** To take in; soak up: *A sponge absorbs water.* **2.** To occupy the full attention of: *completely absorbed by his work.*

ac•cuse (ə kyo͞oz′) *v.* **ac•cused, ac•cus•ing.** To blame (someone) for wrongdoing: *He was accused of the crime.*

ac•quaint•ance (ə kwān′təns) *n.* **1.** Knowledge of or familiarity with something: *acquaintance with the facts.* **2.** A person whom one knows. *Idiom.* **make (someone's) acquaintance** or **make acquaintance with.** To get to know; become familiar with.

ad lib (ăd lĭb′) *adv. & adj.* In an informal manner; without preparation.

ad•mir•ing•ly (ăd mīr′ĭng lē) *adv.* In a way that shows pleasure, wonder, and delight in someone or something: *They gazed admiringly at the statue.*

a•dopt (ə dŏpt′) *v.* To take (a new member) into one's family, tribe, or nation and treat as one's own. —**a•dopt′ed** *adj.: her adopted country.*

ad•vis•er, also **ad•vi•sor** (ăd vī′zər) *n.* A person who gives advice, especially officially or professionally.

af•fec•tion•ate•ly (ə fĕk′shə nĭt lē) *adv.* In a tender and loving manner.

Af•ghan hound (ăf′găn′) *or* (-gən) *n.* A large, slender dog with long, thick hair, a pointed snout, and drooping ears.

ag•ri•cul•ture (ăg′rĭ kŭl′chər) *n.* The science, art, and business of preparing the soil in order to raise useful crops and animals; farming.

a•gue (ā′gyo͞o) *n.* A fever in which there are periods of chills, fever, and sweating.

aisle (īl) *n.* **1.** A passageway between rows of seats, as in a church or theater. **2.** Any passageway, as between counters in a department store.

a•lert (ə lûrt′) *adj.* **1.** Mentally quick; intelligent. **2.** Watchful; attentive: *A good driver must remain constantly alert.*

al•ma•nac (ôl′mə năk′) *or* (ăl′-) *n.* A book containing calendars, statistics, and other information in many different fields.

al•ti•tude (ăl′tĭ to͞od′) *or* (-tyo͞od′) *n.* A height measured usually in relation to sea level or the earth's surface: *flying at an altitude of 5,000 feet.*

am•ble (ăm′bəl) *v.* **am•bled, am•bling.** To walk or move along at a slow, easy pace: *We ambled aimlessly down the street.*

a•midst (ə mĭdst′) *prep.* In the middle of: *a house amidst the trees.*

an•ces•tor (ăn′sĕs′tər) *n.* Any person from whom one is descended, especially if of a generation earlier than a grandparent.

an•te•lope (ăn′tə lōp′) *n., pl.* **an•te•lope** or **an•te•lopes.** A swift-running animal, somewhat like a small deer.

an•tic (ăn′tĭk) *n.* An odd act or gesture; a playful trick or joke.

anx•ious•ly (ăngk′shəs lē) *adv.* In a worried or uneasy manner.

ap•par•ent (ə păr′ənt) *or* (ə pâr′-) *adj.* Easily understood or seen; obvious: *for no apparent reason.*

ap•pen•di•ci•tis (ə pĕn′dĭ sī′tĭs) *n.* A painful swelling of the appendix, which is located in the lower part of the body.

ap•pre•ci•a•tion (ə prē′shē ā′shən) *n.* Thankfulness; gratefulness: *They showed their appreciation with a gift.*

ap•proach (ə prōch′) *v.* To come or go near or nearer to someone or something.

ă pat/ā pay/â care/ä father/ĕ pet/ē be/ĭ pit/ī pie/î fierce/ŏ pot/ō go/ô paw, for/oi oil/o͝o book/
o͞o boot/ou out/ŭ cut/û fur/*th* the/th thin/hw which/zh vision/ə ago, item, pencil, atom, circus

ap•pro•pri•ate (ə prō′prē ĭt) *adj.* Suitable for a particular person, condition, occasion, or place; proper: *appropriate clothes.*

a•quar•i•um (ə kwâr′ē əm) *n., pl.* **a•quar•i•ums** or **a•quar•i•a** (ə kwâr′ē ə). **1.** A water-filled tank for keeping and displaying fish or other water animals, and often water plants. **2.** A place where such animals and plants are displayed to the public.

a•re•na (ə rē′nə) *n.* A place where a contest, show, or performance is held.

a•ro•ma (ə rō′mə) *n.* A pleasant smell.

a•rouse (ə rouz′) *v.* **a•roused, a•rous•ing.** **1.** To awaken from or as if from sleep. **2.** To excite.

ar•range•ment (ə rānj′mənt) *n., pl.* **ar•range•ments.** Plans or preparations: *Make arrangements for a vacation.*

as•ton•ish•ment (ə stŏn′ĭsh mənt) *n.* Great surprise; amazement.

a•stride (ə strīd′) *prep.* With a leg on each side of: *He jumped astride his back.*

as•tron•o•my (ə strŏn′ə mē) *n.* The scientific study of the part of the universe that lies beyond the earth, especially the observation of stars, planets, comets, galaxies, etc.

awk•ward•ly (ôk′wərd lē) *adv.* In a clumsy or uneasy manner.

bach•e•lor (băch′ə lər) or (băch′lər) *n.* A man who has not married.

back-up (băk′ŭp′) *n.* A person standing by and ready to serve as a substitute.

balk (bôk) *v.* To stop short and refuse to go on: *His pony jumped across a deep ravine, and all the others balked.*

bank (băngk) *n.* **1.** Ground, often sloping, along the edge of a river, creek, pond, etc. **2.** A thick mass: *a bank of clouds.*

beck•on (běk′ən) *v.* To signal (someone) to come, as by nodding or waving: *The captain beckoned us over to watch her.*

bed (běd) *n.* **1.** A piece of furniture for resting. **2.** A small piece of ground for growing things: *a bed of flowers.* **3.** Anything that forms a bottom or supporting part: *the bed of a stream.* **4.** A mass of rock, clay, etc. that reaches under a large area and is surrounded by different material. —*v.* **1.** To provide with a bed or sleeping quarters. **2.** To make a bed for (an animal): *She bedded down her horse at night.*

bel•lig•er•ent•ly (bə lĭj′ər ənt lē) *adv.* In a hostile or fighting manner.

bel•low (běl′ō) *n.* **1.** The loud, roaring sound made by a bull or certain other large animals. **2.** A loud, deep shout or cry. —*v.* **1.** To roar as a bull does. **2.** To shout in a deep, loud voice.

be•ret (bə rā′) or (běr′ā′) *n.* A soft, round, flat cap of wool or felt.

be•wil•der (bĭ wĭl′dər) *v.* To confuse greatly; puzzle. —**be•wil′dered** *adj.:* *a bewildered look.*

bin (bĭn) *n.* An enclosed space for storing food, coal, etc.

bi•ol•o•gist (bī ŏl′ə jĭst) *n.* A scientist who studies living things.

bi•ol•o•gy (bī ŏl′ə jē) *n.* The scientific study of living things.

bit¹ (bĭt) *n.* **1.** A small piece or amount. **2.** A brief amount of time.

bit² (bĭt) *n.* **1.** A tool for drilling that fits into a brace or electric drill. **2.** The metal mouthpiece of a bridle, used to control one's horse.

blaze¹ (blāz) *n.* **1.** A brightly burning fire. **2.** Any bright or direct light. —*v.* To burn brightly.

blaze² (blāz) *n.* A white spot on the face of a horse or other animal.

blue•grass (bloo′grăs′) or (-gräs′) *n.* A lawn and pasture grass with bluish or grayish leaves and stems.

Bluegrass Country. An area in central Kentucky noted for its great amount of bluegrass and also for the breeding of racehorses.

bluff (blŭf) *n.* A steep headland, cliff, river bank, etc.

blun·der (blŭn′dər) *n.* A foolish or stupid mistake. —*v.* **1.** To make a stupid mistake. **2.** To move clumsily or blindly; stumble: *A small fly blundered into the spider's web.*

blus·ter·y (blŭs′tər ē) *adv.* Blowing in a loud, violently gusty manner.

board (bôrd) *or* (bōrd) *n.* A group of persons organized to watch over a particular business.

book (bŏŏk) *n.* A set of printed or written pages fastened together along one edge and enclosed between covers. —*v.* To arrange for in advance; reserve or schedule: *He was asked to book tickets to all hit shows.*

book·plate (bŏŏk′plāt′) *n.* A label pasted inside a book and showing the owner's name.

boom[1] (bŏŏm) *n.* A sudden increase: *a boom in car sales.*

boom[2] (bŏŏm) *n.* A long pole extending from the mast of a boat to hold or stretch out the bottom of a sail.

bow·ie knife (bō′ē) *or* (bŏŏ′ē). A long hunting knife with a single-edged blade.

brand (brănd) *n.* **1.** A name or symbol that identifies a product; a trademark. **2.** A mark burned with a hot iron into the hide of cattle, showing ownership. —*v.* To mark with a brand: *Cowboys branded the calves.*

break (brāk) *v.* **broke** (brōk), **bro·ken** (brō′kən), **break·ing**. **1.** To crack or split into two or more parts. **2.** To run or dash suddenly: *The runner broke for home plate.* **3.** To outdo: *break a record.* **4.** To train to obey; tame: *break a wild mustang.*

bron·co (brŏng′kō) *n., pl.* **bron·cos**. A small wild or half-wild horse of western North America.

bronze (brŏnz) *n.* **1.** A mixture of metals made by combining copper, tin, and small amounts of other substances. **2.** A work of art made of bronze.

brow (brou) *n.* **1.** The forehead. **2.** Either of the lines of hair growing above the eyes; an eyebrow. **3.** An expression of the face: *a puzzled brow.*

browse (brouz) *v.* **1.** To inspect in a leisurely and casual way: *browse through a book.* **2.** To look over goods in a store casually without seriously intending to buy them: *browse around in a department store.*

bru·tal (brŏŏt′l) *adj.* Cruel; harsh.

budge (bŭj) *v.* To move or cause to move slightly: *The boulder did not budge.*

bug·gy (bŭg′ē) *n.* **1.** A small, light carriage drawn by a horse. **2.** A baby carriage.

bulge (bŭlj) *n.* An outward curve or a swelling. —*v.* To swell or cause to swell beyond the usual size: *His eyes bulged with surprise.*

bulk·y (bŭl′kē) *adj.* Extremely large.

bur·ble (bûr′bəl) *v.* To bubble; gurgle: *The stream burbled between mossy banks.*

can·cel (kăn′səl) *v.* To call off: *cancel plans for a movie.*

can·vas (kăn′vəs) *n.* **1.** A heavy, coarse cloth of cotton or flax, used for making tents, sails, etc. **2.** An oil painting on canvas.

cap·tiv·i·ty (kăp tĭv′ĭ tē) *n., pl.* **cap·tiv·i·ties**. A period or the condition of being held prisoner. —**cap′tive** *adj. & n.*

car·go (kär′gō) *n., pl.* **car·goes** or **car·gos**. The goods carried by a ship, airplane, etc.

cas·cade (kăs kād′) *n.* **1.** A small waterfall, usually one of many, that flows

---

ă pat/ā pay/â care/ä father/ĕ pet/ē be/ĭ pit/ī pie/î fierce/ŏ pot/ō go/ô paw, for/oi oil/ŏŏ book/
ŏŏ boot/ou out/ŭ cut/û fur/*th* the/th thin/hw which/zh vision/ə ago, item, pencil, atom, circus

over steep rocks. **2.** Anything resembling a cascade: *a cascade of sparks.*

cast (kăst) *or* (käst) *v.* **cast, cast•ing. 1.** To throw: *cast dice.* **2.** To form (an object) by pouring a soft material into a mold and allowing it to harden: *The artist cast the sculpture in bronze.* —*n.* **1.** The actors in a play, movie, etc. **2.** A particular shape formed in a mold: *a cast in plaster of a face.*

cas•u•al•ly (kăzh′oo ə lē) *adv.* In a way that shows little interest and concern. —**cas•u•al** *adj.*

cen•tri•fuge (sĕn′trə fyooj′) *n.* Any device that is basically a chamber whirled about in such a way that its contents are forced toward its outer wall.

cer•e•mo•ny (sĕr′ə mō′nē) *n., pl.* **cer•e•mo•nies.** A formal act or set of acts performed in honor or celebration of an event, such as a wedding, funeral, etc.: *a wedding ceremony.*

chan•nel (chăn′əl) *n.* **1.** The cut or depression in the earth through which a river or stream passes. **2.** A part of a river or harbor deep enough to form a passage for ships.

chant (chănt) *or* (chänt) *n.* A melody, often with many words or syllables sung on the same note. —*v.* To call out in a repeating, rhythmic way.

char•ac•ter (kăr′ĭk tər) *n.* **1.** A person portrayed in a story, play, movie, etc. **2.** A symbol, such as a letter or number, used in giving information, as in printing or writing.

chis•el (chĭz′əl) *n.* A metal tool with a sharp, flat edge, used in cutting and shaping stone, wood, or metal. —*v.* To shape with or use a chisel.

chop (chŏp) *n.* **1.** The jaw. **2.** A small cut of meat that usually contains a bone.

chry•san•the•mum (krĭ săn′thə məm) *n.* A kind of plant that has showy flowers of different colors and sizes.

chuck wagon. A wagon equipped with food and cooking utensils for a team

of workers on the move, as on a cattle drive.

chute (shoot) *n.* An up-and-down or slanting passage down which things can be dropped or slid.

cinch (sĭnch) *n.* **1.** A strap encircling a horse's body and used for holding the saddle or pack. **2.** Something easy; a sure thing.

cin•der (sĭn′dər) *n.* **1.** A piece of partly burned wood or coal. **2. cinders.** Pieces of ash, sometimes packed hard and used to surface racetracks.

cir•cum•stance (sûr′kəm stăns′) *n.* Often **circumstances.** One of the conditions, facts, or events connected with another event, a person, or a course of action. *Idiom.* **under** (or **in**) **the circumstances.** Given these conditions; such being the case.

Civil War. In the United States, the war between the North and the South, lasting from 1861 to 1865. Also called *War Between the States.*

clip (klĭp) *n.* A fast or brisk pace: *move along at a good clip.*

clutch (klŭch) *n.* A tight hold or grip. —*v.* To hold or grasp tightly.

coarse (kôrs) *adj.* Not smooth; rough: *coarse skin; coarse material.*

coax (kōks) *v.* To persuade or try to persuade by gentle urging: *He coaxed the bird into a cage.* —**coax′ing•ly** *adv.*

cob•bled (kŏb′əld) *adj.* Paved with a naturally rounded stone.

cob•ble•stone (kŏb′əl stōn′) *n.* A naturally rounded stone once much used for paving streets.

coil (koil) *n.* Anything made by winding something long and flexible around a center a number of times: *a coil of rope.* —*v.* To wind into a coil or a shape like that of a coil.

col•li•sion (kə lĭzh′ən) *n.* A bumping together; a crash.

col•o•ny (kŏl′ə nē) *n., pl.* **col•o•nies. 1.** A group of people who settle in a distant land but are still governed by their native country. **2. the Colonies.** The 13 British colonies that became the original United States of America.

com·mo·tion (kə mō′shən) *n.* Disturbance; excitement.

com·pete (kəm pēt′) *v.* To take part in a contest: *compete in a race; compete for first prize.*

com·pet·i·tor (kəm pĕt′ĭ tər) *n.* One who takes part in a contest.

com·pe·tent·ly (kŏm′pĭ tənt lē) *adv.* In a satisfactory and capable manner.

com·put·er (kəm pyōō′tər) *n.* A machine that works out an answer through mathematics.

con·ceit·ed (kən sē′tĭd) *adj.* Too proud of oneself.

con·clude (kən klōōd′) *v.* To bring or come to an end.

con·fer·ence (kŏn′fər əns) *or* (-frəns) *n.* A meeting at which people discuss a subject or a number of subjects.

con·fi·dent (kŏn′fĭ dənt) *adj.* Feeling sure; certain.

con·scious (kŏn′shəs) *adj.* Able to see or hear and understand what is happening: *He is hurt but still conscious.*

con·sid·er·a·tion (kən sĭd′ə rā′shən) *n.* Careful thought.

con·sol·ing·ly (kən sōl′ĭng lē) *adv.* In a comforting manner.

con·ster·na·tion (kŏn′stər nā′shən) *n.* Great fear, alarm, or confusion.

con·tent (kən tĕnt′) *adj.* Happy with what one has; satisfied.

con·tin·u·ous (kən tĭn′yōō əs) *adj.* Continuing without stopping; unbroken.

con·tract (kŏn′trăkt′) *n.* A formal agreement between two or more persons or groups. —*v.* (kən trăkt′). **1.** To draw together; make or become smaller: *The pupils of his eyes contracted.* **2.** To arrange or make by a formal agreement: *contract a marriage.*

cor·al (kôr′əl) *n.* A hard, stony substance formed by the skeletons of tiny sea animals grouped together in great numbers.

cor·net (kôr nĕt′) *n.* A musical instrument that is very similar to the trumpet.

coun·ty (koun′tē) *n., pl.* **coun·ties.** In the United States, a group of towns or cities in a state.

cou·pling pin (kŭp′lĭng pĭn) *n.* Something that links or connects, especially something that holds railroad cars together.

court (kôrt) *or* (kōrt) *n.* **1.** A short street enclosed by buildings on three sides. **2.** An area marked and fitted for a sport. **3.** A royal mansion or palace. **4.** The people who assist a king or royal ruler. —*v.* To woo and seek to marry.

court·ship (kôrt′shĭp) *or* (kōrt′-) *n.* The act or period of courting a female.

coy·o·te (kī ō′tē) *or* (kī′ōt′) *n.* A wolflike animal common in western North America.

crack (krăk) *adj.* Excellent; first-rate.

crack the safe. *Idiom.* Break open (rob) the safe, or cash box.

craft·y (krăf′tē) *or* (kräf′-) *adj.* Skilled in sneaky dealing and dishonesty.

crane (krān) *v.* **craned, cran·ing.** To stretch or strain for a better view.

crave (krāv) *v.* **1.** To ask. **2.** To have a very strong desire for.

cre·o·sote (krē′ə sōt′) *n.* An evergreen bush of the western United States and Mexico.

crook (krōōk) *n.* Something bent or curved: *holding a bag of groceries in the crook of his arm.* —*v.* To bend or curve: *The road crooks to the right.*

crotch (krŏch) *n.* A point where a branch separates from a tree; a fork: *the crotch of a tree.*

ă **pat**/ā **pay**/â **care**/ä **father**/ĕ **pet**/ē **be**/ĭ **pit**/ī **pie**/î **fierce**/ŏ **pot**/ō **go**/ô **paw, for**/oi **oil**/ōō **book**/ ōō **boot**/ou **out**/ŭ **cut**/û **fur**/*th* **the**/th **thin**/hw **which**/zh **vision**/ə **ago, item, pencil, atom, circus**

crude (krōōd) *adj.* Not skillfully made or done; rough: *a crude table.*

cud (kŭd) *n.* Food that has been swallowed and brought up to the mouth again for further chewing by animals such as cattle, sheep, etc.

cu•ri•o (kyoŏr′ē ō′) *n.* A rare or unusual object of art.

curt (kûrt) *adj.* **curt•er, curt•est.** Rudely brief in speech or manner: *a curt reply.*

curt•sy (kûrt′sē) *n., pl.* **curt•sies.** A gesture of respect made by bending the knees and lowering the body while keeping one foot forward. —*v.* To make a curtsy.

cus•tom (kŭs′təm) *n.* An accepted thing to do: *Shaking hands when meeting someone is an old custom.*

cut (kŭt) *v.* To separate from the main body of something.

cyl•in•der (sĭl′ən dər) *n.* A figure shaped like a tube.

cym•bal (sĭm′bəl) *n.* **1.** One of a pair of brass, dish-shaped musical instruments, sounded by being struck together. **2.** A single brass plate, sounded by being hit with a drumstick.

daze (dāz) *n.* A stunned or confused condition: *He fell flat and lay there in a daze.*

dead run. A speed that is as fast as possible.

debt (dĕt) *n.* Something, such as money, owed by one person to another.

de•cline (dĭ klīn′) *n.* **1.** A change to a lower level or state: *a decline in prices.* **2.** A downward slope.

de•gree (dĭ grē′) *n.* An academic title awarded by a college or university after completion of a required course of study.

de•ject•ed (dĭ jĕk′tĭd) *adj.* Low in spirits; depressed.

de•pend•a•ble (dĭ pĕn′də bəl) *adj.* Capable of being relied upon, as for support or help; trustworthy.

de•pot (dē′pō) *n.* **1.** A railroad or bus station. **2.** A warehouse or storehouse.

de•spite (dĭ spīt′) *prep.* In spite of: *They won despite many problems.*

de•test (dĭ tĕst′) *v.* To dislike strongly.

de•vice (dĭ vīs′) *n.* **1.** Something that is made, designed, or used for a particular purpose. **2.** A plan, scheme, or trick.

dig•ni•ty (dĭg′nĭ tē) *n., pl.* **dig•ni•ties. 1.** The condition of being worthy or honorable: *a certain dignity in every human being.* **2.** A stately or poised manner.

din•gy (dĭn′jē) *adj.* **din•gi•er, din•gi•est. 1.** Dirty; soiled; grimy. **2.** Drab: *a dingy room; dingy curtains.*

di•plo•ma (dĭ plō′mə) *n.* A document or certificate showing that a person has earned a degree from or completed a course of study at a school, college, or university.

dis•charge (dĭs′chärj′) *or* (dĭs chärj′) *n.* **1.** An act of unloading: *a discharge of freight.* **2.** An act of firing a gun or other weapon.

dis•cour•age•ment (dĭ skûr′ĭj mənt) *or* (-skŭr′-) *n.* **1.** A condition of being with little hope or of being depressed.

dis•gust (dĭs gŭst′) *n.* A feeling of sickness, extreme annoyance, etc.

dis•mal•ly (dĭz′məl ē) *adv.* In a way that shows gloom or depression. —**dis′mal** *adj.*

dis•tin•guished (dĭ stĭng′gwĭsht) *adj.* Recognized as excellent; famous: *a distinguished composer.*

dis•tress (dĭ strĕs′) *n.* The condition of being in need of immediate help. —*v.* To worry (someone).

doo•dle (dōōd′l) *v.* **doo•dled, doo•dling.** To scribble (a design or figure) while thinking about something else.

dor•mi•to•ry (dôr′mĭ tôr′ē) *or* (-tōr′ē) *n., pl.* **dor•mi•to•ries. 1.** A large room providing sleeping quarters for a number of people. **2.** A building for housing a number of persons as at a school.

down (doun) *n.* **1.** Fine, soft, fluffy feathers. **2.** A similar soft, fine covering or substance: *the down on a peach.*

down•sweep (doun′swēp) *n.* A sweep of the arm in a downward direction.

dow•ry (dou′rē) *n., pl.* **dow•ries.** Money or property brought by a bride to her husband.

doze (dōz) *v.* **dozed, doz•ing.** To sleep or appear to sleep lightly; nap. —*n.* A short, light sleep; a nap.

drag (drăg) *n.* Something that slows or stops motion.

dra•mat•ic (drə măt′ĭk) *adj.* Striking in appearance or actions.

draw (drô) *v.* **drew** (drōō), **drawn** (drôn), **draw•ing.** To pull or move so as to cover or uncover: *drew the blanket up to her neck.* —*n.* **1.** A small natural ditch with a shallow bed. **2.** A ·contest ending in a tie.

drear•y (drîr′ē) *adj.* **drear•i•er, drear•i•est.** **1.** Gloomy; dismal: *a dreary January rain.* **2.** Boring; dull.

drib•ble (drĭb′əl) *v.* **drib•bled, drib•bling.** To move (a ball) by bouncing or kicking repeatedly, as in basketball or soccer: *He dribbles the ball.*

dune (dōōn) *or* (dyōōn) *n.* A mass of sand blown by the wind into the form of a hill or ridge.

earth•bound (ûrth′bound′) *adj.* **1.** Unable to leave the surface of the earth: *Until recent times, people were earthbound, moving in horse-drawn vehicles and boats.* **2.** Heading toward the earth: *an earthbound spaceship.*

eaves•drop (ēvz′drŏp′) *v.* **eaves•dropped, eaves•drop•ping.** To listen secretly to the private conversation of others: *hidden behind the door to eavesdrop.*

ech•o (ĕk′ō) *n.* A sound repeated exactly; sound sent back. —*v.* To repeat exactly; send back a sound; imitate.

e•lab•o•rate (ĭ lăb′ər ĭt) *adj.* Planned or made with great attention to many parts or details: *elaborate preparations for the party.*

eld•er (el′dər) *n.* An older person.

em•blem (ĕm′bləm) *n.* An object or picture that comes to stand for something else; a symbol: *The bald eagle is the national emblem of the United States.*

em•ploy•ment (ĕm ploi′mənt) *n.* A job or activity: *He got regular employment on a fishing boat.*

en•dure (ĕn dōōr′) *or* (-dyōōr′) *v.* **en•dured, en•dur•ing.** **1.** To undergo; bear up under. **2.** To put up with.

en•gi•neer (ĕn′jə nîr′) *n.* **1.** A person who is trained in the field of planning and building things, such as roads and bridges. **2.** A person who runs a locomotive. **3.** A person who is skilled in the planning, building, and use of engines or machines.

en•gi•neer•ing a•cad•e•my (ĕn jə nîr′ing ə kăd′ə mē) *n.* A school at which students learn how to design and build structures (buildings, bridges, etc.), machinery, and transportation systems.

en•grave (ĕn grāv′) *v.* **en•graved, en•grav•ing.** To carve or cut a design or letters into a surface: *engrave a name on a plate.*

en•thu•si•as•ti•cal•ly (ĕn thōō′zē ăs′tĭk lē) *adv.* In an eager manner. —**en•thu•si•as′tic** *adj.*

en•ti•tle (ĕn tīt′l) *v.* **en•ti•tled, en•ti•tl•ing.** To give the right to do or have something: *Everyone is entitled to have an opinion.*

e•rect (ĭ rĕkt′) *adj.* Directed or pointing upward; standing up straight: *erect posture.*

ă pat/ā pay/â care/ä father/ĕ pet/ē be/ĭ pit/ī pie/î fierce/ŏ pot/ō go/ô paw, for/oi oil/ōō book/ ōō boot/ou out/ŭ cut/û fur/*th* the/th thin/hw which/zh vision/ə ago, item, pencil, atom, circus

e·vap·o·rate (ĭ văp/ə rāt/) *v.* **e·vap·o· rat·ed, e·vap·o·rat·ing. 1.** To change into the form of a gas. **2.** To disappear; fade: *His confidence evaporated as the airplane was about to land.*

ev·i·dent·ly (ĕv/ĭ dənt lē) *or* (ĕv/ĭ dĕnt/- lē) *adv.* Obviously; clearly: *She is evidently a bad singer.*

ewe (yoō) *n.* A female sheep.

ex·ceed·ing·ly (ĭk sē/dĭng lē) *adv.* To an unusual degree; extremely.

ex·is·tence (ĭg zĭs/təns) *n.* **1.** The fact or condition of being alive; life. **2.** Occurrence; presence.

express rider. A person on horseback who rides between two points, usually some distance apart, without making stops in between.

ex·te·ri·or (ĭk stîr/ē ər) *n.* **1.** The outside, as of a car. **2.** Outward appearance: *a friendly exterior.*

fair¹ (fâr) *adj.* **fair·er, fair·est. 1.** Pleasing to look at; beautiful; lovely: *a fair maiden.* **2.** Light in color: *fair hair; fair skin.*

fair² (fâr) *n.* A gathering for the buying and selling of goods; a market.

faith (fāth) *n.* Confidence or trust in a person, idea, or thing: *You must have faith in yourself.* **Idiom. good faith.** Honesty: *a token of one's good faith.*

fate (fāt) *n.* Something that happens to a person or thing: *The fate of the plane's passengers is still unknown.*

fea·ture (fē/chər) *n.* **1.** An especially important part, quality, or characteristic. **2.** A part of the face.

fee·ble (fē/bəl) *adj.* **fee·bler, fee·blest.** Without strength; weak.

felt (fĕlt) *n.* A smooth, firm cloth made by pressing wool, fur, or other fibers together.

fer·ry (fĕr/ē) *n., pl.* **fer·ries. 1.** A boat used to carry people, cars, goods, etc.; a ferryboat. **2.** The place where a ferryboat docks.

fes·ti·val (fĕs/tə vəl) *n.* An important occasion, celebrated with special customs: *the harvest festival.*

fe·ver·ish·ly (fē/vər ĭsh lē) *adv.* In an intensely disturbed or active manner: *They worked feverishly to finish the job on time.* —**fe/ver·ish** *adj.*

film (fĭlm) *n.* **1.** A movie. **2.** A thin coating, layer, or sheet: *a film of paint.*

fire (fīr) *v.* To treat with heat, as by baking in a kiln or oven.

fire·trap (fīr/trăp/) *n.* A building thought likely to catch fire easily or difficult to escape from in case of fire.

flag·stone (flăg/stōn/) *n.* A flat stone split into slabs for paving.

flash flood. A sudden, violent flood after a heavy rain.

flip·per (flĭp/ər) *n.* A wide, flat, finlike, rubber shoe worn for swimming and skin diving.

flit (flĭt) *v.* **flit·ted, flit·ting.** To move quickly and lightly: *Birds flitted about.*

flog (flŏg) *or* (flôg) *v.* **flogged, flog·ging.** To beat; whip

flush (flŭsh) *v.* To turn red in the face.

flute (floōt) *n.* A high-pitched musical instrument having soft low tones and clear high tones. It is played by blowing into a whistlelike mouthpiece.

fold¹ (fōld) *v.* To bend together, double up, or crease so that one part lies over another: *Fold your paper in half.* —*n.* A line or crease formed by folding.

fold² (fōld) *n.* A pen for sheep or other tame animals.

For·eign Le·gion (fôr/ĭn lē/jən) *or* (fŏr/-) *n.* A former military group in the French army made up of people from all nations and given military duties outside of France.

for·lorn·ly (fôr lôrn/lē) *adv.* In a sad or pitiful manner. —**for·lorn/** *adj.*

for·ma·tion (fôr mā/shən) *n.* **1.** The act of forming or making; development: *the formation of labor unions.* **2.** Something formed geologically: *This formation is called a canyon.*

foun·da·tion (foun dā′shən) *n.* An organization that receives and gives out gifts of money (to schools, hospitals, scientists, etc.).

frame home. A house built with a wooden framework and usually covered with wood siding.

fran·tic (frăn′tĭk) *adj.* Very excited with fear; desperate: *a frantic scream.*

free throw. In basketball, a throw from the foul line, taken by a fouled player and scored as one point if successful.

fret (frĕt) *v.* **fret·ted, fret·ting.** To be or cause to be uneasy or troubled; worry. —*n.* A condition of being troubled; worry; irritation.

frill (frĭl) *n.* A gathered or pleated piece of fancy trimming, such as a lace ruffle.

fringe (frĭnj) *n.* **1.** A decorative border or edge made of hanging cords or thread. **2.** Something like fringe along an edge: *a fringe of eyelashes.*

fu·ri·ous·ly (fyŏŏr′ē əs lē) *adv.* In a fierce or frantic way. —**fu′ri·ous** *adj.*

fur·ther·more (fûr′thər môr′) *or* (-mōr′) *adv.* Moreover; also.

gait (gāt) *n.* A way of walking or running: *a slow gait.*

gam·ble (găm′bəl) *v.* **gam·bled, gam·bling.** To bet money on the outcome of a game or contest. —*n.* A chance; risk; bet.

gen·er·os·i·ty (jĕn′ə rŏs′ĭ tē) *n.* Willingness in giving or sharing.

ge·ra·ni·um (jĭ rā′nē əm) *n.* A plant with rounded leaves and red, pink, or white flowers, often grown in a flower pot.

ges·ture (jĕs′chər) *n.* A motion of the hands, arms, head, or body used while speaking or in place of speech

to help express one's meaning: *The speaker used dramatic gestures.*

gilt (gĭlt) *n.* A thin layer of gold, such as gold-colored paint, applied to a surface.

ging·ham (gĭng′əm) *n.* A light cotton cloth woven in checks, stripes, plaids, or solid colors.

glint (glĭnt) *n.* A gleam; a flash of light.

glut·ton (glŭt′n) *n.* A person or animal that overeats.

gnaw (nô) *v.* **gnawed, gnawed** or **gnawn** (nôn), **gnaw·ing.** To bite or eat away little by little with the teeth.

gon·er (gô′nər) *or* (gŏn′ər) *n.* *Slang.* Someone or something that is dying or beyond help.

gos·ling (gŏz′lĭng) *n.* A young goose.

grab·ble (grăb′əl) *v.* To feel around with the hands; grope; grab.

grand·stand (grănd′stănd′) *or* (grăn′-) *n.* A stand for spectators, as at a stadium.

griev·ous (grē′vəs) *adj.* **1.** Causing grief or pain: *a grievous wound.* **2.** Very serious; grave: *a grievous crime.*

grim·ly (grĭm′lē) *adv.* In a worried or gloomy manner. —**grim** *adj.*

grit (grĭt) *n.* Tiny rough particles, as of sand or stone.

grit·ty (grĭt′ē) *adj.* **grit·ti·er, grit·ti·est. 1.** Of, like, or containing tiny rough particles, as of sand or stone. **2.** Showing courage; brave; refusing to give up.

gust (gŭst) *n.* A sudden, strong wind.

gy·ro·scope (jī′rə skōp′) *n.* A device consisting basically of a disk or wheel that spins rapidly about an axis, or central part.

ha·lo (hā′lō) *n., pl.* **ha·los** or **ha·loes.** A circular band of light, as around the sun or the moon.

ă pat/ā pay/â care/ä father/ĕ pet/ē be/ĭ pit/ī pie/î fierce/ŏ pot/ō go/ô paw, for/oi oil/ŏŏ book/ ŏŏ boot/ou out/ŭ cut/û fur/*th* the/th thin/hw which/zh vision/ə ago, item, pencil, atom, circus

hand (hănd) *n.* A person who does work with his or her hands: *a hired hand.*

haunch (hônch) *or* (hänch) *n.* The hip, buttock, and upper thigh of a person or animal: *The dog settled back on its haunches.*

haz·ard (hăz′ərd) *n.* 1. A chance of being injured, lost, etc.; danger; risk: *Space travel is full of hazards.* 2. Something or someone that is likely to cause harm; a possible source of danger: *a fire hazard.*

head·long (hěd′lông′) *or* (-lŏng′) *adv.* 1. With the head leading; headfirst. 2. At reckless speed or with uncontrolled force: *He rode headlong down the road.*

head·wa·ters (hěd′wô′tərz) *or* (-wŏt′ərz) *pl. n.* The bodies of water that form the source, or beginning, of a river.

heat (hēt) *n.* A single course in a race or contest, which one runs to qualify for the final race.

heave (hēv) *v.* **heaved** *or chiefly nautical* **hove** (hōv), **heav·ing.** 1. To raise or lift, especially with great effort or force: *heaved the pack onto his back.* 2. To throw with or as if with great effort.

heir (âr) *n.* A person who receives or who is entitled to receive the property, rank, title or office of another person after that person dies.

hes·i·tate (hěz′ĭ tāt′) *v.* **hes·i·tat·ed, hes·i·tat·ing.** To be slow to act, speak, or decide; pause in doubt or uncertainty.

hitch (hĭch) *v.* 1. To tie or fasten to something with a rope, strap, loop, etc.: *Get out the wagon and hitch up the old gray mare.* 2. To raise or pull with a tug or jerk: *The hiker hitched the knapsack higher on her shoulders.*

hith·er (hĭth′ər) *adv.* Here: *Little friends, please come hither.*

hoe (hō) *n.* A tool with a flat blade on a long handle, used for breaking up soil, weeding, growing plants, etc.

—*v.* **hoed, hoe·ing.** To dig, weed, etc., with a hoe.

hom·i·ny (hŏm′ə nē) *n.* A food made from grains of corn that have had the outer hulls removed.

hor·ri·fy (hôr′ə fī′) *or* (hŏr′-) *v.* **hor·ri·fied, hor·ri·fy·ing, hor·ri·fies.** To cause to feel fear and terror: *The news horrified the people.*

hud·dle (hŭd′l) *n.* In football, a brief gathering of a team's players to plan the next play. —*v.* **hud·dled, hud·dling.** 1. To crowd together, as from cold or fear. 2. To draw oneself together; curl up: *The little brown rabbit huddled in a ball, afraid for its life.*

im·i·ta·tion (ĭm′ĭ tā′shən) *n.* 1. The act or process of imitating or copying: *learning a song through imitation.* 2. An act of mimicking; copying the actions of someone else: *The comedian does imitations of television actors.*

im·mense (ĭ měns′) *adj.* Of great size, degree, etc.; huge: *immense rocks.*

im·mi·grant (ĭm′ĭ grənt) *n.* A person who leaves his or her native country or region to live in another.

im·pa·tient (ĭm pā′shənt) *adj.* Not able or willing to put up with trouble, hardship, or delay without complaining or becoming angry.

im·pres·sive (ĭm prěs′ĭv) *adj.* Causing an effect of fearful respect.

im·pulse (ĭm′pŭls′) *n.* A sudden inclination or urge; a whim: *acting on impulse.*

in·cin·er·a·tor (ĭn sĭn′ə rā′tər) *n.* A furnace or other device for burning trash.

in·cred·i·ble (ĭn krěd′ə bəl) *adj.* 1. Unbelievable: *an incredible excuse.* 2. Amazing.

in·cu·ba·tor (ĭn′kyə bā′tər) *or* (ĭng′-) *n.* An enclosed space in which a desired temperature can be kept, often used for hatching eggs.

in·di·ges·tion (ĭn′dĭ jĕs′chən) *or* (-dī-) *n.* Upset stomach caused by eating too much or too fast.

in·dus·tri·al (ĭn dŭs′trē əl) *adj.* Of or having something to do with the production of goods in large quantities.

in·ex·pert (ĭn ĕk′spûrt′) *adj.* Not expert; unskilled.

in·her·i·tance (ĭn hĕr′ĭ təns) *n.* **1.** Property, money, etc. received from someone, as a father, after he dies. **2.** Something passed down from previous generations; heritage: *Many American place names, foods, and legends are part of our inheritance from the Indians.*

in·lay (ĭn′lā′) *or* (ĭn lā′) *v.* **in·laid** (ĭn′lād′) *or* (ĭn lād′), **in·lay·ing. 1.** To set (pieces of wood, ivory, metal, etc.) into a surface to form a design. **2.** To decorate by setting in such designs.

in·quir·y (ĭn kwīr′ē) *or* (ĭn′kwə rē) *n.*, *pl.* **in·quir·ies.** A request for information: *many inquiries about the new mail rates.*

in·quis·i·tive (ĭn kwĭz′ĭ tĭv) *adj.* **1.** Eager to learn: *an inquisitive child.* **2.** Especially curious.

in·sa·tia·ble (ĭn sā′shə bəl) *or* (-shē ə-) *adj.* Unable to be satisfied; greedy; never getting enough.

in·spec·tion (ĭn spĕk′shən) *n.* The act of looking at (something) carefully: *an inspection of the elevators.*

in·stall·ment (ĭn stôl′mənt) *n.* One of a series of payments to pay a debt or bill.

in·tent·ly (ĭn tĕnt′lē) *adv.* In a determined or forceful manner.

in·trude (ĭn trōōd′) *v.* **in·trud·ed, in·trud·ing.** To break, come, or force in without being wanted or asked: *Don't intrude on my privacy.* **—in·trud′er** *n.*

i·rons (ī′ərnz) *n.* The flat-based loops or rings hung from either side of a horse's saddle to support the rider's feet in mounting and riding; stirrups.

ir·ri·gate (ĭr′ĭ gāt′) *v.* **ir·ri·gat·ed, ir·ri·gat·ing.** To supply (farmland, crops, etc.) with water by means of streams, ditches, pipes, canals, etc.

ir·ri·tate (ĭr′ĭ tāt′) *v.* **ir·ri·tat·ed, ir·ri·tat·ing. 1.** To make angry or impatient; annoy or bother: *His endless questions irritated me.* **2.** To cause to become sore or inflamed.

jade (jād) *n.* Either of two stones that are usually white or pale green and are used in jewelry and as materials from which art objects are carved.

jigsaw puzzle. Many differently shaped pieces of wood or cardboard that are fitted together to form a picture.

joint (joint) *n.* A point or position at which two or more things are joined. **—adj.** Sharing with someone else: *Mr. and Mrs. Dunn are joint owners of the property.*

ju·ni·per (jōō′nə pər) *n.* An evergreen tree or shrub related to the pines, having small or prickly leaves and bluish berries.

keen (kēn) *adj.* Sharp; excellent; bright.

kum·quat (kŭm′kwŏt′) *n.* A small, thin-skinned, orangelike fruit that may be eaten.

lac·quer (lăk′ər) *n.* A liquid that can be applied to a surface, drying to leave a glossy finish.

land·ing (lăn′dĭng) *n.* A level area at the top or bottom of a set of stairs.

ă pat/ā pay/â care/ä father/ĕ pet/ē be/ĭ pit/ī pie/î fierce/ŏ pot/ō go/ô paw, for/oi oil/ōō book/
ōō boot/ou out/ŭ cut/û fur/*th* the/th thin/hw which/zh vision/ə ago, item, pencil, atom, circus

land·lord (lănd′lôrd′) *n.*   A person who owns a house or apartment building with rooms or living space rented out to others.

las·so (lăs′ō) *or* (lă soo′) *n., pl.* **las·sos** or **las·soes.**   A long rope with a loop that can be pulled tight at one end, used especially to catch horses and cattle.   —*v.* **las·soed, las·so·ing, las·soes.**   To catch with a lasso: *lasso a runaway calf.*

launch (lônch) *or* (länch) *v.*   **1.** To move or set in motion with force: *launch a rocket into space.*   **2.** To move (a boat or ship) into the water.

launch pad.   A platform from which a rocket is launched.

lav·en·der (lăv′ən dər) *n.*   A pale or light purple.   —*adj.* Pale or light purple.

lay-up (lā′ŭp′) *n.*   In basketball, usually a one-handed shot made close to the basket after running in to the basket.

lec·ture (lĕk′chər) *n.*   A speech providing information about a given subject, delivered before an audience or class.

leer·y (lîr′ē) *adj.* **leer·i·er, leer·i·est.** *Informal.*   Suspicious; cautious; watchful.

leg·is·la·ture (lĕj′ĭs lā′chər) *n.*   A group of persons given the power to make and change the laws of a nation or state.

lest (lĕst) *conj.*   For fear that; so as to prevent the possibility that: *Take care lest the flowers become crushed.*

let·down (lĕt′doun′) *n.*   A disappointment: *Losing a game is a letdown.*

li·cense (lī′səns) *n.*   **1.** Legal permission to do or own a certain thing.   **2.** A paper, card, plate, or other proof that such permission has been granted.

li·no·le·um (lĭ nō′lē əm) *n.*   A sturdy, washable material made in sheets, used for covering floors and counters.

liv·er·wurst (lĭv′ər wûrst′) *n.*   A sausage made from liver.

loaf¹ (lōf) *n., pl.* **loaves** (lōvz).   **1.** A shaped mass of bread baked in one piece.   **2.** Any shaped mass of food: *a meat loaf.*

loaf² (lōf) *v.*   To spend time lazily or aimlessly; idle: *We loafed all morning.*

lob·by (lŏb′ē) *n., pl.* **lob·bies.**   A hall or waiting room in a hotel, apartment house, theater, or other public place.

log·i·cal (lŏj′ĭ kəl) *adj.*   **1.** Reasonable: *a logical choice.*   **2.** Able to think clearly and carefully: *a logical mind.*

log·i·cal·ly (lŏj′ĭ kəl lē) *adv.*   In a clear and reasonable manner.

long·horn (lông′hôrn′) *or* (lŏng′-) *n.*   One of a breed of cattle with long, spreading horns, raised in the southwestern United States.

loom (loom) *v.*   To come into view or appear as a large or unclear image: *Clouds loomed behind the mountains.*

loot (loot) *n.*   Stolen goods.   —*v.* To rob of valuable things by violent means.

lope (lōp) *v.* **loped, lop·ing.**   To run or ride with a steady, easy way of moving.

lum·ber¹ (lŭm′bər) *n.*   Wood sawed into boards and planks.

lum·ber² (lŭm′bər) *v.*   To walk or move with clumsiness and often great noise: *Twenty elephants lumbered slowly into the circus tent.*

lu·nar (loo′nər) *adj.*   **1.** Of the moon. **2.** Measured or determined by motions of the moon: *a lunar year.*

lurch (lûrch) *n.*   An unsteady or abrupt swaying movement.   —*v.* To move unsteadily; stagger: *The big, bullying fellow lurched toward Jed.*

lure (loor) *n.*   Something that attracts or appeals, especially with the promise of pleasure or a reward: *the lure of the sea.*

lurk (lûrk) *v.*   **1.** To be or keep out of view, lying in wait or ready to attack: *The pirates lurked in caves along the river.*   **2.** To move about in a sneaky way.

lust (lŭst) *n.*   A strong desire.

main·land (mān′lănd′) *or* (-lənd) *n.*
The land mass of a country or continent as opposed to its islands.

ma·jes·tic (mə jĕs′tĭk) *adj.* Very grand;
splendid: *a majestic oak.*

man·or house (măn′ər hous) *n.* The
main house of an estate.

man·sion (măn′shən) *n.* A large, stately
house.

man·til·la (măn tē′yə) *or* (-tĭl′ə) *n.* A
scarf, usually of lace, worn over the
head and shoulders by women, especially in Spain and Latin America.

man·u·script (măn′yə skrĭpt′) *n.* A
handwritten or typewritten book, paper, or article.

mar·ble (mär′bəl) *n.* Any of several
rocks, often having irregularly colored marks. It is used in buildings
and in making ornaments.

mar·ry (măr′ē) *interj. Archaic.* A word
used to express surprise or emphasis.

marsh (märsh) *n.* An area of low-lying,
wet land; a swamp or bog.

mas·sive (măs′ĭv) *adj.* **1.** Large; heavy
and solid; bulky: *a massive elephant.*
2. Unusually large or impressive: *a
massive head.*

mate (māt) *n.* **1.** One of a matched pair:
Find the mate to this sock. **2.** One of
a pair of animals brought together
for breeding.

medicine man. A member of a North
American Indian tribe who presided
at various ceremonies and practiced
magic and folk medicine.

meek·ly (mēk′lē) *adv.* In a gentle or
peaceful manner. —**meek** *adj.*

meet (mēt) *n.* A gathering of two or
more teams for athletic contests or
games.

men·tal (mĕn′tl) *adj.* Of the mind.

me·sa (mā′sə) *n.* A flat-topped hill or
small plateau with steep sides, common in the southwestern United
States.

mes·quite (mĕ skēt′) *or* (mĕs′kēt′) *n.*
A thorny shrub or tree of southwestern
North America, having feathery leaves
and beanlike pods.

me·thinks (mĭ thĭngks′) *v. Archaic.* It
seems to me.

mid·dlings (mĭd′lĭngz) *n.* The coarse
part of ground grain.

midge (mĭj) *n.* A very small, gnatlike fly.

mi·gra·tion (mī grā′shən) *n.* The act
of moving regularly to a different area,
especially at a certain time of the
year.

mill (mĭl) *v.* To move around in a confused or disorderly manner.

mill·er (mĭl′ər) *n.* A person who works
in, operates, or owns a mill for grinding grain.

mill·pond (mĭl′pŏnd′) *n.* A pond
which is made when water is dammed
up for the purpose of operating a mill.

min·i·a·ture (mĭn′ē ə chər) *or* (mĭn′ə-)
adj. Of a much smaller size than the
usual: *miniature poodles.*

mint (mĭnt) *n.* A large amount, especially of money.

mi·rage (mĭ räzh′) *n.* An imagined
sight in which water that is not really
there and upside-down reflections of
distant objects are seen.

mod·est (mŏd′ĭst) *adj.* **1.** Tending to
play down one's own talents or abil-
ities. **2.** Quiet in manner; shy.

mo·men·tar·y (mō′mən tĕr′ē) *adj.* Lasting only an instant or moment: *I caught
only a momentary glance of her as
she flashed by.*

mo·ray (môr′ā) *or* (mōr′ā) *or* (mə rā′)
n. Any of several long, slippery,
snakelike, tropical ocean fishes that
have sharp teeth and can be dangerous
to swimmers.

ă pat/ā pay/â care/ä father/ĕ pet/ē be/ĭ pit/ī pie/î fierce/ŏ pot/ō go/ô paw, for/oi oil/ŏŏ book/
ŏŏ boot/ou out/ŭ cut/û fur/*th* the/th thin/hw which/zh vision/ə ago, item, pencil, atom, circus

moth·er-of-pearl (mŭ*th*′ər əv pûrl′) *n.* The hard, smooth, pearly layer on the inside of certain oyster shells and other seashells, used to make buttons, jewelry, etc.

mot·to (mŏt′ō) *n.*, *pl.* **mot·toes** or **mot·tos.** Any brief phrase or statement of a guiding principle; a slogan.

mush (mŭsh) *n.* Corn meal, or other meal, boiled in water or milk until thick.

mus·tang (mŭs′tăng′) *n.* A small, wild horse of the North American plains.

muz·zle (mŭz′əl) *n.* **1.** The nose and jaws of certain animals, such as a dog or horse. **2.** The front end of the barrel of a gun.

natural history. The study of living things and natural objects and happenings and of their origins, relationships, and descriptions.

ne·on (nē′ŏn′) *n.* A colorless gas that gives a reddish-orange glow in a vacuum tube and is widely used in electric signs and advertisements.

nour·ish·ment (nûr′ĭsh mənt) *or* (nûr′-) *n.* Anything that a living thing uses to grow or maintain its life; food.

num·skull (nŭm′skŭl′) *n.* A stupid person.

ob·ser·va·tion (ŏb′zûr vā′shən) *n.* **1.** The act of observing, noticing, etc. **2.** Something that has been seen or observed: *writing her observations on the ways ants work.*

oc·cur·rence (ə kûr′əns) *n.* Something that happens; an incident: *a strange occurrence.*

off·spring (ôf′sprĭng′) *or* (ŏf′-) *n.*, *pl.* **off·spring.** **1.** A child or children of a particular parent or parents. **2.** The young of an animal.

old country. The country where one used to live.

o·mit (ō mĭt′) *v.* **o·mit·ted, o·mit·ting.** To leave out; not include: *Omit unnecessary words and ideas.*

orb (ôrb) *n.* **1.** A sphere; a globe. **2.** Also **orb web.** The wheel-shaped web made by certain kinds of spiders.

or·na·ment (ôr′nə mənt) *n.* Something that decorates or makes more attractive or beautiful. —*v.* (ôr′nə mĕnt′). To supply with ornaments: *ornament a carriage with gold.*

out·do (out dō′) *v.* **-did (-dĭd′), -done (-dŭn′), -do·ing.** To do better than: *a person not to be outdone by anyone.*

pace (pās) *n.* **1.** A step made in walking; a stride. **2.** The rate of speed at which a person, animal, or group walks or runs. —*v.* **paced, pac·ing. 1.** To walk up and down or back and forth across. **2.** To set the pace of.

pa·le·on·tol·o·gist (pā′lē ən tŏl′ə jĭst) *n.* A scientist who studies fossils and ancient forms of life.

pan·ick·y (păn′ĭ kē) *adj.* Full of or showing signs of sudden terror.

par·ty (pär′tē) *n.*, *pl.* **par·ties. 1.** A group of persons working together in some activity: *a search party.* **2.** An event in which a group is gathered together for pleasure.

pas·tor (păs′tər) *n.* **1.** A minister who is the leader of a church. **2.** One who cares for a flock of sheep; a shepherd.

pa·trol (pə trōl′) *v.* **pa·trolled, pa·trol·ling.** To walk or travel through (an area) checking for possible trouble.

ped·es·tal (pĕd′ĭ stəl) *n.* A support or base, as for a column or statue.

peer (pîr) *v.* To look hard, searchingly, or with difficulty.

peev·ish (pē′vĭsh) *adj.* Annoyed; irritable; cross.

pen·sion (pĕn′shən) *n.* A sum of money paid regularly as a retirement benefit.

perk·y (pûr′kē) *adj.* Cheerful and brisk; chipper; jaunty.

per·son·al·ly (pûr′sə nə lē) *adv.* **1.** In person or by oneself; without the help of another. **2.** As far as oneself is concerned: *Personally, I can't stand it.*

phy·sics (fĭz′ĭks) *n. (used with a singular verb).* The science of matter and energy and relations between them.

picket line. A rope tied to a pointed stake that has been driven into the ground and used to keep a horse or other animal from wandering or running away.

piece (pēs) *n.* A short distance.

pil·lar (pĭl′ər) *n.* A vertical support for a building; a column.

pine·y (pī′nē) *adj.* A form of the word **piny.**

pin·y (pī′nē) *adj.* **pin·i·er, pin·i·est.** Covered with or consisting of pines: *piny woods.*

pint-cup (pīnt′kŭp) *n.* A container that holds one pint; a small jug.

pin·wheel (pĭn′hwēl′) *or* (-wēl′) *v.* To buck so that the horse jumps up, turns while its feet are in the air, and lands on its back.

pi·o·neer (pī′ə nîr′) *n.* A person who leads the way in a field of science, research, etc.: *a pioneer in the use of liquid fuel in rockets.*

pipe (pīp) *v.* To signal the arrival of (someone) to a ship's crew by blowing on a pipe; to welcome (onto a ship).

pitch (pĭch) *n.* **1.** A line of talk which tries to talk a customer into buying something without thinking. **2.** A throw or toss.

plant (plănt) *or* (plänt) *n.* A factory.

plas·ter (plăs′tər) *or* (plä′stər) *n.* A mixture of sand, lime, and water that hardens to form a smooth solid surface, used for covering walls and ceilings.

pla·za (plăz′ə) *or* (plä′zə) *n.* A public square or similar open area in a town or city.

plot (plŏt) *n.* **1.** A small piece of ground: *a plot of good land.* **2.** The series of actions or events in a story, play, etc. **3.** A secret plan.

plun·der (plŭn′dər) *v.* To take treasures or valuables from; rob.

pom·e·lo (pŏm′ə lō′) *n., pl.* **pomelos.** A grapefruit.

por·rin·ger (pôr′ĭn jər) *or* (pōr′-) *n.* A shallow cup or bowl with a handle.

por·trait (pôr′trĭt′) *or* (-trāt′) *or* (pōr′-) *n.* A painting, photograph, or other likeness of a person, especially one showing the face.

post (pōst) *n.* A military base at which troops are stationed: *an army post.*

pot·hole (pŏt′hōl′) *n.* A deep hole or pit.

pot·ter·y (pŏt′ə rē) *n., pl.* **pot·ter·ies.** Objects, such as pots, vases, or dishes, shaped from moist clay and hardened by heat.

pound (pound) *n.* Also **pound sterling.** The basic unit of money of the United Kingdom.

pox (pŏks) *n. Archaic.* Bad luck.

prairie dog. A burrowing animal of the plains of central North America, having a barklike call and living in large groups.

prank (prăngk) *n.* A playful trick, joke, or caper.

preen (prēn) *v.* To smooth or clean (the feathers) with the beak.

prem·is·es (prĕm′ĭs əz) *n.* Property; someone's land or building.

pre·serve (prĭ zûrv′) *v.* **pre·served, pre·serv·ing.** To protect (food) from spoiling and prepare it for future use, as by freezing, canning, etc.

pro·claim (prō klām′) *or* (prə-) *v.* To announce; declare: *proclaim a holiday.*

ă pat/ā pay/â care/ä father/ĕ pet/ē be/ĭ pit/ī pie/î fierce/ŏ pot/ō go/ô paw, for/oi oil/ŏŏ book/
ŏŏ boot/ou out/ŭ cut/û fur/*th* the/th thin/hw which/zh vision/ə ago, item, pencil, atom, circus

pro·duce (prə dōōs′) *or* (-dyōōs′) *v.* **pro·duced, pro·duc·ing.** **1.** To bring forth (something); yield: *Seeds grow up to produce plants.* **2.** To bring forward; show; exhibit: *The girl produced a snake from her pocket.* —*n.* (prŏd′ōōs) *or* (-yōōs) *or* (prō′dōōs) *or* (-dyōōs). Farm products, such as fruits or vegetables, raised for selling.

prof·it (prŏf′ĭt) *n.* The money made in a business or sale after all costs have been paid.

prone (prōn) *adj.* Lying with the front or face downward.

pro·pose (prə pōz′) *v.* **pro·posed, pro·pos·ing.** To suggest.

pros·per·ous (prŏs′pər əs) *adj.* Successful; enjoying wealth or profit.

prov·en·der (prŏv′ən dər) *n.* Dry food, such as hay, for livestock; feed.

pry (prī) *v.* **pried, pry·ing, pries.** **1.** To raise, move, or force open with or as with a lever: *pry the lid off a box.* **2.** To obtain with difficulty: *pried answers from the child.*

pum·per·nick·el (pŭm′pər nĭk′əl) *n.* A dark bread made from coarsely ground rye.

pu·ny (pyōō′nē) *adj.* **pu·ni·er, pu·ni·est.** Small or inferior in size or strength.

Quak·er (kwā′kər) *n.* A member of the religious group called the Society of Friends. The word "Quaker" is not used officially by the Friends.

quarter horse. One of a breed of strong saddle horses developed in the western United States.

qua·ver (kwā′vər) *v.* To shake, as from fear.

quirk (kwûrk) *n.* A sudden, sharp turn or twist.

rab·bi (răb′ī) *n.* The spiritual leader of a group of people who worship together in the Jewish faith.

raw·hide (rô′hīd′) *n.* **1.** The hide of cattle before it has been tanned. **2.** A whip or rope made of such hide.

re·cede (rĭ sēd′) *v.* **re·ced·ed, re·ced·ing.** **1.** To move back or away from a limit, point, or mark: *after the flood had receded.* **2.** To slope backward.

rec·og·ni·tion (rĕk′əg nĭsh′ən) *n.* Attention or favorable notice; praise: *world recognition for her work in medicine.*

rec·ol·lect (rĕk′ə lĕkt′) *v.* To remember.

re·cov·er (rĭ kŭv′ər) *v.* **1.** To return to a normal condition: *recover after a long illness.* **2.** To regain control over (oneself): *recovered himself enough to speak in public.*

reef (rēf) *n.* A strip or ridge of rock, sand, or coral that rises to or close to the surface of a body of water.

re·fined (rĭ fīnd′) *adj.* Having good manners; elegant.

re·flec·tion (rĭ flĕk′shən) *n.* **1.** An image, or something bounced back, as from a mirror or water. **2.** Serious thought.

ref·uge (rĕf′yōōj) *n.* **1.** Protection; shelter: *seeking refuge in the castle.* **2.** A place of protection or shelter: *a wildlife refuge.*

rein (rān) *n.* Often **reins.** A long, narrow leather strap attached to the bit in a horse's mouth and held by the rider or driver to control the horse.

re·li·a·bil·i·ty (rĭ lī′ə bĭl′ə tē) *n.* The quality of being dependable and of being one who can be trusted.

re·lieve (rĭ lēv′) *v.* To take something from the possession of: *relieved him of his heavy load.*

re·luc·tant (rĭ lŭk′tənt) *adj.* Unwilling: *reluctant to leave.*

re·ly (rĭ lī′) *v.* To depend on; trust confidently: *We rely upon her judgment.*

re·pro·duc·tion (rē′prə dŭk′shən) *n.* **1.** The act or process of copying. **2.** Something that is reproduced; a copy: *a reproduction of a painting.*

rep·tile (rĕp′tĭl′) *n.* Any of a group of cold-blooded animals that have a backbone and are covered with scales or horny plates, such as a snake, turtle, or dinosaur.

re·quest (rĭ kwĕst′) *v.* To ask (a person or persons) to do something.

res·er·voir (rĕz′ər vwär′) *n.* A natural or artificial lake used as a storage place for water.

res·i·dent (rĕz′ĭ dənt) *n.* A person who makes his or her home in a particular place.

re·sume (rĭ zōōm′) *v.* To begin again or continue after a break.

re·tort (rĭ tôrt′) *v.* To make a quick, clever, or angry reply.

re·trieve (rĭ trēv′) *v.* To get back.

re·vive (rĭ vīv′) *v.* **re·vived, re·viv·ing.** To bring back or return to life, to strength, or to consciousness.

rib (rĭb) *n.* One of the main veins of a leaf.

rip·cord (rĭp′kôrd′) *n.* A cord pulled to release a parachute from its pack.

rit·u·al (rĭch′ōō əl) *n.* The form or order of events followed during a religious or other ceremony.

round·house (round′hous′) *n.* A huge, round building for housing locomotives, usually built around a turntable which is used to turn the locomotives around.

rouse (rouz) *v.* **roused, rous·ing. 1.** To wake up; awaken. **2.** To cause to become active or excited.

rove (rōv) *v.* To wander or roam.

roy·al·ty (roi′əl tē) *n.* A king, queen, or other member of a royal family.

ru·in (rōō′ĭn) *n.* Often **ruins.** The remains of a structure or group of structures that has been destroyed or has fallen into pieces from age: *Aztec ruins.* —*v.* To harm beyond repair.

sage¹ (sāj) *n.* A very wise person, usually old and highly respected.

sage² (sāj) *n.* **1.** A plant with grayish-green, spicy-smelling leaves used as flavoring in cooking. **2.** Sagebrush.

san·i·ta·tion work·er (săn′ĭ tā′shən wûr′kər) *n.* One who protects public health by getting rid of sewage and wastes or by studying the subject of getting rid of sewage and wastes.

satch·el (săch′əl) *n.* A small bag or piece of hand luggage, often having a shoulder strap, used to carry books, clothes, etc.

sched·ule (skĕj′ōōl) *or* (-ōō əl) *or* (skĕj′əl) *n.* Any plan showing something to be done within a certain time. —*v.* To plan for a certain time or date. —**sched′uled** *adj.: a scheduled flight.*

scheme (skēm) *n.* **1.** A plan for doing something. **2.** A secret plan. —*v.* **1.** To make up a plan or scheme for. **2.** To plan in a sneaky or secret way. —**schem′ing** *adj.: a scheming person.*

scorn·ful (skôrn′fəl) *adj.* Full of or showing dislike. —**scorn′ful·ly** *adv.*

scringe (skrĭnj) *v.* To shrink down in fear; crouch; move away from.

scrounge (skrounj) *v.* To rummage or search: *scrounging around in the attic looking for old books.*

sculp·ture (skŭlp′chər) *n.* **1.** The art of making figures or designs that have depth, as by carving wood, chiseling stone, or casting metal. **2.** One or more works of art created in this way.

scut·tle (skŭt′l) *v.* To move with quick little steps; scurry.

scythe (sīth) *n.* A tool used for mowing or reaping, having a long, curved blade with a long, bent handle.

Secretary of State. The head of the governmental department that deals with matters between countries.

ă pat/ā pay/â care/ä father/ĕ pet/ē be/ĭ pit/ī pie/î fierce/ŏ pot/ō go/ô paw, for/oi oil/ōō book/
ōō boot/ou out/ŭ cut/û fur/*th* the/th thin/hw which/zh vision/ə ago, item, pencil, atom, circus

sen·sa·tion (sĕn sā′shən) *n.* Something felt sharply and briefly in the mind: *a sensation of having been here before.*

sen·sa·tion·al (sĕn sā′shə nəl) *adj.* **1.** Of feeling or the senses. **2.** Arousing great interest. **3.** *Informal.* Extraordinary; outstanding.

sen·si·tive (sĕn′sĭ tĭv) *adj.* **1.** Easily hurt, damaged, or irritated: *sensitive skin; sensitive feelings.* **2.** Quick to take offense; touchy: *He had big feet and was sensitive about them.*

se·vere·ly (sə vîr′lē) *adv.* In a strict or forbidding manner. —**se·vere′** *adj.*

shav·er (shā′vər) *n.* **1.** An electric razor. **2.** *Informal.* A young boy; lad.

shoulder blade. Either of the two large, flat bones that form the rear of the shoulder.

shy (shī) *adj.* **1.** Easily startled; timid: *a shy animal.* **2.** Bashful; reserved: *a shy person.* —*v.* **shied, shy·ing, shies.** To move suddenly, as if startled.

sieve (sĭv) *n.* A strainer; any meshwork used for straining, sifting, etc.: *Drain the vegetables in the sieve.* —*v.* **sieved, siev·ing.** To sift.

sil·i·ca (sĭl′ĭ kə) *n.* A chemical compound, found in sand and other substances, used in making glass, concrete, and other materials.

sil·ver·smith (sĭl′vər smĭth′) *n.* A person who makes and repairs articles of silver.

sin·is·ter (sĭn′ĭ stər) *adj.* **1.** Suggesting evil. **2.** Promising trouble.

skep·ti·cal·ly (skĕp′tĭ kə lē) *adv.* In a doubting or disbelieving manner.

slab (slăb) *n.* A broad, flat, thick piece of something, as of cake, stone, or cheese.

slate (slāt) *n.* **1.** A fine-grained rock that splits into thin layers with smooth surfaces. **2.** A writing tablet made of this or a similar material. **3.** A record of past performance: *starting with a clean slate.*

slink (slĭngk) *v.* **slunk** (slŭngk), **slink·ing.** To move in a quiet, secret way.

slip (slĭp) *n.* **1.** A young, slender person or a small, frail thing: *A slip of a child was leading the big horse.* **2.** A part of a plant cut or broken off for planting; a cutting.

smart (smärt) *v.* To feel a sharp, stinging pain.

snor·kel (snôr′kəl) *n.* Breathing equipment used by skin divers, consisting of a plastic tube curved at one end and fitted with a mouthpiece.

snout (snout) *n.* The long, pointed nose, jaws, or front part of the head of an animal.

so·ber·ly (sō′bər lē) *adv.* Seriously.

soft drink. A beverage, often carbonated, such as cola or a flavored soda.

sol·emn (sŏl′əm) *adj.* Serious.

sol·id·ly (sŏl′ĭd lē) *adv.* Completely; fully. —**sol′id** *adj.*

sol·vent (sŏl′vənt) *n.* A liquid that can dissolve another substance, or change it from a solid to a liquid.

sooth·ing·ly (sōō′thĭng lē) *adv.* In a comforting manner.

sow (sou) *n.* A full-grown female pig.

spec·i·men (spĕs′ə mən) *n.* A sample of a group or a part of a whole.

spec·ta·tor (spĕk′tā′tər) *n.* Someone who watches an event.

spell (spĕl) *v.* To relieve (someone) from work for a short time by taking a turn.

spi·der (spī′dər) *n.* A frying pan having a long handle and short legs.

spur (spûr) *n.* A U-shaped device with a point or sharp-toothed wheel behind, worn on the heel of a rider's boot and used to urge a horse on.

squint (skwĭnt) *v.* To look with the eyes partly open.

stage (stāj) *n.* A step in development: *a disease in its early stages.*

stag·ger (stăg′ər) *v.* To move or stand unsteadily, as if carrying a great weight.

stalk (stôk) *v.* To walk in a stiff, proud manner.

stand (stănd) *n.* **1.** A small place for the display of goods for sale; a booth, stall, or counter: *a flower stand.* **2.** A military position prepared for defense against attack.

stark (stärk) *adj.* **stark•er, stark•est.** Unadorned; bare; grim.

starting block. A device that gives a runner a rigid surface against which to place his or her feet at the start of a race.

starting gate. A mechanically operated barrier used as a starting device for a race.

stat•ic (stăt′ĭk) *adj.* Not moving.

stealth•i•ly (stĕl′thə lē) *adv.* In a quiet manner, so as to avoid notice.

sting•ing•ly (stĭng′ĭng lē) *adv.* In a way that feels like sharp, smarting pain.

sting•ray (stĭng′rā′) *n.* Also **sting ray.** An ocean fish having a broad, flattened body and a long, whiplike tail with a sharp, poison-bearing spine that can cause great harm.

stir•rup (stûr′əp) *n.* A loop or ring with a flat base, hung by a strap from either side of a horse's saddle to support the rider's foot.

strag•gler (străg′lər) *n.* One who strays or falls behind. —**strag′gle** *v.*

strand (strănd) *v.* To leave in a difficult or helpless position.

stream•lined (strēm′līnd′) *adj.* Smoothly constructed so as to be able to move easily through a fluid.

stretch (strĕch) *n.* A straight section of a course or track leading to the finish line.

strew (strōo) *v.* **strewed, strewn** (strōon) or **strewed, strew•ing.** To spread here and there; scatter.

stride (strīd) *v.* To walk vigorously with long steps. *Idiom.* **take in (one's) stride.** To handle without fuss.

stroll•er (strō′lər) *n.* Someone who walks or wanders at a leisurely pace.

strut (strŭt) *v.* To walk in a stiff, self-important manner.

stu•di•o (stōo′dē ō′) or (styōo′-) *n.* An artist's workroom.

sub•urb (sŭb′ûrb′) *n.* An area where people live that is near a city.

suc•ces•sion (sək sĕsh′ən) *n.* A group of persons or things arranged or following in order: *a succession of sharp sounds.*

suc•cu•lent (sŭk′yə lənt) *adj.* Full of juice or sap; juicy: *succulent berries.*

sul•phur (sŭl′fər) *n.* Also **sulfur.** A pale-yellow powder used in some medicines.

sun•fish (sŭn′fĭsh′) *v.* To buck by bringing one shoulder of the horse nearly to the ground, raising it, and then repeating this with the other shoulder.

su•perb (sŏo pûrb′) or (sə-) *adj.* Excellent: *a superb meal.*

surf (sûrf) *n.* **1.** The waves of the sea as they break upon a shore or reef. **2.** The white foam of breaking waves.

sur•rey (sûr′ē) *n.* A horse-drawn carriage with four wheels and two seats.

sur•vey (sər vā′) or (sûr′vā′) *v.* **1.** To look over the parts or features of; view broadly: *surveyed the neighborhood from a rooftop.* **2.** To examine; investigate: *surveyed the damage done by the storm.* —*n.* (sûr′vā′). **1.** A view of a broad area, field, or subject. **2.** A study of a group of persons or things.

sus•tain (sə stān′) *v.* To keep alive; supply with needed nourishment.

swim[1] (swĭm) *v.* To move oneself through water by means of movements of the body or parts of the body.

swim[2] (swĭm) *v.* To feel faint or dizzy.

sym•pa•thize (sĭm′pə thīz′) *v.* To share or understand another's feelings.

ă pat/ā pay/â care/ä father/ĕ pet/ē be/ĭ pit/ī pie/î fierce/ŏ pot/ō go/ô paw, for/oi oil/ŏŏ book/ ŏŏ boot/ou out/ŭ cut/û fur/*th* the/th thin/hw which/zh vision/ə ago, item, pencil, atom, circus

tam·bou·rine (tăm′bə **rēn′**) *n.* An instrument consisting of a small drumhead stretched over a narrow rim that is fitted with small metal disks that jingle when the drumhead is struck or when the instrument is shaken.

tan·ger·ine (tăn′jə **rēn′**) *n.* A fruit related to the orange but somewhat smaller, having deep-orange skin that peels easily.

tas·sel (tăs′əl) *n.* A bunch of loose threads or cords bound at one end and hanging free at the other, used as a decoration on curtains, clothing, etc.

'ta·ter (tā′tər) *n.* A potato.

tat·tered (tăt′ərd) *adj.* Torn or worn to shreds; ragged: *tattered clothes.*

taut (tôt) *adj.* **1.** Pulled or drawn tight: *sails taut with wind.* **2.** Strained; tense: *his taut and angry face.*

tav·ern (tăv′ərn) *n.* An inn for travelers.

tech·nique (tĕk **nēk′**) *n.* A step-by-step method of carrying out and completing a difficult task or problem.

ten·ant (tĕn′ənt) *n.* A person who pays rent to use or occupy land, a building, or other property owned by another.

tend (tĕnd) *v.* To look after.

ten·der[1] (tĕn′dər) *adj.* **1.** Easily crushed or bruised. **2.** Not tough: *tender meat.*

tender[2] (tĕn′dər) *n.* A railroad car attached to the locomotive, carrying fuel and water.

ten·ta·tive·ly (tĕn′tə tĭv lē) *adv.* In an uncertain, not definite manner.

tex·tile (tĕk′stəl) *or* (-stīl′) *n.* **1.** Cloth or fabric, especially when woven or knitted. **2.** Fiber or yarn that can be made into cloth.

throng (thrông) *or* (thrŏng) *n.* A large group of people or things crowded together.

thrust (thrŭst) *v.* To push or drive forcibly: *thrusting our way through the crowd.* —*n.* A force that tends to move an object, especially an object such as an airplane or rocket.

tie (tī) *n.* Something that unites or draws people closer together: *the ties of friendship.*

tit·ter (tĭt′ər) *v.* To utter a soft, nervous giggle.

tou·sle (tou′zəl) *v.* To disarrange or rumple.

tra·di·tion·al (trə dĭsh′ə nəl) *adj.* Of or in accord with custom.

trans·port (trăns pôrt′) *v.* To carry from one place to another: *transport passengers.* —*n.* (trăns′pôrt′) **1.** The act or process of transporting: *the transport of goods by ship.* **2.** A vehicle, as an aircraft, used to transport passengers or freight.

tri·um·phant·ly (trī ŭm′fənt lē) *adv.* In a successful and victorious way.

trom·bone (trŏm bōn′) *or* (trŏm′bōn′) *n.* A brass wind instrument that is somewhat similar to the trumpet. Some trombones change pitch by using a slide, and some use valves.

trough (trôf) *or* (trŏf) *n.* A long, narrow container, especially one for holding water or feed for animals.

trudge (trŭj) *v.* To walk in a heavy-footed way; plod.

tu·ba (tōō′bə) *or* (tyōō′-) *n.* A large brass wind instrument having a deep tone, using several valves to change its pitch.

tu·ber·cu·lo·sis (tōō bûr′kyə lō′sĭs) *or* (tyōō-) *n.* A lung disease of human beings and animals.

tuf·fet (tuf′ĭt) *n.* **1.** A clump or tuft of grass. **2.** A low, small seat.

tun·dra (tŭn′drə) *n.* A cold, treeless area of arctic regions, having only low-growing plant life.

tusk (tŭsk) *n.* A long, pointed tooth, usually one of a pair, projecting outside of the mouth of certain animals, such as the elephant or walrus.

twi·light (twī′līt′) *n.* **1.** The time when the sun is a little bit below the horizon. **2.** The way in which the sky is lighted during this time, especially after a sunset.

twine (twīn) v. **1.** To twist together, as threads. **2.** To twist or coil about: *A vine twined the fence.*

un·ru·ly (ŭn roo′lē) adj. **un·ru·li·er, un·ru·li·est.** Difficult or impossible to control.

urge (ûrj) v. **urged, urg·ing. 1.** To push, force, or drive onward; encourage: *urging the horses with shouts and cracks of the whip.* **2.** To recommend strongly; press forcefully. —n. A strong desire or impulse.

vain·ly (vān′lē) adv. In an unsuccessful way. —**vain** adj.

ve·loc·i·ty (və lŏs′ĭ tē) n., pl. **ve·loc·i·ties.** Speed.

ven·der, also **ven·dor** (vĕn′dər) n. A person who sells; a peddler.

ven·ture (vĕn′chər) v. **ven·tured, ven·tur·ing. 1.** To place oneself in danger; dare: *to venture sailing across the ocean in a small boat.* **2.** To undertake something without being sure of success.

ver·i·ta·ble (vĕr′ĭ tə bəl) adj. Without doubt or question; real: *a veritable success.*

ves·sel (vĕs′əl) n. A ship, large boat, or similar craft.

vol·ca·no (vŏl kā′nō) n., pl. **vol·ca·noes** or **vol·ca·nos. 1.** Any opening in the crust of the earth through which hot, melted rock, dust, ash, and hot gases are thrown forth. **2.** A mountain or other peak formed by the material thrown forth in this way.

vul·ture (vŭl′chər) n. Any of several large birds that generally have dark feathers and a bare head and neck and that feed on dead animals.

wa·ger (wā′jər) n. A bet. —v. To bet.

wash (wŏsh) or (wôsh) n. The dry bed of a stream.

weird (wîrd) adj. **weird·er, weird·est. 1.** Mysterious and often frightening. **2.** Strange or odd.

whick·er (hwĭk′ər) v. To whinny or neigh, as a horse. —n. A whinnying or neighing sound, as made by a horse.

whirl·wind (hwûrl′wĭnd) or (wûrl′-) n. A mass of air that rotates, often violently, about a region, as a tornado.

whop (hwŏp) v. To strike; beat.

wil·der·ness (wĭl′dər nĭs) n. An unsettled area left in its natural condition.

wist·ful·ly (wĭst′fəl ē) adv. In a manner of sadly longing or wishing.

wit (wĭt) n. Often **wits.** Understanding; intelligence: *using one's wits.*

with·er (wĭth′ər) v. To dry up or cause to dry up from lack of water: *The flowers withered in the vase.*

with·ers (wĭth′ərz) pl. n. The highest part of the back of a horse or similar animal, between the shoulder blades.

wit·less (wĭt′lĭs) adj. Lacking intelligence or wit; stupid or dull.

wool·ly (wool′ē) adj. **wool·li·er, wool·li·est. 1.** Of or covered with wool. **2.** Rough; disorderly: *a wild and woolly frontier town.*

wres·tle (rĕs′əl) v. **wres·tled, wres·tling.** To fight by struggling and trying to bring the other person to the ground.

yearn (yûrn) v. To have a deep, strong desire; be filled with longing: *She yearned for company.*

yuc·ca (yŭk′ə) n. Any of several plants of dry regions of southern and western North America, having stiff, pointed leaves and a large cluster of whitish flowers.

ă pat/ā pay/â care/ä father/ĕ pet/ē be/ĭ pit/ī pie/î fierce/ŏ pot/ō go/ô paw, for/oi oil/oo book/ oo boot/ou out/ŭ cut/û fur/th the/th thin/hw which/zh vision/ə ago, item, pencil, atom, circus

DEFGHIJ-D-8   210/798